The GartnerGroup Glossary of Information Technology Acronyms and Terms

Third Edition

About Gartner Direct Products and GartnerGroup

Gartner Direct Products is a one-stop shopping source offering more than 2,000 GartnerGroup reports — including Executive Reports, Strategic Analysis Reports, Dataquest reports and Datapro reports. In addition, it offers the complete GartnerGroup audiotape library — including all conferences, Symposium presentations, conference documentation in both print and electronic formats, and all audio teleconferences. Customers may also subscribe to GartnerGroup periodicals, newsletters, and technology-training audios. All Gartner Direct Products are marketed through the "Virtual IT Bookstore" at www.gartnerdirect.com. Customers may also call 203-363-7150.

As the world's leading authority on IT, GartnerGroup provides clients with a wide range of products and services in the areas of IT advisory services, measurement, research, decision support, analysis and consulting. Founded in 1979, with headquarters in Stamford, Conn., GartnerGroup is at the center of a global community of more than 11,000 client organizations served by analysts in 80 locations worldwide. GartnerGroup's unique capabilities and resources help bring clarity to the direction of the world's hottest and most volatile industry. To learn more about GartnerGroup, or to become a client, visit www.gartner.com or call 203-316-1111.

The GartnerGroup Glossary of Information Technology Acronyms and Terms

Third Edition

Managing Editor: Robin Whiting

Editors:
George Hoza, Jean Kendall, Lou Latham, Gisela Moriarty, Edward Younker

Design and layout:
Gay Christie, Leigh Conover, Beverly Morlang

October 1999

Order code #5604

ISBN 1-891234-02-1

Published by:
Gartner Direct Products, Two Stamford Landing, Stamford, Connecticut 06902-7649, U.S.A.

Introduction

This Glossary is a comprehensive collection of information technology (IT) acronyms and terms. The definitions and illustrations were written by GartnerGroup analysts. The book is updated every year so that new terms can be included and the obsolete discarded.

Due to the proliferation of acronyms in speech as well as in written communications, the definitions in this Glossary are attached to their acronym forms. Therefore, under ATM, the reader will find "asynchronous transfer mode" and its definition, whereas under "asynchronous transfer mode," the reader will find the cross reference "See ATM."

Entries are arranged alphabetically, ignoring spaces, hyphens and slashes. Numbers and symbols can be found at the beginning of the book. The editors have chosen to reflect correct capitalization, using lowercase unless terms are product names, associations or industry standards.

The GartnerGroup Glossary of Information Technology Acronyms and Terms

Third Edition

Contents

Numbers

#

1Base-5
One megabit per second (Mbps) transmission over twisted-pair configuration.

10Base-x series
Any of several Institute of Electrical and Electronics Engineers (IEEE) specifications for baseband networks using the Ethernet protocol. It includes:

1. 10Base-2: 10 megabits per second (Mbps) baseband network using thin Ethernet coaxial cable.
2. 10Base-5: 10 Mbps baseband network using thick Ethernet coaxial cable.
3. 10Base-F: The IEEE specification for baseband Ethernet over fiber-optic cabling.
4. 10Base-FB: Part of the 10Base-F specification providing a synchronous signaling backbone that allows additional segments and repeaters to be connected to the network.
5. 10Base-FL: Part of the 10Base-F specification that is designed to replace the Fiber-Optic Inter-Repeater Link (FOIRL) standard providing Ethernet over fiber-optic cabling.
6. 10Base-FP: Part of the 10Base-F specification that allows the organization of a number of end nodes into a star topology without the use of repeaters.
7. 10Base-T: IEEE standard enabling telephone (unshielded twisted-pair) cable to be used for Ethernet local-area networks (LANs).

10BROAD-36
Broadband 10 megabits per second (Mbps) network running over thick coaxial cable.

100Base-T
100-megabit-per-second (Mbps) standard for copper cabling used with Fast Ethernet, often used to mean Fast Ethernet with copper cabling.

100Base-VG
Local-area network (LAN) standard of the Institute of Electrical and Electronics Engineers (IEEE) 802 committee for transmission of 100 megabits per second (Mbps) over unshielded twisted pair (UTP), promoted originally by Hewlett-Packard and AT&T, among others. With 100VG-AnyLAN, it is an alternative to 100Base-T with Fast Ethernet.

100VG-AnyLAN
Method of local-area network (LAN) transmission based on 100Base-VG that builds on aspects of both Token Ring and Ethernet to run at 100 megabits per second (Mbps) with resilience and high realization of potential. It is generally considered technically better than Fast Ethernet, the alternative, but less successful in the marketplace.

2B+D
The Integrated Services Digital Network (ISDN) Basic Rate Interface (BRI) which is comprised of two 64 Kbps bearer (B) channels and one 16 kilobits per second (Kbps) D channel.

2PC (two-phase commit)

23B+D
The Integrated Services Digital Network (ISDN) Primary Rate Interface (PRI), which is comprised of 23 64 kilobits per second (Kbps) bearer (B) channels and one 64 Kbps D channel.

24x7 (24 hours a day, seven days a week) or 24x365 (24 hours a day, 365 days a year)
Continuous availability: 24 hours a day, seven days a week. A continuously available system exhibits two characteristics: high availability and continuous operations. High availability means that the service tolerates unscheduled outages. Continuous operations means that the service does not require scheduled downtime.

3-D visualization
Uses interactive graphics to represent and manipulate high-volume multidimensional data as graphical objects with a wide range of characteristics (e.g., x/y/z axes, size, color, shape, vibration, movement).

3-D Web sites
A Web site (e.g., created in VRML — Virtual Reality Modeling Language) providing a virtual space for visitors to explore.

3GL (third-generation language)
A high-level programming language such as FORTRAN, COBOL, BASIC, Pascal or C, which compiles to machine language.

3270
IBM's interactive communications terminal standard used to communicate with an IBM mainframe or compatible system.

3380
An IBM direct-access storage device (DASD) family first introduced in 1980.

3390
An IBM family of direct-access storage devices (DASD) first introduced in 1989.

3420
A family of IBM half-inch open-reel tape drives introduced in 1970, offering densities of up to 6,250 bits per inch.

3480
An IBM cartridge tape subsystem first introduced in 1984.

3745
An IBM front-end processor (FEP) introduced in 1988.

3780
A batch protocol used to communicate with an IBM mainframe or compatible system.

3880
A family of IBM direct-access storage device (DASD) controllers introduced in 1980, supporting a wide range of devices (3340, 3344, 3350, 3370, 3375 and 3380).

3990
An IBM direct-access storage device (DASD) controller family introduced in 1987, supporting a wide range of devices (3380, 3390, 9340 and RAMAC).

4GL (fourth-generation language)
A high-level language suitable for end-user or programmer data access and capable of reasonably complex data manipulation. It includes two categories of software development tools: application generators for production applications, and information generators for decision-support applications. 4GLs are relatively nonprocedural and easier to use than 3GLs (e.g., COBOL, FORTRAN and C), but are less powerful and more wasteful of computer resources. GartnerGroup identifies three types of 4GL:

- A procedural language integrated with a database management system. Examples include Ideal (Computer Associates) and Natural (Software AG).
- An information generator. Examples include FOCUS (Information Builders), Nomad 2 (Must Software) and Ramis (Computer Associates).

- A code generator or nonprocedural tool. Examples include SQLForms (Oracle) and Telon (Computer Associates). These tools are also called lower-CASE tools.

80x86

A family of Intel microprocessors used in IBM and IBM-compatible PCs and workstations. Includes the 80286, 80386 and 80486. The Pentium and Pentium II are members of the same family, but the numerical designations have been dropped.

802.x series

Any of several Institute of Electrical and Electronics Engineers (IEEE) specifications covering network protocols. Includes:

1. 802.1D: Standard for spanning tree.
2. 802.10: Standard for packet tagging for security within local-area networks (LANs), also used by some companies to tag packets for virtual LANs.
3. 802.12: Standard that specifies the physical layer and the Media Access Control (MAC) sublayer of the datalink layer of the Open Systems Interconnections (OSI) 7-Layer Model.
4. 802.1AB: Draft standard for Gigabit Ethernet over unshielded twisted pair (UTP).
5. 802.1P: A draft standard.
6. 802.1Q: Draft standard for virtual LANs.
7. 802.1Z: Draft standard for Gigabit Ethernet.
8. 802.3: Broadband bus networking system that uses Carrier Sense Multiple Access with Collision Detection (CSMA/CD) protocol. "Ethernet" has become the generic name, despite being one trademarked version of 802.3.
9. 802.4: Standard that governs broadband bus and broadband token bus; usually used in industrial applications.
10. 802.5: Standard that governs Token Ring Networking systems.
11. 802.6: Standard that governs metropolitan area networks (MANs).

A

AA (automated attendant)
A device that is connected to a private branch exchange (PBX). Automated attendants are connected to voice mail systems. When a call comes in, this device answers it.

AAC (ATM access concentrator)
A device used to concentrate a variety of services such as frame relay, Internet Protocol (IP), video, etc., over a single ATM network access connection.

AAEC (American Association of Electronic Commerce)

AAL (ATM adaptation layer)
The "glue" that connects traditional packet and frame structures and multimedia data types with short, fixed-length asynchronous transfer mode (ATM) cells. It is where non-ATM data is converted to ATM format by filling the 48-byte fixed-length cells at the user-to-network interface (UNI). Forms the top layer of the ATM version of the Broadband Integrated Services Digital Network (B-ISDN) protocol stack. AAL is divided into two sublayers: Convergence Sublayer and Segmentation and Reassembly Sublayer.

A and B signaling
A type of in-band signaling used in T1 transmission, in which one bit, robbed from each of the 24 subchannels in every sixth frame, is used for carrying dial and control information.

AAR (Automatic Alternative Routing)
Automatic switching of a call to other routes when first-choice routes are unavailable.

AARP (AppleTalk Address Resolution Protocol)

ABAP (Advanced Business Application Programming — SAP)
The core tool for the development of SAP R/3.

ABC (activity-based costing)
An improved approach to understanding where and why costs are incurred within an enterprise. It provides the information for activity-based management, which focuses on the decisions and actions needed to reduce costs and increase revenue. ABC differs from traditional cost accounting in explicitly recognizing that not all cost objects place an equal demand on support resources.

ABEND (abnormal end)

ABI (application binary interface)
A set of specifications provided by AT&T that enable vendors that have chosen the same microprocessor to build object-code-compatible systems. ABIs enable compatibility only among products built on the same microprocessor architectures.

ABM (Asynchronous Balanced Mode)
A High-Level Data Control Link Control (HDLC) type supporting peer-oriented, point-to-point communications between two stations.

ABR (auto baud rate)
Automatic detection of transmission speed by sampling the first character of a message and adjustment to match.

ABR (Available Bit Rate)
An asynchronous transfer mode (ATM) service category, defined by the ATM forum and conceptually similar to a frame relay network, in which a minimal cell rate (MCR) will be guaranteed and

bursts can be supported if the network resources allow it.

abstract syntax
A machine-independent data structure description (OSI term).

Abstract Syntax Notation 1 (See ASN.1)

AC (alternating current)

ACA (Application Control Architecture — Digital Equipment)

ACA (Automatic Circuit Assurance)
A PBX feature that assists the customer in identifying possible trunk malfunctions.

"A" carrier
A non-wireline cellular carrier.

ACC (ATM access concentrator)

Accelerated Graphics Port (See AGP)

access charge
The cost assessed to communications users for access to the local or regional exchange to send or receive calls. It also includes access to specialized telecommunications services such as interexchange, interstate message toll telephone network for originating and receiving interstate toll calls, as well as access to the customer's local access and transport area (LATA).

access code
The digit or digits that a user must dial to be connected to an outgoing trunk facility.

access control
Hardware, software, and administrative tasks that monitor system operation perform user identification, and record system accesses and changes.

Access Control Facility 2 (See ACF2)

access control list (See ACL)

access line
The connection to the customer's local telephone company for origination of local and long-distance calls. Also known as local loop or trunk.

access method

1. That part of a computer's operating system responsible for formatting data sets and their direction to specific storage devices. Examples from the mainframe world include Virtual Storage Access Method (VSAM) and Indexed Sequential Access Method (ISAM).
2. In local area networks, the technique and/or program code used to arbitrate the use of the communications medium by granting access selectively to individual stations. Examples are Carrier Sense Multiple Access with Collision Detection (CSMA-CD) and token passing.

access point (See AP)

access router
An access device with built-in basic routing protocol support, specifically designed to allow remote local-area network (LAN) access to corporate backbone networks. Access routers are not designed to replace backbone routers or to build backbone networks. They usually have limited protocols, few ports and low speed.

access to 3270 Data Stream
A facility that enables user-written programs to become "users" of terminal-based applications on an IBM mainframe. Common use would be in accessing applications under Customer Information Control System (CICS), Information Management System (IMS) and others.

accounting rate
The charge per traffic unit — a unit of time or information content, — covering communications between zones controlled by different telecommunications authorities. Accounting rates are used to establish international tariffs.

ACD (automatic call distributor)
A specialized phone system that handles many incoming calls. ACD is used for a variety of order-taking functions, such as call to help desks or dispatching of service technicians. It is designed to distribute a large volume of incoming calls uniformly to a number of operators or agents, e.g., for airline reservations.

ACE (Advanced Computing Environment)
A consortium founded in April 1991 whose goal was to establish at least source code compatibility between Santa Cruz Operation (SCO) and System V Release 4 (SVR4) Unix systems on either reduced instruction set computer (RISC) or Intel processors, as well as source compatibility of Windows NT systems on RISC or Intel systems. The primary founding members were Digital Equipment, Compaq Computer, MIPS Computer Systems, SCO and Microsoft.

A+ certification
A microcomputer service technician credential issued by the Computing Technology Industry Association (CompTIA).

ACF (Advanced Communications Function)
The generic name for a family of IBM licensed programs consisting mainly of VTAM, TCAM, NCP and SSP programs that use the principles of Systems Network Architecture (SNA) and include the distribution of function and resource sharing.

ACF2 (Access Control Facility 2 — Computer Associates)
A host-based security subsystem. ACF2 is also called CA-ACF2.

ACF/NCP (See NCP)

ACF/VTAM (Advanced Communications Function/Virtual Terminal Access Method)
Part of the IBM family of Systems Network Architecture (SNA) communications products; provides support for LU 6.2, the logical unit for IBM's Advanced Program-to-Program Communications (APPC).

ACH (automated clearinghouse)

ACIA (asynchronous communications interface adapter)

ACID (atomicity, consistency, isolation, durability)
Four well-established tests for verifying the integrity of business transactions in a data-processing environment.

ACK/NAK/END (Acknowledged/Not Acknowledged/Inquiry)

ACL (access control list)
Manages users and their access to files and directories. Access control requires linking users with content. User information is stored in a directory, and content is referenced in ACLs.

ACM (Association for Computing Machinery)
The premiere professional association of computer (principally software) professionals. The ACM is heavily represented in the academic community.

ACMS (Application Control and Management System)
Digital Equipment's transaction processing (TP) monitor.

acoustic coupler
A device that allows a telephone handset to be used for access to the switched telephone network for data transmission. Digital signals are modu-

lated as sound waves, and data rates are typically limited to a range of 300 bits per second (bps) to 1,200 bps.

ACP (array control processor)

ACP (Associate Computer Professional)
A level of information technology (IT) credential issued by the Institute for Certification of Computer Professionals (ICCP) requiring basic knowledge of information processing (a core exam) and one programming language.

ACPI (Advanced Configuration and Power Interface)

A-CPR (ambulatory computer-based patient record system)

ACR (Allowed Cell Rate)
ATM Forum-defined parameter for asynchronous transport mode (ATM) traffic management.

ACR (architecture conformance review)
Designed to achieve an alignment between information technology strategy and a major external force — vendors. It is a periodic, formal review of the enterprise's objectives and enterprise information architecture (EIA). It is intended to provide vendors with a clear direction regarding the enterprise's technology requirements during the next five years — requirements that will dictate acquisitions and determine vendor participation. The ACR, with the EIA, provides the enterprise with a structure to build and maintain a clear and comprehensive architectural vision, and the means to manage (along with vendors in a positive working relationship) the implementation of that vision from a product perspective.

ACR (attentuation-to-crosstalk ratio)

ACSE (Association Control Service Element)
An ISO standard specifying how application processes on two remote machines must initiate and terminate a communications session. This session is called an association.

ACSLS (Automated Cartridge System Library Software)

ACT (application sources, characterization and testing)
A mnemonic for GartnerGroup's network profiling process.

ACT I (application, channel, technology and industry)
A GartnerGroup acronym, representing the "survival locations" for integrated document management (IDM) vendors. A survival location is a market segment where a vendor can develop sustainable competitive advantage. A critical mass of sustainable competitive advantage is necessary for a vendor to thrive in the long term in any market.

active data dictionary
A facility for storing dynamically accessible and modifiable information relating to midrange-system data definitions and descriptions.

active-matrix liquid crystal display (See AMLCD)

Active Server Pages — Microsoft Exchange (See ASP)

ActiveX
An application programming interface (API) that enhances Microsoft's OLE protocol. Often compared to Java, ActiveX facilitates various Internet applications, and therefore extends and enhances the functionality of Microsoft's Internet Explorer browser. Like Java, ActiveX enables the

development of interactive content. When an ActiveX-aware browser encounters a Web page that includes an unfamiliar feature, it automatically installs the appropriate applications so the feature can be used. For ActiveX to be effective, Web pages must conform to standards established by Microsoft. While not a direct replacement for Java, ActiveX will allow Microsoft and other Windows software to gain some of the portability of Java applets.

activity-based costing (See ABC)

actuator
The mechanism that positions the disk read-write head over the selected track.

ACU (automatic calling unit)
A unit, which may or may not be integrated within a modem, that automatically dials calls based on digits supplied by the attached business machine.

ACU (Automatic Client Update)

AD (applications development)
A process that includes the following steps:

1. Identifying a need
2. Defining the requirements
3. Planning the overall application structure or architecture
4. Developing the code or programming instructions
5. Monitoring progress
6. Testing results

A/D (analog to digital)

adaptive control
A control strategy that automatically changes the type or influence of control parameters to improve overall control system performance.

adaptive differential pulse code modulation (See ADPCM)

adaptive equalization
Equalization that is adjusted during transmission in order to compensate for line characteristics.

adaptive routing
Routing that automatically adjusts to network changes, such as changes of traffic pattern, to find the most efficient path for transmission.

ADC (advanced data control)

ADC (analog-to-digital conversion)
A method of sampling and encoding an analog signal to create a digital signal.

ADC (automated data collection)
Devices such as bar-code systems, optical character recognition, radio frequency identification devices, and magnetic media recording that convert disparate information into computer records.

ADCCP (Advanced Data Communications Control Procedure)
A bit-oriented protocol developed by the American National Standards Institute (ANSI).

AdDMD (Administrative Directory Management Domain)
A directory management domain run by a postal, telegraph and telephone (PTT) authority.

address

1. Coded representation of the origin or destination of data. Multiple terminals on one communications line, for example, each have a unique address.
2. Group of digits that makes up a telephone number.
3. In software, a location in memory that can be specifically referred to in a program.

Address Resolution Protocol (See ARP)

address translation
The process of changing the identifier associated with an item of data, or an instruction, to the actual location in main storage where it is held.

ADE (applications development environment)

ADF (Applications Development Facility — IBM)

ADF (automated document factory — GartnerGroup)
An architecture and set of processes that prepares and positions enterprises to manage the process of creating and delivering mission-critical, high-volume digital documents using factory production techniques that appropriately mechanize document production. The raw materials, including data and preparation instructions, enter the ADF, where they are transformed into digital documents and prepared for delivery.

Adjunct Switch Application Interface (See ASAI)

ADLC (Asynchronous Data Link Control)
An IBM Systems Network Architecture (SNA)-compatible protocol for asynchronous connection of remote terminals.

ADM (applications development and maintenance)

AdMD (Administrative Management Domain)
A Message Handling System/Service (MHS) management domain run by a postal, telegraph and telephone (PTT) authority.

Administrative Directory Management Domain (See AdDMD)

Administrative Management Domain (See AdMD)

ADMS (Access Device Messaging System)

ADO (ActiveX Data Object — Microsoft)

Adobe Type Manager (See ATM)

ADP (automatic data processing)

ADPCM (adaptive differential pulse code modulation)
A speech-coding method that calculates the difference between two consecutive speech samples in standard pulse code modulation (PCM) coded telecommunications voice signals. This calculation is encoded using an adaptive filter and, as a result, allows analog voice signals to be carried on a 32 Kbps digital channel in half the space PCM uses.

ADF

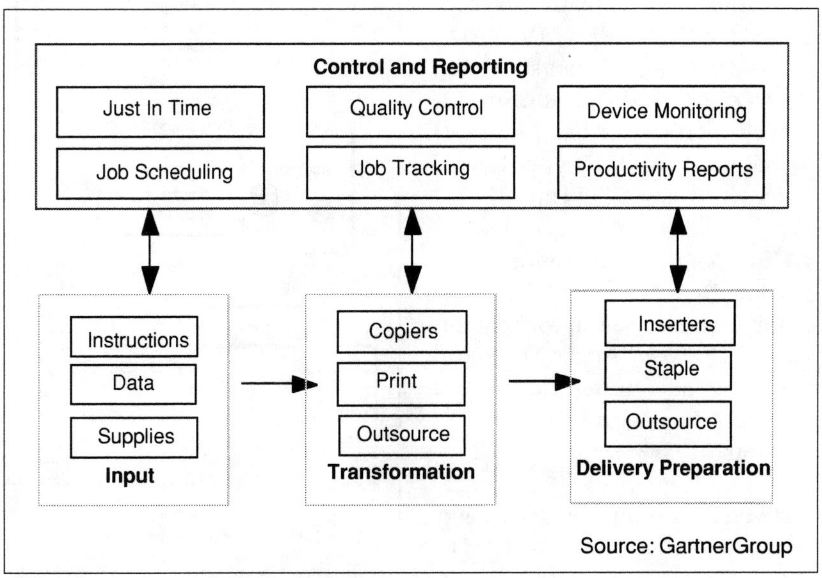

The Automated Document Factory Architecture

ADSI (Active Directory Services Interface)

ADSI (Analog Display Services Interface)

ADSL (asymmetric digital subscriber line)
A group of technologies known as digital subscriber line (DSL). ADSL allows cable TV, video, telephony, and other multimedia services to be sent over voice-grade twisted-pair cable carrying from 1.5 megabits per second (Mbps) to 8 Mbps downstream, and from 16 kilobits per second (Kbps) to 640 Kbps upstream (hence the designation "asymmetric"), over distances from 2 km. to 6 km. without the use of repeaters. ADSL uses adaptive digital filtering, which adjusts to compensate for noise and other problems on the line.

ADSM (ADSTAR Distributed Storage Manager)
An IBM software product that enables a user to manage storage, data access and backup across multivendor enterprisewide networks. ADSM supports five different server platforms and 10 different client platforms. Server platforms supported are IBM's VM, MVS, AIX, OS/400 and OS/2. Clients supported are DOS, OS/2, Macintosh, SunOS, Novell NetWare, AIX, Microsoft Windows, HP-UX, Digital Equipment Ultrix and SCO Unix.

ADSP (Apple Datastream Protocol)
A transport mechanism for communication between Apple Macintosh systems and Digital Equipment Virtual Address Extension (VAX) systems.

ADSTAR (Automated Document Storage and Retrieval — IBM)

ADSTAR Distributed Storage Manager (See ADSM)

ADT (abstract data type)

ADT (Access Developer's Toolkit — Microsoft)

AD technology profile
A GartnerGroup method of assessing an enterprise and its methodology. It includes:

- Development process profile: Life cycle coverage, ease of use, change management, methodologies supported, project management, information model, templates/componentware.
- Development technology profile: Work-group support, development platform, repository,

ADSL

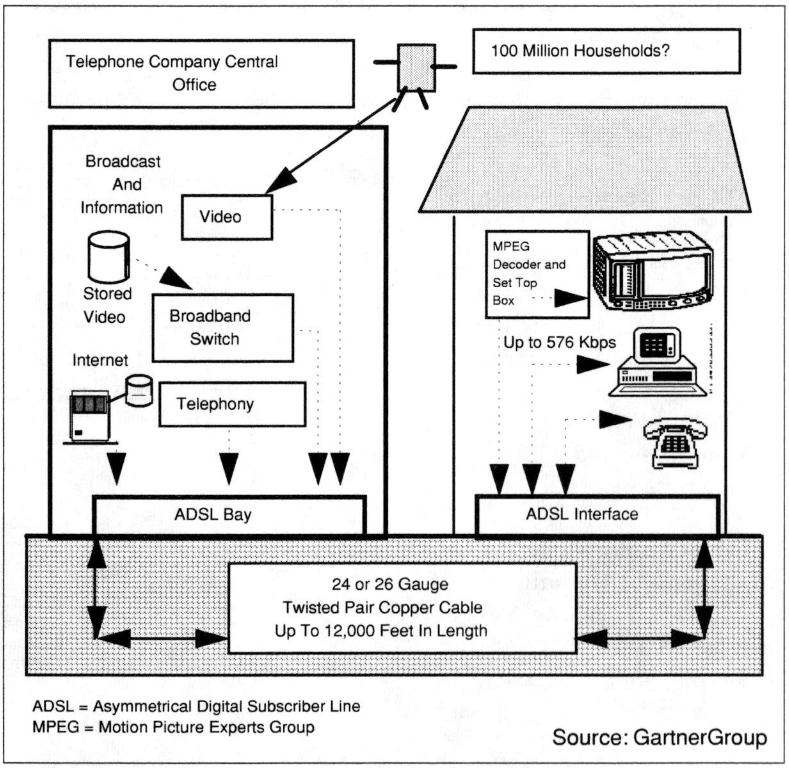

Asymmetric Digital Subscriber Line Technology

object-oriented (OO) component concepts, technical quality, openness, integration.

- Target environment profile: Execution platforms, human interface, database management systems, middleware supported, portability, communications protocols, execution technology, reliability.
- Application capabilities profile: Application topology, application types, complexity supported, transaction volume, security, usability support, type of users supported.
- (Built-in) execution environment profile: Application servers, middleware, database gateways, wrapper facilities, workflow engine, rules engine, dynamic repartitioning.

Advanced Business Application Programming — SAP (See ABAP)

Advanced Communications Function (See ACF)

Advanced Communications Function/Virtual Terminal Access Method (See ACF/VTAM)

Advanced Computing Environment (See ACE)

Advanced Data Communications Control Procedure (See ADCCP)

Advanced Function Printing (See AFP)

Advanced Intelligent Network (See AIN)

Advanced Intelligent Tape (See AIT)

Advanced Interactive Executive (See AIX)

Advanced Linking and Embedding (See ALE)

Advanced Metal Evaporated (See AME)

Advanced Mobile Phone Service (See AMPS)

advanced payer revised DRG (See APR-DRG)

Advanced Peer-to-Peer Networking (See APPN)

Advanced Peer-to-Peer Networking Topology and Accounting Management (See APPNTAM)

Advanced Planner and Optimizer (See APO)

Advanced Program-to-Program Communications (See APPC)

Advanced Research Projects Agency Network (See ARPANET)

advanced ship notice (See ASN)

advanced technology
A technology that is still immature but promises to deliver significant value, or that has some technical maturity but still has relatively few users. Among current examples: artificial intelligence, agents, speech and handwriting recognition, virtual reality and 3-D visualization, smart cards, real-time collaboration, enhanced user authentication, data mining, and knowledge management.

advanced technology group (See ATG)

ADW (Applications Development Workbench)

AEC (architecture, engineering and construction)

AEP (AppleTalk Echo Protocol)

AERM (alignment error-rate monitor)
Monitor used in network and transmission troubleshooting.

affiliates
Web-based counterparts of the industry-based manufacturer representatives that sell multiple manufacturers' product lines. Affiliates (satellite sites) sell other manufacturers' or retailers' (sponsoring merchants) products from a Web site. The user clicks on a product at the affiliate site, but the sales are actually transacted at the sponsoring merchant's e-commerce site (not the affiliate's). Affiliate programs differ from portal tenancy arrangements, which are more complex and differ from electronic marketplace tenancy arrangements, since electronic marketplaces charge subscription fees, as well as take title to the goods in some cases.

AFIPS (American Federation of Information Processing Societies)
An organization of computer-related societies. Its members include The Association for Computer Machinery; The Institute of Electrical and Electronic Engineers Computer Group; Simulation Councils, Inc.; and American Society for Information Science.

AFP (Advanced Function Printing)
An IBM all-points-addressable enterprisewide print architecture. IBM has delivered AFP platforms for AS/400 and OS/2 environments, which has enabled IS organizations to build enterprisewide AFP architectures for distributed printing.

AFP (AppleTalk Filing Protocol)
A standard way to display the filing system of a server to Apple Macintosh clients.

AFPDS (Advanced Function Printing Data Stream)

agent
An independent program or process running on each system element to be managed. Various vendors provide network, operating system, database and application agents that collect information, determine threshold exceptions, execute recovery actions, and store parameter and event information.

agent profile (See AP)

agent technology
Software that acts as an intermediary for a person by performing some activity. Agents can "learn" an individual's preferences and are intended to act in the person's best interest. For example, an agent for a purchasing manager could learn the corporate specifications. The agent can determine when inventory is low or search the Internet for the lowest cost supplier. It may even be possible to use an agent to negotiate and complete a transaction.

AGP (Accelerated Graphics Port)
An Intel technology for desktop systems. It increases system performance by offloading graphic requirements from the system bus to a bus dedicated to video processing.

AGVS (automated guided vehicle system)

AHP (analytical hierarchy process)
A process that uses hierarchical decomposition to deal with complex information in multicriteria decision making, such as information technology vendor and product evaluation. It consists of three steps:

1. Developing the hierarchy of attributes germane to the selection of the IT vendor.
2. Identifying the relative importance of the attributes.
3. Scoring the alternatives' relative performance on each element of the hierarchy. Developed by Thomas Saaty while he was teaching at the University of Pennsylvania's Wharton School of Business, the AHP is recognized as the leading theory in multicriteria decision making.

AI (artificial intelligence)
A wide-ranging discipline of computer science that at its core seeks to make computers behave more like humans. The term was coined by John McCarthy of the Massachusetts Institute of Technology in 1956. AI attempts to resolve problems by "reasoning," similar to the process used by the human mind. AI involves the capability of a machine to learn (to remember results produced on a previous trial and to modify the operation accordingly in subsequent trials) or to reason (to analyze the results produced in similar operations and select the most favorable outcome). Today, applications of artificial intelligence include voice recognition, robotics, neural networks and expert systems (i.e., systems that can make decisions an expert would otherwise have to make to, for example, forecast financial performance, or diagnose illnesses).

AIA (Applications Integration Architecture)
A set of Digital Equipment architecture and product development programs intended to provide a common application programming interface (API) across the VAX/VMS and Ultrix operating systems.

AIAG (Automotive Industry Action Group)

AIDC (automatic identification data capture)

AIF (Application Integration Feature — IBM)

AIIM (Association for Information and Image Management)
A Maryland-based organization dedicated to promoting development of systems that store, retrieve and manage document images.

AIM
A proprietary benchmark designed and administered by AIM Technology, Santa Clara, Calif. AIM measures the performance of multiuser Unix systems. AIM is routinely quoted by system vendors and often required in requests for proposals.

AIMS (Association for the Integration of Network Management Systems)
European vendor group set up with the objective of addressing end-user needs and providing integration of existing management applications, while helping to define the needs of systems developers for standards and open frameworks that will support the interoperation of higher-level management applications. Originally set up as an independent organization, AIMS formally joined the Network Management Forum on 3 August 1992, in order to foster a closer collaboration of efforts.

AIN (Advanced Intelligent Network)
A U.S. variant of intelligent network (IN) technology evolving from earlier research work and specifications carried out by Bellcore.

AIOS (Application Infrastructure & Operations — SAP)
A service providing answers to common challenges that enterprises encounter with the initial implementation issues of SAP products.

AIT (Advanced Intelligent Tape)
The first 8-millimeter helical-scan tape drive designed and manufactured by Sony's tape streaming division using advanced metal evaporated media. Sony has differentiated its AIT drive from other 8-millimeter tape drives with a unique media feature on the tape cartridge called memory in cassette (MIC).

AIX (Advanced Interactive Executive)
The Unix operating system delivered by IBM for its mainframe, workstation and PC hardware.

A/L (ArchiveLink — SAP)
An interface that enables enterprises to link traditional storage archives with SAP R/3. A/L is the product of a partnership between SAP and iXOS Software.

A-law encoding
Encoding according to ITU Recommendation G711, used with European 30-channel pulse code modulation (PCM) systems that comply with ITU Recommendation G732. It employs nonuniform quantifying to obtain the desired compression characteristic.

AIChE (American Institute of Chemical Engineers)

ALE (Advanced Linking and Embedding)
SAP AG's proprietary middleware.

ALE (Application Link Enabling)

alert
A message that an application or operating system may display to notify the user of certain conditions.

algorithm
A process for calculations involving manipulation of numbers.

Alignment Error-Rate Monitor (See AERM)

ALL-IN-1
Digital Equipment's VAX/VMS-based second-generation integrated office information system.

Allowed Cell Rate (See ACR)

all points addressable (See APA)

Alpha
Digital Equipment's 64-bit reduced instruction set computing (RISC) microprocessor.

alternate buffer
Two input/output buffers that are alternated to provide continuous throughput.

Alternate Mark Inversion (See AMI)

alternate voice/data circuits (See AVD circuit)

alternative routing
Method of routing whereby a secondary communications path is used if the usual one is not available.

ALU (arithmetic logic unit)
The core element of a central processing unit (CPU) which actually carries out the arithmetic computations.

ALUW (application logical unit of work)
A design container that developers define for allocation across client/server environments. It is useful in designing enterprise client/server applications of a scope and complexity beyond traditional applications.

AM (amplitude modulation)
A form of modulation in which the amplitude of the carrier is varied in accordance with the instantaneous value of the modulating signal.

AM (asset management)
A system of practices intended to address shortcomings, inefficiencies, waste and unavoidable failures in managing technology and information technology equipment. It involves five major areas:

1. Requisition
2. Procurement
3. Deployment
4. Maintenance
5. Retirement strategies

At its core is an integrated data repository that contains:

- Asset tracking — technical information about the equipment or software
- Portfolio information — acquisition and financial details
- A Contracts database — summarizing key software and maintenance contracts terms and conditions

AMA (automatic message accounting)
An automatic recording system that documents all the necessary billing data of subscriber-dialed long-distance calls.

ambient noise
Communications interference present in a signal path at all times.

AME (Advanced Metal Evaporated)
A media formulation manufactured by Sony for use in its consumer and computer product lines.

AME (Automated Methods Environment)
Ernst & Young's delivery tool for Navigator. It automates methodology and project-level support for several team roles.

American Federation of Information Processing Societies (See AFIPS)

American Medical Informatics Association (See AMIA)

American National Standards Institute (See ANSI)

American Standard Code for Information Interchange (See ASCII)

ALUW

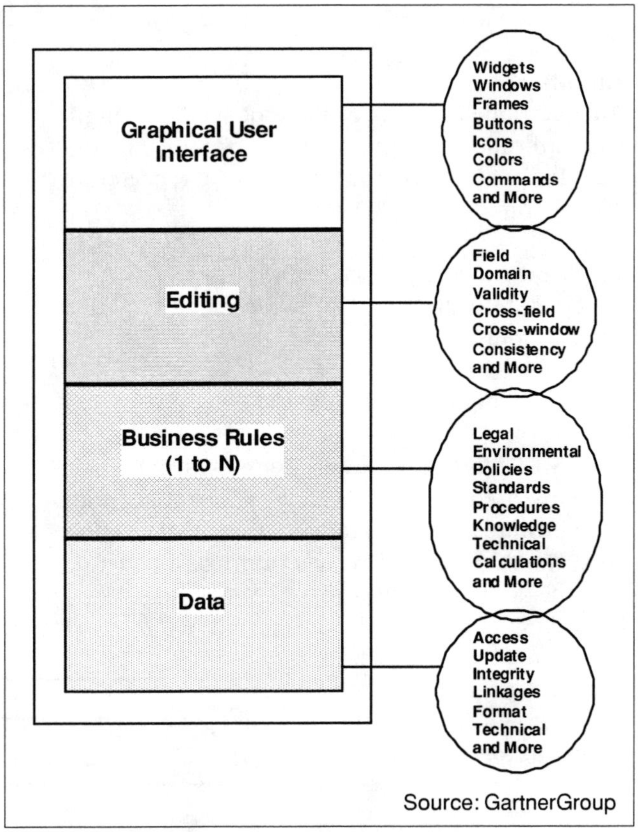

Application Logical Unit of Work

AMF (annual maintenance fee)

AMI (Alternate Mark Inversion)
A digital signaling method in which the signal carrying the binary value alternates between positive and negative polarities; zero and one values are represented by the signal amplitude at either polarity, while no-value "spaces" are at zero amplitude. Also called bipolar.

AMIA (American Medical Informatics Association)
A not-for-profit organization dedicated to the development and application of medical informatics in the support of patient care, teaching, research and healthcare administration. The AMIA serves as an authoritative body in the field of medical informatics and represents the United States in the international arena of medical systems and informatics in international forums.

AMIS (Audio Messaging Interchange Specification)
An enhanced key system feature for voice/call processing that enables enterprise locations to transfer and forward voice messages between systems. It is a voice processing standard that specifies the procedures to network voice processing systems, regardless of who manufactures the system.

AMLCD (active-matrix liquid crystal display)
A key flat panel display (FPD) technology.

amplifier
An electronic component that boosts the strength or amplitude of a transmitted, usually analog, signal; functionally equivalent to a repeater in digital transmissions.

amplitude
A departure of the value of a wave or alternating current from its average value.

amplitude modulation (See AM)

AMPS (Advanced Mobile Phone Service)
The term used by AT&T's Bell Laboratories (prior to divestiture in 1984) to refer to its cellular technology. The AMPS standard has been the foundation for the industry in the United States, although it has been slightly modified in recent years.

AMR (automated medical record)

AMS (Application Management Specification — Tivoli)
A set of application-programming interfaces from Tivoli that enable the consistent definition of applications for deployment and management.

AMS (automation management system)
A subsystem of the warehouse management system. It controls automated material-handling equipment such as carousels, pick to light, in-line scales, and conveyors. The AMS is designed to provide a standardized interface between the warehouse management system and the automated material-handling equipment.

ANA (Article Numbering Association)

analog
Information presented in the form of a continuously varying signal. A transmission is conveyed by modulating (varying) the frequency, amplitude, or phase of a carrier.

analog loopback
A technique for testing transmission equipment and devices which isolates faults to the analog signal receiving or transmitting circuitry, where a device such as a modem echoes back a received (test) signal that is then compared with the original signal.

AM

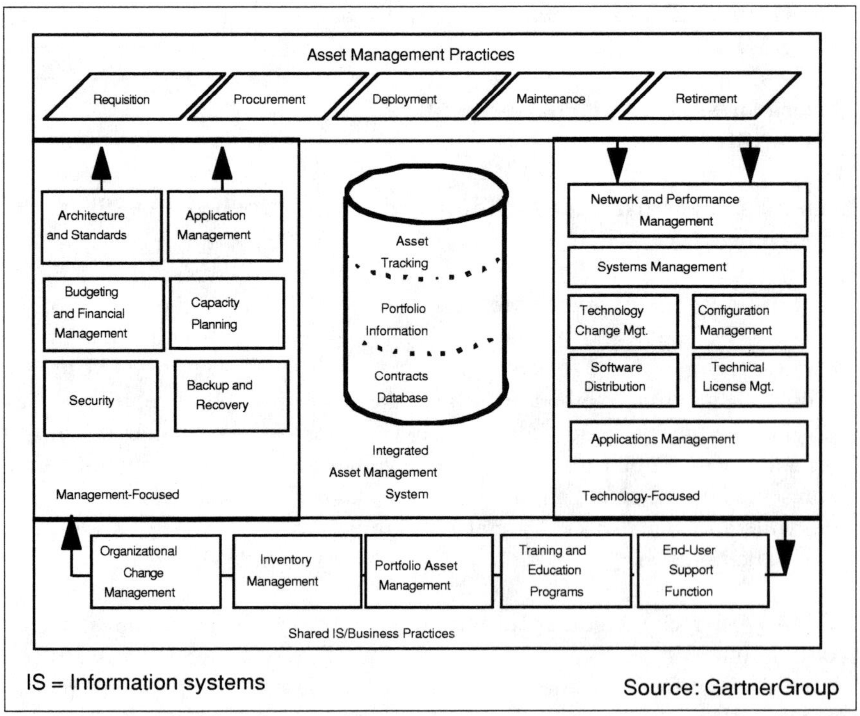

Integrated Asset Management Practices

analog signal
A signal in the form of a continuous wavelike pattern representing a physical quantity, such as voltage, which reflects variations in some quantity, such as loudness of the human voice. Analog signaling is generic to the public switched telephone network (PSTN), as well as to certain other audio frequency and radio frequency facilities such as broadcasting. A digital baseband signal generated by a business machine must be converted to analog form in order to be transmitted over an analog facility, e.g., a voice grade telephone line. This process is performed by a modem.

analog-to-digital conversion (See ADC)

analog transmission
Transmission of a continuously variable signal as opposed to a discretely variable signal. Also called analog signaling.

analytical hierarchy process (See AHP)

anchor
A fragment of information in a hypertext document to which a link is attached, enabling connection to another document.

ANDF (Architecture-Neutral Distribution Format)
The Open Software Foundation's (OSF's) format enabling distribution of a single version of an application to computers with different hardware and software architectures.

ANI (automatic number identification)
A series of digits, in either analog or digital form, which tells a user the originating number of the incoming phone call. Caller ID is the most familiar form of ANI.

anisochronous data channel
A communications channel capable of transmitting data but not timing information. More commonly known as asynchronous data channel.

ANS (Assured Networks Services — Cisco)

ANSI (American National Standards Institute)
In the United States, ANSI serves as a quasi-national standards organization. It provides "area charters" for groups that establish standards in specific fields. These groups include the Institute of Electrical and Electronics Engineers (IEEE) and the Electronic Industries Association (EIA). ANSI is unique among the world's standards groups as a nongovernmental body granted the sole vote for the United States in the International Organization for Standardization (ISO). This status is part of the reason ANSI bends over backward to limit its role to that of facilitator, or catalyst, in the production of standards.

ANSI X series
Any of a number of standards administered by ANSI, including:

1. ANSI X3B11: The evolving standards for smaller-format optical storage subsystems.
2. ANSI X9.9: U.S. Electronic Data Interchange (EDI) standard for message authentication in banking.
3. ANSI X.12: U.S. Electronic Data Interchange (EDI) standard.

antenna
A device used to transmit and/or receive radio waves. The physical design of the antenna determines the frequency range of transmission and reception.

ANX (Automotive Network Exchange)
Established by the Automotive Industry Action Group (AIAG) to offer extranet-based applications to suppliers of Chrysler, Ford and General Motors.

AOCE (Apple Open Collaboration Environment)
Provides a top-level application programming interface (API) for applications developers and a

service provider interface for various back-end providers within the Macintosh operating system. With Vendor Independent Messaging (VIM) in its architecture, it offers pure AOCE for Macintosh-only development, and a VIM interface for portability among Macintosh, Windows and DOS.

AOR (architecture objectives review)
As part of enterprise information management, is focused on achieving an alignment between business and information technology strategies. This alignment was explored in some detail throughout the 1980s. In fact, more than 45 different methods are now being used throughout the industry.

AP (access point)
The basic building block of a roaming wireless local-area network (LAN) infrastructure. APs attach to a wired backbone and provide wireless connectivity to all devices within range of the AP. As devices move out of the range of one AP, they move into the range of another.

AP (agent profile)
A basic agent technology that enables the user to be selective about what reaches the desktop. It describes users' information interests in words, concepts and relationships, not in a simulation of artificial intelligence. When invoked on a user's behalf, APs can be applied to real-time broadcasts, office applications including e-mail and distributed filing systems such as Microsoft Exchange. Technically, an AP is an inquiry that is reused against new, incoming information to determine if, when and to whom information should be delivered.

APA (all points addressable)
A monitor or printer that can place a dot or mark at any x,y coordinate within the limit of its resolution.

Apache
An open-source Web server.

aperture
The diameter of a parabolic antenna.

APG (Ambulatory Patient Group)

API (application programming interface)
A set of calling conventions that defines how a service is invoked through software. An interface that enables programs written by users or third parties to communicate with certain vendor-supplied software.

APIA (Application Program Interface Association)

APICS (American Productivity and Inventory Control Society)

APM (Advanced Power Management)

APO (Advanced Planner and Optimizer)
SAP's supply-chain-planning suite. Its primary components are Supply Chain Cockpit, Demand Planning, Supply Network Planning and Deployment, Production Planning and Detailed Scheduling and Global Available to Promise (ATP). Key functional elements in the first release include full pegging, rule-based ATP with multilevel material checking, and simultaneous material and capacity planning.

APPC (Advanced Program-to-Program Communications)
The programming interface to LU 6.2, IBM's protocol for peer relationship program-to-program communications under Systems Network Architecture (SNA). APPC is the Systems Application Architecture (SAA) interface for cooperative processing.

Apple Open Collaboration Environment (See AOCE)

AppleShare
Apple software for the Apple Macintosh environment, which enables the sharing of files and network services.

application management (See AM)

applications development (See AD)

applet
A small program that runs within an application. Applets are commonly used to make otherwise static World Wide Web pages more interactive. Some examples are: animated graphics, games, configurable bar charts, and scrolling messages. Applets also play an important role in network computers (NCs). They increase an NC's independence from the server because they do not have to communicate with the operating system (resident on the server) to function once the applet has been received by the NC.

AppleTalk Address Resolution Protocol (See AARP)

AppleTalk Filing Protocol (See AFP)

AppleTalk Remote Access (See ARA)

AppleTalk Update-Based Routing Protocol (See AURP)

application
A specific use for the computer such as for accounts payable or payroll. The term is sometimes used in place of "application program," "software" or "program," which are used to process data for the user. Examples of programs and software include both prepackaged productivity software such as spreadsheets, word processors, or customized larger packages designed for multiple users (e.g., Lotus Notes, e-mail and general-ledger software).

application binary interface (See ABI)

application, channel, technology and industry (See ACTI)

Application Control and Management System (See ACMS)

application generator
A tool or toolset that is more sophisticated than simple query/report facilities, and that enables reasonably complex interactive or batch applications to be created at a higher level more easily than the compiler languages mentioned under "traditional processing." Code that is generated should be compiled rather than interpreted for better performance.

Application Infrastructure and Operations — SAP (See AIOS)

application integration
The process of a) keeping redundant copies of data (in independently designed applications) consistent and/or b) enabling end-users to access data and functionality from independently designed applications on a single user interface.

application layer
The top of the seven-layer Open Systems Interconnection (OSI) model, generally regarded as offering an interface to, and largely defined by, the network user. It is the end-user layer in IBM's Systems Network Architecture (SNA).

application logical unit of work (See ALUW)

application management
Consists of the following:

- Application element management — applies the 12 key AM disciplines to the individual physical components that comprise the application.
- Application topology management — applies the 12 key AM disciplines to the logical-applications architecture. The logical architecture comprises the interrelationships of the physical

architecture of application elements plus the technical infrastructure elements on which the application components reside.

- Service-level management — includes defining and measuring logical application-level service metrics, such as scheduled uptime, application availability and application performance (response time and throughput).
- Business process management — uses information systems (IS) to improve the business process (e.g., to improve productivity, profitability and customer satisfaction).

Application Management Specification (See AMS)

application platform
The upper four layers of the Open Systems Interconnection (OSI) Reference Model.

application portfolio analysis
A tool to divide current and proposed applications into three categories — utility, enhancement and frontier — based on the degree to which they contribute to the enterprise's performance. The utility category is essential but does not enhance the corporate performance (e.g., payroll); the enhancement category does improve the enterprise performance based on the use of information technology (IT) (e.g., documentation automation); and the frontier category is aimed at greatly improving enterprise performance (e.g., through aggressive use of rules-based decision support) but usually entails substantial risk. The management issues for each category are, respectively, cost, opportunity identification and innovation. The planning process should consider the best balance among the three categories to gain optimal future performance and the appropriate value from the application of IT.

application program
Software programs in a system are either application programs or supervisory programs, also called system software. Application programs contain instructions that transfer control to the system software to perform input/output and other routine operations, working through the application programming interface (API).

application programming interface (See API)

applications development (See AD)

application server
1. A hardware server designated to run applications (but not a database).
2. A single runtime executable that contains modules of application logic.
3. Systems software used to host the business logic tier of applications — i.e., to manage, optimize, monitor, secure, scale and make its functionality accessible.

For three-tier applications, the application server is the fundamental enabling technology. It enables the management of the business logic of an application in the middle tier, and it enables access to the middle tier from the user interface tier of the application. In a service-oriented architecture, an application server is the host for the application services and also plays the role of a fundamental enabling technology. Transaction processing (TP) monitors, object request brokers (ORBs) and object transaction monitors (OTMs) are native application server products.

application sharing
The ability of two or more participants to have equal and simultaneous control over the content of a document inside an application (e.g., a word processing document, spreadsheet or conference slide) over a wide-area network (WAN), local-area network (LAN) or modem connection. Enables users in different locations to work together on the same documents, with shared control and editing capabilities. A component of data conferencing.

Applications Integration Architecture (See AIA)

applications outsourcing
An outsourcing arrangement for a wide variety of application services including new development, legacy systems maintenance, offshore programming, management of packaged applications, year 2000 services, transitioning service retooling, and reskilling and staff augmentation. While this form of outsourcing generally involves a transfer of staff, the use of the term has recently broadened to include arrangements where this is not the case, as in reskilling or staff augmentation. It does not include systems integration activities.

application-specific integrated circuit (See ASIC)

applications portfolio analysis (See APA)

application sources, characterization and testing (See ACT)

Application System (See AS)

Application System/400 (See AS/400)

APPN (Advanced Peer-to-Peer Networking)
IBM's APPN is an extension of Systems Network Architecture (SNA) Low-Entry Networking (LEN, also known as Physical Unit 2.1), which provides dynamic multipath routing among nodes.

APRC (Amdahl Peer-to-Peer Remote Copy)

APR-DRG (advanced payer revised DRG)
An enhanced diagnosis-related group (DRG) scheme that provides more granular, appropriate groupings.

APS (advanced planning and scheduling)

AQ (Advanced Queuing)

Application Server

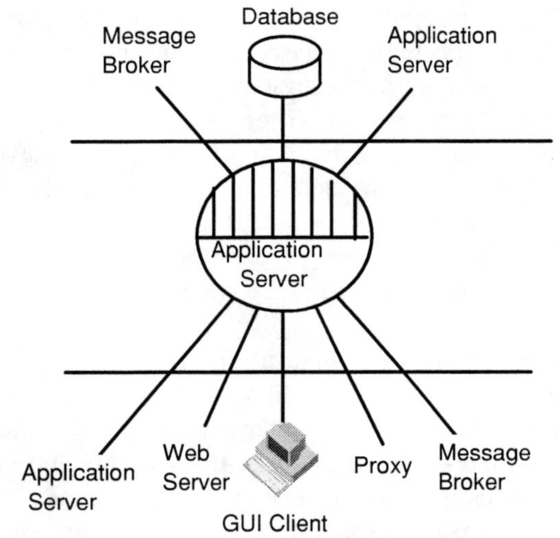

GUI = Graphical user interface

Source: GartnerGroup

Application Server Topology

AQL (acceptable quality level)

ARA (AppleTalk Remote Access)
Protocol enabling remote Macintosh users to have direct access to information on a network, via a dial-up connection.

ARC (additional resource charge)

Archie
An Internet search tool used to look for file names; derived from Archive.

architecture

1. In reference to computers, software or networks, the overall design of a computing system and the logical and physical interrelationships between its components. The architecture specifies the hardware, software, access methods and protocols used throughout the system.

2. A framework and set of guidelines to build new systems. IT architecture is a series of principles, guidelines or rules used by an enterprise to direct the process of acquiring, building, modifying and interfacing IT resources throughout the enterprise. These resources can include equipment, software, communications, development methodologies, modeling tools and organizational structures.

architecture conformance review (See ACR)

architecture implementation review
Designed to enable an alignment between information technology (IT) strategy and implementation, this review, which involves IS managers and end users, assures that tactical initiatives such as product acquisitions support the enterprise information architecture and, therefore, the business and technology objectives. The AIR can be a periodic, formal review or it can be ongoing (e.g., each time the enterprise distributes a request for proposal for IT equipment).

Architecture-Neutral Distribution Format (See ANDF)

architecture objectives review (See AOR)

Architecture of Integrated Information Systems (See ARIS)

ArchiveLink (See A/L)

ARCnet (Attached Resource Computer Network)
A 2.5 megabits per second (Mbps) baseband, token-bus local-area network (LAN) in bus or star topologies developed by Datapoint in the late 1970s. Versions can support coax, twisted pair, or fiber cabling.

ARD (application requirements definition)

Arden Syntax
The Arden Syntax for Medical Logic Modules (MLMs) is a de facto standard in healthcare for coding clinical information (e.g., to generate clinical alerts, suggest interpretations or diagnoses, and guide compliance with protocols).

ARIS (Architecture of Integrated Information Systems)
Suite of software tools developed by IDS Sheer that allows the user to design business processes and to measure their impact.

arithmetic logic unit (See ALU)

ARL (U.S. Army Research Library)

ARM (Application Resource Measurement)

ARP (Address Resolution Protocol)
Internet protocol (IP) used in IPv4 to map an IP address to a media access control (MAC) address.

ARPA (Advanced Research Projects Agency — U.S. Department of Defense)

Architecture

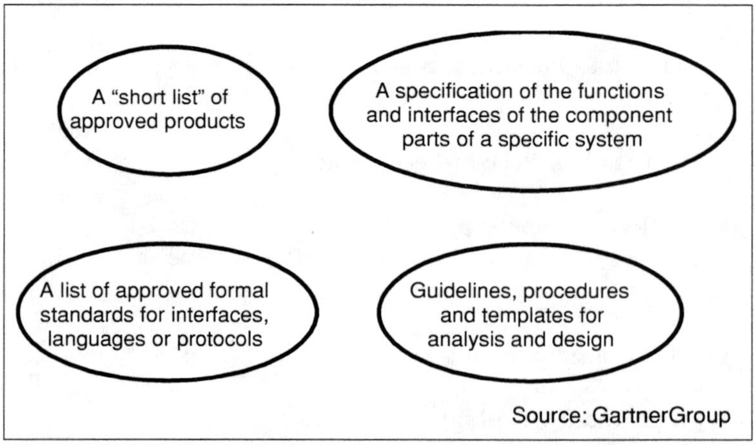

What is IT Architecture?

ARPANET (Advanced Research Projects Agency Network)
The ARPANET, the forerunner of the Internet, was a pioneering long-haul network funded by the AROA. It served as the test bed for many areas of internetwork technology development and testing, and acted as the central backbone during the development of the Internet. The ARPANET was built using packet-switching computers interconnected by leased lines.

ARQ (automatic repeat request)
An error control technique that requires retransmission of a data block which contains detected errors.

ARS (automatic route selection)
Provides automatic routing of outgoing calls over alternative customer facilities based on the dialed long-distance number.

artificial intelligence (See AI)

Artificial Life/emergent computation
Produces complex behavior from the interaction of many simple behaviors (as in societies of ants and bees). Uses include simulation and planning.

ARU (audio response unit)
A device that provides prerecorded spoken responses to digital inquiries from a telephone caller once the connection is established. Also called voice response unit (VRU).

ARUP (AppleTalk Update-Based Routing Protocol)
Encapsulates AppleTalk traffic in the header of a foreign protocol, enabling the connection of separate AppleTalk networks through a different network.

AS (Application System)
IBM's second-tier fourth-generation language/decision support system (4GL/DSS) program product.

AS (autonomous system)
An administrative domain. All members of an AS that share route information can handle traffic to and from any destination.

AS (Netscape Application Server)

AS/400 (Application System/400)
IBM's midrange system that replaced the IBM System/36 and System/38 product families.

ASA (average speed of answer)
A standard quantitative method for measuring the speed at which call center calls are answered.

ASAI (Adjunct Switch Application Interface)
An AT&T product that provides a detailed set of technical specifications for having an outside computer control an AT&T private branch exchange (PBX).

ASAP
A collective term for Mesa Group's management-focused tool and related services for automatically characterizing and analyzing all Lotus Notes applications in an enterprise. ASAP is a breakthrough technology for a software "Notes archaeologist" function. (Microsoft acquired Mesa in March 1998.)

ASC (Authorized Microsoft Support Center)

ASCB (application system control block)

Ascend Tunnel Management Protocol (See ATMP)

ASCII (American Standard Code for Information Interchange)
A standard table of seven-bit designations for digital representation of uppercase and lowercase Roman letters, numbers and special control characters in teletype, computer and word processor systems.

Some IBM systems use similar code called Extended Binary-Coded Decimal Interchange Code (EBCDIC). Since most computer systems use a full byte to send an ASCII character, many hardware and software companies have made their own nonstandard and mutually incompatible extensions of the official ASCII 128-character set into a 256-character set.

ASCOM (asynchronous communication)

ASI (application-specific interface)

ASIC (application-specific integrated circuit)
A chip on which the pattern of connections has been set up exclusively for a specific function.

ASM (abnormal situation management)
The process of and systems supporting the handling of a deviation to the normal procedures involved with the control and management of a manufacturing or other production process.

ASN (advanced ship notice)
An electronic data interchange (EDI) transaction that identifies the contents of a container that is en route from a supplier to a customer. It is also known as UCC transaction set 856.

ASN (autonomous system number)
A number assigned to a local network, registered into the carrier's routing community and placed under the umbrella of an administrative domain called an autonomous system (AS).

ASN.1 (Abstract Syntax Notation 1)
A specification language adopted by the International Telecommunications Union (ITU) for the Open Systems Interconnection (OSI) Reference Model, described in ITU Recommendations X.409, X.208, and X.209.

ASO (automated system operations)
Often referred to as "lights-out operations." This is a combination of hardware and software that allows a computer installation to run unattended — that is, without the need for a human operator to be physically located at the site of the installation.

ASP (Active Server Pages — Microsoft Exchange)
A technology introduced by the Mesa Group in September 1997 that automatically senses whether the user's browser supports ActiveX. If it does, the applet is downloaded; if not, the ASP runs the applet on the server and broadcasts the result to the client, essentially switching dynamically between Stage 0 (time sharing) and Stage 2 (applet-based clients). (Microsoft acquired Mesa in March 1998.)

ASP (average selling price)

ASR (automatic speech recognition)

ASRS or AS/RS (automated storage and retrieval system)

asset management (See AM)

Associate Computer Professional (See ACP)

Association Control Service Element (See ACSE)

Association for Computing Machinery (See ACM)

Association for Information and Image Management (See AIIM)

Association for the Integration of Network Management Systems (See AIMS)

associativity
The ability to link computer-aided design (CAD) data and models together in a manner that allows

design changes to be reflected automatically. Unidirectional or downstream associativity permits model changes to automatically change downstream data such as drafting, analysis or computer-aided manufacturing (CAM) data. Bidirectional associativity allows downstream changes, such as in drawings, to change the model.

ASTD (American Society for Training and Development)

ASTM (American Society for Testing and Materials)

asymmetric digital subscriber line (See ADSL)

asynchronous
Characterized by not having a constant time interval between successive bits, characters or events. Transmission generally uses one start and one stop bit for character element synchronization (often called start-stop transmission).

Asynchronous Balanced Mode (See ABM)

asynchronous data link control (See ADLC)

asynchronous transfer mode (See ATM)

asynchronous transmission
A process in which each information character, and sometimes each word or small block, is individually synchronized, usually by the use of start and stop elements.

AT
Control language for dial-up modems developed by modem pioneer Hayes Microcomputer Products. Use of these commands is one of the characteristics that makes a modem "Hayes compatible."

AT (advanced technology)

ATA (Advanced Technology Attachment)

ATE (automatic test equipment)

ATG (advanced technology group)
The role of the ATG is to provide a continuing stream of technology opportunities to the enterprise. It typically takes the lead in prototype and pilot projects.

ATL (automated tape library)

Atlas
Unix International's graphical user interface (GUI).

ATM (Adobe Type Manager)
A program that enables the user to view type of any size with the highest resolution the user's monitor can provide.

ATM (asynchronous transfer mode)
A wide-area network (WAN) technology, a transfer mode for switching and transmission that efficiently and flexibly organizes information into cells; it is asynchronous in the sense that the recurrence of cells depends on the required or instantaneous bit rate. Thus, empty cells do not go by when data is waiting. ATM's powerful flexibility lies in its ability to provide a high-capacity, low-latency switching fabric for all types of information, including data, video, image and voice, that is protocol-, speed- and distance-independent. ATM supports fixed-length cells 53 bytes in length and virtual data circuits between 45 megabits per second (Mbps) and 622 Mbps. Using statistical multiplexing, cells from many different sources are multiplexed onto a single physical circuit. The fixed-length fields in the cell, which include routing information used by the network, ensure that faster processing speeds are enabled using simple hardware circuits. The greatest benefit of ATM is its ability to provide support for a wide range of communications services while providing transport independence from those ser-

vices. An example is ATM's time independence; there is no relationship between the application clock and the network clock. Ironically, first implementations of ATM will augment local-area network (LAN) transport (and then the WAN it was designed for).

ATM (automated teller machine)
A public banking machine that is usually hooked up to a central computer through leased local lines and a multiplexed data network.

ATM access concentrator (See AAC)

ATM adaptation layer (See AAL)

ATM Forum
An international body, mostly composed of networking vendors, that sets standards for — and promotes the use of — asynchronous transfer mode networking.

ATMP (Ascend Tunnel Management Protocol)
Layer 3 tunneling protocol, developed by Ascend Communications, that performs Internet Protocol (IP) encapsulation at the communications server, thus enabling remote users to connect into their networks over the Internet.

ATO (assemble to order)

atomicity, consistency, isolation, durability (See ACID)

Attachment Unit Interface (See AUI)

attenuation
A decrease in the magnitude of the current, voltage, or power of a signal in transmission between points because of the transmission medium. Attenuation is usually expressed in decibels.

Audio Messaging Interchange Specification (See AMIS)

audio response unit (See ARU)

Audiotex
A communications system that enables a host computer to pass data to a voice mail computer — a store-and-forward mechanism for digitized voice — where the data is interpreted and delivered over the telephone.

AUI (autonomous unit interface or attachment unit interface)
Most commonly used in reference to the 15-pin D-type connector and cables used to connect single- and multiple-channel equipment to an Ethernet transceiver.

AUNet (Asian UUNet)

AURP (AppleTalk Update-Based Routing Protocol)

authentication service
A mechanism, analogous to the use of passwords on time-sharing systems, for the secure authentication of the identity of network clients by servers and vice versa, without presuming the operating system integrity of either (e.g., Kerberos).

auto baud rate (See ABR)

AUTODIN (Automatic Digital Network — U.S. Military)

automated attendant (See AA)

automated attendant system
Processor-controlled system that performs most attendant functions, such as answering calls, extending them to station users, taking messages, and providing assistance. The system provides voice prompts to which users reply via any standard 12-button dial pad.

automated backup
Delivers the most basic form of storage availability, — recoverable data. Most enterprises are struggling with the implementation of this function. It is a conceptually complex and labor-intensive process. Backup design must address multiple elements (e.g., hardware, network, file system and application) across heterogeneous platforms and geographically dispersed sites. Labor intensive, departmental processes are replaced with automated, enterprise-level solutions to increase availability.

automated data collection (See ADC)

automated document factory — GartnerGroup (See ADF)

Automated Methods Environment (See AME)

automated system operations (See ASO)

automated teller machine (See ATM)

Automated Work Distributor (See AWD)

Automatic Alternative Routing (See AAR)

automatic call distributor (See ACD)

automatic calling unit (See ACU)

Automatic Circuit Assurance (See ACA)

automatic error correction
A transmission system feature that automatically detects and corrects a proportion of errors in a received signal. It performs fault detection and isolation and reconfigures the system, dynamically invoking redundant components without the need to bring the system down.

automatic message accounting (See AMA)

automatic message-switching center
In a communications network, the location at which data is automatically routed according to its destination.

automatic number identification (See ANI)

automatic repeat request (See ARQ)

automatic restart — "warm" recovery
Resumption of operation after a system failure with minimal loss of work or processes (as opposed to a cold restart, which requires a complete reload of the system with no processes surviving).

automatic route selection (See ARS)

automation management system (See AMS)

Automotive Network Exchange (See ANX)

autonegotiation
Automatic adjustment to transmission type or speed.

autonomous system (See AS)

autonomous system number (See ASN)

autonomous unit interface (See AUI)

autopartitioning
A 10Base-T feature that causes an Ethernet hub to stop forwarding packets if it detects too many sequential collisions.

autosensing
Automatic adjustment to differing operating conditions or to transmission type or speed.

auto topology
A feature of network management systems that automates the creation of a graphical network configuration map.

autovectorizing
Software used in technical document control systems to convert certain bit-mapped data to geometrical values.

AUTOVON (automatic voice network — U.S. military)

A/UX (Apple's UNIX product)

AV (audiovisual)

available bit rate (See ABR)

available to promise
The uncommitted portion of a company's inventory or planned production. This figure is frequently calculated from the master production schedule and is maintained as a tool for order promising.

avatar
Computer representation of users in a computer-generated 3-D world, used primarily in chat and entertainment Web sites. Potential business applications include customer support, training or sales, where avatars in an enterprise's Web site help out potential customers through text or audio links.

AVD circuits (alternate voice/data circuits)
Circuits that have been conditioned to handle both voice and data traffic.

average inventory
In an inventory system, this is the sum of one-half the lot sizes plus the reserve stock in formula calculations.

average speed of answer (See ASA)

AVL (automatic vehicle locator)

AVS (Advanced Visual Systems)

AWD (Automated Work Distributor)
A suite of imaging, telephony and work management software tools developed by DST Systems. AWD uses AS/400, Windows NT, and various UNIX servers and supports OS/2 and Windows clients.

AWG (American wire gauge)

AWK
A text parser named after its developers — Aho, Weinberger and Kernighan.

AWS (automatic warehousing system)

AWT (Abstract Windowing Toolkit)

B

B1
Mandatory labeled security protection. A class of computer system security defined by the U.S. Department of Defense. In a military context, B1 systems offer a higher degree of security than C2 systems by enforcing the concept of information sensitivity classifications (e.g., unclassified, confidential, secret, top secret) with corresponding user clearance requirements. B1 security has little or no relevance to commercial applications.

B2B (Business-to-Business Procurement — SAP)

B2B or BTB (business-to-business)

backbone
A high-speed line or series of lines that forms the fastest (measured in bandwidth) path through a network. It often acts as a metanetwork.

backbone network
A high-speed transmission facility, or an arrangement of such facilities, designed to interconnect lower-speed distribution channels or clusters of dispersed user devices.

backbone router
A router designed to be used to construct backbone networks using leased lines. Backbone routers typically do not have any built-in digital dial-up wide-area network (WAN) interfaces.

back end
The server side of a client/server system.

background task
A task performed by a system during the time when its primary application is idle.

backhaul
The terrestrial link between an earth station and a switching or data center.

backoff algorithm
The formula for a contention network to determine when to reattempt to access the network after collision.

backplane
The physical connection between the interface cards and the data and power distribution buses in a network device such as a router, hub, or switch.

backup server
A software or hardware system that copies or "shadows" the contents of a server, providing redundancy.

balanced-to-ground
With a two-wire circuit, the impedance-to-ground on one wire equals the impedance-to-ground on the other wire.

Balun
Balanced/unbalanced. In the IBM cabling system, this refers to an impedance-matching device used to connect balanced twisted-pair cabling with unbalanced coaxial cable.

band
1. The range of frequencies between two defined limits.
2. In relation to wide-area telephone service (WATS), the specific geographical area the customer is entitled to call.

bandpass filter
A circuit designed to allow a single band of frequencies to pass, neither of the cutoff frequencies being zero or infinity.

bandwidth
1. The range of frequencies, expressed in hertz (Hz), that can pass over a given transmission channel. The bandwidth determines the rate at which information can be transmitted through the circuit: the greater the bandwidth, the more information that can be sent in a given amount of time. Bandwidth is typically measured in bits per second (see "modem"). Increasing bandwidth potential has become a high priority for network planners due to the growth of multimedia, including videoconferencing, and the increased use of the Internet.

2. The signal-to-noise ratio (SNR) of a modulated signal is tested within a range of frequencies on either side of the carrier frequency. This range is also called a bandwidth. In the case of videodiscs, it is often 15 kilohertz (KHz) on either side, or a bandwidth in measuring SNR often returns a different SNR, with SNR degrading as bandwidth increases.

3. The amount of information that can be effectively handled by a given device at a given time. Typically measured in bits per second (bps), the bandwidth of a fast modem can be up to 25,000 bits per second. This is fine for pages of text but is much more of an issue when dealing with complicated graphical images or full-motion, full-screen video at more than 10 million bps.

Bandwidth On Demand Interoperability Group (See BONDING)

BANI (Bell Atlantic Network Integration)

Bank Global Trust Enterprise
On 21 October 1998, eight leading banks announced they would form a global trust enterprise to provide certificate authority services for business-to-business e-commerce. The first member banks were ABN Ambro, Bank of America, Bankers Trust, Barclays Bank, Chase Manhattan, Citibank, Deutsch Bank and Hypo Vereinsbank. This initiative was renamed Identrus in early 1999.

Banking Industry Technology Secretariat (See BITS)

BAPI (Business Application Programming Interface — SAP)
A set of documented, server-side interfaces to one or more R/3 processes that effectively package multiple internal functions to enable programmatic access to such higher-order tasks as checking customer numbers, providing product descriptions, selecting products, creating quotations, or creating orders.

barrel nut connector (See BNC)

BASDA (Business and Accounting Software Developers Association)

baseband
Transmitting a signal in its original form and not changed by modulation. A baseband signal can be analog (e.g., originating from a telephone set) or digital (e.g., originating from a computer).

base station
Within a mobile radio system, a fixed radio station providing communication with mobile stations and, where applicable, with other base stations and the public telephone network.

BASIC (Beginner's All-Purpose Symbolic Instruction Code)
A high-level algebraic programming language developed at Dartmouth College in the 1960s and

widely taught to beginning programmers. It is simple to use but lacks speed.

Basic Encoding Rules (See BER 1)

Basic Input/Output System (See BIOS)

Basic Rate Access (See B-channel)

Basic Rate Interface (See BRI)

Basic Telecommunications Access Method (See BTAM)

BASIS
SAP's proprietary middleware, between the SAP graphical user interface (GUI) and the R/3 application servers, that optimizes and enhances traditional operating system (OS) and relational database management system (RDBMS) functions.

BASR (Buffered Automatic Send/Receive) (See ASR)

batch data interface (See BDI)

batch processing
The processing of application programs and their data individually, with one being completed before the next is started. It is a planned processing procedure typically used for purposes such as preparing payrolls and maintaining inventory records.

battery backup
Provision of sufficient battery backup to enable the nonvolatile storage of data and graceful system shutdown in the event of a power interruption.

baud or baud rate
A unit of signaling speed. The speed in baud is the number of discrete changes per second in some aspect of a signal (e.g., voltage in a wire). It is now obsolete and has been replaced by "bits per second" (bps). The two terms were roughly synonymous until modems began to exceed 2,400 bits per second, but they have diverged more widely as modem speed has increased. Modems now use coding techniques to transmit more than one bit per baud, making their true baud ratings irrelevant.

Bayonet Neill Concelman (See BNC)

BBNS (Broadband Network Services)
IBM's architecture for implementing high-speed multimedia networks. It is designed to be complementary to existing asynchronous transfer mode (ATM) standards and the implementers' agreements developed by the ATM Forum.

BBP (business-to-business procurement)

BBS (bulletin board system or service)
An information systems communications initiative for sharing information and experience via a dial-up message center.

BC (business continuity)
Recovery of normal operations following the loss of resources, facilities, or technology.

"B" Carrier
Wireline Cellular Company.

BCC (block check character)
A control character appended to blocks in character-oriented protocols. Used for determining if the block was received in error in longitudinal and cyclic redundancy checking.

BCD (binary-coded decimal)
A binary-coded alphanumeric notation in which each of the decimal digits is represented by a binary numeral; e.g., in binary-coded decimal notation that uses the weights 8-4-2-1, the number 23 is represented by 0010 0011 (compare its representation by 10111 in the pure binary numeration system).

B-channel (Basic Rate Access)
Provides access to two 64 kilobit per second (Kbps) data channels as defined in the International Telecommunications Union's (ITU's) Recommendation I.420 as 2B (2B+D).

BCM (business continuity manager)
The person responsible for business recovery planning (BRP) and business continuity planning (BCP).

BCOCA (Bar Code Object Content Architecture)

BCP (business continuity plan)
The plan to be used in the event of some kind of incident (such as fire, flood, restricted access to a building) to ensure that important business processes can continue to function at an acceptable level with minimal impact on customers, service levels and contractual, legal or regulatory requirements. It should also encompass the recovery of those processes to full function.

BCP (business continuity planning or business continuation plan)
A broad disaster recovery approach whereby enterprises plan for recovery of the entire business process. This includes a plan for workspaces, telephones, workstations, servers, applications, network connections and any other resources required in the business process.

BCS (Balanced Cluster Service — Cubix)

BCV (business continuance volume)

BDC (Backup Domain Controller)

BDC (block down conversion)

BDI (batch data interface)
An interface used within SAP's R/3 enterprise resource planning (ERP) system to permit developers to load data into R/3 on a batch basis.

BDLC (Burroughs Data Link Control)
A bit-oriented protocol similar to High-level Data Link Control (HDLC). (Burroughs is now part of Unisys.)

BDLS (bidirectional loop switching)
The ability of fiber rings to be recovered in either of two directions, typically by using two pairs of fiber in the ring.

beacon
In token-ring and fiber distributed data interface (FDDI) networks, a frame indicating a serious prob-

BCP

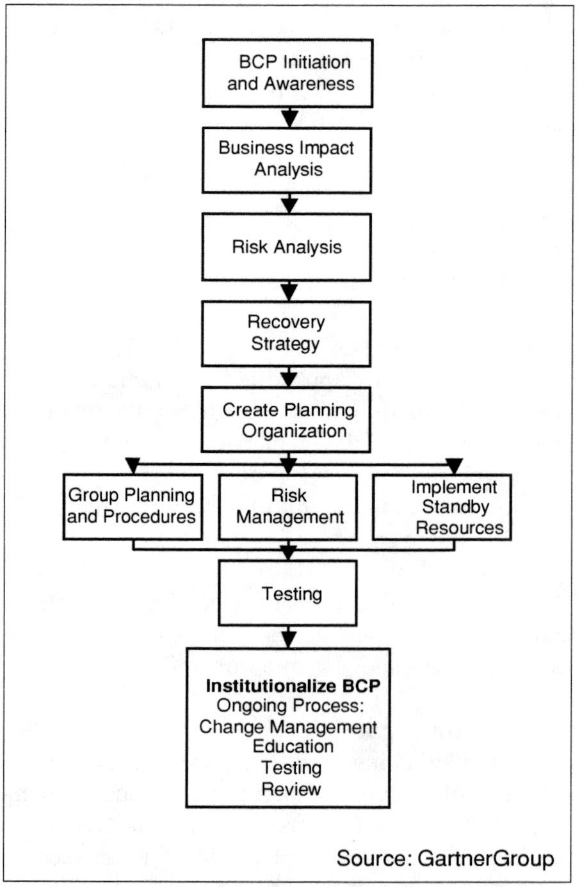

The Business Continuity Planning Process

lem, and containing the address of the station(s) that is/are down.

beam width
Angular width of an antenna radiation pattern, or beam, within which the radiation exceeds some proportion of the maximum.

beatdown
The condition a switch suffers when it becomes congested and cells or cell streams representing Layer 3 virtual local-area network (VLAN) packets are missed or dropped, leading to the VLAN becoming unstable. Also known as virtual circuit (VC) starvation on an asynchronous transfer mode (ATM) network and transit VLAN starvation on a non-ATM network.

BECN (Backward Explicit Congestion Notification)

Beginner's All-Purpose Symbolic Instruction Code (See BASIC)

Bell Communications Research (See Bellcore)

Bellcore (Bell Communications Research)
A jointly owned, financed and centrally staffed organization of the seven regional holding companies (RHCs). It was established by the AT&T divestiture for the purpose of establishing telephone network standards and interfaces and includes much of the former Bell Labs. Among other activities, it performs testing and coordination for the procurement of much of the RHC equipment.

Bell operating company (See BOC)

benchmarking
The comparison between vendor performance and designated benchmark organizations or indexes. An index is a publicly available indicator for a factor that is associated with a pricing element.

- Internal benchmarking is the continuous process of measuring a company's products, services and practices to determine whether the best possible job is performed with the resources at hand. This can include comparing similar functions of different operating units in an organization or comparing the operations of a specific division from one year to the next.
- External benchmarking is the continuous process of measuring a company's products, services and practices and comparing them with those of another company. This can include comparisons with industry peers, functional leaders, or best-in-class performers.

bend loss
Attenuation in fiber cabling resulting from a bend being at too great an angle or from distortion within the cable.

bend radius
The radius of the smallest circle possible when bending a cable, if transmission is not to be faulty.

BER (bit error rate)

BER 1 (Basic Encoding Rules)
The Open Systems Interconnection (OSI) language for transfer syntax description.

Berkeley 4.2Bsd
The Unix version developed by the University of California at Berkeley, which dominated technical computing applications until it was merged with AT&T's System V Unix operating system through an agreement between AT&T and Sun Microsystems. The merger was completed in System V release 4 (SVR4).

Berkeley Internet Name Daemon (See BIND)

Berkeley Software Distribution (See BSD)

Berkeley Software Distribution Sockets (See BSD)

BERT (Bit Error Rate Test or Bit Error Rate Tester)

beta test
The stage at which a new product is tested under actual usage conditions.

BETRS (basic exchange telephone radio system)

BGP (Border Gateway Protocol)
The interdomain routing protocol implemented in Transmission Control Protocol/Internet Protocol (TCP/IP) networks.

BGP-4 (Border Gateway Protocol-4)
A Border Gateway Protocol-based networking redundancy service. It enables an enterprise to route Information Protocol (IP) traffic destined for the same IP address via different network connections. In a BGP-4 environment, when a transmission comes from an Internet Service Provider (ISP's) network, it will look for the primary router that connects to the enterprise's location. If that router becomes unavailable, the transmission will automatically be redirected to the backup router without interrupting the original transmission.

BI (business intelligence)

1. The class of applications and tools by which end users without a high degree of computer literacy may access, analyze and act on information. BI applications evolve from spreadsheets, executive information systems, text management systems using content-based retrieval methods, and decision support systems.

2. A user-centered process of exploring data, data relationships and trends, thereby helping to improve overall decision making. This involves an interactive process of accessing data (ideally stored in a data warehouse) and analyzing it, thereby deriving insights, drawing conclusions and communicating findings with the purpose of effecting positive change within an enterprise. There are four major product segments that constitute BI: interactive query tools, reporting tools, decision support systems, executive information systems.

BIA (business impact analysis)
Business impact analysis identifies the cost (financial and nonfinancial) of a set of business processes that are not functioning correctly. It is one of the early steps required for preparing a disaster recovery plan (DRP) or a business continuity plan (BCP). Without this step, it is difficult for the business continuity manager (BCM) to balance the cost of the DRP/BCP against the potential loss.

BiCMOS (bipolar complementary metal-oxide semiconductor)

bid
An attempt to gain control over a line in order to transmit data, usually associated with the contention style of sharing a single line among several terminals.

bidirectional loop switching (See BDLS)

big-endian
A method of storing or transmitting data where the most significant bit or byte is presented first. See little-endian.

BI IDA (business intelligence information delivery architecture)
A key element of business intelligence (BI) implementation planning deals with the means and mechanisms for providing the needed data and information to users. Information delivery via desktop databases, intermediate servers, client/server database applications, or Web server interaction presents a challenge to most enterprises and many

users. The BI IDA provides a framework and implementation model for evaluating and prioritizing users' needs as well as matching those needs to the evolving delivery approaches and technologies.

bill-of-material processor
Computer applications supplied by many manufacturers for maintaining, updating and retrieving bill-of-material information on direct-access files.

BiMOS (bipolar metal oxide semiconductor)
An integrated circuit technology.

binary code
Representation of quantities expressed in the base-2 number system.

binary-coded decimal (See BCD)

binary digit (See bit)

binary large object (See BLOB)

Binary Synchronous Communications (See BSC)

binary table (See byte)

BIND (Berkeley Internet Name Daemon)
A public domain code used for name resolution.

bindery
A database used by a workstation or network operating system to store internal data such as user or node definitions.

biometrics
A method of identification or authentication that measures a unique physical or behavioral biological characteristic. To identify an individual a computer can use one of three things: something that person knows (e.g., a password), something he or she has (e.g., a token or a credit card), or something he or she is (e.g., a fingerprint). Biometrics is the study of what people are and, in the context of computing, it is a computer's ability to recognize an individual according to a physiological uniqueness, like a fingerprint, a face, a voice, or even the iris in an eye.

BIOS (Basic Input/Output System)
The part of an operating system that links the specific hardware devices to the software. It obtains the buffers required to send information from a program to the hardware/desktop receiving the information.

biphase coding
A bipolar coding scheme developed for Ethernet use where the clocking information is embedded into, and recovered from, the synchronous data stream without the need for separate clocking leads.

bipolar
1. The predominant signaling method used for digital transmission services, such as digital data service (DDS) and T1, in which the signal carrying the binary value successfully alternates between positive and negative polarities. Zero and one values are represented by the signal amplitude at either polarity, while no-value "spaces" are at zero amplitude.

2. A type of integrated circuit that uses both positively and negatively charged currents, characterized by high operational speed and cost. Also called Alternate Mark Inversion.

bipolar metal oxide semiconductor (See BiMOS)

bipolar violation
Modified bipolar signaling in which a control code is inserted into the original digital format.

B-ISDN (Broadband ISDN)
A high-speed (greater than ISDN primary rate), asynchronous, time division multiplexed transmission facility, or an arrangement of such facilities,

designed to provide a wide range of audio, video and data applications in the same network.

Bisync (binary synchronous communications)

bit (binary digit)
The minimum unit of binary information as stored in a computer system. A bit can have only two states, on or off, which are commonly called ones (1) and zeros (0). The combination of ones and zeros determines which information is entered into and processed by the computer.

BitBLT (bit block transfer)

Bitbus
A serial, low-speed network developed by Intel Corp. in 1983 for sensor and factory-level controlling devices.

bit interleaving
A method of time-division multiplexing where inputs are sampled so that the sequence and number of bits are maintained, facilitating synchronization.

bit mapped
Generally refers to the ability of a device (e.g., monitor or printer) to read and display a vast number of picture elements, or pixels.

BITS (Banking Industry Technology Secretariat)
The technology arm of the Bankers Roundtable, whose membership comprises the top 125 bank holding companies in the United States. BITS' mission is to help banks develop electronic-banking and e-commerce initiatives, and to address and resolve critical industry issues (e.g., competitive disintermediation and reduction of infrastructure costs).

bits per inch (See bpi)

bits per second (See bps)

BIW (Business Information Warehouse — SAP R/3)

BizTags
Microsoft "bridges" that translate between different Extensible Markup Language (XML) schemas.

BizTalk
A Microsoft-proposed Extensible Markup Language (XML) schema.

blanking interval
The area in a video signal that falls between frames. It is often used to accommodate data such as synchronizing information.

BLERT (Block Error Rate Test/tester)
A test conducted by transmitting a known blocked bit pattern, comparing the pattern received with the pattern transmitted, and counting the number of blocks containing errored bits.

BLOB (binary large object)
A generic term used to describe the handling and storage of long strings of data by database management systems. A BLOB is a category of data type including media formats such as audio and video, characterized by its large size, which can place extreme demands on storage systems and network bandwidth.

block
A group of bits or bytes treated as a unit.

block check character (See BCC)

block down conversion
The conversion of a full satellite band to a lower frequency (e.g., from SHF to UHF or VHF).

block error rate
In data communications testing, the ratio between the total number of blocks transmitted in a

given message and the number of blocks in that message received in error; a measure of the quality of a data transmission.

Block Error Rate Test or Block Error Rate Tester (See BLERT)

blocking
The inability to interconnect two lines in a network because all possible paths between them are already in use.

Blowfish
A public-domain algorithm developed by Bruce Schneier.

Blue Book
Recommendations approved in 1988 by Comite Consultatif International Telegraphique et Telephonique (CCITT). CCITT is now the International Telecommunications Union Telecommunications Standards Sector (ITU).

BNC (Bayonet Neill Concelman or barrel nut connector)
A type of coaxial cable connector (named for its inventors) with a plug that is turned after insertion to ensure that the pins stay inserted.

BOB (Business Object Broker)
SAP's message broker for R/3.

BOC (Bell operating company)
One of 23 Bell telephone companies whose primary business is providing local telephone service to customers. These companies were spun off from AT&T as a result of divestiture, and were reorganized into seven Bell regional holding companies (RHCs). (There are now five.) BOCs are allowed to market, but not manufacture, telephone equipment. BOCs handle intra-LATA (local access and transport area) traffic, and are also referred to as "local-exchange carriers" (LECs). The BOCs, under their respective RHCs, are:

- Ameritech: Illinois Bell, Indiana Bell, Michigan Bell, Ohio Bell and Wisconsin Bell.
- Bell Atlantic: Bell of Pennsylvania, Diamond State Telephone, Chesapeake and Potomac Company, Chesapeake and Potomac of Maryland, Chesapeake and Potomac of Virginia, and Chesapeake and Potomac of West Virginia. Now merged with NYNEX (New York Telephone and New England Telephone).
- BellSouth: Southern Bell and Southeastern Bell.
- SBC Communications (formerly Southwestern Bell or Southwestern Bell Telephone): Now merged with Pacific Telesis Group (Alascom, Pacific Telephone and Nevada Bell).
- US West: Northwestern Bell, Mountain Bell and Pacific Northwest Bell.

BOI (business object interface)
Application programming interfaces (APIs) published by Baan for their enterprise resource planning (ERP) system to permit access to functions within that set of applications.

BOM (bill of material)
A listing of all the subassemblies, parts and raw materials that go into a parent assembly showing the quantity of each required to make an assembly. There are many formats for bills of material, including single-level, indented, modular (planning), transient, matrix and costed.

BONDING (Bandwidth On Demand Interoperability Group)
A consortium of more than 40 data communications equipment vendors and service providers that have joined together to create a standardized inverse multiplexing protocol for interoperative purposes. The resultant specification is also sometimes referred to as the BONDING specification.

bookmark
Pointer to an Internet address kept within a Web client (browser).

boot
To start a computer system. A boot from a power-off condition is called a "cold boot" while merely reinitializing the system is called a "warm boot."

bootp (bootstrap protocol)
A protocol defined by the Internet Engineering Task Force (IETF) and used to remotely boot systems that communicate with the Transmission Control Protocol/Internet Protocol (TCP/IP) suite. IP address, configuration, and software load are a few of the things that can be accomplished with bootp.

BOP (beginning of partition)

Border Gateway Protocol (See BGP)

Border Gateway Protocol-4 (BGP-4)

BOT (beginning of tape)

BOT (build-operate-transfer)
A process used in several Asia/Pacific countries that allows foreign companies to build a telecommunications network in the country, operate it for a period and then transfer ownership to the government.

bottleneck
The operation with the least capacity in a total system with no alternative routings; the total system can be effectively scheduled by simply scheduling the limiting operation.

bounce
The return of an undeliverable e-mail.

BPA (business process automation)
The automation of complex business processes and functions beyond conventional data manipulation and record-keeping activities, usually through the use of advanced technologies. It focuses on "run the business" as opposed to "count the business" types of automation efforts and often deals with event-driven, mission-critical, core processes. BPA usually supports an enterprise's knowledge workers in satisfying the needs of its many constituencies.

bpi (bits per inch)
A measurement used to calculate the number of bits stored in a linear inch of a track on a disk, tape, or other recording surface.

BPI (business process improvement)

BPM (business process management)
Outsourcing of an entire business process, such as logistics, sales support, billing and processing, and customer service, to a vendor. Also called business process outsourcing.

BPM (business process modeling)
A process that links business strategy to information technology (IT) systems development to ensure business value. It combines process/workflow, functional, organizational and data/resource views with underlying metrics such as costs, cycle times and responsibilities to provide a foundation for analyzing value chains, activity-based costs, bottlenecks, critical paths and inefficiencies.

BPO (business process outsourcing)
The delegation of one or more IT-intensive business processes to an external provider that, in turn, owns, administrates and manages the selected processes, based upon defined and measurable performance metrics.

BPR (business process re-engineering)
The fundamental analysis and radical redesign of business practices and management systems, job definitions, organizational systems, and beliefs and behaviors to achieve dramatic performance improvements. BPR uses objective, quantitative methods and tools to analyze, redesign and implement

innovative business transformation processes and their supporting organization structures, performance standards, information and delivery systems, and management decision-making processes to achieve dramatic improvements in financial performance, product/service quality and customer satisfaction. Information technology is a key enabler for business process re-engineering.

BPR analytical techniques
Mathematical, graphical, logical and managerial algorithms for describing and modeling business processes, information systems or management decision-making systems.

BPR methodology
An integrated set of management policies, project management procedures, and modeling, analysis, design and testing techniques for analyzing existing business processes and systems; designing new processes and systems; testing, simulating and prototyping new designs prior to implementation; and managing the implementation process.

BPR tools
Combinations of techniques and software products that allow electronic capture, analysis, testing, simulation, reconfiguration, and persistent memory of business and systems models

bps (bits per second)
The basic unit of measurement for serial data transmission capacity. Represented as Kbps, or kilobit/s, for thousands of bits per second; Mbps, or megabit/s, for millions of bits per second; Gbps, or gigabit/s, for billions of bits per second; Tbps, or terabit/s, for trillions of bits per second. The numbers are not exact: Kbps is really 1024 bits per second, and so on. This is because capacity expands exponentially, not sequentially.

BPSK (binary phase-shift keying)

BQM (Business Quality Messaging)
A multivendor marketing initiative that is intended to proffer the benefits of message-based communications in packaged Windows applications. Launched in conjunction with the Electronic Messaging Association (EMA) show in April 1997, BQM was initially positioned as a convergence of message-queuing middleware (MQM) and interpersonal messaging (e.g., e-mail), with the interests of the latter group being represented by EMA. BQM continues to be more closely aligned with the EMA than with any other industry association.

BR (business routing)
A GartnerGroup category of call routing used for sales or service functions. The general objective is to determine, as transparently as possible, the caller's needs, business value and relationship, and ultimately to automate the call's routing to a resource. The process is usually driven by multiple databases, with each factor considered becoming a decision or value point.

BRA (Basic Rate Access — Canada and Europe) (See BRI)

break
An interruption to a transmission; frequently a provision permitting a controlled terminal to interrupt the controlling computer.

breakout box
A device that allows access to individual points on a physical interface connector (e.g., EIA RS-232-C) for testing and monitoring.

breakout panel
A breakout box mounted as a component in some larger device.

BRI (Basic Rate Interface — United States, known as BRA in Canada and Europe)
The Integrated Services Digital Network (ISDN) Basic Rate Interface consists of two 64-kilobit per

second (Kbps) data or voice channels, which are designated as B (bearer) channels. The interface also has a 16-Kbps signaling or packet data channel designated as the D (delta) channel. The interface is, therefore, often referred to as 2B+D.

bridge
A relatively simple device that passes data without examining it. Bridges interconnect networks, or network segments, running the same protocols. Operating at the MAC Layer, they are protocol independent; the decision as to whether to forward a signal depends only on the address. There are various special types of bridges: encapsulating, translating, and source routing (q.v.) are the main categories.

bridge/router
Strictly, this provides bridging at Level 2 and routing at Level 3, but this very precise meaning has been largely superseded by a looser categorization that includes any device that combines the functions of bridge and router. Also called brouter.

broadband
A general term for communications at speeds above 1.5 megabits per second (Mbps) and usually at or above T3. The term has an analog heritage where it referred to bandwidths greater than 20 kilohertz (KHz). Broadband channels are used for many communications applications, including high-speed voice and data communications, radio and television broadcasting and some local-area networks (LANs).

Broadband ISDN (See B-ISDN)

Broadband Network Services (See BBNS)

broadcast
1. Delivery of a transmission to two or more stations at the same time, such as over a bus-type local network or by satellite.
2. Protocol mechanism whereby group and universal addressing is supported.

broadcast storm
Excessive one-to-many or many-to-many transmissions, especially troublesome on Ethernet networks.

brownout operation
In response to heavy demand, main system voltages are sometimes lowered, leading to brownouts in which power is not lost but reduced.

browser
A software program on a client system used to locate and display Hypertext Markup Language (HTML) documents on an intranet or the Internet. Browsers are most often used to access World Wide Web pages. Most browsers can display graphics and photographs as well as text, and can present multimedia information, including sound and video, which may require additional applets called plug-ins. Netscape Navigator and Microsoft Internet Explorer are examples of browsers.

BRP (business recovery planning)
Mathematical, graphical, logical and managerial algorithms for describing and modeling business processes, information systems, or management decision-making systems.

BRU (business requirement unit — GartnerMeasurement)
A unit of measure developed to compensate information systems (IS) organizations for performing up to business requirements. The unit cost to deliver server environments to the corporation can then be calculated by accumulating all the delivered BRUs and dividing them by the total cost to operate the environment. BRUs are determined by IS functions delivered by the IS organization, weighted by importance, scaled for size, and added together to provide a total. Scaling is performed by use of the size of the usable gigabytes associated with the business system. The usable gigabyte calculation takes into account the ability of a server platform to use system-managed storage.

BS7799
The Code of Practice for Information Security Management published by the British Standards Institute (BSI) in 1995, to provide a basis for organizational security standards and to enable the establishment of mutual trust among networked sites. Many information security service providers, primarily in the United Kingdom, are offering services associated with BS7799. Its scope is geography-neutral, so it could be implemented by enterprises anywhere.

BSA (Business Software Alliance)
A software industry coalition whose stated missions include industry education and copyright enforcement.

BSC (Binary Synchronous Communications)
A half-duplex, character-oriented data communications protocol originated by IBM in 1964. It includes control characters and procedures for controlling the establishment of a valid connection and the transfer of data. Also called bisync. Although still in widespread use, it has largely been replaced by IBM's more efficient protocol, Synchronous Data Link Control (SDLC), which is under Systems Network Architecture (SNA).

BSC (bisynchronous communication)

BSD (Berkeley Software Distribution)
A version of Unix developed at the University of California.

BSD (Berkeley Software Distribution) sockets
Interprocess communications for creating distributed application programs; corresponds to the Session Layer (5) of the Open Systems Interconnection (OSI) model.

BSI (British Standards Institute)

BSN (Backward Sequence Number — ISDN term)

BSS (Business Solution Server)
A platform for development and execution of complete line-of-business (LOB) applications. A unit of BSS development abstraction is a business process, not a program. Architecturally, a BSS is a framework of business processes. Technologically, BSSs may rest on a variety of technologies, exposed to developers via business application programming interfaces (APIs).

BTAM (Basic Telecommunications Access Method)
IBM's lowest-level input/output (I/O) macro-routine support for providing communications programs on a host computer.

BTB or B2B (business-to-business)

BTC (business-to-consumer)

BTU (British thermal unit)

BU (business unit)

buffer
A storage device used to compensate for a difference in rate of data flow, or time of occurrence of events, when transmitting data from one device to another.

bug
An unexpected problem with software or hardware. Typical problems are often the result of external interference with the program's performance that was not anticipated by the developer. Minor bugs can cause small problems like frozen screens or unexplained error messages that do not significantly effect usage. Major bugs may not only affect software and hardware, but could also have unintended effects on connected devices or integrated software and may damage data files.

build-operate-transfer (See BOT)

bulletin board service (See BBS)

bulletin board system (See BBS)

bundling
Packaging multiple features and products together for a single price.

buoyancy effect
The explosion in the number of applications and application providers caused by the increase in the ease of applications development that arises from the increasing robustness and standardization of base platforms and middleware.

Burroughs Data Link Control (See BDLC)

burst
In data communications, a sequence of signals counted as one unit in accordance with some specific criterion or measure.

bursty
Data that is transmitted in uneven spurts.

bus

1. Physical transmission path or channel. Typically an electrical connection with one or more conductors, wherein all attached devices receive all transmissions at the same time.
2. Local network topology, such as that used in Ethernet and the token bus, where all network nodes listen to all transmissions, selecting certain ones based on address identification. It involves some type of contention-control mechanism for accessing the bus transmission medium.

BUS (Broadcast and Unknown Server)

Business Application Programming Interface — SAP (See BAPI)

business continuity
A comprehensive plan consisting of procedures and facilities designed to keep the critical processes of a business running without interruption.

business continuity manager (See BCM)

business continuity plan (See BCP)

business continuity planning or business continuation plan (See BCP)

business impact analysis (See BIA)

business intelligence (See BI)

business intelligence information delivery architecture (See BI IDA)

Business Object Broker (See BOB)

business object interface (See BOI)

business process
An event-driven, end-to-end processing path that starts with a customer request and ends with a result for the customer. Business processes often cross departmental and even organizational boundaries.

business process automation (See BPA)

business process improvement (See BPI)

business process management (See BPM)

business process modeling (See BPM)

business process outsourcing (See BPO)

business process re-engineering (See BPR)

Business Quality Messaging (See BQM)

business recovery planning (See BRP)

business requirement unit (See BRV)

business routing (See BR)

Business Software Alliance (See BSA)

Business Solution Server (See BSS)

Business Workflow (See BW)

bus topology
An equal-access network design in which all devices are connected to a single linking cable with two distinct ends.

BW (Business Workflow — SAP)
The workflow component introduced by SAP with release 3.0 of R/3. SAP Business Workflow provides the infrastructure and tools to allow business processes to be managed, automated and analyzed.

B/W (Basis/Workflow)

bypass
Any of several configurations of alternative transmission arrangements whose purpose is to avoid the local telephone company switched network. "Service" bypass involves using the telephone company's own (cheaper) facilities, while "facilities" bypass involves privately owned fiber or radio transmission.

byte (binary table)
A group of eight bits handled as a logical unit. In text files, a byte is equivalent to a single character such as a letter, number or punctuation mark.

C

C
The programming language created by Dennis Ritchie at the former Bell Laboratories in 1972. C provides very precise control of the computer's operation.

C++
An extension to the C language defined by Bjarne Stroustrop at Bell Laboratories in 1986. As a superset of C, it provides additional features for data abstraction and object-oriented programming. C++ can be used to develop programs for almost all computers. Together, C and C++ are the principal programming languages in use today (1998).

CA (Computer Associates International)

CA (continuous availability)

CAB (Cabinet File)

cable
An assembly of one or more conductors within a protective sheath.

Cableless Local Area Network (See CLAN)

cable modem
The fastest of the current Internet connection technologies. Cable modems are devices that enable very high-speed data access via a cable TV network. Fast cable modems can transfer a megabyte (Mbyte) of information in less than one second.

CAC (Call Admission Control)
In asynchronous transfer mode (ATM), a function that checks whether network resources are available to support the quality of service (QOS) and traffic parameters of an incoming call.

CAC (Connection Admission Control)

cache
A temporary storage area for instructions and data near a computer's central processing unit (CPU), usually implemented in high-speed memory. It replicates information from main memory or storage in a way that facilitates quicker access, using fewer resources than the original source. Because data is closer to the CPU, it can be retrieved more quickly.

caching server
A device that efficiently stores frequently requested data from protocols such as Hypertext Transport Protocol (HTTP) and File Transfer Protocol (FTP) and has the ability to "prefetch" additional data at

CA

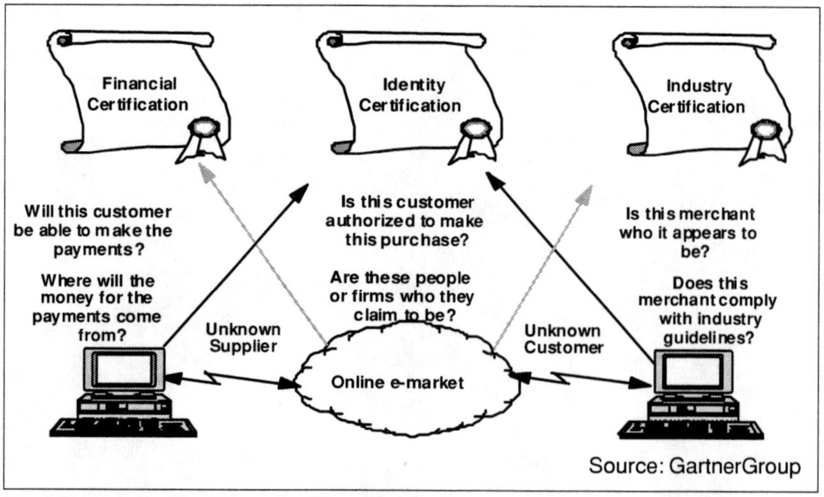

Certificate Authorities in Electronic Commerce

preset intervals. A network caching server has the ability to listen on the network and intercept protocol requests on its associated Transmission Control Protocol (TCP) ports. This alleviates the need to have the enterprise's browser configured to "know" where the server sits on the network.

CACS (Customer Administration Center System)
Allows a PBX user to administer station and switching features as well as obtain traffic and other measurements from one or more private branch exchange (PBX) switching locations via an interactive terminal.

CAD (computer-aided design)
High-speed workstations or personal computers that use specialized software and input devices such as graphic tablets and scanners for specialized use in architectural, electrical and mechanical design. With few exceptions, CAD systems rely extensively on graphics.

CADAM (Computer-Aided Design and Manufacturing)
A computer-aided design program by IBM consisting of three-dimensional construction, modification, analysis and display (geometrical representation) of mechanical parts, including a control system for automated machine tools to manufacture the parts.

CAD/CAM (computer-aided design/computer-aided manufacturing)

CADD (computer-aided design and drafting)
Interactive graphic programs that automate the methodologies of drafting and design layouts. A few programs are successful enough so that it is difficult to justify designing layouts manually. Applications include integrated circuits and printed circuit boards.

CAE (computer-aided engineering)
An area of automated manufacturing and design technology for building end products that had its roots in finite element methods, but today it includes all types of performance systems, e.g., heat transfer, structural, electromagnetic, aeronautics and acoustic analysis. Major improvements have been in the architecture, mechanical, electronic and electrical-engineering disciplines.

CAFM (Computer-aided facilities management)

C

CAGR (compound annual growth rate)
Average yearly growth rate during a specified period.

CAI (Common Air Interface)
An interface for digital cordless communications, adopted by the British Department of Trade and Industry (DTI)

CA-IDMS (Computer Associates' Integrated Data Management System)

CAL (Client Access License)

call
Any demand to set up a connection. Also used as a unit of telephone traffic.

call accounting system
A device that tracks outgoing calls and records data for reporting. See call detail recording (CDR) and station message detail recording (SMDR).

Call Admission Control (See CAC)

call center
A group or department where employees receive and make high volumes of telephone calls. Call centers can have internal customers (e.g., help desks) or external customers (e.g., customer service and support centers).

The call center uses a variety of technologies to improve the management and servicing of the call. A contact center is a networked unit integrated from a media perspective (e.g., e-mail, Internet, fax, data) and a functional perspective (linked to a central database, working in concert with other sales and service channels such as direct sales, Web sites, and partners/distributors).

call detail recording (See CDR)

caller ID
A telephone service that records the telephone numbers of incoming calls, it is a form of automatic number identification (ANI). Caller ID systems can be integrated with customer databases to streamline call management processes. This integration gives the agent receiving a call instantaneous access to relevant information about the caller. For example, when a customer calls, that customer's name immediately appears on the agent's computer screen. The screen might include information about the product a customer purchased and the purchase date. The system could also display the client's previous call history, information about other products the customer owns and price promotions on products that might also be appealing to that caller, based on a profile in the database.

call information logging
Automatic recording of chargeable calls made on a private branch exchange (PBX) system, with details of extension number, exchange line number, time, call duration and digits dialed. This can be used for call accounting or billing.

CallPath
An IBM proprietary standard that covers switch and application interfaces and client/server architectures.

call processing
The sequence of operations performed by a switching system from the acceptance of an incoming call through the final disposition of the call.

call record
All recorded data pertaining to a single call.

CALS (Continuous Acquisition and Life Cycle Support, originally Computer-Aided Acquisition and Logistics Systems)
A joint project of industry and the U.S. Department of Defense to exchange technical-support information in digital form. Now dubbed "Commerce at Light Speed," it has become a set of peacetime programs for integrating electronic commerce initiatives, intended to enhance the development of pro forma and de facto standards (particularly for graphics exchanges) and to drive new methods for concurrent manufacturing in the automotive, aerospace, electronics and heavy-equipment industries. CALS is a useful way for manufacturing enterprises to combine a number of productivity-enhancing initiatives under one umbrella.

CAM (computer-aided manufacturing)
The manufacturing of goods controlled and automated via computer and robot. Frequently used in conjunction with computer-aided design (CAD).

CAMA (centralized automatic message accounting)
An automatic message accounting system that is located at an exchange but that serves various adjacent exchanges.

campaign management system (See CMS)

Canadian Information Processing Society (See CIPS)

CANDA (computer-assisted new drug application)

CAP (carrierless amplitude phase modulation)
A multilevel, multiphase encoding method for transmitting data over twisted pair lines. It is a superset of the legacy protocol used by analog modems. It is simple to implement in silicon, uses less power than

discrete multitone (DMT), is supported by Paradyne and a number of original equipment manufacturer (OEM) providers, and is currently in use in several Internet service provider (ISP) generic digital subscriber line (DSL) services.

CAP (competitive access provider)
A U.S. provider of bypass services for telecommunications.

capabilities exchange (See CEX)

Capability Maturity Model (See CMM)

capacity requirements planning (See CRP)

CAPE (concurrent art-to-product environment)
CAPE represents the third wave of design. It requires a wide variety of synergistic applications to work together, including visualization, rapid prototyping, analysis, materials selection, machining and cost estimation. Key to CAPE are application frameworks, data management and product geometry exchanges, so that any person who is involved in product design and approval can participate in the process.

CAPE II (collaborative art-to-product environment)

CAPE application-specific elements
Technological components that are necessary for a specific application area. Application-specific elements are grouped into three vertical application markets — mechanical design, process plant design and electronics design — which account for the majority of industrial design activity.

CAPE base elements
The seven generic elements that represent the technological foundation and underpinning of the CAPE systems architecture including hardware independence, software architecture, framework incorporation, application integration, data exchange, data management and enterprise pricing policies.

CAPP (computer-aided process planning)
Application software used to develop work instructions and product manufacturing or assembly steps in discrete manufacturing operations.

CAPS (Compugraphic Automated Publishing System)

CAR (committed access rate)
Internet quality of service uses CAR to classify and rate limit customer traffic and manage excess traffic according to the network policy.

card (circuit)
The individual boards that carry the necessary circuits for particular functions; these cards (or boards) are designed to fit expansion slots provided by many computer manufacturers.

card cage
A frame for holding circuit cards in a midsize computer system. Also referred to as a card chassis.

CARGOIMP
Electronic data interchange (EDI) standard for international air cargo, developed by the International Air Transport Authority (IATA).

carrier alarm
An alarm condition that occurs when excessive zeros or all zeros are transmitted.

carrier detect (See CD)

carrier frequency
The frequency of a carrier wave, measured in cycles per second, or Hertz, that is modulated to transmit signals.

carrierless amplitude phase modulation (See CAP)

carrier loss
An alarm condition that occurs when 32 consecutive zeros are transmitted.

Carrier Sense Multiple Access with Collision Detection (See CSMA/CD)

carrier signaling
Any of the signaling techniques used in multichannel carrier transmission. The most commonly used techniques are in-band signaling, out-of-band signaling, and separate channel signaling.

carrier system
The means of obtaining a number of channels over a single path by modulating each channel on a different carrier frequency and demodulating at the receiving point to restore the signals to their original frequency.

cartridge
In optical technology, an enclosure, generally of plastic, in which an optical medium is kept for protection; also called a "cassette." Some vendors captivate their media in the cartridges (this mode is called "spin in"), providing a window for the light beams; others remove the medium from the cartridge inside the drive.

Cartridge Memory (See CM)

cascade control
A control strategy that uses the output of one controller as the setpoint for another.

cascading faults
Network faults (outages) that generate other faults.

cascading hubs
A hierarchy of hubs enabling many local-area network (LAN) segments to be connected to a backbone efficiently but without great expense.

CASE (computer-aided software engineering)
An umbrella term for a collection of tools and techniques that are said by their distributors to promise revolutionary gains in analyst and programmer productivity. The two prominent delivered technologies are application generators and PC-based workstations that provide graphics-oriented automation of the front end of the development process.

CASE analysis and design tools
Graphical, interactive tools for the analysis and design phases of application software development.

case-based reasoning (See CBR)

cash concentration and disbursement plus addendum
One of the primary message formats necessary for enterprise-initiated payments to traverse the U.S. national banks' clearinghouse system. The format is limited to a single addendum record (one invoice, one payment), and many banks can process it.

CASE Data Interchange Facility (See CDIF)

CASE Data Interchange Format (See CDIF)

CASE tools for client/server applications
Software development tools (higher-level than remote procedure call compilers) specifically oriented toward the design and implementation of client/server applications.

CAST
A Canadian-designed telecommunications algorithm named after its designers, Carlisle Adams and Stafford Tavares. CAST is used by Nortel Networks and Entrust Technologies.

CAT (Communications Authority of Thailand)
The exclusive operator of Thailand's international telecommunications services to the rest of the world.

Set up in 1976, it has challenged the Telephone Organization of Thailand's (TOT's) dominance in the domestic services sector and, apart from international telecommunications services, provides data communications, mobile and satellite services. It also has some regulatory and licensing powers and operates Thailand's postal service.

catalog
Data sets grouped and placed permanently in a storage device for use when required.

Category, cabling
A series of five grades of unshielded twisted-pair (UTP) cabling defined by the Electronic Industries Association/Telecommunication Industry Association (EIA/TIA)-586 standard. It includes:

1. Category 1: Used for voice communications; not normally used for data.
2. Category 2: Used for data transmission up to 4 megabits per second (Mbps).
3. Category 3: Used in 10Base-T networks.
4. Category 4: Used in Token-Ring networks transmitting up to 16 Mbps.
5. Category 5: Now becoming the standard for local area networks transmitting at up to 100 Mbps.

CATIA (Computer-Aided Three Dimensional Interactive Application)

CATV (community antenna television)
1. Commonly known as "cable TV." Television signals are received at a selected site by and retransmitted to subscribers via a cable network. Additional channels, not normally available in that area, can also be transmitted.
2. Data communications based on radio frequency (RF) transmission, generally using 75-ohm coaxial cable as the transmission medium. CATV offers multiple frequency-divided channels, allowing mixed transmissions to be carried simultaneously.

CAU (Controlled Access Unit)
Intelligent hub on a Token-Ring Network (IBM term).

CAV (Constant angular velocity)
One of two standards for rotating storage media in which the disk spins at the same rate at all times. The other, constant linear velocity (CLV), spins the disk more slowly on the inside tracks where the circumference is smaller.

CB (Component Broker)
An object request broker (ORB)-based message broker from IBM, focused on solving the problem of application integration. It will enable enterprises to build applications that draw on the enterprise applications' resources.

C-band
The portion of the electromagnetic spectrum, approximately 4 gigahertz (GHz) to 6 GHz, used primarily for satellite and microwave transmission.

CBC (cipher block chaining)
A Data Encryption Standard (DES) mode of operation.

CBD (component-based development)
A set of reuse-enabling technologies, tools and techniques that allow applications development (AD) organizations to go through the entire AD process (i.e., analysis design, construction and assembly) or through any particular stage via the use of predefined component-enabling technologies (such as AD patterns, frameworks, design templates) tools and application building blocks.

CBDS (Connectionless Broadband Data Service)
A European metropolitan-area networking term similar in many respects to Switched Multimegabit Data Service.

CBL (Common Business Language)

CBP (constraint-based programming)
A technique that looks for a workable solution by reducing the search space (i.e., possibilities) by processing the necessary conditions to be satisfied. Configuration engines, planning and scheduling systems are among its most successful applications.

CBQ (class-based queuing)
A mechanism that defines various levels of service for access to the Internet and can be used with or without Resource Reservation Protocol (RSVP). CBQ divides traffic into queues and assigns each a specific amount of network bandwidth.

CBR (case-based reasoning)
An artificial-intelligence problem-solving technique that catalogs experience into "cases" and correlates the current problem to an experience. CBR is used in many areas, including pattern recognition, diagnosis, troubleshooting and planning. These systems are easy to maintain in comparison to rule-based expert systems.

CBR (constant bit rate)
An asynchronous transfer mode (ATM) service category, defined by the ATM Forum, that guarantees a constant bandwidth with low delay, jitter and cell loss. Circuit emulation is a typical application.

CBR (content-based retrieval)
Search methodology for retrieving information based on words or phrases in the text.

CBT (computer-based training)
A training method that uses a mixture of software, disks and manuals to convey information. Trainees work at their own pace, often over an extended period.

CBX (computerized branch exchange)

CC (closed caption)

CC (concurrent copy)

CC (control code)
A multibit code reserved for controlling hardware, such as printers.

CCA (Compatible Communications Architecture)
A protocol for transmission of asynchronous data over X.25 lines.

CCD (charge-coupled device)
A semiconductor device capable of both photodetection and memory, which converts light to electronic impulses. One-and two-dimensional CCD arrays are used in scanners to perform the first stage in converting an image into digital data. They are particularly attractive because they can step the signals from each detector across the array in response to a clock signal, permitting each scan line to be read through a single electrical connection.

CCIR (Comite Consultatif International de Radio Communications/Consultative Committee on International Radio)
Now part of the International Telecommunications Union (ITU).

CCIS (Common Channel Interoffice Signaling)
An electronic means of signaling between any two switching systems independent of the voice path.

CCITT (Comité Consultatif International Telegraphique et Telephonique)
Abbreviation of the French name for the International Telegraph and Telephone Consultative Committee (Comite Consultatif International

Telegraphique et Telephonique). In March 1993, the name was changed to the International Telecommunications Union Telecommunications Standards Sector. The ITU is a specialized Agency of the United Nations based in Geneva and coordinates and fosters cooperation in the use of international telecommunications systems.

CCITT Group III (Also now called ITU Group III)
The original standard for compression and decompression for facsimile.

CCITT Group IV (Also now called ITU Group IV)
The optimized standard for black-and-white office documents. Neither Group III nor Group IV handles color. Both are required to reduce bandwidth and storage demand.

CCL (common-carrier line)
A form of access charge paid by interexchange carriers (IXCs) to local-exchange carriers (LECs). A usage-sensitive portion is included, even though the actual costs to the LECs are not usage-sensitive.

CCM (clinical context manager)

C/CM (content and component management)

CC/ME (Computational chemistry/molecular engineering)

CCMS (Computing Center Management System — SAP)
The integral part of the R/3 BASIS component that provides management services to SAP R/3. It also provides a management console and some selected sets of management application programming interfaces (APIs) to SAP administrators.

CCN (common control node)

ccNUMA (cache-coherent nonuniform memory access)

C conditioning
A type of line conditioning that controls attenuation, distortion and delay distortion so they lie within specific limits.

CCOW (Clinical Context Object Workgroup)
A consortium of more than 20 clinical information systems vendors and pioneering end-user organizations.

CCP (Certified Computer Professional)
A level of information technology (IT) credential issued by the Institute for Certification of Computer Professionals (ICCP) requiring four years of industry experience, a core exam and either two or more specialty exams or one specialty program and two languages.

CCR (consumer-controlled routing)

CCR (Customer-controlled reconfiguration)

CCS (Common Channel Signaling)
Part of Integrated Services Digital Network (ISDN) known as Signaling System 7, which uses Common Channel Interoffice Signaling (CCIS).

CCS (Common Communications Support — IBM)
Systems Application Architecture (SAA) specifications for communications.

CCS (computer-communications services)

CCSA (Common Control Switching Arrangement.)
Switching facilities connected by the telephone company to corporate tie-line networks.

CCSA access
The provision of inward and outward service between the private branch exchange (PBX) and the Common Control Switching Arrangement (CCSA) network.

CCSS7 (Common Channel Signaling System Number 7)
An ITU-specified signaling protocol used in high-speed digital networks to provide communication between intelligent network nodes.

CCTA (Central Computer and Telecommunications Association)

CCTO (client configure-to-order)

CCTV (Closed circuit television)

CD (carrier detect)
A signal indicating that a connection has been made. Also known as Received Line Signal Detector (RLSD).

CD (compact disc)
The trademarked name for the laser-read digital audio disc, 12 centimeters in diameter, developed jointly by Philips and Sony.

CDA (compound document architecture)

CDA (Compound Document Architecture — Digital Equipment)
A proprietary method for describing and interchanging data, which may include rich text, synthetic graphics, scanned images, voice, relational and spreadsheet-like tables, and full-motion video.

CDBS (Connectionless Broadband Data Service)
European high-speed, packet switched wide-area network (WAN) networking standard, similar to Switched Multimegabit Data Service (SMDS).

CDDI (Copper Distributed Data Interface)
A method, favored by the American National Standards Institute (ANSI), of transmitting Fiber Distributed Data Interface (FDDI) signals over copper media. CDDI runs on both shielded and unshielded twisted-pair cabling, unlike the similar Shielded Distributed Data Interface (SDDI) proposal from IBM.

CDD/Plus (Command Data Dictionary/Plus)
Digital Equipment's active, distributed data dictionary system that provides a single logical repository for data definitions and descriptions.

CDE (Common Desktop Environment — COSE)
The first user interface specification (based on Motif) from the Common Open Software Environment (COSE) group, a consortium of major vendors dedicated to standardizing Unix.

CDE (Cooperative Development Environment — Oracle)

CDF (Channel Definition Format)
Microsoft's effort at standardizing the marketplace for push delivery. Push is the automatic delivery of content, data or software to a desktop receiver, server receiver or storage system. Delivery to the desktop or to servers can be handled in three basic ways: through a persistent, open connection; through automated polling; and through multicasting, a one-to-many form of broadcasting. Content and data have been pushed through enterprises for years. Trading-room floors of financial institutions and manufacturing operations are examples of early adopter markets for push, also known in the pre-Internet days as "publish and subscribe" or "event-driven computing." Electronic mail and list servers are also examples of push delivery at work.

CDG (CDMA Development Group)

CD-I (Compact Disc-Interactive)

CDIA (Certified Document Imaging Architect)
An information technology (IT) certification issued by the Computing Technology Industry Association (CompTIA).

CDIF (CASE Data Interchange Facility)
An effort by vendors, users and researchers organized solely to outline standards to address information-bridging challenges. The focus for CDIF is to define a standard whereby any one tool only provides one import and export interface to enable the effective exchange of information with any other CDIF-compliant tool.

CDIF (CASE Data Interchange Format)
The primary interchange standard for computer-aided software engineering (CASE) tools.

CDLA (Computer Dealers and Lessors Association)
A trade association of North American-based computer dealers and lessors. The principal purpose of the organization is to promote professional integrity among its members. It also promotes alternate instruments for computer financing.

CDM (Competitor displacement marketing)

CDMA (code division multiple access)
A user access technique based on the simultaneous transmission and reception of several messages, each of which has a coded identity to distinguish it from the other messages.

CDO (care delivery organization)

CDO (Collaboration Data Object)
An event-based architecture, formerly known as Active Messaging.

CDPD (cellular digital packet data)
Transmission of digital data over a cellular network. With it, data moves at 19.2 kilobits per second (Kbps) over ever-changing unused intervals in the voice channels. It allows cellular networks to offer remote and mobile computing.

CDR (call detail recording)
See also station message detail recording (SMDR).

CDR (continuous data recognition)

CD-R (compact-disc-recordable)
A standard and technology that enables users to write on and read from a compact disc. This new technology is compatible with existing CDs and CD players in that a CD-ROM drive can read any CD, and a user-written CD can be read by any CD-ROM drive.

CD-ROM (compact disc read-only memory)
A version of the standard compact disc intended to store general-purpose digital data. CD-ROMs can store a wide variety of data such as music, video and graphics. CDs are often used by software companies to deliver programs like word processing or spreadsheet applications, because they store significantly more data (650 Mbytes) than a typical floppy disk .

CDS (cell directory service)
A core Distributed Computing Environment (DCE) server component provided for applications to locate resources. It functions primarily as a naming service, which provides a mapping between a logical name and a physical address.

CDS (Control Data Set)

CDSS (clinical decision support system)
An application that enhances decision making by health caregivers by providing context-sensitive advice relating to clinical situations.

CDV (cell delay variation)
One of three negotiated quality of service (QOS) parameters defined by the ATM Forum.

CDVT (cell delay variation tolerance)
Parameter defined by the ATM Forum for ATM traffic management.

CDW (corporate data warehouse)

CE (concurrent engineering)
A collaborative, team-based approach for designing products that combines multiple departments and disciplines into a project team.

CE (customer engineer)

CE (Windows CE)
A lightweight, micro-kernel-based operating system targeted at non-PC devices, licensed by Microsoft for use in pocket-sized devices called HPCs (handheld PCs), and expected to appear in new-form-factor information appliances in the arenas of commercial enterprise and consumer electronics.

CE-Based Windows Terminal (See CEWT)

CEC (central electronics complex)
The term generically used to refer to the central processing unit (CPU), and includes the power unit, service units, console and other units, but not any peripherals. Within a sysplex or coupled complex it is any serial-numbered processor (which may be made up of multiple engines). Within a parallel sysplex complex, it is a single parallel processor that can house multiple engines. (Today this is an uncommon configuration.)

CEC (Commission of the European Community)
The executive body of the European Community (EC). One of its tasks is to draw up proposed EC-wide legislation in areas such as telecommunications for submission to the European Parliament for enactment into EC-wide law. It also has powers to enforce EC legislation where required.

CEFACT (Center for Facilitation of Procedures and Practices, Administration, Commerce and Transport)
A body that is under the auspices of the United Nations Economic Commission for Europe and is responsible for the United Nations rules for Electronic Data Interchange for Administration, Commerce and Transport (UN/EDIFACT).

cell
1. A block of fixed length identified by a label at Layer 1 of the Open Systems Interconnection (OSI) reference model. It is the fundamental building block of asynchronous transfer mode (ATM) and Broadband Integrated Services Digital Network (B-ISDN).

CDSS

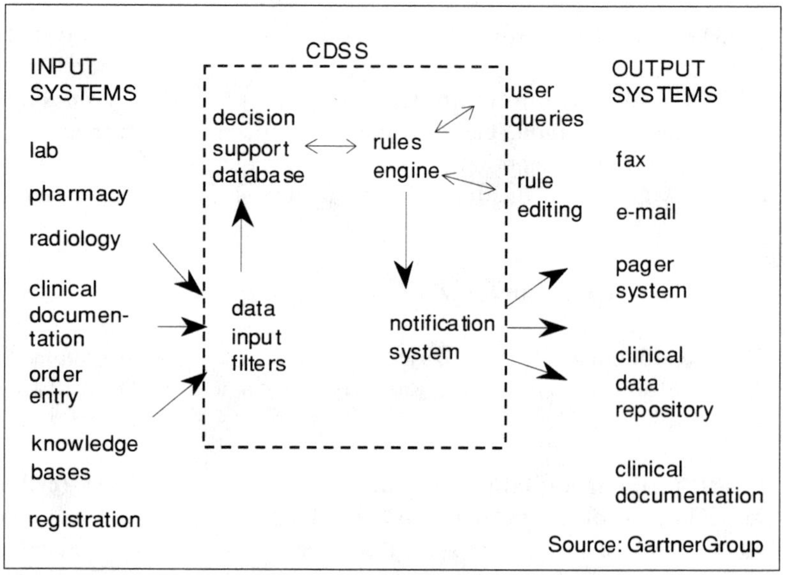

Information Flow in Clinical Decision Support System

2. The storage position of one unit of information such as a character, bit, or word.
3. Also used to describe a precise location in an electronic spreadsheet where specific row and column coordinates intersect.
4. In data transmission, a fixed number of bytes of data sent together, as opposed to a frame, which is of variable length.
5. In mobile communications, the basic geographic unit of a cellular system. Also, the basis for the generic industry term "cellular."

cell controller
A supervisory computer used to sequence and coordinate multiple machines and operations.

cell delay variation (See CDV)

cell delay variation tolerance (See CDVT)

cell directory service (See CDS)

Cell Loss Ratio (See CLR)

cell relay
A transmission mode that utilizes fixed-length cells as the bearer mechanism, as with asynchronous transfer mode (ATM), which uses 48 bytes of payload plus five overhead bytes as the standard cell size.

Cell Splitting
A means of increasing the capacity of a cellular system by subdividing or splitting cells into two or more smaller cells.

Cell Transfer Delay (See CTD)

cellular
Wireless services in the 800 megahertz (MHz) radio spectrum.

cellular digital packet data (See CDPD)

Cellular Multi-Processing (See CMP)

cellular radio
Technology employing low-power radio transmission as an alternative to local loops for accessing the switched telephone network. It differs from older forms of mobile telephony in that service is provided through a large number of areas or cells that are served by a low-power transmitter in each cell, rather than through a single high-power transmitter for the entire region. Because any given frequency can be reused in each cell, the number of subscribers that can be served is multiplied dramatically. Users can be stationary or mobile.

CEMS (Contrat d'Enterprise Maintenance et Service)
IBM's Extended Service Agreement (ESA) offering in France.

CEN (Comité Européen de Normalisation/European Standards Institute)

CENELEC (Comité Européen de Normalisation Electrique/European Electrical Standards Institute)

Center for Facilitation of Procedures and Practices, Administration, Commerce and Transport (See CEFACT)

center of excellence
A central clearinghouse for knowledge capital that is used across all business transformation projects.

central electronics complex (See CEC)

centralized automatic message accounting (See CAMA)

centralized dispatching
Organization of the dispatching function into one central location. This often involves the use of data collection devices for communication between the

centralized dispatching function, which usually reports to the production control department, and the shop manufacturing departments.

Centralized Vehicle Scheduler (See CVS)

central office (See CO)

central processing unit (See CPU)

Centrex
Centrex switching equipment is located in the central office (exchange) and enables subscribers to access facilities normally provided by a separate private branch exchange (PBX). It can be located in a central office or on a large customer's premises.

CEPT (European Conference of Postal and Telecommunications Administrations)
Formed in 1959, CEPT underwent a major reform during the early 1990s. CEPT's involvement in standardization and operational activities has been transferred to other bodies, leaving CEPT to deal solely with the regulatory issues affecting postal and telecommunications sectors across Western and Eastern Europe.

CERDIP (Ceramic dual in-line package)

CERN (Conseil Européen pour la Recherche Nucléiare)

CERT (computer emergency response team)
Formed as part of an information security response for enterprises facing significant security risks. Besides technical specialists capable of dealing with specific threats, it should include people who can train executives to respond to urgent and potentially hostile questions from the media, regulatory agencies, emergency services, stockholders, unions, neighbors and competitors. It will operate in conjunction with other teams, including site security and public relations, but its most important relationships are with the disaster recovery and business resumption teams.

certificate authority
Either internal or third-party entities that affirm or electronically vouch for an individual's identity. They are used to vouch for the identity of a device, such as a Web server, a network router, or an application. The certificate is backed by a profile stored in a database that is referenced to retrieve a public key, or to check attributes such as permissions and roles.

certificate revocation list (See CRL)

certification (See accredited certification)

Certified Computer Professional (See CCP)

Certified Document Imaging Architect (See CDIA)

Certified Network Professional (See CNP)

certified records manager (See CRM)

CES (Consumer Electronics Show)

CEU (continuing education unit)

CEWT (CE-Based Windows Terminal)
A device running the Microsoft CE Windows operating system, which is a smaller version of the Windows operating system, for a range of mobile handheld communications, entertainment or consumer electronics devices other than PCs.

CEX (capabilities exchange)
A method whereby applications "understand" device attributes such as screen size, color vs. monochrome, resolution, amount of storage and bandwidth available.

CF (coupling facility)

CFAR (collaborative forecasting and replacement)

CFB (cipher feedback)
A DES (data encryption) mode of operation.

CFCC (coupling facility control code)

CFI (Computer-Aided Design Framework Initiative)
A nonprofit organization formed to develop framework standards to facilitate the integration of CAD tools, particularly in the electronics design arena.

CFML (Cold Fusion Markup Language)
The server-side declarative script used as an extension to Hypertext Markup Language (HTML) by Cold Fusion, a utility that enables users to create interactive, dynamic Web applications without the need for Common Gateway Interface (CGI) programming.

CFONB (Comité Francais d'Organisation et de Normalisation Bancaire)
The CFONB has defined a convention for representing residual conversion errors in a single byte stored as centimes plus 5. For example, an error of 3 centimes would be represented by a value of 2 and an error of 2 centimes would be represented by a value of 7.

CGA (Color Graphics Adapter)
The first color video adapter, introduced by IBM in 1981. It displays four colors simultaneously.

CGI (Common Gateway Interface)
A data-passing specification used when a Web server must send or receive data from an application such as a database. A CGI script passes the request from the Web server to a database, gets the output, and returns it to the Web client.

Chai driver
Hewlett-Packard's version of enterprise Java technology for embedded-systems efforts.

Challenge Handshake Authentication Protocol (See CHAP)

change integration
Occurs at the back end of the change management process to coordinate and schedule requested changes, with the goal of reducing downtime and risk.

change management
Automated support for development, rollout and maintenance of system components (i.e., intelligent regeneration, package versioning, state control, library control, configuration management, turnover management and distributed impact sensitivity reporting).

channel
1. In data communications, a one-way path along which signals can be sent between two or more points.
2. In telecommunications, a transmission path (one-or two-way) between two or more points provided by a common carrier.

channel assembly
A sales channel initiative aimed at offloading much of the system assembly task from the initial manufacturers to an intermediate dealer or distributor. The reseller or distributor then assembles the system to the buyer's specifications.

channel bank
The equipment typically used in a telephone central office that performs multiplexing of lower-speed, digital channels into a higher-speed composite channel. The channel bank also detects and transmits signaling information for each channel

and transmits framing information so that time slots allocated to each channel can be identified by the receiver.

channel capacity
An expression of the maximum data traffic that can be handled by the channel.

Channel Definition Format (See CDF)

channel service unit (See CSU)

CHAP (Challenge Handshake Authentication Protocol)
A security protocol used to provide challenges and responses with encryption that allows access between data communications systems prior to and during data transmission. CHAP uses challenges to verify that a user is allowed access to a system. See also Password Authentication Protocol.

character-oriented
Generally refers to a type of information display in which the information is limited to that which may be displayed in a fixed array of rows with a fixed number of positions per row. Character-oriented displays have very poor graphics capabilities. The most popular character-oriented terminals are IBM's 3270 family and Digital Equipment's VT family.

charge-coupled device (See CCD)

check digit
A number added to each character in a coded system which allows for the detection of errors; through the use of a mathematical formula, recording errors such as number reversals can be noted. See also parity bit.

checksum
A value calculated from a block of data, used to detect errors in transmitted data.

CHESS (Comprehensive Health Enhancement Support System)
An ongoing research project at the University of Wisconsin focused on providing seriously ill patients with free computers loaded with educational software, access to databases with information about their diagnosed illnesses and access to support groups.

chief information officer (See CIO)

chief knowledge officer (See CKO)

chief technology officer (See CTO)

CHIME (College of Healthcare Information Management Executives)

CHIN (community health information network)
An encompassing term to describe any community-based network open to (and perhaps required for) all healthcare organizations.

chip
An integrated circuit that is the foundation of computer processing and data storage. It holds the logic circuitry that responds to and processes the basic instructions that run all types of computers. Chips are used in everything from watches and calculators to personal computers (PCs) and high-performance computers.

CHIP (client host interface processor)

CHIPCo (Clearing House Interbank Payments Company)
A private company responsible for CHIPS, a clearing system (serviced by the New York Clearing House) that processes very large payments (valued at an average of $1.4 trillion a day) in more than 27 countries. CHIPCo is governed by a 10-member

board of directors representing some of the world's largest banks. CHIPCo's efforts are now concentrated on an effort to simultaneously release, net and settle CHIPS transactions during the day to minimize risk by disallowing bank overdrafts.

CHMIS (community health management information system)

choke packet
A packet sent to a transmitter which informs it that congestion exists and requests that it reduce its sending rate.

CHRP (Common Hardware Reference Platform)
An effort, subsequently abandoned by Apple Computer, IBM and others to establish a multivendor system architecture for the PowerPC processor.

CI (competitive intelligence)
A knowledge management (KM) application that creates perspective and provides actionable advice by capturing large amounts of formal and informal information; organizing these sources of information; storing them in order to access them at time of need; using the information to create reports and advisories; making the supporting information available to users on demand; and reposting CI reports so workers can access them as the need arises.

CI (Computer Interconnect)
The local-area network (LAN) used in a Virtual Address Extension (VAX) cluster.

CIC (circuit identification code)
An end-point identifier (ISDN term).

CICS (Customer Information Control System)
An IBM subsystem (transaction-processing monitor) for implementing transaction-processing (TP) applications. CICS is IBM's strategic general-purpose subsystem for implementing TP applications. CICS invokes customer-written application programs in response to transactions entered at teleprocessing terminals and provides the services needed by those applications to retrieve and update data in files and respond to the terminal that invoked them.

CICS/SM (Customer Information Control System/System Manager for AIX)
The Unix-environment CICS management capability.

CIDR (classless interdomain routing)
The successor to class-oriented domains for Internet routing, it allows for better allocations of Internet addresses. It combines a number of Class C Internet Protocol (IP) addresses to reduce the burden on routing tables in the Internet.

CIF (common intermediate format)

CIF (customer information file)
A system that consolidates customer account information and combines it with basic demographic information to create a current snapshot of a customer relationship. CIFs are often a central component of integrated banking application packages and are primarily used to support operational activities with current, as opposed to historical, data. See also MCIF.

CIFS (Common Internet File System)

CIL (Component Integration Labs)

CIM (Common Information Model)
Within the Web-based Enterprise Management (WBEM) proposal, the new name applied to Hypermedia Management Schema (HMMS) by the Desktop Management Task Force. See also HMMS.

CIM (computer-integrated manufacturing)
The integration of manufacturing operations by integrating human systems, information systems and manufacturing systems. The goal of such systems is to combine electronically the systems

and functions necessary to manufacture products more effectively.

CIM (customer information management)
The systematic support of business strategy through customer knowledge.

CIM Series/400
Introduced by IBM in October 1990 as the first series of products that meet IBM's CIM architecture. It was designed with the AS/400 midrange computer as the core engine and includes software designed to tie together engineering, business and controls systems by linking PS/2s, AS/400s and RS/6000s.

CIO (chief information officer)
The person responsible for planning, choosing, buying and installing a company's computer and information-processing operation. Originally called data-processing managers, then management information system (MIS) directors, CIOs develop the information technology (IT) vision for the company. They oversee the development of corporate standards, technology architecture, technology evaluation and transfer; sponsor the business technology planning process; manage client relations; align IT with the business; and develop IT financial management systems. They also oversee plans to reinvest in the IT infrastructure, as well as in business and technology professionals. They are responsible for leading the development of an IT governance framework that will define the working relationships and sharing of IT components among various IT groups within the corporation.

CIP (Channel Interface Processor)

CIP (Classical Internet Protocol)

cipher block chaining (See CBC)

cipher feedback (See CFB)

CIPS (Canadian Information Processing Society)
A Canadian organization that provides information technology (IT) certification.

CIR (committed information rate)
In a frame relay network, the minimum speed to be maintained between nodes.

CIRC (Cross-interleaved Reed-Solomon code)

circuit
1. A continuous electrical connection between any two points.
2. The means of two-way communication between two or more points.
3. A group of electrical/electronic components connected to perform a specific function. See also channel.

circuit board
A flat card with connections for electronic components; part of an electronic system.

circuit, four-wire
Communications path using four wires, two for each direction of transmission.

circuit grade
The data-carrying capability of a circuit; the grades of circuit are broadband, voice, subvoice, and telegraph.

circuit identification code (See CIC)

circuit switching
Temporary direct connection of one or more channels between two or more points to provide the user with exclusive use of an open channel with which to exchange information. A discrete circuit path is set up between the incoming and outgoing lines, in

contrast to message switching and packet-switching, in which no such physical path is established. Also called line switching.

circuit, two-wire
A circuit formed by two conductors that are insulated from each other, which can be used as a one-way transmission path, a half-duplex path, or a duplex path.

CIS (clinical information systems)

CIS (customer information system)

CISC (complex instruction set computer)
A computer in which individual instructions may perform many operations and take many cycles to execute, in contrast with reduced instruction set computer (RISC). Examples include IBM System/370, Digital Equipment VAX, Motorola 68020 and Intel 80386.

CISO (chief information security officer)

CIT (Computer Integrated Telephony)
Digital Equipment's program that provides a framework for integrating voice and data in an applications environment. The telephone and terminal on the desktop are synchronized so that the arriving call appears on the terminal's screen and the data can be efficiently exchanged within an organization. CIT supports inbound and outbound telecommunications applications. For inbound calls, the application will recognize the caller's originating phone number through automatic number identification, or the dialed number through Dialed Number Identification Service (DNIS). It will then match the information to database records and automatically deliver the call and the data to a call center or agent. In an outbound application, dialing can be automated, thus increasing the number of connected calls.

CKO (chief knowledge officer)
An emerging trend among early adopters of enterprisewide knowledge management (KM) is to formalize a chief knowledge officer (CKO) position. The CKO articulates and champions the KM vision, proactively leads the enterprise to implement and sustain KM, and is the ultimate role model for knowledge users, creators and sharers.

CL (coupling link)

CL/1
A client/server database access product developed by Network Innovations, a subsidiary of Apple Computer.

CLA (Corporate License Agreement — Novell)
A licensing agreement option under Novell's "Customer Connections" program. It offers an alternative for midsize organizations that have made an upfront purchase of $25,000 but cannot qualify for Novell's Master License Agreement (MLA).

cladding
In fiber optic cable, a colored, low refractive index material that surrounds the core and provides optical insulation and protection to the core.

CLAN (cableless LAN)
A local-area network (LAN) network where radio, microwave, or infrared links take the place of physical cables. Also known as wireless LAN (WLAN).

class
A specification that defines the operations and the data attributes for a set of objects.

class-based queuing (See CBQ)

Classical IP over ATM
A specification for running Internet Protocol over asynchronous transfer mode (IP over ATM) as defined in RFC 1577. This differs from traditional

IP, whose Address Resolution Protocol (ARP) uses broadcasts to learn remote addresses.

classless interdomain routing (See CIDR)

class of exchange
The ranking assigned to a switching point in the telephone network determined by its switching functions, interrelationships with other exchanges, and transmission requirements. Also called class of office.

class of service (See COS)
1. In X.25 networks, refers to the speed at which the data circuit-terminating equipment (DCE) and the data terminal equipment (DTE) communicate.
2. In telephony, the categorization of telephone subscribers according to specific types of telephone usage.

Clearing House Interbank Payments Company (See CHIPCo)

Cleartext operation
An option permitting a user to bypass a device's crypto functions, enabling communication with nonsecure terminals and enabling data to be sent or stored in clear mode.

clear to send (See CTX)

CLEC (competitive local-exchange carrier)
Provides competition in the local telephone services market. Two types of CLECs will likely emerge: the local-services reseller or aggregator that buys local services in volume at wholesale prices and resells them to the market, and "hybrid" resellers — carriers that will build portions of the local network band and buy the remaining service components.

CLI (call-level interface)

CLI (command-line interface)

C library
A group of tested application-level routines in C language used by programmers to develop applications.

client
A system or a program that requests the activity of one or more other systems or programs, called servers, to accomplish specific tasks. In a client/server environment, the workstation is usually the client.

client library (See CTLIB)

client/server (See C/S)

client/server architecture
The division of an application into separate processes capable of operating on separate central processing units (CPUs) connected over a network.

Client/Server Interface (See C/SI)

client/server model
In most cases, the "client" is a desktop computing device or program "served" by another networked computing device. Computers are integrated over the network by an application, which provides a single system image. A client can be served by multiple servers.

Clinical Context Object Workgroup (See CCOW)

clinical decision support system (See CDSS)

clinical information systems (See CIS)

Clinical Resource Management System (See CRMS)

clipping

1. Loss of parts of words or of syllables in the operation of voice-actuated devices.
2. Distortion of a signal that has reached the limit of its modulation parameter (e.g., amplitude) and can no longer be effectively modulated.

CLLM (Consolidated Link Layer Management)

CLNS (Connectionless Network Service)
An Open Systems Interconnection (OSI) Network Layer service that does not require a circuit to be established before transmitting. The familiar TCP/IP service used by the World Wide Web is of this type.

clock, clocking
Repetitive, regularly timed signals used to control synchronous processes.

closed-loop MRP (closed-loop material requirements planning)
A system built around MRP that also includes production planning, master production schedule, and capacity requirements planning. Once the planning phase is complete and the plans have been accepted as realistic and attainable, the execution functions come into play. These include the shop floor control functions of input/output measurement, detailed scheduling and dispatching, as well as anticipated delay reports from both the shop and vendors, purchasing follow-up and control, and other functions. The term "closed loop" implies that not only is each of these elements included in the overall system, but also that there is feedback from the execution functions so the planning can be kept valid at all times.

closed user group (See CUG)

CLR (Cell Loss Ratio)
One of three negotiated quality of service (QOS) parameters defined by the Asynchronous Transfer Mode (ATM) Forum.

cluster
Two or more terminals connected to a single point or node.

cluster controller
A device that handles the remote communications processing for multiple (usually dumb) terminals or workstations.

clustered system
An architecture that ties together uniprocessor, symmetric multiprocessing (SMP) and/or massively parallel processing (MPP) systems with all nodes sharing access to disks. Also called a shared-disk system.

clustering
The capability to define resources on one or more interconnected midrange systems as transparently available to users and applications from within the specified group of loosely coupled systems in a local-or metropolitan-area network. Examples include Digital Equipment Virtual Address Extension (VAX) clusters and the Lotus Transparent Computing Facility.

CLV (constant linear velocity)
One of two standards for rotating storage media, in which the disk spins at a higher speed on the outside tracks than on the inside tracks (where the circumference is smaller), so that all data moves past the head at the same rate. The other standard is constant angular velocity (CLV), in which the disk spins at the same rate at all times.

CM (Cartridge Memory)
A Linear Tape Open (LTO) tape format feature. It consists of an embedded, noncontacting, passive radio frequency interface that accesses 4 kilobytes (Kbytes) of nonvolatile memory. It stores metadata and data without consuming drive resources.

CM (configuration management)
A function that enables impact/dependency analysis of application components. There are two views of configuration management. The first is a microcosmic view that looks at a single device or system and the knobs, dials, switches, buffers and settings individually for the device or system. The second is a macrocosmic view that looks at these settings and components as well as the relationships and the dependencies among them.

CM (contact management)
Stand-alone CM applications that enable individuals or multiple users to manipulate and share contact information. CM is now integrated into vendors' messaging offerings and office suites.

CM (ContextManager)
Used by applications to join or leave a context and to indicate the start and end of a context change.

CM (contract management)

CM (course management)
The administrative module that is used to place a structure around computer-based training (CBT) content to:

1. Create a recommended set and order of courses based on job description, skills assessment results or regulatory requirements.
2. Provide a "registrar" function, where students "sign in" to take classes they need.
3. Perform tracking and reporting, keeping track of the results of the course taken, how well the student performed in the course, and what the student should take next. This information would be stored and forwarded to other human resources (HR) systems.

CMC (common messaging calls)
A set of calls developed by the X.400 API Association (XAPIA) for use on top of any existing messaging system. Programmers developing applications using these calls may request services of whatever messaging system is accepting the call. The number of calls is limited to the most popular messaging and directory lookup functions. CMC is similar to simple Messaging Application Programming Interface (MAPI) in its breadth of services, but provides greater portability of applications.

CMDE (Comparex Multiplatform Data Exchange)

CMIP (Common Management Information Protocol)
The Open Systems Interconnection (OSI) protocol for the exchange of network management information.

CMIP end-to-end management
The ability of a global enterprise to manage all the technical and functional components of business applications that run in a distributed, heterogeneous world, including servers, workstations, networking equipment, databases and middleware.

CMIP over LLC (See CMOL)

CMIP over TCP/IP (See CMOT)

CMIS (Common Management Information Standard)
An Open Systems Interconnection (OSI) standard that defines the network monitoring and control function.

CML (chemical markup language)

CMM (Capability Maturity Model — Software Engineering Institute)
The Software Engineering Institute's (SEI's) Capability Maturity Model — and the SCE process based on it — offers an initial basis for defining software development processes for regulatory purposes. The model formalizes the process of determining orga-

nizational maturity and provides a road map for improvement.

CMMS (computer(ized) maintenance management system)
Application software used to provide for work and materials management of maintenance activities in a manufacturing organization. See also EAM.

CMNS (Connection Mode Network Service)
Extends local X.25 switching to Ethernet, Token-Ring, or Fiber Distributed Data Interface (FDDI).

CMOL (CMIP over LLC)
A proprietary network management draft developed jointly by 3Com and IBM that specifies using Common Management Information Protocol (CMIP) over Logical Link Control (LLC) to provide network management of devices on mixed-media local-area networks (LANs).

CMOS (complementary metal-oxide semiconductor)
A semiconductor technology that uses less power and generates less heat (enabling higher circuit density), but is typically slower than bipolar technologies.

CMOT (CMIP over TCP/IP)
Use of the Common Management Information Protocol (CMIP) to manage gateways in a Transmission Control Protocol/Internet Protocol (TCP/IP) Internet.

CMP (Cellular Multi-Processing)
A heterogeneous server technology from Unisys that can run any combination of operating systems (OSs).

CMP (crisis management planning)
An approach that limits the impact of a threat or event — such as an environmental accident or loss of confidence by employees — on an enterprise.

CMS (cable management system)

CMS (campaign management system)
A database marketing application used by marketers to design multichannel marketing campaigns and track the effect of those campaigns, by customer segment, over time.

CMS (certificate management system)

CMS (Change Management System — Aldon Computer Group)

CMS (Clinical Management System — IDX)

CMS (Color Management System — Kodak)

CMS (content management strategy)
The intent of CMS is to define, for everyone in the enterprise, how content is to be used. The CMS for an enterprise should lay out the philosophy and direction for future content use. It should be the result of a joint effort between content managers — i.e., the information resource center (IRC), information systems (IS) and Internet/intranet administrators — and the individual business units.

CMS (contract management system)

CMS (Conversational Monitor System)
A single-user interactive operating system that was implemented for and together with the Virtual Machine (VM) environment. Its prime function has historically been software development. An emerging use within the departmental arena is to house production applications. The CMS file system is oriented toward small files rather than large, however, and CMS is not generally suitable for mission-critical applications.

CMS (customer management solutions)
A method of interaction between a company and its customers (including suppliers, wholesalers

and end users) that is intended to provide measurable benefits.

CMV (controlled medical vocabulary)
An approved list of terms coded in a fashion that facilitates the use of the computer. Controlled vocabularies are essential if clinical applications are to function as intended. Widely used systems include the American College of Radiology (ACR) Code, Current Procedural Terminology (CPT), Diagnostic and Statistical Manual of Mental Disorders (DSM-IV) and the International Classification of Diseases, Ninth Revision (ICD-9).

CMYK
Refers to the traditional four-color printing process incorporating four inks (cyan, magenta, yellow, and black). The majority of printed color paper and photographic documents incorporate the CMYK process.

CNC (computer numerical control)

CNE (Certified NetWare Engineer)

CNI (Coalition for Networked Information)

CNLP (Connectionless Network Protocol)
The Open Systems Interconnection (OSI) version of the Internet Protocol (IP).

CNOS (corporate network operating system)
An evolved, service-rich network operating system (NOS) that provides the service underpinnings for local-area network (LAN)-based middleware. Enterprise-satisfying NOS solutions fall along two lines. Infrastructure NOSs will continue to develop the directory, network management and wide-area network (WAN) support services to build the horizontal infrastructure. Application support NOSs will tightly integrate with desktop operating systems, providing the best base for advanced workgroup and collaborative applications, in a fashion that can be termed "shrink-wrapped client/server."

CNP (Certified Network Professional)
An information technology (IT) certification by the Network Professional Association (NPA) requiring two years of experience, two vendor certifications and a passing grade on the core fundamentals exam.

CNS (converged network services)
The delivery of voice, data, video and other network services over a single infrastructure.

CO (central office)
The telephone company's centralized switching facility, where subscriber loops terminate. The CO handles a specific geographic area, identified by the first three digits (NXX) of the local telephone number.

CO (Contract Option — Lotus)

coaxial cable
Cable consisting of an outer conductor surrounding an inner conductor, with a layer of insulating material in between. Such cable can carry a much higher bandwidth than a wire pair.

COBIT (Control Objectives for Information and Related Technology)
An auditing standard.

COBOL (Common Business Oriented Language)
A language compiler compliant, at the high level of required modules, with the American National Standards Institute (ANSI) X3.23-1985 standard.

COCOT (customer-owned, coin-operated telephone)

CODASYL (Conference on Data Systems Languages)

Codd's Rule Zero
Ted Codd, whose theoretical work on relational databases stimulated the today's plethora of relational products, defined a fundamental "Rule Zero" for classifying relational database management systems (RDBMSs). The intent of this rule was to help enterprises focus on the requirement for a consistent integrity layer in the RDBMSs they evaluated: "For any system that is advertised as, or claimed to be, a relational database management system, that system must be able to manage databases entirely through its relational capabilities, no matter what additional capabilities the system may support."

codec (coder/decoder)
A device used to convert analog signals, such as speech, music, or television, to digital form for transmission over a digital medium, and back again to the original analog form. One is required at each end of the channel.

code division multiple access (See CDMA)

coder/decoder (See codec)

COL (Component Object Library)
Microsoft's distributed OLE/Component Object Model (COM) uses a non-CORBA object request broker (the Component Object Library) running on a proprietary Distributed Computing Environment-like underpinning (Object RPC).

COLD (computer output to laserdisc)
Microfiche replacement system. COLD systems offer economies as a replacement medium when rapid or frequent access to archived documents is necessary. Typically, a 12-inch optical-disc platter holds approximately 1.4 million 8.5-by-11-inch pages of information, equal to 7,000 fiche masters.

Cold Fusion Markup Language (See CFML)

Collaboration Data Object (See CDO)

collaborative planning, forecasting and replenishment (See CPFR)

collision
Overlapping transmissions that interfere with one another. This occurs when two or more devices attempt to transmit at or about the same instant.

Color Graphics Adapter (See CGA)

COLS (commercial online service)
A company that provides its subscribers with access to a data base, via a modem and telephone line, for a fee.

COM (Component Object Model — Microsoft)
A robust component architecture in Microsoft's desktop operating system. A distributed version of COM (i.e., DCOM — the Distributed Component Object Model) enables the development of applications in which components are distributed over several computers (e.g., a client and one or more servers).

COM (computer output to microfilm or microfiche)
A system in which digital data is converted into an image on dry processed microfilm.

COM+
The next generation of Microsoft Transaction Server (MTS) and Component Object Model (COM).

Comdex (Computer Dealers' Exposition)

COMINT (Communications Intelligence)

Comité Consultatif International de Radio Communications (See CCIR)

Comité Consultatif International Telegraphique et Telephonique (See CCITT)

Comité Francais d'Organisation et de Normalisation Bancaire (See CFONB)

Command Data Dictionary/Plus (See CDD/Plus)

commercial online service (See COLS)

commercial parallel processing (See CPP)

Commission of the European Community (See CEC)

Committed Access Rate (See CAR)

committed information rate (See CIR)

Common Air Interface (See CAI)

Common Business Oriented Language (See COBOL)

common carrier
An organization in the business of providing regulated telephone, telegraph, telex and data communications services.

common-carrier line (See CCL)

Common Channel Interoffice Signaling (See CCIS)

Common Channel Signaling (See CCS)

Common Channel Signaling System Number 7 (See CCSS7)

Common Communications Support (See CCS)

common control
An automatic switching arrangement in which the control equipment necessary for the establishment of connections is shared, being associated with a given call only during the period required to accomplish the control function.

Common Control Switching Arrangement (See CCSA)

Common Desktop Environment (See CDE)

Common Gateway Interface (See CGI)

Common Hardware Reference Platform (See CHRP)

Common Information Model (See CIM)

Common Management Information Protocol (See CMIP)

Common Management Information Protocol over Logical Link Control (LLC) (See CMOL)

Common Management Information Protocol over Transmission Control Protocol/Internet Protocol (See CMOT)

Common Management Information Standard (See CMIS)

common messaging calls (See CMC)

Common Object Request Broker Architecture (See CORBA)

Common Open Software Environment (See COSE)

Common Programming Interface (See CPI)

Common Programming Interface for Communications (See CPI-C)

Common User Access (See CUA)

Common Workflow Framework for Java (See CWF/Java)

COMMS (customer-oriented maintenance management system)

communication
Transmission of information between points of transmission and reception, without alteration of sequence or structure of the content. May include data, voice, video or other content. Also "communications."

communication controller
A dedicated computer with special processing capabilities for organizing and checking data and handling information traffic to and from many remote terminals or computers, including functions such as message switching.

communication protocol
The exchange of a special sequence of control characters between a computer and a remote terminal to establish synchronous communications.

communication satellite
An earth satellite designed to act as a telecommunications radio relay. A communication satellite is usually positioned in geosynchronous orbit 35,800 kilometers (23,000 miles) above the equator so that it appears from earth to be stationary in space, but may also be in low earth orbit (LEO) 150-200 miles from earth.

Communications Authority of Thailand (See CAT)

Communications Oriented Production Information and Control System (See COPICS)

community antenna television (See CATV)

community health information network (See CHIN)

community of practice
People associated and interlinked in a communication or knowledge network because of their shared interest or shared responsibility for a subject area. Examples include: people who hold similar job functions (e.g., project managers, department managers, team leaders or customer service agents); all the people on a project team; and people interested in specific technologies (e.g., e-commerce or network management). Communities continually emerge and dissolve, and their membership, processes and knowledge continually change and evolve. See also knowledge management (KM).

compact disc (See CD)

compact disk read-only memory (See CD-ROM)

compandor
The combination of a compressor at one point in a communications path, for reducing the volume range of signals, followed by an expandor at another point, for restoring the original volume range. It is designed to improve the ratio of the signal to the interference entering the path between the compressor and expandor.

COMPARE (Compliance Progress and Readiness)
A scale introduced by GartnerGroup in April 1997 to assist business units, enterprises or business partners in measuring their progress toward year 2000 compliance.

COMPARE Operational Readiness Evaluation — GartnerGroup (See CORE)

comparison-shopping agent
Comparison-shopping agents are pieces of software code that automatically crawl from Web site to Web site gathering information to assist consumers in making purchasing decisions — e.g., locating a particular product at the lowest price.

compatibility
The characteristic of data processing equipment by which one machine may accept and process data prepared by another machine without conversion or code modification.

Compatible Communications Architecture (See CCA)

competency center
An organizational structure used to coordinate information technology (IT) skills with an enterprise. Competency centers provide expertise for project or program support, acting both as repositories of knowledge and resource pools for multiple business areas. Skills-based competency centers, the most common type in an information services (IS) organization, are used for applications development, software language skills, data management, Internet development and network design. Within the business, it is also increasingly common to find competency centers (or shared services) for travel, finance and human resources. Repository-based competencies act exclusively as sources of information.

competitive access provider (See CAP)

competitive intelligence (See CI)

competitive local-exchange carrier (See CLEC)

complementary metal-oxide semiconductor (See CMOS)

complex instruction set computer (See CISC)

Compliance Progress and Readiness (See COMPARE)

compliance unit (See CU)

component-based development (See CBD)

Component Broker (See CB)

Component Object Library (See COL)

Component Object Model (See COM)

composite application
An emerging applications architecture in which functionality and data from multiple applications are exploited to present an integrated user interface. A composite application is one that has the appearance of a single application (from the point of view of the end user) but is, in fact, composed of multiple, independently designed applications. They defragment the end user's view into data, providing, for example, a "customer-centric" perspective in which all relevant information on a customer is accessible from a single user interface. The enabling software required for a composite application is essentially a hub for connections between back-end (often legacy) systems and systems designed to interact with end users (e.g., Windows clients, Web servers and integrated computer-telephony systems).

compound document
Any document containing more than one data type, which may include rich text, vector graphics and raster images.

compound document architecture (See CDA)

Comprehensive Health Enhancement Support System (See CHESS)

comprehensive production architecture (See CPA)

Compressed Serial Link Internet Protocol (See CSLIP)

compression
1. The removal of redundancy in a signal to save bandwidth or storage space.

2. The application of any of several techniques that reduce the number of bits required to represent information in data transmission or storage, therefore conserving bandwidth and/or memory.
3. In the specific context of digital image representation, the process of compacting the data based on the presence of large white or black areas in common business documents, printed pages and engineering drawings. The International Telecommunications Union Telecommunications Standards Sector digital facsimile standards contain standard one-and two-dimensional compression/decompression algorithms.

compressor
An electronic device that compresses the volume range of a signal.

CompTIA (Computing Technology Industry Association)

Computer-Aided Acquisition and Logistics Systems (See CALS)

computer-aided design (See CAD)

computer-aided design and drafting (See CADD)

Computer-Aided Design and Manufacturing (See CADAM)

Computer-Aided Design Framework Initiative (See CFI)

computer-aided drafting and design (See CADD)

computer-aided engineering (See CAE)

computer-aided manufacturing (See CAM)

computer-aided process planning (See CAPP)

computer-aided software engineering (See CASE)

computer-based patient record (See CPR)

Computer-Based Patient Record Institute (See CPRI)

computer-based training (See CBT)

Computer Dealers and Lessors Association (See CDLA)

computer emergency response team (See CERT)

Computer Graphics Augmented Design and Manufacturing System (See CADAM)

computer-integrated manufacturing (See CIM)

Computer Integrated Telephony (See CIT)

Computer Interconnect (See CI)

computerized branch exchange (See CBX)

computer(ized) maintenance management system (See CMMS)

computer network
An interconnection of two or more computer systems, terminals, and/or communications facilities.

computer output to laserdisc (See COLD)

computer output to microfilm or microfiche (See COM)

Computer Software and Engineering (See CSE Systems)

Computer Supported Telephony Architecture (See CSTA)

Computer Support for Cooperative Work (See CSCW)

computer-telephony integration (See CTI)

computer to PBX interface (See CPI)

Computing Center Management System — SAP (See CCMS)

Computing Technology Industry Association (See CompTIA)

COM-R (computer output to microfiche replacement)

COMTI (COM Transaction Integrator — Microsoft)

concentrator
A device that merges many low-speed asynchronous channels into one or more high-speed synchronous channels to achieve economies of data transmission.

concurrent art-to-product environment (See CAPE)

concurrent backup
A system-level facility to allow a database or disk file to be backed up to another disk or to magnetic tape while it is still open for application access.

concurrent database restore
A system-level facility to allow a database or portion thereof to be restored while the database is still open for application access.

concurrent engineering (See CE)

concurrent use
A way to measure the usage of software licenses. Software can be licensed in one of the following ways: individual (it cannot be shared with other users); site (a limited number of people can use the software); concurrent use (usage is limited to a maximum number of users at a particular time.) The software vendor usually sets the guidelines on the type of software license. Monitoring is facilitated by the vendor or by the user. When software usage is measured by the user, the vendor can require a user to supply detailed reports or can rely on the user's pledge. Enterprises can avoid liability and save money by accurately measuring the number of users.

conditioning
A procedure that restricts transmission impairments of a circuit to certain specified limits.

conductor
1. Any equipment, such as a wire or cable, that can carry an electric current.
2. One wire of a multiwire cable.

configuration management (See CM)

connection
The establishment of a communication path for the transfer of information as per agreed-upon conventions.

connectionless
The interconnection model in which communication takes place without first establishing a connection.

Connectionless Broadband Data Service (See CBDS)

Connectionless Network Service (See CLNS)

connectionless service
In a connectionless service, no fixed path is set up between sender and recipient. Every unit of data that is exchanged is self-contained in that it contains all the necessary control and address information to ensure correct delivery, e.g., packet switching.

Connection Mode Network Service (See CMNS)

Connection-Oriented Network Protocol (See CONP)

connection-oriented service
A service in which a connection (real or virtual) is set up and maintained for the duration of the communication. See also circuit switching.

connect time
The amount of time that a circuit, typically in a circuit switched environment, is in use. See also holding time.

Connect via System/370 Channel as SNA Device
A hardware connection to a System/370 channel emulating a Systems Network Architecture (SNA) device (e.g., 3174) to accommodate high-speed and bulk data transfers where communication and Token Ring Network (TRN) connections are not appropriate.

CONP (Connection-Oriented Network Protocol)
An Open Systems Interconnection (OSI) protocol enabling connection-oriented operation to upper-layer protocols.

console
The part of a computer used for communicating between the user and the system. A cathode ray tube (CRT) terminal with mouse and keyboard is the most common type.

consolidated service desk (See CSD)

consolidation effect
The reduction in the number of vendors that can afford to supply all of the hardware, operating systems and middleware necessary to compete effectively.

constant angular velocity (See CAV)

constant bit rate (See CBR)

constant linear velocity (See CLV)

constraint-based programming (See CBP)

constraint management
The ability to define model topology in the form of geometric constraints such as parallelism or tangency.

consulting

1. Management consulting — Tier 1 (executive): assistance regarding setting or execution of corporate business strategy or vision; Tier 2 (business): assistance regarding business processes (re-engineering) or change management.
2. IS consulting — includes systems architecture design or development and IS organizational planning.
3. Application or technical consulting — includes application project management and development, technology assessment, and product tuning.

contact
Part of a switch designed to touch a similar contact, enabling current to flow, and designed to break this union, causing current to cease.

contact center
A multichannel — phone, fax, interactive voice response (IVR), speech recognition, e-mail, Web, video — multipurpose organization that handles sales, marketing and customer service transactions for a variety of constituencies (customers, prospects and supply chain), in a logically consolidated but physically disaggregated environment.

contact database
Software that holds names and addresses and is used for appointments for the purposes of keeping track of sales and prospects.

contact management (See CM)

content
Commercial publishing content refers to individual documents that can be graphic, textual or illustrative in nature, or amalgamations of documents that can be combined into individual articles or complete publications.

content-based retrieval (See CBR)

contention
A method of line control in which the terminals request to transmit. If the channel in question is free, transmission proceeds; if it is not free, the terminal must wait until it becomes free.

content management strategy (See CMS)

context
Refers to meanings that are clear to the sender or receiver (e.g., application or person), either because they are stated elsewhere in the message or because they have been predefined (e.g., the number "30" means "30 pounds of flour" in one message and "30 cases of orange soda" in another message). Sender and receiver may have different interpretations of meaning (i.e., different context). For example, "customer" could be the party that pays the freight bill in a billing application, but the receiver of the item (which might not be the payer) in a warehousing application.

ContextManager (See CM)

ContextParticipant (See CP)

continuity check
In common-channel signaling, a test performed to check that a path exists for speech or data transmission.

Continuous Acquisition and Life Cycle Support (See CALS)

continuous improvement
A manufacturing methodology used to improve overall quality by continuously increasing precision in part specification.

continuous operations
Those characteristics of a data-processing system that reduce or eliminate the need for planned downtime, such as scheduled maintenance. One element of 24x7 operation.

continuous process improvement (See CPI)

continuous production
A production system in which the productive units are organized and sequenced according to the steps to produce the product. The routing of the jobs is fixed, and setups are seldom changed.

continuous quality improvement (See CQI)

Continuous Variable Slope Delta Modulation (See CVSD)

Contrat d'Enterprise Maintenance et Service (See CEMS)

control character
A character inserted into a datastream to signal the receiving station to perform a function or to identify the structure of the message. Newer protocols are moving away from character-oriented control procedures toward bit-oriented control procedures.

control code (See CC)

Controlled Access Unit (See CAU)

controlled medical vocabulary (See CMV)

Control-M
A single multiplatform product from New Dimension Software, based on a robust three-tier architecture, which enables users to manage production control and scheduling across multiple platforms.

Control Objectives for Information and Related Technology (See COBIT)

Control Program for Microcomputers (See CP/M)

control signals
Signals which pass between one part of communication system and another to control the system.

converged network services (See CNS)

convergence
The folding together of broadcast and consumer technologies with the accountability and interactivity of applications such as those deployed on the World Wide Web.

conversational
A program or a system that carries on a dialog with terminal users, alternately accepting input and then responding to the input quickly enough for the users to maintain their train of thought. See also interactive.

Conversational Monitor System (See CMS)

conversion
The process of preparing, capturing and indexing paper files to digital files.

cookie
A permanent code placed in a file on a client computer's hard disk by a server that the client has visited. The code uniquely identifies, or "registers," that user and can be accessed for number of marketing and site-tracking purposes.

Cooperation
NCR's third-generation office information system and end-user computing initiative.

cooperative processing
The splitting of an application into tasks performed on separate computers. Physical connectivity can occur via a direct channel connection, a local-area network (LAN), a peer-to-peer communication link or a master/slave link. The application software can exist in a distributed processing environment, but this is not a requirement.

coordination mechanics
A term coined by Coordination Technology's founder, Anatole Holt. It generally refers to a class of workflow that is heuristic in nature; i.e., a higher form of workflow concentrating on human behavior.

COPICS (Communications Oriented Production Information and Control System)
IBM's mainframe material requirements planning product. Several versions are now supported, including COPICS-D (defense) and a version using IBM's DB2.

Copper Distributed Data Interface (See CDDI)

COPS (Common Open Policy Service)

CORAS (Corporate Access Server)

CORBA (Common Object Request Broker Architecture)
An Object Management Group (OMG) interoperability standard for object-oriented applications communicating over heterogeneous networks.

Cordless Telephone version 2 (See CT2)

Cordless Telephone version 3 (See CT3)

CORE (COMPARE Operational Readiness Evaluation — GartnerGroup)
The CORE risk assessment and reporting steps are used to define business operational risks, to report risks to management, investors, regulators and customers in a consistent form, and to determine when contingency and recovery strategies are required.

CORE (Council of Registrars)

Corporate License Agreement (See CLA)

corporate network operating system (See CNOS)

corporate property management software (See CPMS)

Corporate Time (See CT)

corporate trade exchange (See CTX)

corporate trade payment (See CTP)

Corporation for Open Systems (See COS)

correspondence-tracking application (CTA)

COS (class of service)
An Internet service provider (ISP) offering that prioritizes which traffic is delivered before other traffic. With COS, when an ISP's network is not congested, all traffic is treated equally. When the network is congested, however, traffic that has been designated as a higher priority will be delivered first, while lower priority traffic will be held in a queue until the higher-class traffic has been transmitted.

COS (Corporation for Open Systems)
An organization started in 1986 to hasten the introduction of products and services that are interoperable, that come from many vendors and that are based on international standards.

COSE (Common Open Software Environment)
A group formed to promote interoperability and portability across Unix platforms. The group's first project was the Common Desktop Environment (CDE), spearheaded by Hewlett-Packard, SunSoft, IBM and Novell.

cost center
The smallest segment of an organization for which costs are collected. The criteria in defining cost centers are that the cost be significant and the area of responsibility be clearly defined. A cost center may not be identical to a work center. Normally, it would encompass more than one work center.

costed bill of material
A form of bill of material that, besides providing the normal information such as components, quantity of each, and effectivity data, also extends the quantity of every component in the bill by the cost of the components.

COTS (commercial off-the-shelf)

country code
In direct distance dialing, a code characterizing a particular country. Codes corresponding to the world numbering plan start with a single digit that identifies a particular geographical area. This can be followed by one or two extra digits.

course management (See CM)

CP (central processor)

CP (ContextParticipant)
Used by a clinical content manager (CCM) to inform participating applications that the context has changed.

CPA (comprehensive production architecture)
Enables simultaneous and cost-effective production and archiving in print and Internet formats by integrating five key processes: document cre-

ation and retrieval, assembly and formatting, internal archiving, prepress and printing and Internet publishing.

CPAF (Cost Plus Award Fee)

CPBX (cordless PBX)

CPE (customer premises equipment)
Any telephone apparatus — including telephone handsets, private branch exchange (PBX) switching equipment, key and hybrid telephone systems, and add-on devices — that is physically located on a customer's property, as opposed to being housed in the telephone company's central office or elsewhere in the network.

CPFR (collaborative planning, forecasting and replenishment)
One of a number of industry and vendor initiatives to establish data models and process models for collaborative activities such as replenishment. Under these collaborative scenarios, trading partners compare their plans and jointly resolve discrepancies or problem areas to obtain a single agreed-upon plan. This reduces supply chain uncertainty and thus can dramatically cut cycle times and inventory levels.

CPI (Common Programming Interface — part of IBM's SAA)

CPI (computer to PBX interface)
A gateway providing 24 digital pulse code modulation (PCM) channels at an aggregate rate of 1.544 megabits per second (Mbps). Developed by Nortel Networks (formerly Northern Telecom). See also DMI.

CPI (continuous process improvement)
A methodology for improving production, driven by formal metrics and measurement programs, including methodology upgrades.

CPI-C (Common Programming Interface for Communications)
A superset of IBM communications verbs containing bits of Advanced Program-to-Program Communications/Virtual Machine (APPC/VM), Transparent Services Access Facility (TSAF) and Server/Requester Programming Interface (SRPI). It provides a high-level interface to APPC.

CPG (consumer packaged goods)

CPM (cent per minute)

CPM (critical path method or critical path management)
The series of activities and tasks in a project that do not have built-in slack time. Any task in the critical path that takes longer than expected lengthens the total time of the project.

CP/M (Control Program for Microcomputers)
The first major operating system for personal computers, introduced by Digital Research in the late 1970s. In 1981, it was largely supplanted by PC-DOS from IBM, licensed from Microsoft.

CPMS (corporate property management software)
Software whose basic functionality is to produce basic rent rolls and feed to general ledger; to track simple information about leased or owned property (e.g., renewal dates, term dates, amount of square footage and basic breakdown of divisions or departments in space for space allocation); and to capture data regarding parties to agreement and basic contract information.

CPP (commercial parallel processing)
The use of parallel-processing systems for complex commercial-type applications.

CPR (computer-based patient record)
A system that contains electronically maintained information about an individual's health status and

C

care. It focuses on tasks directly related to patient care, unlike other healthcare information systems that support providers' and payers' operational processes (which may, however, serve as source or feeder systems for the CPR). The CPR completely replaces the paper medical chart and thus must meet all clinical, legal and administrative requirements.

CPRI (Computer-Based Patient Record Institute)
The Computer-Based Patient Record Institute defines a CPR, from a user's perspective, as an "electronic patient record that resides in a system designed to support users through availability of complete and accurate data, practitioner reminders and alerts, clinical decision support systems, links to bodies of medical knowledge, and other aids." In an attempt to help clarify the terminology and the strategy for healthcare organizations (HCOs) pursuing a computer-based patient record, GartnerGroup has defined a CPR, from a technical perspective, as an architecture containing a variety of IT initiatives, each intended to automate part of the patient record.

cps (characters per second)

CPS (certificate policy statement)

CPT (Current Procedural Terminology)
A widely used controlled medical vocabulary authored by the American Medical Association, this system describes medical and surgical procedures in a hierarchical format with six major sections and more than 7,300 codes. A series of two-digit modifiers are used to increase specificity, allowing the reporting of a procedure under specific circumstances.

CPT-4 (Current Procedural Terminology, version 4)
One of the standard code formats and definitions included in the Uniform Billing codes.

CPU (central processing unit)
The component of a computer system that controls the interpretation and execution of instructions. The CPU of a PC consists of a single microprocessor, while the CPU of a more powerful mainframe consists of multiple processing devices, and in some cases, hundreds of them. The term "processor" is often used to refer to a CPU.

CPW (commercial processing workload)

CQI (continuous quality improvement)
A program to continually improve the quality-, cost-, time-, information-and touch-based factors of the goals and processes a corporation has determined are right for it.

CR (computed radiography)

CRC (camera-ready copy)

CRC (cyclic redundancy check)
An error detection technique using a polynomial to generate a series of two 8-bit block check characters that represent the entire block of data. These block check characters are incorporated into the transmission frame and then checked at the receiving end.

create, retrieve, update, delete (See CRUD)

CREDIT (Compliance Rating for EMU-Dependent IT Systems — GartnerGroup)

crisis management planning (See CMP)

critical-path method or management (See CPM)

critical-path scheduling
A project-planning and monitoring system used to check progress toward the completion of a project by scheduling events, activities, milestones, etc.

critical ratio
A dispatching rule that calculates a priority index number by dividing the time to due date remaining by the expected elapsed time to finish the job. Typically ratios of less than 1.0 are behind, ratios greater than 1.0 are ahead, and a ratio of 1.0 is on schedule.

critical success factor (See CSF)

CRL (certificate revocation list)
"Hot lists" that identify certificates that have been withdrawn, canceled or compromised or that should not be trusted because of other identified reasons. CRLs should be replicated to all subscribing servers to a specific root certificate authority.

CRM (certified records manager)
Helps to develop a strategy, implement and run a records retention plan and provide the expertise needed to make classification and retention judgments.

CRM (customer relationship management)
A business strategy designed to optimize profitability, revenue and customer satisfaction. To realize CRM, an enterprise must implement processes and technologies that support coordinated customer interactions throughout all channels.

CRMS (Clinical Resource Management System)
A suite of six integrated decision support products from HBO & Company (HBOC) Payor Solutions Group that provides an information infrastructure for health plan medical management reporting and analysis.

CRM

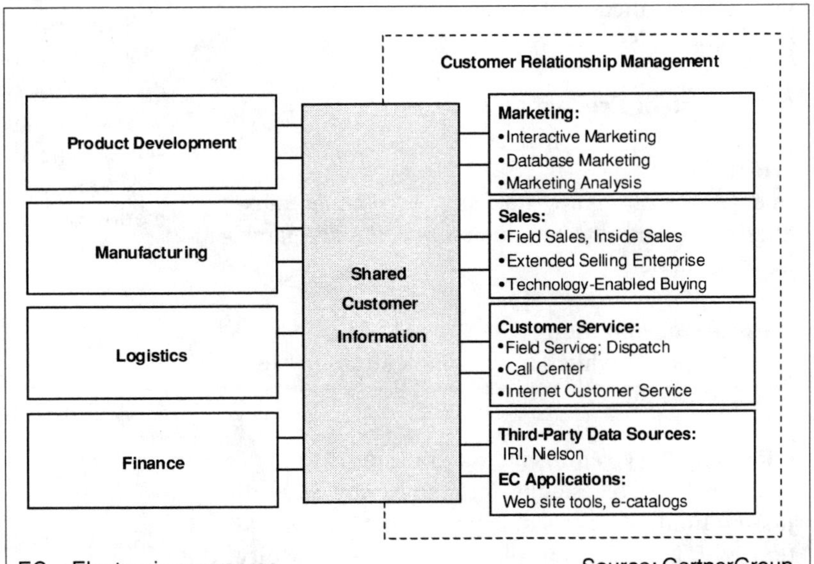

EC = Electronic commerce

Source: GartnerGroup

Customer Relationship Management: A Shared View of the Customer Throughout the Enterprise

cross-assembler program
Symbolically coded input running on one computer that produces machine language output for another computer. See also cross-compiler.

crossbar switch
A switch having multiple vertical and horizontal paths and a means for interconnecting any one of the vertical paths within any one of the horizontal paths.

cross-certification
A process by which two enterprises are able to recognize and trust each other's certificates.

cross-compiler
A program that translates instructions from a high-level language on one computer to the machine language of another computer — the one on which the program is to be run.

C

cross-modulation
Interference caused by two or more carriers in a transmission system interacting through nonlinearities in the system.

crossover cable
A cable with wires that cross over so the terminating ends of the cable have opposite wire assignments. See straight-through cable.

crosspoint
1. A switching element that can be mechanical or electronic.
2. A two-state semiconductor switching device having a low transmission system impedance in one state and a very high one in the other.

cross-posting
The act of posting an Internet message to multiple topic groups at the same time.

cross section
Signal transmission capacity of a transmission system, usually measured in the number of two-way voice channels.

Cross System Product (See CSP)

crosstalk
Interference or an unwanted signal from one transmission circuit detected on another, usually parallel, circuit.

crosstalk attenuation
The extent to which a communications system resists crosstalk.

CRP (capacity requirements planning)
The functions of establishing, measuring and adjusting limits or levels of capacity that are consistent with a production plan. The term "capacity requirements planning" in this context is the process of determining how much labor and machine resources are required to accomplish the tasks of production.

CRS (call reporting system)

CRS (Customer Relationship Solutions)
An IBM business unit.

CRT (cathode ray tube)

CRTC (Canadian Radio-Television and Telecommunications Commission)

CRU (customer replaceable unit)

CRUD (create, retrieve, update, delete)
Guidelines for defining how different people or communities within an organization deal with data elements owned by the organization.

CS (computer science)

C&S (calendaring and scheduling)

C/S (client/server)
The splitting of an application into tasks performed on separate computing devices — a programmable workstation such as a personal computer (PC) and a server. The PC (the client) does some of its own processing, while the server typically stores information and software. The two sides are connected by a local-area network (LAN) or wide-area network (WAN).

CS 1 (Capability Set 1)

CSA (Calendaring and Scheduling API)

CSA (client services applications)

CSA (Customer Services Agreement)
A contract under which IBM provided maintenance and other bundled services with Computer Sciences Corp. (CSC).

CSCW (Computer Support for Cooperative Work)
A networked system in which computers play an active role in collaboration within workgroups.

CSD (consolidated service desk)
An organizational structure that contains the people and skills (physically or virtually), tools (i.e., systems and network management platforms, and utilities), and procedures that deliver service and support to customers. It provides base functions for problem tracking, escalation, notification and resolution, and tightly integrates with asset and change management. It is guided by a service-level agreement (SLA).

C-SET
A chip card electronic-payment implementation supported by French consortium Europay. It is not compliant with the international Secure Electronic Transaction (SET) standard, so it requires software at the merchant site to convert SET transactions to C-SET, allowing for interoperability between the two standards but adding cost and time to the transaction itself. Europay France, formed in January of 1996, includes: Credit Mutuel, Credit Agricole, Credit Industrial et Commercial, Banques Populaires, the Post, Europay France and Europay International.

CSF (critical success factor)
A methodology, management tool or design technique that enables the effective development and deployment of a project or process.

CSI (Computer Security Institute)

C/SI (Client/Server Interface)
An interface published by Sybase and delivered with release 4.0 of its SQL Server product. Open Client, which resides on the client, is an application programming interface (API) that allows applications or third-party products to access SQL Server or Open Server. Open Server is a set of protocols that allows communications with other servers, and can provide gateways to critical data that is not managed by the native SQL server.

C/Side
Navision's proprietary 32-bit development environment, which includes an application-specific database and proprietary 4/GL.

CSLIP (Compressed SLIP)
Extension of Serial Link Internet Protocol (SLIP) that allows just the header information to be sent on a SLIP connection.

CSM (component supplier management)

CSM (customer service management)

CSMA/CD (Carrier Sense Multiple Access with Collision Detection)
A local-area network (LAN) access technique in which multiple stations connected to the same channel can sense transmission activity on that channel and defer the initiation of transmission while the channel is active. Sometimes called contention access.

CSP (Cross System Product)
IBM's strategic fourth-generation language (4GL). It presents self-contained development and execution environments that IBM has posted among all System/370 and System/390 environments, as well as the 8100 and PC. Enhancements have included library management, structured programming constructs and limited relational support.

CSR (continuous speech recognition)

CSR (customer service representative)

CSRC (Comparex Synchronous Remote Copy)

CSR Guides
Product and procedure guides for customer service representatives (CSRs). They should include detailed information about a company's products, services, procedures and policies, and are essential for providing quality service to all customers. The guides may be online, on paper or both.

CSS (cascading style sheets)

CSS (customer service and support)
Systems such as help desks and sales and marketing systems that provide front-line support with back-end linkage for interaction with customers (e.g., tracking, resolution and escalation). A CSS tracking system tracks and reports inquiries resolved during the initial contact and those that require follow-up.

CSTA (Computer Supported Telephony Architecture)
A European Computer Manufacturers Association standard for linking computers to telephone systems.

CSU (channel service unit)
A device found on digital links that transfers data faster than a modem (in a range from 56 kilobits per second to 1.5 megabits per second) but does not permit dial-up functions. It also performs certain line-conditioning and equalization functions, and responds to loop-back commands sent from a central office. A CSU is the link between digital lines from the central office and devices such as channel banks or data communications devices.

CT (computer tomography)

CT (Corporate Time)
The stand-alone version of the same calendaring technology that Corporate Software & Technology (CS&T) is licensing to Hewlett-Packard (HP) for OpenTime and with some modifications to Netscape for SuiteSpot.

CT2/CAI
A standard for digital mobile telephony. Cordless Telephone version 2 (CT2) uses 4 megahertz (MHz) of channel frequency between 864.1 MHz and 868.1 MHz. CAI (Common Air Interface) enables CT2 manufacturers' handsets to communicate with other manufacturers' base stations.

CT3 (Cordless Telephone version 3)
A technology for digital cordless telephony developed by Ericsson. Many of the principles of CT3 are being incorporated into Digital European Cordless Telephone (DECT).

CTA (correspondence-tracking application)
A blend of integrated document and output management (IDOM) technologies that facilitates high-volume document routing and response, and a strong example of an overlooked document-enabled vertical application (DEVA).

CTD (Cell Transfer Delay)
One of three negotiated quality of service (QOS) parameters defined by the Asynchronous Transfer Mode (ATM) Forum.

CTD (Centura Team Developer)

CTG (Computer Task Group)

CTI (computer-telephone integration)
The intelligent linking of computers with switches, enabling coordinated voice and data transfers to the desktop.

CTLIB (Client Library)
Sybase's application programming interface (API) set required for users to exploit the System 10 version of its SQL Server database management system.

CTO (chief technology officer)
The CTO has overall responsibility for managing the physical and personnel technology infrastruc-

ture including technology deployment, network and systems management, integration testing, and developing technical operations personnel. CTOs also manage client relations to ensure that service objective expectations are developed and managed in the operations areas.

CTP (corporate trade payment)
An electronic-commerce standard format that was established in the early 1980s using bank-developed transaction sets. It was retired in 1996.

CTS (Component Transaction Server)

CTS (corporate technology strategy)

CTX (clear to send)
A control circuit that indicates to the data terminal equipment that data can or cannot be transmitted.

CTX (corporate trade exchange)
An electronic-commerce standard format that allows for inclusion of 9,999 "addenda" records in addition to the primary financial records (i.e., amount being moved, bank routing number and checking-account number).

CU (compliance unit)
A logical partition of applications and data to be upgraded together.

CUA (Common User Access — part of SAA)
IBM's attempt to set a common graphical user interface (GUI) standard. CUA specifies conventions for the dialog between a user and the computer, but has not caught on as a broadly accepted market standard.

CUG (closed user group)
A set up that restricts access to and from one or more terminals to other members of the user group (found on packet switched systems, e-mail, etc.).

cumulative lead time
The longest length of time involved to accomplish the activity in question. For any item planned through material requirements planning, it is found by reviewing each bill-of-material path below the item, and whichever path adds up to the greatest number defines cumulative material lead time.

CUOD (Capacity Upgrade On Demand — IBM)

current loop
A transmission technique that recognizes current flows rather than voltage levels. It was traditionally used in teletypewriter networks incorporating batteries as the transmission power source.

Current Procedural Terminology (See CPT)

Current Procedural Terminology, version 4 (See CPT-4)

custom configuration
A computer system built to order (i.e., to the customer's specifications).

Customer Administration Center System (See CACS)

customer contact center
While traditional call centers handle voice-only customer contact, this term includes all types of channels of customer contact, including voice, e-mail, World Wide Web, faxes, video kiosks and mail. This is an inbound and outbound service-based environment in which agents handle all types of contact regarding sales, service, collections and some other functions.

Customer Information Control System (See CICS)

Customer Information Control System/System Manager for AIX (See CICS/SM)

customer information file (See CIF)

customer information management (See CIM)

customer management solutions (See CMS)

customer premises equipment (See CPE)

customer relationship management (See CRM)

customer service and support (See CSS)

Customer Services Agreement (See CSA)

customized network management
Tools to allow assignment of levels of network management functions and capabilities to selected nodes throughout the network. With this, the degree of centralization vs. decentralization of network management can be varied depending on the environment.

custom key set
Specialized multibutton telephones designed expressly for a particular private branch exchange (PBX). Unlike the locking buttons on normal key telephones, the buttons on a custom key set are used to communicate with the system and are typically nonlocking buttons. Custom key set buttons can be arranged to activate specific features such as speed dialing and executive override, as well as to select lines.

cutover
The physical changing of lines from one system to another, usually at the time of a new system installation.

CVD (Chemical vapor deposition)

CVO (Credentialing Verification Organization)

CVS (Centralized Vehicle Scheduler)
A vehicle production scheduling system based on Ilog's Optimization Suite of software components.

CVSD (Continuous Variable Slope Delta Modulation)
A speech-encoding and digitizing technique that uses one bit to describe the change in the slope of the curve between two samples, rather than the absolute change between the samples. Sampling is usually done at 32 kilobits per second (Kbps).

CWF (Common Working File)

CWF/Java (Common Workflow Framework for Java)
An object-oriented framework developed by CSE Systems that enables developers to build and integrate applications based on the CSE/WorkFlow engine.

CXI (Common X interface)

CXML (Commerce Extensible Markup Language)

cyber library
An electronic version of a physical library that is implemented on behalf of workers for information self-service.

cyclic redundancy check (See CRC)

D

DA (data administration)

DA (data administrator)
An information systems (IS) employee who can help gather information about the operational data and assist in designing the data model that will be used for the data warehouse database management system (DBMS).

D/A (digital-to-analog)

DAA (Data Access Arrangement)
An interface device once used to interconnect customer-owned data terminal equipment (DTE) to the telephone network, it is now generally integrated into such directly attached devices.

DAA (distributed applications architecture)
Architectures in which the computational and data processing requirements of an application are performed by two or more computer systems. Most computational and data processing elements are statically assigned. Architectures include client/server, peer-to-peer and other cooperative processing approaches.

DAAS (Desktop Acquisition and Asset Services — IBM)

DAC (data access control)

DAC (digital-to-analog converter)

DAC (dual-attached concentrator)
In Fiber Distributed Data Interface (FDDI), a concentrator that can be attached to both rings and can also be dual-homed from the master ports of other FDDI concentrators.

DACS (digital access and cross-connect system)
An AT&T term for a digital cross-connect system (DCS).

DADI (directly addressable device interface)

DAE (Disk Array Enclosure — Clarion)

DAE (Distributed Automation Edition)
IBM software for writing factory-floor applications independent of the distributed data, LAN protocol or terminal type.

daemon
A Unix process initiated during system boot and activated automatically and/or periodically to perform a particular task.

daisychaining
The connection of multiple devices in a serial fashion. An advantage of daisychaining is savings in transmission facilities. A disadvantage is that if a device malfunctions, all of the devices daisychained behind it are disabled.

DAL (Data Access Language)
From Apple Computer, a database interface — itself a superset of Structured Query Language (SQL) — that enables access to Macintoshes or non-Apple computers.

DAL (dedicated access line)

DAMA (Demand Assigned Multiple Access)
Allocation of communication satellite time to earth stations as the need arises.

DAO (Data Access Object)

DAP (Directory Access Protocol)
A protocol for working among X.500 Directory Service Agents.

DAP (Distributed Applications Platform)

DAPP (data analysis and provider profiling)
DAPP vendors are those that provide healthcare value-added analytic applications to support analysis of administrative data for the purposes of network management, actuarial and underwriting, medical management and performance measurement — including Health Plan Employer Data and Information Set (HEDIS) reporting.

DARPA (Defense Advanced Research Projects Agency)
The U.S. government department that developed the Transmission Control Protocol/Internet Protocol (TCP/IP) ARPANET protocol architecture.

DAS (Dual-Attached Station)
In Fiber Distributed Data Interface (FDDI), a device that is attached to both the primary and secondary rings.

DASD (direct-access storage device)
Generic nomenclature for a storage peripheral that can respond directly to random requests for information; usually denotes a disk drive.

DASS (Digital Access Signaling System)
The original British Telecom (BT) Integrated Services Distributed Network (ISDN) signaling developed for single-line and multiline Integrated Digital Access (IDA) but used in the BT ISDN pilot service for single-line IDA only.

DASSII
A message-based signaling system based on the International Organization for Standardization (ISO) model, developed by British Telecommunications and its suppliers for multiline integrated digital access to the public network. DASSII is the updated version of Digital Access Signaling System (DASS).

DAT (digital audiotape)
A magnetic tape that stores audio data converted to digital form.

DAT (Dynamic Address Translation)
The change of a logical storage address to an actual storage address.

data
Raw facts and figures that a computer processes into usable information. Data such as cash receipts mean little until processed into information such as an open receivable balance.

Data Access Arrangement (See DAA)

DAP

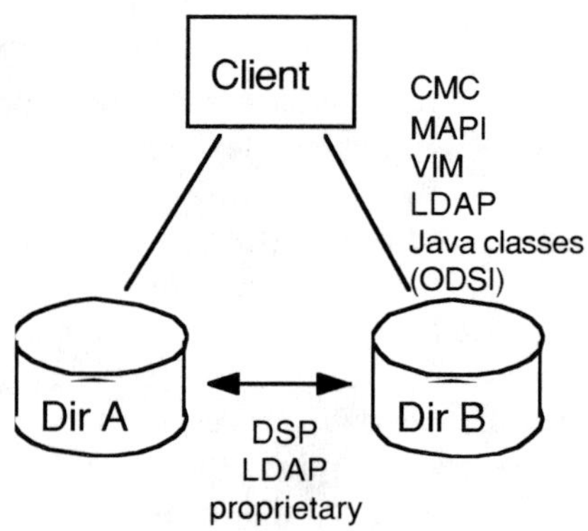

* from clients to servers and from servers to other servers

CMC = Common messaging calls
DSP = Digital signal processor
LDAP = Lightweight Directory Access Protocol
MAPI = Messaging Application Programming Interface
ODSI = Open Directory Service Interface
VIM = Vendor Independent Messaging

Source: GartnerGroup

Directory Access Protocol

Data Access Language (See DAL)

data administrator (See DA)

data analysis and provider profiling (See DAPP)

Database 2 (See DB2)

database administrator (See DBA)

Database/Data Communication (See DB/DC)

Database Library (See DBLIB)

database management system (See DBMS)

Database Manager
IBM's relational database management system offered as part of OS/2 Extended Edition.

database partitioning
The practice of separating a database into portions that may reside on more than one disk volume or more than one system.

data center
The department in an enterprise that houses and maintains back-end information technology (IT) systems and data stores — its mainframes, servers, and databases. In the days of large, centralized IT operations, this department and all the systems resided in one physical place, hence the name data center. With today's more distributed computing methods, single data center sites are still common, but are becoming less so. The term continues to be used to refer to the department that has responsibility for these systems, no matter how dispersed they are.

data circuit
A communications facility that enables transmission of data in either direction, in either analog or digital form.

data collection and mining
The process in which an enterprise collects information about customer behavior and preferences and saves this information in data stores. This information is then mined to identify customers for different marketing campaigns or service options.

data communications
1. The transmission, reception and validation of data.
2. Data transfer between a data source and a data destination via one or more data links, according to appropriate protocols, by means of an electromagnetic transmission system.

data communications equipment (See DCE)

data compression
A technique that saves storage space by eliminating gaps, empty fields, redundancies or unnecessary information to shorten the length of records or blocks.

data concentration
Collection of data at an intermediate point from several low- and medium-speed lines for retransmission across high-speed lines.

data conversion
The process of changing data from one form of representation to another.

Data Country Code (See DCC)

data definition language (See DDL)

data dictionary
A repository of information about data that supplies the meaning of the data, its relationship to other data, its origin, its usage and its format. The dictionary assists management, database administrators, systems analysts and application programmers in effectively planning, controlling and evaluating the

D

collection, storage and use of data. A data dictionary manages data categories such as alias, data elements, data records, data structure, data stores, data models, data flows, data relationships, processes, functions, dynamics, size, frequency, resource consumption and other user-defined attributes.

Data Encryption Standard (See DES)

Data Exchange Interface (See DXI)

Data Extract (See DXT)

Data Facility Data Set Services (See DFDSS)

Data Facility Hierarchical Storage Manager (See DFHSM)

Data Facility Product (See DFP)

Data Facility Sort (See DFSORT)

Data Facility Storage Management Subsystem (See DFSMS)

datagram
A packet of data that can be delivered through a packet-switched system without reference to previous packets addressed to the same destination.

Datagram Delivery Protocol (See DDP)

data integrity
A performance measure based on the rate of undetected errors.

Data Interchange Format (See DIF)

Data Interpretation System (See DIS)

Data Language/1 (See DL/1)

Data Line Interface (See DLI)

data link
Any serial data communications transmission path, generally between two adjacent nodes or devices and without any intermediate switching nodes.

data link control

1. Procedures to ensure that both the sending and receiving devices agree on synchronization, error detection and recovery methods, and initialization and operation methods for point-to-point or multipoint configurations.
2. The second layer in the International Organization for Standardization (ISO) Reference Model for Open Systems Interconnection.

Data Link Control Layer
Layer 2 of the Systems Network Architecture (SNA) architectural model, which is responsible for the transmission of data over a particular physical link. It corresponds approximately to the Data Link Layer of the Open Systems Interconnection (OSI) model.

Data Link Layer
The logical entity in the Open Systems Interconnection (OSI) model concerned with transmission of data between adjacent network nodes; it is the second layer in the OSI model, between the Physical and the Network Layers.

Data Link Switching (See DLS)

data logging
Recording data about events in the time sequence in which they occur.

data management/middleware
Manages the efficient storage, retrieval, security and integrity of any kind of information.

data manipulation language (See DML)

data mart
A data mart contains a subset of the data in the data warehouse, and is built upon a data model tailored

for a specific application or business function. Unlike a data warehouse, a data mart contains only the data that is required for a particular process, application or workgroup, and typically offers much faster query performance than a data warehouse. A data mart can be either a physical construction (with its own separate database) or a logical one (a high-level abstraction of the data warehouse data model). Enterprises choosing between physical and logical data marts must decide whether the performance benefits of a physical data mart will outweigh the associated CPU, networking, maintenance and support costs of an additional database.

data migration interface (See DMI)

data mining
The process of discovering meaningful correlations, patterns and trends by sifting through large amounts of data stored in repositories, using pattern recognition technologies as well as statistical and mathematical techniques.

data network identification code (See DNIC)

Data-Over-Cable Service Interface Specification (See DOCSIS)

data over voice (See DOV)

Data Packet Network (See DPN)

data PBX
A switch that allows a user on an attached circuit to select from other circuits, usually one at a time and on a contention basis, for the purpose of establishing a through connection. A data private branch exchange (PBX) is distinguished from a PBX in that only digital transmission, and not analog, is supported.

data rate
The speed at which a channel carries data, measured in bits per second (bps).

data service unit (See DSU)

data set
An infrequently used term for modem.

data synchronization
A form of embedded middleware that allows applications to update data on two systems so that the data sets are identical. These services can run via a variety of different transports but typically require some application-specific knowledge of the context and notion of the data being synchronized.

data terminal equipment (See DTE)

data voice private network (See data VPN)

Data Mining

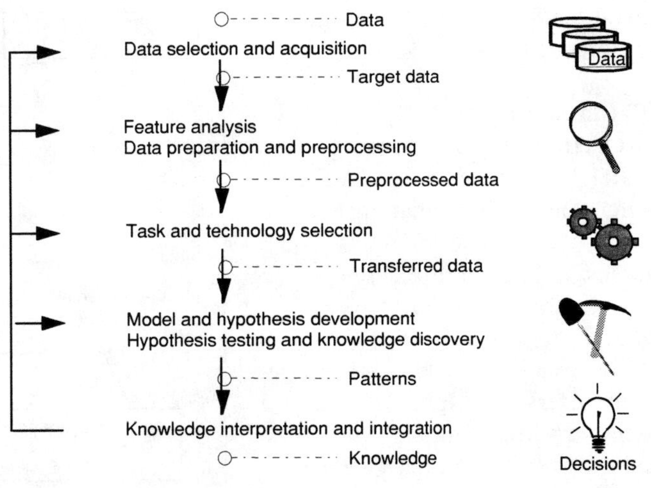

Source: GartnerGroup

The Data Mining Process

D

data VPN (data voice private network)
A trademarked voice service offered by Sprint and GlobalOne.

data warehouse (See DW)

date export formats
A year may be stored in an application as 1998 but displayed as 98, and the export file may represent the year as 98 or 1998, accordingly. If the date is exported as two digits, the application importing the date may store this value incorrectly.

date windowing
When the year is entered as two digits, the software must interpret this information to establish the full four-digit year implied.

DAVAR (dealer-assisted value-added reseller)

dB (decibel)
The unit for measuring the relative strength of a signal parameter such as power or voltage. The number of decibels is 10 times the logarithm (base 10) of the ratio of the power of two signals or the ratio of the power of one signal to a reference level.

DB (database)
An electronic filing system organized by fields, records and files. A field is a single piece of information; a record is one complete set of fields; and a file is a collection of records.

DB2 (Database 2 — IBM)
IBM's relational database management offering, originally built for Multiple Virtual Storage (MVS) systems. It uses Structured Query Language (SQL) as its data manipulation and definition language. IBM has also released versions of DB2 for OS/2 and AIX/6000.

DBA (database administration)

DBA (database administrator)
The person responsible for managing data, namely data set placement, database performance, and data recovery and integrity at a physical level.

DBCS (double-byte character set)

DB/DC (Database/Data Communication)
This acronym refers to IBM's collection of transaction managers and database managers, e.g., Customer Information Control System (CICS), Information Management System (IMS), Database 2 (DB2) and SQL/DS.

DB/file distribution management
Selective distribution of all or part of a central database to selected remote midrange systems.

Data Warehouse

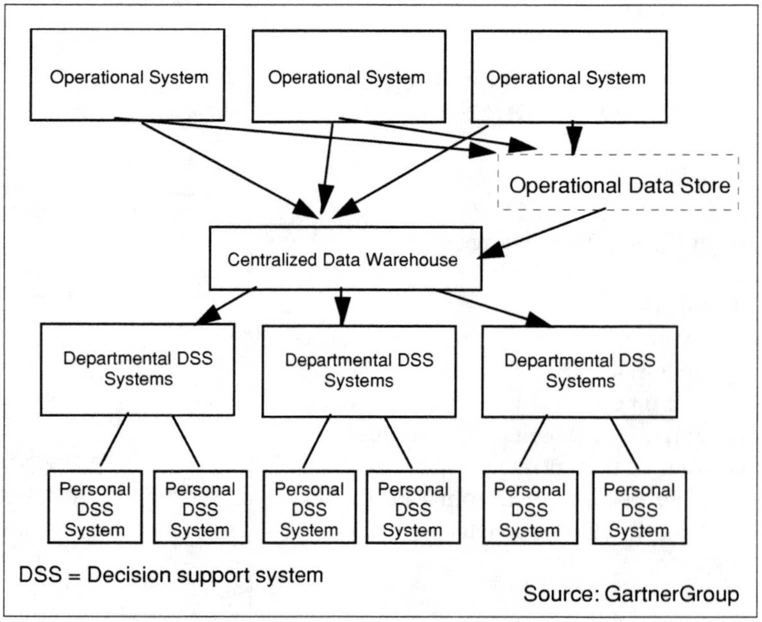

Data Warehouse Example

DBLIB (Database Library)
The native application programming interface (API) for Sybase's SQL Server.

DBM (database marketing)

DBMS (database management system)
A software package that enables end users or application programmers to share data. It provides a systematic method of creating, updating, retrieving and storing information in a database (DB). DBMSs are generally also responsible for data integrity, data access control, and automated rollback, restart and recovery.

DBS (direct broadcast satellite)
A wireless technology for broadcasting by transmitting a compressed high-speed video signal via satellite.

DC (direct current)

DC (distributed computing)

DC (distribution center)

DCA (Document Content Architecture — IBM)

DCB (data communications bureau)

DCC (Data Country Code)
One of two formats from the Asynchronous Transfer Mode (ATM) Forum for address usage. Also see ICD.

DCD (document content description)

DCE (data communications equipment)
Equipment that performs the functions required to connect data terminal equipment (DTE) to the data circuit. In a communications link, it is either part of the network, an access point to the network, a network node, or equipment at which a network circuit terminates. In the case of an RS-232-C connection, the modem is usually regarded as DCE while the user device is considered data terminal equipment (DTE). In an ITU X.25 connection, the network access and packet-switching node is viewed as the DCE.

DCE (Distributed Computing Environment)
An Open Software Foundation (OSF) initiative to create a vendor-neutral networking and distributed computing environment to support distributed applications, by integrating the appropriate technology or combination of technologies into a single environment while addressing interoperability, standards and security. DCE integrates remote procedure calls, presentation services, a naming directory, security, threads (sequential flows of control

DCE

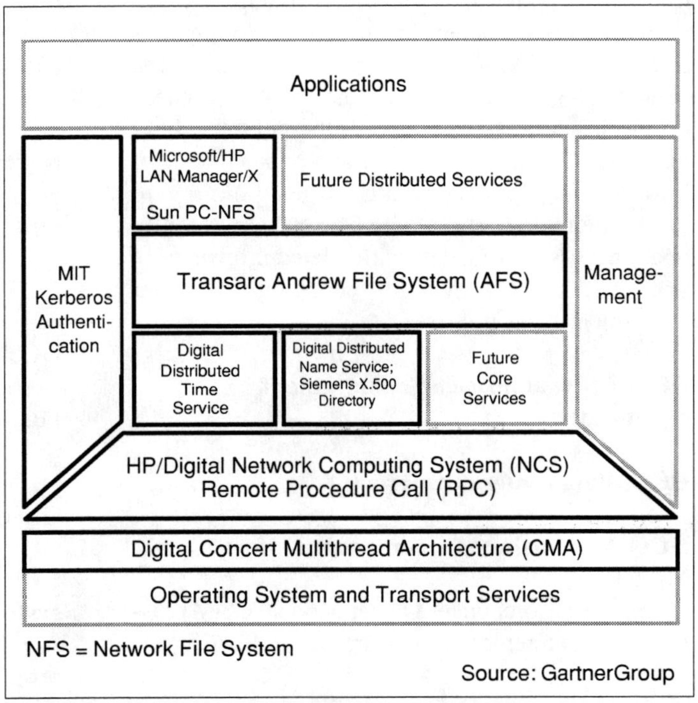

Open Software Foundation's Distributed Computing Environment Architecture

similar to tasks), time services (to synchronize clocks) and a distributed file system.

DCF (Document Composition Facility)
Program used in IBM's Professional Office System (PROFS) for creating text. Also known as SCRIPT/VS.

DCM (demand chain management)

DCM (document component management)
DCM applies the principles of managing entire documents to managing parts of documents. Every significant unit of information is identifiable as a separate entity and is subject to the same core library services (check in/check out, version control, security) that integrated document management (IDM) provides on complete documents or sections of documents. Structural markup — i.e., using Standard Generalized Markup Language (SGML) or Extensible Markup Language (XML) — within the document identifies the components of information. Unlike IDM, information about the content — metadata or "attributes" — is captured on the inside and embedded in the content rather than stored on the outside as a separate index of information. This is essential when pointing to information elements required for selective reuse, updating, associating data with related information, storing translations, validity checking and other component-level processes.

DCME (dynamic cache management enhanced)

DCO (data center outsourcing)

DCOM (Distributed Component Object Model)
Microsoft's Component Object Model (COM) distributed via a remote procedure "call" (RPC).

D conditioning
Conditioning that controls the harmonic distortion and the signal-to-noise ratio of a signal so that they lie within specified limits.

DCS (digital cellular service)
Digital wireless services provided in the cellular spectrum (800 MHz).

DCS (digital communications system)

DCS (digital cross-connect system)
A computerized facility allowing DS1 lines (1.544 Mbps) to be remapped electronically at the DS0 level (64 Kbps). This means that DS0 channels can be individually rerouted and reconfigured into different DS1 lines.

DCS (distributed control system)
Forerunner of open control system (OCS). DCs are used to control the manufacturing processes in continuous and batch process manufacturing industries such as petroleum refining, pulp and paper, and chemical manufacturing. Key elements include: sensors for input, actuators for output, controllers to execute control algorithms and interfaces with humans for operational control and engineering configuration.

DCT (digital cordless telephone)

DCT (discrete cosine transformation)
A video compression algorithm similar to Fast Fourier Transform (FFT) but easier to compute.

DDA (Distributed Data Architecture)
Groupe Bull's scheme for data interoperability.

DDBMS (distributed database management system)
A DBMS that enables end users or application programmers to view a collection of physically separate databases as one logical single-system image. The concept that is most fundamental to

the DDBMS is location transparency, meaning the user should not be conscious of the actual location of data.

DDC (Display Data Channel)
To simplify installation, the Video Extended Standards Association (VESA) has developed the DDC standards to allow plug and play. The monitor and the system unit communicate to agree on the configuration options that both sides can support.

DDCMP (Digital Data Communications Message Protocol)
A synchronous protocol developed by Digital Equipment Corp.

DDD (direct distance dialing)
A telephone exchange service that enables the telephone user to call long distances without operator assistance.

DDE (Dynamic Data Exchange)
A limited method of sharing data between two applications or files. When data is used in both files, with DDE it can be automatically updated in the other. Both applications must be in use, and DDE does not work over a network. OLE is a more sophisticated development.

DDI (Digital Document Interchange)
The Compound Document Architecture format for encoding revisable form text, graphics and image information.

DDI (direct dialing in)
If the private branch exchange (PBX) and the local public exchange are suitable, callers can dial direct to an extension, bypassing the operator.

DDL (data definition language)
A language for describing the data model for a user database, i.e., the names and access paths for the data and how they are interrelated. For some software products, DDL describes the logical, not the physical, data. Other products use it to describe both.

DDM (distributed data management)
A form of cooperative processing in which some portion of the database management system executes on two or more nodes.

DDN (Defense Data Network)

DDN (digital data network)

DDNS (Dynamic Domain Name Service)

DDP (Datagram Delivery Protocol)
AppleTalk network layer protocol.

DDP (distributed data processing)
The use of computer systems or intelligent terminals within an enterprise to perform data processing and/or storage functions. The devices may or may not be interconnected via transmission facilities.

DDS (digital data service)
A dedicated digital data transmission service that operates over interconnected, point-to-point digital private lines.

DDS (digital data storage)

DDW (distributed data warehouse)

deadlock
Occurs in a network when two users each try to access a file the other has locked.

debit/credit benchmark
A discredited performance measurement for online transaction processing (OLTP) throughput. The debit/credit transaction, sometimes called ET-1, simulates an automated teller machine (ATM) function. It has been replaced by TPC-A and TPC-B, defined by the Transaction Processing Performance Council (TPC).

deblocking
Separating blocked data into individual logical records.

decentralized
The description for an application that is distributed, but originates with the IS organization, has central applications development, and is centrally supported.

decibel (See dB)

decision support system (See DSS)

decision trees/fault models (See DT/FM)

DECnet
Digital Equipment's family of peer-to-peer, Ethernet-based network products.

DECnet end node
Interconnected support that enables a midrange system to act as an end node in a DECnet network.

DECOmni (DEC Open Manufacturing Network Interface)
Digital Equipment's version of the Open Systems Interconnection (OSI) Manufacturing Message Service protocol to be used for control-level device communications.

DECT (Digital European Cordless Telephone)
An interface specification for European digital mobile telephony. An access technology for "distance communications" with voice, data and video services, depending on the network accessed. DECT employs 10 carrier frequencies between 1.88 gigahertz (GHz) and 1.9 GHz.

DECtp
Digital Equipment's name for its entire online transaction processing (OLTP) marketing program.

DECwrite
Digital Equipment's compound document editor. It is based on the editor engine from Frame Technologies.

dedicated circuit
A line for communications used by one person exclusively at each end.

Defense Advanced Research Projects Agency (See DARPA)

Defense Message System (See DMS)

DEIS (Defense Enterprise Integration Services)

delay
In communications, the wait time between two events, such as the time when a signal is sent until the time it is received.

delay announcement
Associated with automatic call distribution (CACD) capability, delay announcement provides a recorded announcement to incoming calls that are delayed and placed in queue.

delay distortion
The change in a signal from the transmitting end to the receiving end resulting from the tendency of some frequency components within a channel to take longer to be propagated than others.

delimiter
In data communications, a character that separates and organizes elements of data.

delta modulation
A method of representing a speech waveform (or other analog signal) in which successive bits represent increments of the waveform. The increment size is not necessarily constant.

Demand Assigned Multiple Access (See DAMA)

demand management
The function of recognizing and managing all the demands for products to ensure that the master scheduler is aware of them. It encompasses the activities of forecasting, order entry, order promising, branch warehouse requirements, interplant orders and service parts requirements.

demilitarized zone (See DMZ)

demodulation
The process of retrieving data from a modulated carrier wave; the reverse of modulation.

DEN (Directory-Enabled Networks)
An initiative formed by Microsoft and Cisco to define a directory schema foundation for common network objects as well as for the use of Lightweight Directory Access Protocol (LDAP) as a query protocol. Microsoft and Cisco have turned over control of the DEN specification to the Desktop Management Task Force (DMTF), which has incorporated the DEN specification under its Common Information Model. The DEN specification is continuing to evolve, providing a logical specification and representation of network elements stored in a directory service that is independent of physical implementation details. A separate effort within the Internet Engineering Task Force (IETF) is working to develop a Common Open Policy Service (COPS) protocol to establish a common query and response protocol between policy servers and consumers of policy information.

dense wave division multiplexing (See WDM)

dependent demand
Demand is considered dependent when it is directly related to or derived from the demand for other items or end products. Such demand is thus calculated and does not have to be forecast. A given inventory item may have both dependent and independent demand at any given time.

Dependent Logical Unit Requester (See DLUR)

derivation equipment
Equipment used to produce narrowband facilities from a wider band facility. Commonly used on alternate voice/data (AVD) circuits to derive telegraph-grade lines from unused portions of a voice circuit.

DES (Data Encryption Standard)
A security specification developed by IBM in 1977. Still in use today, it is available at no charge from many online bulletin boards and is based on a single key encryption algorithm. If user A wants to send an encrypted file to user B, user A would first encrypt it with a private key (sometimes referred to as a "secret" key). User B would then decrypt the file with an identical private key. Recipients must prearrange for possession of the appropriate key for decryption to take place.

design synthesis
The set of technological capabilities for modeling, simulating and analyzing product designs. Also known as conceptual design or top-down design.

Desktop Management Interface (See DMI)

desktop services
Acquisition, maintenance and ongoing management of PC hardware and software assets.

desktop videoconferencing
The ability of two or more geographically separated users to meet via their personal computers. A typical system involves a PC, a monitor-mounted camera, a network connection, and special software that facilitates the exchange of video and audio.

despreading
In spread spectrum technology, the correlation by which the data is rejoined.

destination field
A field in a message header that contains the address of the station to which a message is being directed.

destination point code and origination point code (See DPC/OPC)

Deutsche Institut fur Normung (See DIN)

DEVA (document-enabled vertical application)
A GartnerGroup concept that explores the application of integrated document and output management (IDOM) technologies in specific industries for support of vertical (or sometimes horizontal) processes. Examples of industries and related processes include insurance (claims processing), engineering (technical document management), pharmaceuticals (new drug application), financial services (retirement processing) and cross-industry applications (call-center support).

DFDSS (Data Facility Data Set Services)
A member of IBM's Data Facility family of software products. It provides copy, dump-restore and direct access storage device (DASD) space management functions.

DFHSM (Data Facility Hierarchical Storage Manager a.k.a. DFSMShsm)
A member of IBM's Data Facility family of software products. It provides automatic space and availability management among a hierarchy of storage.

DFL (design for logistics)

DFP (Data Facility Product)
Originally called MVS/DFP, it was the MVS component that contained the access methods and handled catalog management. This facility was later renamed DFSMSdfp.

DFS (Distributed File System — Transarc)
A Distributed Computing Environment standard that provides users with a common file system across different operating systems. When files are moved, DFS tracks the new location by storing its address in a database. DFS also eases backup difficulties by automating regular backup routines across each cell through a backup server.

DFSMS (Data Facility Storage Management Subsystem)
The conceptual repackaging of IBM's Data Facility family of products and Resource Access Control Facility (RACF). It is intended to simplify the management and use of external storage resources by providing a device-independent means of requesting services by data set.

DFSMSdfp (DFSMS Data Facility Product) (See DFP)

DFSMShsm (DFSMS Hierarchical Storage Manager) (See DFHSM)

DFSORT (Data Facility Sort)
A member of IBM's Data Facility family of software products. It provides high-performance rearrangement of data.

DHCF (Distributed Host Command Facility)
A function that helps create or support the link between a terminal and an application.

DHCP (Dynamic Host Configuration Protocol)
An Internet Engineering Task Force (IETF) Transmission Control Protocol/Internet Protocol (TCP/IP) specification for allocating Internet Protocol (IP) addresses and other configuration information based on network adapter addresses. It enables address pooling and allocation and simplifies TCP/IP installation and administration.

DHTML (dynamic HTML)
Both Microsoft and Netscape have announced dynamic Hypertext Markup Language (HTML) products that enhance the HTML specification to add dynamic access to data as well as dynamic configuration of Web pages. These are not to be confused with dynamically generated HTML through a Common Gateway Interface (CGI) or server application programming interface (API) — e.g., ISAPI or NSAPI — gateway.

DIA (Display Industry Association)

DIA (Document Interchange Architecture — part of SAA)
Defined by IBM as a set of services performed by peer communications processes. DIA functioned as a set of communication programs — i.e., software that uses communication facilities such as Systems Network Architecture (SNA) — to carry out functions requested by users, which can be people, application programs or devices.

diagnostic programs
Software routines used to check equipment malfunctions and to pinpoint faulty components.

Dialed Number Identification Service (See DNIS)

dial-up
The process of, or the equipment or facilities involved in, establishing a temporary connection via the switched network.

dial-up line
A circuit that is established by a switched circuit connection; generally refers to a common-carrier telephone network.

dibit
Two data elements (bits) treated as one information element.

DICOM (Digital Imaging and Communications in Medicine)
A communication standard developed by the American College of Radiology/National Electrical Manufacturers Association, relied on by digital radiology systems, Picture Archive and Communication System (PACS), teleradiology, and acquisition devices — such as computed radiography (CR), computer tomography (CT) and magnetic resonance (MR).

DIF (Data Interchange Format)
A file format developed for VisiCalc, the first electronic spreadsheet. Still used today as a means for transferring files to and from spreadsheets.

Differential Phase-Shift Keying (See DPSK)

Diffie-Hellman
The first widely deployed public-key algorithm developed. Held primarily by Cylink, it passed into the public domain in September 1997.

digital
The representation of information in discrete binary form as either "1" or "0"; discontinuous in time, as opposed to the analog representation of information in variable but continuous waveforms.

digital access and cross-connect system (See DACS)

Digital Access Signaling System (See DASS)

digital audiotape (See DAT)

digital cellular service (See DCS)

digital cross-connect system (See DCS)

Digital Data Communications Message Protocol (See DDCMP)

digital data service (See DDS)

Digital Document Interchange (See DDI)

Digital European Cordless Telephone (See DECT)

Digital Imaging and Communications in Medicine (See DICOM)

digital linear tape (See DLT)

digital loopback
A technique for testing the digital processing circuitry of a communications device. It can be initiated locally or remotely via a telecommunications circuit; the device being tested will echo back a received test message (after first decoding and then re-encoding it) the results of which are compared with the original message.

digital mock-up (See DMU)

digital modem
A system component that enables communication over digital access facilities with a remotely located system connected to the public network over analog facilities.

Digital Multiplexed Interface (See DMI)

digital network
A network incorporating both digital switching and digital transmission.

Digital Private Network Signaling System (See DPNSS)

digital signal
A discrete or discontinuous signal; one whose various states are discrete intervals apart.

Digital Signal Level 0-4 (See DS-0 through DS-4)

digital signal processor (See DSP)

digital signature
A core function of a public key infrastructure (PKI). A digital signature can prove identity because it is created with the private key portion (which only the key holder should access) of a public/private key pair. Digital signatures most commonly prove the identity of the sender of a secure message or a transaction for purposes of nonrepudiation.

Digital Signature Algorithm (See DSA)

digital simultaneous voice and data (See DSVD)

Digital Speech Interpolation (See DSI)

Digital Standard Relational Interface (See DSRI)

digital subscriber line (See DSL)

digital switching
The process of establishing and maintaining a connection under stored program control where binary-encoded information is routed between an input and an output port.

Digital Table Interchange Format (See DTIF)

digital videodisc (See DVD)

digital videodisc read-only memory (See DVD-ROM)

digitize
To convert or express an analog form in a digital format.

digitizer
A purely graphical input device — i.e., a computer-aided design/computer-aided manufacturing (CAD/CAM) system digitizer used in computer-aided engineering (CAE) for converting locations into storable electronic impulses — with a surface on

which a location or a point is selected and then automatically converted into a digital X-Y coordinate suitable for transmission to a computer.

DIMM (dual in-line memory module)
A memory packaging and form factor that allows for a wider data path to memory, higher memory capacities in systems, and potentially easier upgrading than traditional single in-line memory modules (SIMMs).

DIN (Deutsche Institut fur Normung)
1. German national standards organization.
2. A German standard for cable connectors.

DIN connector
Multipin connector to the German standard used in some Macintosh and IBM PC computers and in some network processor panels.

DIP (Document Image Processing)
A system that offers the ability to scan, digitize, and store documents (e.g., invoices) as images.

DIP (dual in-line package)
A method of packaging electronic components for mounting on printed circuit boards.

DIP switch
A dual in-line switch that allows the user open or closed electrical pathways. It is frequently used to reconfigure computer components and peripherals.

direct-access storage device (See DASD)

direct broadcast satellite (See DBS)

Direct Department Calling (See DDC)

direct dialing in (See DDI)

direct digital control
The use of computers for machine and process control by direct interface to sensors, valves and other control devices.

direct distance dialing (See DDD)

direct memory access (See DMA)

direct numerical control
A system connecting a set of machines to a common memory for part-program or machine-program operation.

Directory Access Protocol (See DAP)

Directory-Enabled Networks (See DEN)

directory services
Middleware that locates the correct and full network address for a mail addressee from a partial name or address. A directory service provides a naming service and extends the capabilities to include intelligent searching and location of resources in the directory structure.

directory system agent (See DSA)

direct sequence spread spectrum (See DSSS)

"dirty" protocols
Many Internet Protocol (IP) applications assume that direct IP connectivity exists between hosts. In today's Internet or extranets, this is often not true. The problems of limited IP address space has caused many enterprises to use private request for comment (RFC) 1918 addresses. These addresses cannot be routed and, for enterprises to connect to the Internet or to communicate in an extranet, address translations or application proxies must be used. For applications that exchange their IP addresses between the client and the server, these "dirty" IP address are not valid when one or both of the end

systems exist on an RFC 1918 network. In addition, without using special techniques, applications like File Transfer Protocol (FTP) will not work when an enterprise uses private RFC 1918 addresses.

DIS (Data Interpretation System)
A marketing-oriented decision support system (DSS) product from IBM.

DIS (draft international standard)

DISA (Data Interchange Standards Association)

DISA (Defense Information Systems Agency)

DISA (direct inward system access)

disaster recovery (See DR)

disaster recovery plan (See DRP)

disaster recovery planning (See DRP)

disconnect signal
A clear-forward/clear-back signal.

discrete cosine transform (See DCT)

discrete-event simulation
A modeling technique where the traffic is represented as sequences of messages, packets or frames.

discrete multitone (See DMT)

discretionary security controls
An operating-system security rating of C2 or higher based on U.S. Department of Defense trusted computer system evaluation criteria.

discussion database
A database designed specifically for the capture, exchange and storage of ideas. The most popular discussion database today is IBM/Lotus Development's Notes product.

disk drive
A storage device attached to a computer that reads from, writes to and stores information on a floppy disk or hard disk.

diskless workstation
A computer attached to a LAN that has neither hard nor diskette drives, depending instead on the file server for all data storage.

disk mirroring
The duplication of disks and controllers so that two access paths exist in case a failure occurs on one of them.

Disk Operating System (See DOS)

Disk Operating System/Virtual Storage Extended (See DOS/VSE)

DISN (Defense Information Systems Network)

DISOSS (Distributed Office Support System)

DISP (Directory Information Shadowing Protocol)

dispatching
The selecting and sequencing of available jobs to be run at individual workstations and the assignment of these jobs to workers.

Display Data Channel (See DDC)

Distance Vector Protocol
Any routing protocol derived from the Bellman-Ford algorithm such as DECnet Phase IV, RIP, HELLO, and IGRP. The routers using this protocol create a network map by communicating in a periodic and progressive sequence.

distortion
The unwanted change in a waveform that occurs between points in a transmission system.

distributed applications architecture (See DAA)

Distributed Automation Edition (See DAE)

Distributed Component Object Model (See DCOM)

Distributed Computing Environment (See DCE)

distributed control system (See DCS)

Distributed Data Architecture (See DDA)

distributed database
A database whose objects (tables, views, columns and files) reside on more than one system in a network, and can be accessed or updated from any system in the network.

distributed database management system (See DDBMS)

distributed data management (See DDM)

Distributed Data Processing (See DDP)

distributed DB — read
Availability of a distributed, location-transparent database residing on multiple system nodes whereby location of and access to information are transparently managed by the system rather than by applications at each node. Remote access may be read-only or read/update.

Distributed File System (See DFS)

distributed function
A form of cooperative processing in which some of the application program logic executes on one node, possibly with a database, and the rest of the application resides on another node, possibly along with presentation services.

Distributed Host Command Facility (See DHCF)

Distributed Internet Applications Architecture for Financial Services (See DNafs)

distributed lock manager (See DLM)

Distributed Management Environment (See DME)

distributed memory parallel processors (See DMPP)

distributed naming and directory services
Directory facilities available transparently to all systems in the network allowing cross-network resource location and access. Directories can be maintained centrally and independently of each midrange system operation. More than one copy of the main directory at multiple nodes could be used to improve directory access performance.

Distributed Naming Service (See DNS)

Distributed Object Computing Architecture (See DOCA)

Distributed Object Management Facility (See DOMF)

Distributed Office Support System (See DISOSS)

distributed OLTP monitor
An online transaction processing (OLTP) monitor implementation that enables deployment of the application across multiple systems with minimal application programmer involvement or foreknowledge.

distributed parallel processing (See DPP)

distributed presentation
A form of cooperative processing in which some of the presentation handling executes on one node and the rest of the presentation, along with the remainder of the application and the database, executes on another node.

Distributed Print Architecture (See DPA)

distributed processing
A data-processing organizational concept under which computer resources of a company are installed at more than one location with appropriate communication links. Processing is performed at the user's location, generally on a minicomputer, and under the user's control and scheduling. This is in contrast to a large, centralized computer system which handles processing for all users. It is also the ability of an application to run on one or more nodes of a multiplatform network. The user need not be aware of the physical location of the data or the application software. The application can operate using cooperative processing, but this condition is not necessary.

Distributed Queue Dual Bus (See DQDB)

Distributed Relational Data Architecture (See DRDA)

Distributed Request (See DR)

distributed resource management (See DRM)

Distributed System Object Model (See DSOM)

distributed systems
Refers to computer systems in multiple locations throughout an organization working in a cooperative fashion. The system at each location serves the needs of that location but also is able to receive information from, and supply information to, other systems within the network.

Distributed Systems License Option (See DSLO)

distributed systems management (See DSM)

Distributed Systems Network (See DSN)

Distributed Systems

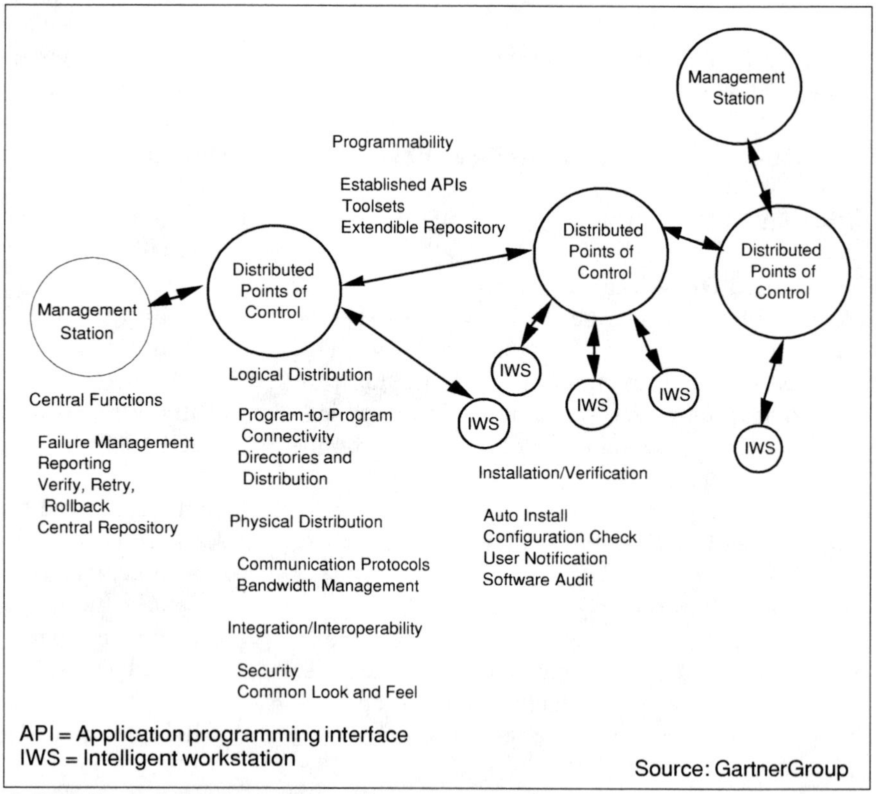

A Distributed Systems Example

Distributed Unit of Work (See DUOW)

distribution management system (See DMS)

distribution requirements planning (See DRP)

distribution service
Middleware that ensures a mail package is delivered to the specified addressee.

divestiture
The Justice Department's legal action against AT&T leading to the terms of the Modified Final Judgment. AT&T agreed to the 1982 Consent Decree, and in 1984 it relinquished ownership and control of its 22 wholly owned local Bell telephone operating companies. They were separated into seven independent Regional Bell Holding Companies (RBHCs).

DL/1 (Data Language/1)
The "language" in which the application programmer specifies requirements to IBM's Information Management System/Database Manager (IMS/DB).

DLCI (data link connection identifier)

DLI (Data Line Interface)
The point at which a data line is connected to a telephone system.

DLL (down line load)

DLL (Dynamic Link Library)
A windows and OS/2 feature.

DLM (distributed lock manager)
An architecture critical to maintaining locking consistency across multiple processing nodes and maintaining coherency between the multiple database buffer pools that exist on those different nodes.

DLS or DLSw (Data Link Switching)
An IBM-developed technique for carrying Systems Network Architecture (SNA) and NetBIOS over Transmission Control Protocol/Internet Protocol (TCP/IP). DLS "tunnels" or encapsulates SNA traffic using the transport services of TCP/IP. Upon entry into a router-based intranet, SNA traffic is placed into TCP segments, which are then sent across the network as IP datagrams. Intermediate routers along the session path "see" only standard IP datagrams and addresses, with no need to recognize SNA information flowing through them. At the destination router, TCP/IP headers are stripped off, and the original SNA traffic is sent in "native" mode to an SNA network or destination device using SNA addresses.

DLT (digital linear tape)
A linear recording tape drive designed by Digital Equipment and sold to Quantum in 1993. The technology became a de facto standard for backup and archive applications in 1997.

DLUR (Dependent Logical Unit Requester)
A technology that performs a "gateway" type of conversion to get the Systems Network Architecture (SNA) traffic onto Advanced Peer-to-Peer Networking/High-Performance Routing (APPN/HPR) sessions.

DMA (direct memory access)
A facility that permits data transfers directly into or out of main storage without passing through the processor's general registers; either performed independently of the processor or on a cycle-stealing basis.

DMA (Document Management Alliance)

DME (Distributed Management Environment)
A mix of network management specifications endorsed by the Open Software Foundation (OSF).

DME (domestic medical equipment)

DMI (data migration interface)
An interface published by SAP for the R/3 enterprise resource planning (ERP) system to support the batch process required to load data into an R/3 database as part of a migration to R/3 from another application.

DMI (Desktop Management Interface)
An architecture specification defined by the Desktop Management Task Force (DMTF) designed to give vendors and users a common vendor- and protocol-neutral framework to manage desktop systems, servers, peripherals, and components.

DMI (Digital Multiplexed Interface)
A gateway providing 23 digital channels plus one signaling channel at an aggregate rate of 1.544 megabits per second (Mbps). Developed by AT&T. See also CPI.

DML (data manipulation language)
The language by which an application programmer invokes functions from a database management system (DBMS) product to access and manipulate data.

DMP (distributed message passing)

DMPP (distributed memory parallel processors)
Massively parallel processing machine without shared-memory capabilities; also known as "loosely coupled."

DMS (Defense Message System)
A protocol that is not intended for use over the Internet; it is to be run over the Defense Information Systems Network (DISN). Connectivity between DMS and other systems is to be handled through gateways called Multifunction Interpreters (MFIs).

DMS (distribution management system)
Another term for warehouse management system (WMS). Some people use the term DMS because the system is used to control the activities within a distribution center. The terms DMS and WMS can be used interchangeably.

DMT (discrete multitone)
A frequency division method for transmitting data over twisted pair lines using 256 frequencies in the 64 kilohertz (KHz) to 1.1 megahertz (MHz) range. It is a more sophisticated signaling method that has more robust error correction and bandwidth management features. DMT is the official standard for generic digital subscriber line (xDSL) signaling.

DMU (digital mock-up)
A 3-D application used to simulate mechanical designs.

DMX (Document Manager for Microsoft Exchange)
A software component developed by Eastman Software that adds document management services to Microsoft Exchange.

DMZ (demilitarized zone)
Technical jargon for the protected subnet between an intranet and the public Internet.

DNA (Digital Network Architecture — Digital Equipment)

DNA (Distributed InterNet Applications)

DNafs (Distributed Internet Applications Architecture for Financial Services)
An applications development framework from Microsoft that is 75 percent industry-neutral Component Object Model (COM) object libraries, and 25 percent financial-services extensions for support of existing industry standards — e.g., Open Financial Exchange (OFX) for banking, Olife and Objx for insurance, and Federal Internet Exchange (FIX) and Society for Worldwide Interbank Financial Telecommunications (SWIFT) for securities — as well as financial-services-specific logic to address

specific integration issues and standard definitions for various transaction participants.

DNC (digital numeric control)
Software used to control machine tools or other devices that use pre-programmed motion control to remove material from a stock piece as part of the manufacturing process. It is usually stored in a general-purpose computer and distributed to multiple devices on demand.

DNIC (data network identification code)
A four-digit number assigned to public data networks.

DNIS (Dialed Number Identification Service)
DNIS is a feature of 800 and 900 lines. The long-distance carrier transmits the DNIS of the incoming call to identify the numbers the person is calling. Those DNIS digits may be received via in-band or out-of-band format, Integrated Services Digital Network (ISDN), or data channel.

DNS (Distributed Naming Service)
A DECnet service that enables a network resource to be named independently of its physical location. Using DNS, a database could be referred to as "Sales," regardless of where it was located or relocated.

DNS (Domain Naming System)
The online distributed database system that serves as the map between names and Internet addresses.

DOCA (Distributed Object Computing Architecture)
An applications architecture on which System Software Associates (SSA) has largely based its BPCS 6.0 product for the enterprise resource planning (ERP) market. It has tools to enable interoperability.

DOCSIS (Data-Over-Cable Service Interface Specification)
A standards-based set of specifications managed by the MCNS partners (Comcast Cable Communications, Cox Communications, Tele-Communications, and Time Warner Cable) for residential cable modems.

document component management (See DCM)

Document Composition Facility (See DCF)

document-enabled vertical application (See DEVA)

Document Image Processing (See DIP)

document imaging
The conversion (i.e., digitizing) of paper documents into electronic documents by using a scanner or similar device, and the subsequent storage and management of those electronic images.

Document Interchange Architecture (See DIA)

document management
An application or middleware that performs data management tasks tailored for typical unstructured documents (including compound documents). It may also manage the flow of documents through their life cycles.

Document Manager for Microsoft Exchange (See DMX)

Document Object Model (See DOM)

document rendering
The ability to control the appearance of a document.

document representation standards
Internal data streams that can support the transport of text, data, graphics, image and, in the future, voice and video.

document-type definition (See DTD)

DOM (Document Object Model)
A standard for defining hierarchies of document objects (e.g., document, element, attribute) and how they can be processed by a standard set of programmatic calls (i.e., application programming interfaces between applications and documents) for traversing, identifying and manipulating those hierarchies.

domain
1. A group of nodes on a network forming an administrative entity.
2. On the Internet, a part of the naming hierarchy that refers to groupings of networks based on organization type or geography.

domain name
A unique identifier for an Internet site. Consists of at least two (but sometimes more) parts separated by periods (e.g., http://www.info-edge.com). Top-level domains for Web sites must be registered with the Web Internet Registry, and a yearly fee (currently $50) must be paid to maintain the registry.

Domain Naming System (See DNS)

DOMF (Distributed Object Management Facility)
Hewlett-Packard's (HP's) DOMF is based on the Common Object Request Broker Architecture (CORBA) standard from the Object Management Group (OMG). DOMF provides a location-transparent object-communication mechanism across heterogeneous networks by using the DCE standard.

DOMS (Distributed Object Management System — a.k.a. HD-DOMS, from HyperDesk)

DOMSAT (domestic communications satellite)

DOS (Disk Operating System)
An operating system that resides in main memory and in mass storage. It is the command-driven operating system that is standard for IBM PC and compatible computers and uses disks for data storage.

DOS/VSE (Disk Operating System/Virtual Storage Extended)
The low-end operating system for IBM's S/370 architecture computers. DOS/VSE typically operates on smaller machines, especially in nonadvanced environments.

dot pitch
On a display screen or picture tube, the distance between two dots of the same color. Generally, the finer the dot pitch (typical values are 0.26 to 0.28 mm) the smoother the image, but smaller is not necessarily always better. Since there are a variety of different phosphor coating technologies that dictate the distance between adjacent phosphor triads or strips, there are considerable variations in how different manufacturers measure dot pitch.

dots per inch (See dpi)

Double-Byte Character Set Support
Support for system and application use of double-byte character sets as required for Far Eastern national language support.

double supertwisted nematic (See DSTN)

DOV (data over voice)
A technology that transmits data and voice simultaneously over twisted-pair copper wiring and is used primarily with local Centrex services or a special customer premises private branch exchange (PBX). Data rates for Centrex operation are 9.6 kilobits per second (Kbps) and 19.2 Kbps.

downlink
The portion of a satellite circuit extending from the satellite to the earth. Compare with uplink.

download
The process of bringing a file down to a computer through a network and typically from a server, or some other computing device. Download times can be greatly effected by the method of connection to the network.

downsizing
The process of moving computing work to smaller computers.

downtime
The total time a system is out of service due to equipment failure.

DP (data processing)

DP (distribution point)

DPA (Distributed Print Architecture)
International Organization for Standardization (ISO) standard 10175, which defines print objects, attributes and protocols for submitting print requests across heterogeneous systems. Designed to provide a distributed printing system with high levels of interoperability, robustness, reliability and stability.

DPC (Data Processing Center)

DPCM (Differential Pulse Code Modulation)

DPC/OPC (destination point code and origination point code)
An Integrated Services Digital Network (ISDN) term.

DPE (Disk Processor Enclosure — Clarion)

dpi (dots per inch)
A measurement of resolution; e.g., the number of pixels per inch on a cathode ray tube display.

DPL (Distributed Program Link)

DPN (Data Packet Network)
The public packet networking product by Nortel Networks (formerly Northern Telecom).

DPA

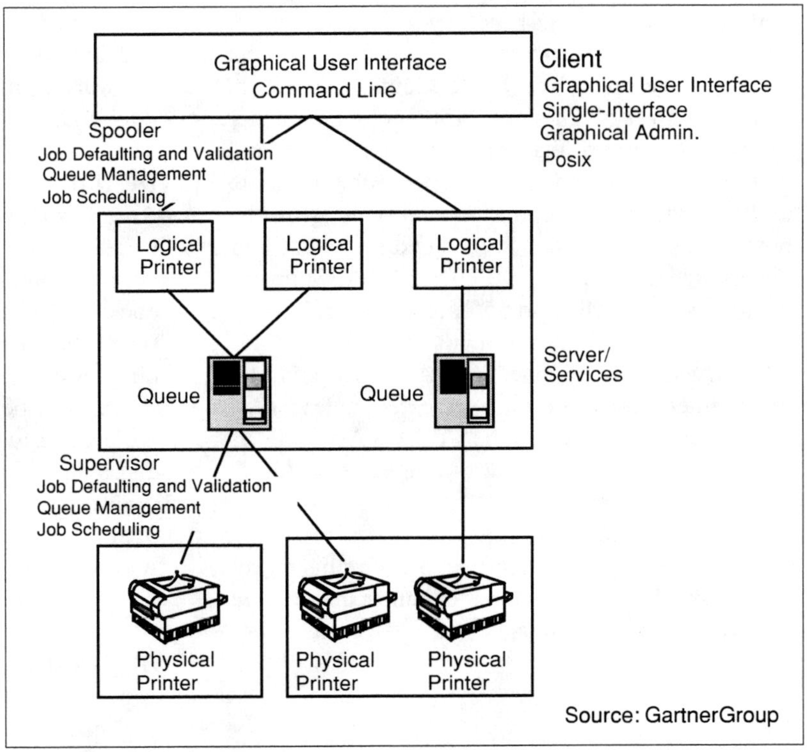

Distributed Print Architecture

DPNSS (Digital Private Network Signaling System)
A standard developed by British Telecommunications and other United Kingdom private branch exchange (PBX) suppliers. It enables PBXs from different vendors to be connected with E1 lines and pass calls transparently between each — as if the phones were extensions of the same PBX.

DPP (distributed parallel processing)
Distribution of a job to whichever processor or network is best equipped to handle the job at that time.

DPSK (Differential Phase-Shift Keying)
See phase modulation.

DQDB (Distributed Queue Dual Bus)
The Media Access Control technique used by the IEEE 802.6 Metropolitan Area Networking (MAN) standard. It is based on the Queued Packet Synchronous Exchange (QPSX) technology conceived at the University of Western Australia in 1985, and further developed by QPSX Communications. DQDB is a very high-speed (150 Mbps), distance-insensitive network that transports both voice and data. It uses a form of asynchronous time division multiplexing. By watching for empty cells on the buses, it avoids the need to pass tokens, as in Fiber Distributed Data Interface (FDDI). DQDB supports data rates of 45 Mbps to 155 megabits per second (Mbps) and isochronous circuits up to 1.44 Mbps. DQDB, which was designed for MAN usage, complements emerging asynchronous transfer mode (ATM) networks on the wide-area network (WAN) side, as 802. 6 uses the same format and cell size as ATM.

DR (disaster recovery)
1. The use of alternative network circuits to re-establish communications channels in the event that the primary channels are disconnected or malfunctioning.
2. Methods and procedures for returning a data center to full operation after a catastrophic interruption (e.g., including recovery of lost data).

DR (Distributed Request)
One of the four functional elements of IBM's Systems Application Architecture Distributed Relational Database strategy that systematically executes a single Structured Query Language (SQL) statement accessing multiple databases.

DRAM (dynamic random-access memory)
A computer memory chip that requires electronic refresh cycles to preserve data stored for manipulation by logic chips.

DRDA (Distributed Relational Data Architecture)
IBM's architecture for enterprisewide data access, announced in July 1990. The architecture is designed to homogenize the way data is defined and accessed across IBM's different hardware/software platforms, as well as address multilingual coding standards.

DRM (distributed resource management)
An evolving discipline consisting of a set of software, hardware, network tools, procedures and policies for enabling distributed enterprise systems to operate effectively in production. DRM embraces solutions for the daily monitoring, resource planning, system administration, change management, operations, performance and other initiatives that are needed to maintain effective productivity in a distributed networked computing environment.

drop
A connection point between a communicating device and a communications network.

DRP (disaster recovery plan)
A plan developed to ensure the timely recovery of information technology (IT) assets and services

following some kind of catastrophe, such as fire, flood, hardware failure, etc.

DRP (disaster recovery planning)
Operational procedures for ensuring recovery of hardware and communications assets and recovery of data.

DRP (distribution requirements planning)
The process of assessing from where products and services should be deployed, and determining the stock-keeping unit (SKU) and location level replenishment plan.

DRP (Distribution Resource Planning — J.D. Edwards & Co.)

Dry Line
A T1 line not providing span power.

DS (decision support)

DS (Netscape Directory Server)

DSA (Digital Signature Algorithm)
Developed by the National Institute of Standards and Technology (NIST) for use with the Digital Signature Standard.

DSA (directory system agent)
The electronic-messaging component that receives requests for addresses, looks them up and returns the address.

DSA (Dynamic Server Architecture)
From Informix Software, DSA is a parallel, scalable architecture that supports large databases running on massively parallel, loosely coupled, symmetric multiprocessing (SMP) and uniprocessor computers. DSA is designed to be independent of platforms and transparent to applications.

DSC (digital selective calling)

DSC2 (Deschutes Slot 2 — Intel)

DSI (Digital Speech Interpolation)
When speech is digitized, it can be cut into slices such that no bits are transmitted when a person is silent. As soon as speech begins, bits flow again.

DSL (digital subscriber line)
DSL technology high-speed network or Internet access over voice lines. There are various types: asymmetric DSL (ADSL), high-bit-rate DSL (HDSL), symmetric DSL (SDSL), very-high-bit-rate DSL (VDSL), and a recent variant of ADSL called G.Lite. The whole group is sometimes referred to as "xDSL."

D

DSLO (Distributed Systems License Option)
An IBM software license option that is available to IBM customers with a basic license for the software product that allows them to copy certain IBM-licensed material for the purpose of installing multiple systems.

DSM (distributed systems management)
A technology for managing the interconnected parts of a system. As managed items — i.e., components of applications, nodes, links or subsystems — become active, they must notify their manager of their status. DSM tools are capable of dealing with a limited number of distinct elements and require a strong directory.

DSMPU (digital signal-processing microprocessor)

DSN (Distributed Systems Network)
The network architecture developed by Hewlett-Packard.

DSOM (Distributed System Object Model)
IBM's distributed object technology, which originated on OS/2 and AIX and could be ported to other operating environments, including Windows. DSOM

is a follow-up to System Object Model (SOM), an operating-system extension that provides object-oriented programming (OOP) mechanisms such as method dispatching and inheritance to OS/2. DSOM is a Common Object Request Broker Architecture (CORBA)-compliant system.

DSP (digital signal processor)
A specialized computer chip optimized for high data rates needed to process digitized wave forms, particularly those derived from analog sources. Often used in equipment requiring voice digitization.

DSP (Directory Synchronization Protocol)

DSRI (Digital Standard Relational Interface)
Digital Equipment's proprietary, low-level application programming interface (API) to Rdb.

DSRL (Dynamic Selection of Runtime Location)

DSS (decision support system)
A system designed to support strategic (vs. operating) decisions. Decision support systems enable the computer rather than the user to make decisions. The system tends to be user-friendly and emphasizes ad hoc query, reporting and analysis capabilities. This is in contrast to online transaction processing, which focuses on low-cost, fast-response and predictably structured applications.

DSSI (Digital Storage Systems Interconnect)

DSSS (direct sequence spread spectrum)
A technology for third-generation wireless LAN (WLAN) systems. It has the ability to deliver twice the bandwidth per node, per access point than frequency hop (FH) and is more resilient to certain types of multipath interference.

DSTN (double supertwisted nematic)
A type of flat-panel display screen.

DSU (data service unit)
A simplified modem for the transmission of digital data over a private line or for limited distance communications over the public switched telephone network (PSTN), where it is not necessary to comply with all the requirements for a high-speed modem.

DSU (disk storage unit)

DSVD (digital simultaneous voice and data)
Technology used in some modems to integrate voice with data for simultaneous use.

DSx
In telephony, one of many digital signal levels each providing a specific bandwidth, including:

1. DS-0: Digital Signal Level 0, a standard 64 kilobit per second (Kbps) digital voice signal or channel.
2. DS-1: Digital Signal Level 1, in which 24 voice channels are multiplexed into one 1.544 megabit per second (Mbps) (United States) or 2.048 Mbps (Europe) T1 digital channel.
3. DS-1C: Digital Signal Level 1C; a 3.152 Mbps digital signal carried on a T1 C facility.
4. DS-2: Digital Signal Level 2; the 6.312 Mbps digital signal carried on a T2, or 8.448 Mbps digital signal carried on an E2 (CEPT) facility.
5. DS-3: Digital Signal Level 3; the 44 Mbps digital signal carried on a T3 facility, or 34.368 Mbps digital signal carried on an E3 (CEPT) facility.
6. DS-4: Digital Signal Level 4; the 273 Mbps digital signal carried on a T4, or 139.264 Mbps digital signal carried on an E4 (CEPT) facility.

DSX-1 Interface
The channel service unit (CSU) interface to which a T1 line is attached — either a RJ48C or a DB15 female connection.

DT (dumb terminal)

DTA (desktop administrator)

DTB (desktop broadcasting)

DTD (document-type definition)
Extensible Markup Language (XML)-defined document grammars. The data elements/markup tags, along with any other defined data element attributes, can be thought of as the document's metadata. DTDs can also be thought of as providing a "schema" and "data dictionary" for the document. Using a DTD, an XML parser can validate a document for conformance to a particular document type.

DTE (data terminal equipment)
End-user devices, such as terminals and computers that connect to data circuit-terminating equipment (DCE), which either generate or receive the data carried by the network. In RS-232-C connections, designation as either DTE or DCE determines the signaling role in handshaking. In an ITU X.25 interface, it is the device or equipment that manages the interface at the user premises.

DT/FM (decision trees/fault models)
Problem resolution technology offerings can be divided into three groups: keyword search/natural language search (KS/NLS); learning network/ association models (LN/AMs); and DT/FMs.

DTIF (Digital Table Interchange Format)
The Compound Document Architecture-specified format used for the storage and interchange of documents that contain data tables, formulas and spreadsheets.

DTL (diode-transistor logic)

DTM (Date Time Module)

DTMF (dual-tone multifrequency signaling)
The basis for operation of push-button telephone sets. DTMF is a method of signaling in which a matrix combination of two frequencies, each from a group of four, is used to transmit numerical address information. The two groups of four frequencies are: 697 hertz (Hz), 770 Hz, 852 Hz; 941 Hz; 1209 Hz, 1336 Hz, 1477 Hz; and 1633 Hz.

DTP (desktop publishing)

DTP (Distributed Transaction Processing — part of CICS)

DTV (digital television)

Dual 56
Two switched 56 kilobit per second (Kbps) calls made between videoconferencing equipment to enable data transfer at 112 Kbps. The videoconferencing equipment performs a two-channel inverse-multiplexing procedure to assure channel alignment.

Dual-Attached Concentrator (See DAC)

Dual-Attached Station (See DAS)

dual in-line memory module (See DIMM)

dual in-line package (See DIP)

dual-tone multifrequency signaling (See DTMF)

dumb terminal
A terminal not performing local processing of entered information; serves only as an input/output device for an attached or network-linked processor.

dump
To transfer all information from a record to another storage medium, e.g., copying from memory to a printer.

DUOW (Distributed Unit of Work — part of DRDA)
Part of IBM's classification of distributed-database capabilities; a self-contained set of Structured Query Language (SQL) requests accessing data that may be situated at multiple physical locations. Each SQL request can access only one system. One of the four functional elements of IBM's Systems Application Architecture (SAA) Distributed Relational Data Architecture (DRDA) strategy that coordinates the systematic execution of multiple SQL statements accessing multiple databases.

DUP (Data User Part — ISDN term)

duplex circuit
A circuit used for transmission in both directions at the same time.

Duplex Ethernet
Ethernet at 20 megabit per second (Mbps) speeds using two data paths. It is only suitable for use with Ethernet switching hubs.

Duplex Signaling (See DX)

duplex transmission
Simultaneous, two-way, independent transmission. Often called full-duplex transmission (FDX).

DVD (digital versatile disk)

DVD (digital videodisc)
An optical disk with the ability to store large quantities of video data.

DVD-ROM (digital videodisc read-only memory)
A read-only format of digital videodisc (DVD) that was designed specifically for the personal computer (PC) market. Physically, DVD discs take on the same 5 1/4-inch footprint used in CD-ROMs. DVD discs, however, are loaded much more densely with data, and storage capacities start at 4.7 gigabytes (Gbytes).

DVI (digital video interface)

DVMRP (Dynamic Vector Multicast Routing Protocol)
An internetworking gateway protocol based on Routing Information Protocol (RIP), which uses a dense-mode Internet Protocol (IP) multicast scheme.

DW (data warehouse)
A central computer repository that stores all (or significant portions of) the data collected by an enterprise's multiple business systems. Data from online transaction-processing applications and other sources is selectively collected, extracted, sorted and cleaned. Then it is stored in a data warehouse, which is usually housed in an enterprise mainframe server.

DW (Development Workbench)

DWDM (dense wave division multiplexing — See WDM)

DX (Duplex Signaling)
A signaling system that occupies the same cable pair as the voice path yet does not require filters.

DXF (data exchange format)

DXI (Data Exchange Interface)
A frame-based protocol for customer premises equipment to access Switched Multimegabit Data Ser-

vice (SMDS). It is based on High-Level Data Link Control (HDLC) format and designed to operate over serial lines.

DXT (Data Extract)
An IBM-licensed program designed for use with user-written exits to support data extraction from a variety of Multiple Virtual Storage (MVS) files.

dyadic
A multiprocessor design term that IBM introduced with the 3081. Multiple Virtual Storage (MVS) sees a dyadic processor as two processors running as one.

dynamic adaptive routing
Automatic selection and use of alternative communications paths among two or more midrange systems of the same supplier in the event of a congested, faulty or downed circuit within the preferred data path.

Dynamic Address Translation (See DAT)

Dynamic Bandwidth Allocation
The process of determining current traffic loads over a channel, and automatically increasing or decreasing the bandwidth of the channel to optimize overall utilization efficiency.

dynamic database restructuring
The ability to change the relational-database structure, table capacities and security without unloading and reloading the database.

Dynamic Data Exchange (See DDE)

dynamic DNS (dynamic Domain Naming Service)

dynamic hardware reconfiguration
The ability to add or delete midrange system hardware components and modify operating-system hardware configuration tables by operator control without turning power off and reinitializing the operating system.

Dynamic Host Configuration Protocol (See DHCP)

dynamic HTML (See DHTML)

Dynamic Link Library (See DLL)

dynamic RAM (See DRAM)

dynamic routing
A method of wide-area network (WAN) transmission that uses a router to select the most appropriate path for each section of data packet transmission along a network.

Dynamic Server Architecture (See DSA)

Dynamic Vector Multicast Routing Protocol (See DVMRP)

E

E (Erlang)
In telecommunications, a unit of traffic intensity. One Erlang is the intensity at which one traffic path would be continuously occupied (e.g., one call-hour per hour or one call-minute per minute). Generally referred to as 36 CCS. Related terms include:

- Erlang B: A traffic-engineering formula used when traffic is random and there is no queuing. It assumes that blocked callers either automatically use another route or blocked calls disappear entirely.
- Erlang C: A traffic engineering formula used when traffic is random and queuing is provided. It assumes that all callers will wait indefinitely until a line becomes available.

E1
A European standard digital facility with a transmission speed of 2.048 megabits per second (Mbps). For digital signal level 1 (DS1), 24 voice channels are multiplexed onto one E1 channel. In the United States, a 1.544 Mbps channel is used (i.e., T1).

E.164
The International Telecommunications Union-T (ITU) recommendation for international telecommunications numbering, especially for Integrated Services Digital Network (ISDN) and Switched Multimegabit Data Service (SMDS). It is a 10-digit phone number with the freedom of choice in all digits implemented in 1997.

E3
A European standard digital facility with a transmission speed of 34.368 megabits per second (Mbps). For digital signal level 3 (DS3), 32 voice channels are multiplexed onto one E3 channel. In the United States, a 44 Mbps channel is used (i.e., T3).

E-4GL (enterprise fourth-generation language)

E-AD (enterprise applications development)
Platform-specific E-AD tools are optimized for specific environments (e.g., the AS/400 or Unix), generally at the expense of supporting more heterogeneous environments.

EAI (enterprise application integration)

EAM (enterprise asset management)
An application software suite consisting of an integrated set of application types — e.g., computer maintenance management system (CMMS), financial, human resources, abnormal situation management (ASM) — operating in concert to maximize or optimize the return generated by an enterprise's physical assets.

EAM (equipment asset management)
The planning and control of equipment purchase and use so as to maximize return on investment (ROI) and minimize total cost of ownership (TCO).

EAROM (electrically alterable read-only memory)

EARS (Electronic Authoring and Routing System)
Digital Equipment workflow application built by Digital's field organization using ALL-IN-1 mail and FMS, the forms system native to ALL-IN-1.

earth station
Ground-based equipment used to communicate via satellites. See also ground station.

EAS (Extended Area Service)
An option whereby the telephone subscriber can pay a higher flat rate to obtain wider geographical coverage without additional per-call charges.

EASDAQ (European Association of Securities Dealers Automated Quotations)
Authorized by the Belgian Banking and Finance Commission, the EASDAQ stock exchange has a small market but high standards of regulation. Recent European Union directives dictate that authorization in Belgium permits EASDAQ to operate its trading system in all other member states. The EASDAQ Rule Book has been closely modeled on National Association of Securities Dealers Automated Quotations (NASDAQ's) rules, allowing companies to comply with the information requirements of the Securities and Exchange Commission (SEC) in the United States, thus easily allowing companies to dual-list on NASDAQ and EASDAQ.

EATE (electronic automatic test equipment)

EAX (Electronic Automatic Exchange)
A term used by the General Telephone Company for electronic exchange equipment.

EBCDIC (Extended Binary-Coded Decimal Interchange Code)
An 8-bit alphanumeric code developed by IBM. Similar to (and now largely eclipsed by) American Standard Code for Information Interchange (ASCII).

e-bill (electronic bill)

EBIS (enterprise business intelligence suites)
Suites that offer multiple styles of common BI functionality, including ad hoc query, reporting, charting, multidimensional viewing (OLAP) and light analysis (e.g., trending).

EBO (Enterprise Business Operations)

EBP (electronic bill presentment)

EBPP (electronic bill presentment and payment)

EBR (electronic batch record)
A transaction that captures all of the relevant steps and measurements associated with the production of a product that is produced using batch-manufacturing methods.

EBSD (electronic business software division)

EBU (European Broadcasting Union)

EC (engineering change)
A revision to a parts list, bill of material, engineering drawing or engineering part model authorized by the engineering department. Changes are usually identified by a control number and are made for safety, cost reduction or functionality reasons. Also called ECO (engineering change order) or ECN (engineering change notice).

ECAD (electronic computer-aided design)

ECAE (electronic computer-aided engineering)

E carrier
A time division multiplexed digital transmission facility operating at an aggregate data rate of 2.048 megabits per second (Mbps) and above.

e-carrier services
High-speed, private-line digital transmission services, defined by the European Conference of Postal and Telecommunications Administrations (CEPT) for Europe, that provide large-volume transmission between two stations. E1, the most common e-carrier service, operates at an aggregate data rate of 2.048 megabits per second (Mbps) and consists of 24 separate channels. (E2 and E3 are rated at 8.448 Mbps and 34.368 Mbps, respectively.) Only E1 and E3 are widely supported. In the United States, T-carrier services are provided, although the corresponding data rates are not identical.

E-CASE (enterprise computer-aided software engineering)
A category of enterprise application development (E-AD) tools that are generally noninterpretive, generate Common Business Oriented Language (COBOL) or C, and may have integrated modeling capabilities in their integrated development environments.

e-cash (electronic cash)
Digital money, typically in the form of downloadable "digital coins" that can be stored in an online bank account, on a personal computer (PC) or on a smart card. Driven by Web-based payment schemes, electronic cash is today primarily aimed at exploiting very-small-value transactions (e.g., less than $20 or $1, or even less than a penny). Worldwide, very-small-value transactions make up trillions of dollars worth of commerce annually. Making these transactions more convenient will be big business when electronic-cash technology matures.

e-catalog (electronic catalog)
Used for buying and selling and as an aggregation tool in electronic marketplaces (EMs).

ECC (Elliptical Curve Cryptosystems)
An algorithm forwarded for commercial use by Canadian vendor Certicom. It is implemented using public-key algorithms combined with elliptic curves. The curves construct "elements" and "rules of combining" to produce groups which, in turn, create cryptographic algorithms.

ECC (enterprise cooperation community)
Enterprise cooperation roles represent the knowledge management (KM) emphasis on sharing. They form a community with other enterprise cooperation roles in other enterprises sharing best practices in the co-evolution of processes and technology. The ECC is linked together through the technology and practices it is championing. This approach requires that all roles use the technology. Enterprise cooperation roles are leveraged when a few users learn new practices and technology, and they pass on this knowledge to more performance-focused roles, and ultimately to the entire white-collar staff.

ECC (error-correcting code)
The diagnostic code used to correct data-storage errors and isolate hardware failures. Based on a concept of simultaneous polynomial equations, the read-back process generates a correction profile over the incorrect data. All ECCs have a very small but finite failure rate (i.e., some uncorrectable errors will either appear as correctable or appear as having no error at all). In either situation, bad data is passed as verified and valid.

ECD (electrochromeric display)

ECD (energy conversion device)

echo
A wave that has been reflected or otherwise returned with sufficient magnitude and delay for it to be perceived as a wave distinct from the one directly transmitted.

echo cancellation
A technique used in higher-speed modems that allows for the isolation and filtering of unwanted signal energy resulting from echoes from the main transmitted signal.

echo check
A method of checking data transmission accuracy, whereby the data received is returned to the sending end for comparison with the original data.

echoplex
Pertaining or referring to the printing of keyboarded characters on return of the signal from the other end of the line, using full-duplex transmission, to ensure that the data was received correctly at the other end.

Echo Return Loss (See ERL)

echo suppressor
A mechanism used to suppress interference on long-distance analog connections; it suppresses the transmission path opposite in direction to the one in use. This feature is necessary for voice transmission but often interferes with data transmission.

ECKD (extended count key data)

ECL (emitter-coupled logic)
A type of bipolar (i.e., a category of chip design) transistor characterized by extremely fast switching speeds.

ECM (enterprise client migration)

ECMA (European Computer Manufacturers Association)

ECN (Electronic Commerce Network — C1)
A catalog-hosting environment managed by MCI that enables suppliers to shift catalog and transaction management off-site. Suppliers need only to have Internet access and provide updates in either batch or real-time to their catalogs. Buyers access ECN to view and interact with supplier catalogs.

ECO (electronic-commerce outsourcing)
The partial or complete outsourcing of the technologies and business processes a company requires to engage in electronic commerce with its trading partners.

ECO (engineering change order)

e-COMM
A French consortium and the "smart card" electronic-payment implementation it supports, which is compliant with the international Secure Electronic Transfer (SET) standard.

e-commerce (electronic commerce)
The use of communication technologies to transmit business information and transact business. Taking an order over the telephone is a simple form of e-commerce. Commerce conducted via the Internet is also called e-commerce, but commercial exchanges on the Internet are only one of several advanced forms of e-commerce that use different technologies, integrated applications and business processes to link enterprises. Business-to-business e-commerce focuses on transactions and communication, specifically the electronic exchange of information,

E-Commerce

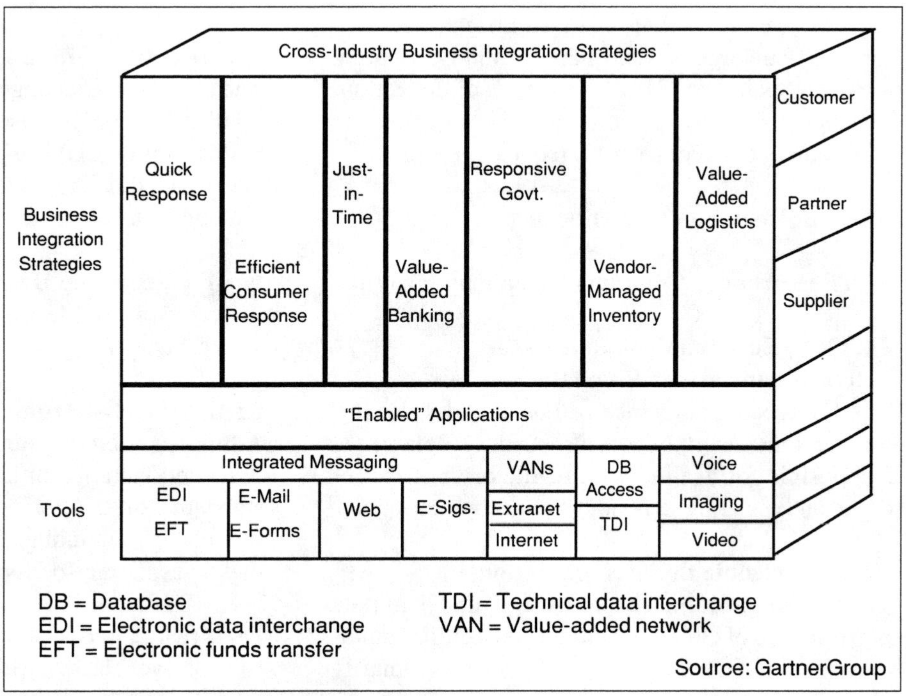

The Components of Electronic Commerce

goods, services and payments. Key business processes that are carried out by e-commerce include procurement, order entry, transaction processing, payment, inventory, fulfillment and customer support.

economic life
The remaining period over which the property is expected to be economically usable with normal repairs and maintenance.

economic value added (See EVA)

ECP (electronic check presentment)
The electronic presentation of check data to processing banks. In the first ECP phase, one bank presents a second bank with electronic check information based on the check's magnetic-ink character recognition (MICR) line, which states the correct customer account and the amount of the payment. Electronic presentment is then followed by the paper check, speeding the clearing process by one day and enabling banks to use credited account balances a day earlier — a significant benefit, especially to large banks. In the second ECP phase, the check is imaged at the first bank of collection; the paper or the image is not passed to the second bank unless the second bank requests it.

ECR (efficient customer response)

ECTF (Enhanced Computer Telephony Forum)

ECTRA (European Committee for Telecommunications Regulatory Affairs)
The European Conference of Postal and Telecommunications Administrations (CEPT) committee responsible for dealing with regulatory issues predominantly relating to nonradio telecommunications.

EDA (electronic design automation)
The use of a computer to design and simulate performance of electronic circuits on a chip. Similar to automatic test equipment, which tests primarily chips in electronic systems.

EDA (Embedded Document Architecture)

EDA/SQL (Enterprise Data Access/Structured Query Language)
A product from Information Builders, EDA provides a common interface between a wide range of Structured Query Language (SQL) programs and SQL databases. Queries on data from different types of databases can be queried simultaneously using EDA.

EDD (electronic document distribution)
Distribution of information without the use of paper. The goal is to enable viewers to actively interact with a document, directing the document to display information on request. The complexity of this task is compounded by the addition of media unsupported by print (e.g., sound and animation). EDD market problems are twofold: limiting technology and lack of acceptance by end users.

edge gateway (See EGW)

EDI (electronic data interchange)
The electronic exchange of trading documents (e.g., invoices and orders) used for electronic commerce. Until recently, EDI was typically conducted through value-added networks (VANs). It is now gradually moving to the Internet.

EDIF (Electronic Data Interchange Format)
A standard for defining the exchange of electronic data.

EDIFACT (Electronic Data Interchange for Administration, Commerce and Transportation)
A United Nations initiative to produce a universal standard for a total approach to electronic data interchange including syntax, data elements and messages. See also UN/JEDI.

EDL (Enterprise Definition Language)
EDL defines classes, which are user-specified groupings of storage objects based on a combination of

node, path, file name, ownership or other filters. Classes are used to collect, analyze and manage storage resources by application, owner, location, node or some other installation-defined criteria.

EDM (electronic document management)

EDM (EMC Data Manager)
Backup and recovery software for the relational database management system (RDBMS) environment developed by EMC. It is considered to be a high-end replacement for EMC's Epoch Systems.

EDM (enterprise desktop manager)
A software application used to manage the total desktop environment. It includes functions such as software distribution and installation, configuration management, change management, and hardware and software inventory.

EDO (extended data output)
A fairly simple, pin-compatible derivative of standard fast-page mode asynchronous memory. EDO can improve memory performance by as much as 20 percent or 30 percent by shortening the page mode cycle of traditional memory. It can be used for dynamic random-access memory (DRAM) or video random-access memory (VRAM). It does not command a significant premium over standard page-mode DRAM.

EDP (electronic data processing)

EDS (Electronic Data Systems)

EDUCOM
A consortium of leading colleges and universities seeking to transform education through the use of information technology (IT).

EEMA (European Electronic Mail Association)

EEPROM (Electrically Erasable Programmable Read-Only Memory)
An EPROM that can be erased or updated by electrical signal, often done remotely.

EESD (enterprise electronic software distribution) (See ESD)

EFCI (Explicit Forward Congestion Indicator)
In an asynchronous transfer mode (ATM) network, one of two feedback mechanisms used by the available bit rate (ABR) service category to inform the source of the network resources available to it.

EFF (Electronic Frontier Foundation)

effective address
A logical or actual location in memory.

effective isotropic radiated power (See EIRP)

e-finance (electronic financial services)
Electronically enabled access to financial services. It is not a delivery (i.e., institution-centric) vehicle, but a vehicle of access (i.e., customer-centric).

e-form (electronic form)
An automated and interactive template for capturing, processing, displaying and creating output from defined sets of business data.

EFS (electronic financial services) (See e-finance)

EFT (electronic funds transfer)
The electronic exchange of information between financial institutions, which results in debits and credits.

EFT/POS (electronic funds transfer/point-of-sale)
Allows direct transfer of funds during a retail transaction.

E

EGA (enhanced graphics adaptor — IBM)

EGP (Exterior Gateway Protocol)
The Transmission Control Protocol/Internet Protocol (TCP/IP) used by exterior routers to move data from one autonomous system to another.

EGW (edge gateway)
The perimeter switching technology that offers users the interface to a variety of virtual public data services.

EHLLAPI (Emulator High-Level Application Program Interface)
An IBM communications feature.

EHR (Enterprise Office Human Resources)

EI (enterprise integration or integrator)

EIA (Electronic Industries Association — U.S.)

EIA (enterprise information architecture)
Enterprise-specific definition of rules defining the use of middleware in third-generation office systems. The EIA rules include application programming interfaces (APIs) and protocols addressing interoperability and portability of applications, whether acquired or developed internally. The EIA is a living specification requiring constant management and regular review for enhancement.

EIA interface
A standardized set of signal characteristics (i.e., duration, voltage and current) specified by the Electronic Industries Association. Includes:

1. EIA/TIA-232: Standard for unbalanced circuits up to 64 kilobits per second (Kbps), formerly RS-232.
2. EIA/TIA-449: Like EIA/TIA 232 but can run at speeds of up to 2 megabits per second (Mbps). Formerly RS-449.
3. EIA-530: Standard for balanced (formerly RS-422) and unbalanced (formerly RS-423) transmission.
4. EIA/TIA-586: Standard describing the various grades of unshielded twisted-pair (UTP) cabling.

EIAJ (Electronic Industries Association of Japan)

EIA/TIA (Electronic Industries Association/ Telecommunications Industry Association)

EIDE (Enhanced Integrated Drive Electronics)
An interface that supports larger capacities than standard Integrated Drive Electronics (IDE) and allows for more peripherals to attach to the interface, providing some incremental flexibility and expandability.

EIGRP (Enhanced Interior Gateway Routing Protocol)
An Interior Gateway Protocol (IGP) that transfers packets from one network to another adjacent one.

EIM (enterprise information management)
EIM is an architecture-management approach for resolving architectural differences within office information system (OIS) implementations. EIM is a tool for strategic planning comprising the enterprise information architecture (EIA) and a set of strategic IS management practices. By applying EIM to their enterprises, users have been able to migrate from the incompatible systems of the 1980s to the interoperable systems of the 1990s.

EIRP (effective isotropic radiated power)
The combination of transmitted power and antenna gain.

EIS (executive information system)
An application program specifically designed for use by the corporate executive. Presentation of

material is often structured after the "board briefing book" concept. Detailed information on the summarized charts is often made available by using a concept known as "drilling." The EIS acts as a usable interface to a database of company information. It automates high-level analysis and reporting, and typically has a user-friendly graphical interface.

EISA (Extended Industry Standard Architecture)
Originally developed as an alternative 32-bit master bus to IBM's Micro Channel master bus for its PS/2 family of micro computers. Unlike the Micro Channel, one of the design goals of the EISA bus was to enable the use of add-on cards developed for IBM's PC and PC/AT computers.

EJB (Enterprise JavaBeans)
The EJB specification defines a way to build server-side, transactional Java-based components. It was developed by Sun Microsystems in collaboration with IBM, Netscape, Oracle and other vendors.

EKA (enterprise knowledge architecture)
The table of contents, or "yellow pages," for information bases accessible through the information services of the intranet, including e-mail and Lotus notes. It enables an end user to navigate to enterprise resources using a hyperlink to the specific Web page, narrowing the search before launching a search inquiry.

EKTS (Electronic Key Telephone System)

EL (electroluminescent)

ELAN (emulated LAN)
The emulated local-area networks (LANs) that occur in a campus environment where asynchronous transfer mode (ATM) and a packet-based LAN technology are installed in the same network. ELANs are the ATM logical subnets that emulate LANs, which have been standardized and operational since the LAN emulation (LANE) 1.0 specification, and later were advanced in LANE 2.0 and Multiprotocol Over ATM (MPOA). Multiple ELANs may comprise many Ethernets or Token Rings.

Electrically Erasable Programmable Read-Only Memory (See EEPROM)

Electromagnetic Interference (See EMI)

electromagnetic spectrum
The entire range of wavelengths or frequencies of electromagnetic radiation extending from gamma rays to the longest radio wave and including visible light. See also radio frequency.

Electronic Authoring and Routing System (See EARS)

Electronic Automatic Exchange (See EAX)

electronic batch record (See EBR)

electronic cash (See e-cash)

electronic catalog (See e-catalog)

electronic check presentment (See ECP)

electronic commerce (See EC)

Electronic Commerce Network — C1 (See ECN)

electronic-commerce outsourcing (See ECO)

electronic data interchange (See EDI)

Electronic Data Interchange for Administration, Commerce and Transportation (See EDIFACT)

Electronic Data Interchange Format (See EDIF)

electronic design automation (See EDA)

electronic document distribution (See EDD)

electronic financial services (See e-finance)

electronic form (See e-form)

electronic funds transfer (See EFT)

electronic funds transfer/point-of-sale (See EFT/POS)

electronic mail (See e-mail)

Electronic Mail Association (See EMA)

electronic marketplace (See e-marketplace)

electronic marketplace manager (e-marketplace manager)

electronic medical record (See EMR)

electronic meeting systems
A class of software products that can make medium-size and large meetings more productive by supporting and automating all or some of these meeting-management activities: agenda planning and management, brainstorming, voting, commenting, evaluating alternatives and some task-specific support (e.g., project planning).

electronic merchandising (See e-merchandising)

electronic messaging
The sending and receiving of messages and, increasingly, data through a network. Like paper messaging, it is accomplished through a number of tasks, including composition, assembly, addressing, posting, sorting, routing and delivery.

Electronic Messaging Association (See EMA)

electronic messaging utility (See EMU)

electronic output strategy (See EOS)

Electronic Publishing Management System — Dataware Technologies (See EPMS)

electronic software distribution (See ESD)

electronic switching system (See ESS)

electronic tandem network (See ETN)

electronic whiteboard
A large, touch-sensitive screen attached to a personal computer (PC). Users view the PC's output on the screen and control it by touching a finger (or a specially designed inkless pen) to the menu options and icons.

elevation
The angle between the horizon and an antenna's beam.

ELF (extremely low frequency)

ELFExT (equal-level far-end crosstalk)

Elgamal
A public-key system that gets its security from the difficulty of calculating discrete logarithms in a finite field.

Elliptical Curve Cryptosystems (See ECC)

ELS (enterprise library service)

EMA (Electronic Messaging Association — formerly Electronic Mail Association)
An electronic-mail industry organization and forum for development standards and policies for such systems as e-mail, voice mail and facsimile. It has played a role in bringing together various application programming interface (API) factions to develop the Common Mail Call specification.

EMA (Enterprise Management Architecture — Digital Equipment)

e-mail (electronic mail)
Any communications service that permits the electronic transmission and storage of messages (generally text or graphics) and attached or enclosed files. Some e-mail systems are limited to communication between end users on the same network; others have gateways that allow end users to send messages to other designated computer systems or worldwide over the Internet. Once sent, the messages (also called e-mail) are stored in electronic mailboxes until the recipient retrieves them. Most Internet service providers (ISPs) also provide e-mail services. Many enterprises use e-mail software to simplify communication between employees or with people outside the enterprise. (Internal e-mail transmitted via corporate networks usually takes minutes to arrive.)

e-mail response management system (See ERMS)

e-mall
An Internet retail site with a wide range of merchants from numerous industries.

e-market maker
A third-party intermediary that provides value-added services for buyers and sellers trading on the Web.

e-marketplace (electronic marketplace)
A network service shared by multiple individuals and enterprises where information about products and services is shared electronically among enterprises, and where those products and services may be purchased without the aid of voice or paper-based exchanges. Electronic marketplaces are the translation of actual commercial and consumer marketplaces (e.g., shopping malls) to the virtual environment. Examples of EMs include the Internet, membership-based online services, bulletin boards, interconnected private networks and value-added third-party networks.

e-marketplace manager (electronic marketplace manager)
Any entity capable of implementing and managing an online e-marketplace, including hub-and-spoke groups, trading co-ops, value networks and other EMs. Online services, individual merchants, Internet service providers (ISPs), telephone companies and systems integrators all offer some level of e-marketplace management.

Embedded Structured Query Language (See ESQL)

E-Marketplace

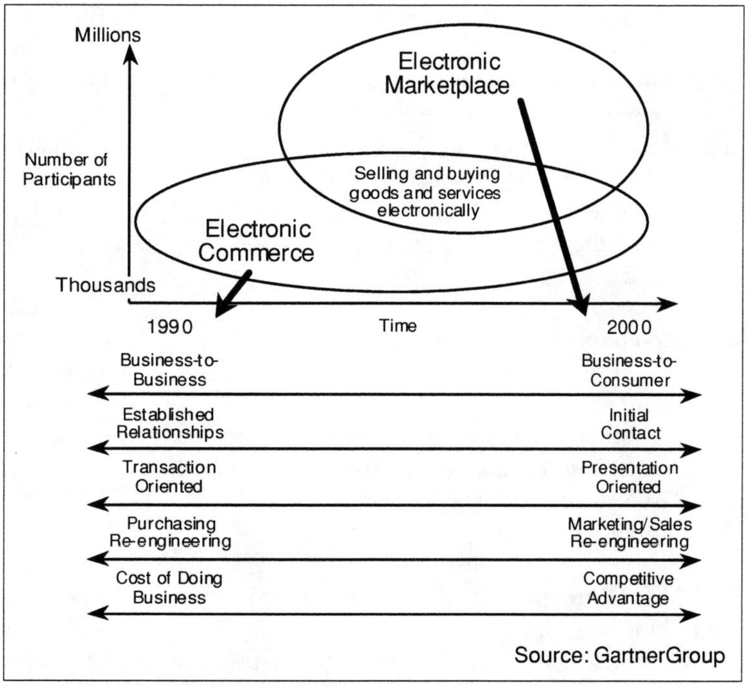

Electronic Commerce vs. Electronic Marketplaces

EMC Data Manager (See EDM)

EMEA (Europe, Middle East, Africa)

e-merchandising (electronic merchandising)
E-merchandising systems assist retailers in creating, executing and managing merchandising strategies, product assortment, pricing and promotions on the Web.

emergency access
An emergency alarm system integrated into the private branch exchange (PBX) switching system that can be implemented by uniquely ringing all station instruments to indicate an emergency condition.

emergency dialing
Allows all system users the ability to use preassigned two-or three-digit numbers that translate to outside exchange numbers (e.g., local police, fire department or ambulance service).

EMF (enterprise middleware framework)

EMI (electromagnetic interference)
The energy given off by electronic circuits and picked up by other circuits. Based on the type of device and operating frequency, EMI can be reduced by shielding. Minimum acceptable levels are detailed by the Federal Communications Commission (FCC).

emitter-coupled logic (See ECL)

emoticon
A text rendition of a face viewed sideways, created from punctuation marks (e.g.,:-)). Used in e-mail and UseNet newsgroups to denote an emotion. (From emotive icon.)

EMPAC (Enterprise Maintenance Planning and Control)
An enterprise asset management (EAM) product from Indus International.

EMPI (enterprise master person index)
The critical first step to safely sharing information on patients and members within the integrated delivery system (IDS). At a minimum, EMPIs uniquely identify patients, persons or members, and cross reference patient, person or member identification numbers to link patient information stored in disparate systems.

employee self-service (See ESS)

EMR (electronic medical record)
Used to compile computerized patient healthcare information, EMR generally deals with information only in the form of document images or text formatted for output to a printer or for video display. It does not ordinarily handle discrete data such as is usually stored in a database management system.

EMS (Enterprise Management System — BindView)

EMS (Enterprise Messaging Server — Microsoft)
Former name for Microsoft Exchange, an enterprisewide messaging and mail system. Rolled into Exchange, it and other planned products will ship as a single system: a workgroup-focused, enterprise-scoped platform for standards-based messaging, groupware, work flow, document management and "information exchange" through a single, multimedia mailbox.

EMS (enterprisewide marketing system)
A new class of vendors created by marketing automation systems (MAS).

EMS (equipment management system)
The subsystem of a warehouse management system (WMS). It controls automated material-handling equipment such as carousels, pick to light, in-line scales, and conveyors. The EMS is designed to provide a standardized interface between the ware-

house management system and the automated material-handling equipment.

EMS (Expanded Memory Specification)

EMU (electronic messaging utility)
A GartnerGroup concept describing a solid base of interworking electronic messaging provided as a utility service like electricity. The EMU is sturdy enough to bear the anticipated increase in number and size of messages, sufficiently generalized to ensure readability of attachments and well-connected to the world beyond the boundary of the enterprise. The EMU provides open interfaces to make its services available to end users and applications.

EMU (enterprise messaging utility)
A stable infrastructure for electronic messaging.

EMU (European monetary union)

emulate
To imitate one system with another, so that the imitating system accepts the same data, executes the same computer programs and achieves the same results as the imitated system.

Emulated LAN (See ELAN)

Emulator High-Level Application Program Interface (See EHLLAPI)

EN (end node)
A node that only sends and receives information and cannot route and forward information to another node.

encapsulating bridge
A bridge used to connect two segments (built on one type of medium) with a different type of medium. An example of a bridge of this sort is where an Fiber Distributed Data Interface (FDDI) ring acts as a backbone for the interconnection of several bridged local-area networks (LANs).

encapsulation
The binding and the hiding of the underlying implementation of an object's data and operations. The data is wrapped in a particular type of protocol header. The set of operations that is accessible is the object's interface. See tunnelling.

encryption
The process of systematically encoding a bit stream before transmission so that an unauthorized party cannot decipher it.

end node (See EN)

End System Designator (See ESD)

End System to Intermediate System (See ES-IS)

end-to-end services
Services offered by the lower three layers of the Open Systems Interconnection (OSI) Reference Model.

end-to-end storage management
A component of an overall systems-management infrastructure that improves application availability by reducing the number of storage-related outages and minimizing the length of the outages when they occur.

end user
An individual who uses a computer to perform a business or personal activity. Technical personnel are generally not considered end users when they are programming or operating the computer for technical purposes, though they are when they perform other tasks.

end-user computing (See EUC)

end-user training (See EUT)

engineering change (See EC)

engineer procure construct (See EPC)

engineer-to-order (See ETO)

Enhanced Integrated Drive Electronics (See EIDE)

Enhanced Interior Gateway Routing Protocol (See EIGRP)

Enhanced Parallel Sysplex Offering (See EPSO)

enhanced private shared communications service (See EPSCS)

Enhanced Private Switched Communications Service (See EPSCS)

ENQ (enquiry)
In data communications, a request for a response from another terminal. It is used to obtain identification or an indication of the other station's status.

enterprise applications development (See E-AD)

enterprise applications
Software products designed to integrate computer systems that run all phases of an enterprise's operations to facilitate cooperation and coordination of work across the enterprise. The intent is to integrate core business processes (e.g., sales, accounting, finance, human resources, inventory and manufacturing). The ideal enterprise system could control all major business processes in real time via a single software architecture on a client/server platform. Enterprise software is expanding its scope to link the enterprise with suppliers, business partners and customers.

enterprise business intelligence suites (See EBIS)

enterprise-class
A term referring to the ability of a given tool or product to handle complex processes or services.

enterprise computer-aided software engineering (See E-CASE)

enterprise console
A key component of event-management systems, comprised of applications' component maps, autodiscovery mechanisms, agents that send information to a manager and a correlation engine (at the agent level, the mid-level manager and the console level).

enterprise content
An all-encompassing term for print and digital (i.e., text, video and audio) information resources, internally produced (i.e., internal documents and discussion groups) and externally available (i.e., news, research and reference).

enterprise cooperation community (See ECC)

Enterprise Data Access/Structured Query Language (See EDA/SQL)

Enterprise Definition Language (See EDL)

enterprise desktop manager (See EDM)

enterprise grade
Products that integrate into an infrastructure with a minimum of complexity and offer transparent proxy support.

enterprise information architecture (See EIA)

enterprise information management (See EIM)

Enterprise JavaBeans (See EJB)

enterprise knowledge architecture (See EKA)

Enterprise Maintenance Planning and Control (See EMPAC)

enterprise master person index (See EMPI)

Enterprise Messaging Server (See EMS)

enterprise messaging utility (See EMU)

enterprise operations center (See EOC)

enterprise resource planning (See ERP)

enterprise scheduling system (See ESS)

Enterprise Server — Netscape (See ES)

Enterprise Server Offering (See ESO)

enterprise server platform (See ESP)

Enterprise Service Agreement (See ESA)

enterprise solutions
Solutions designed to integrate multiple facets of a company's business through the interchange of information from various business process areas and related databases. These solutions enable companies to retrieve and disseminate mission-critical data throughout the organization, providing managers with real-time operating information.

Enterprise Storage Array (See ESA)

enterprise support management (See ESM)

Enterprise Systems Architecture (See ESA)

Enterprise Systems Connection (See ESCON)

enterprise TCO (See ETCO)

enterpriseware (enterprise-class software)

enterprisewide asset management (See EAM)

enterprisewide marketing system (See EMS)

enterprisewide web (See EWW)

entropy encoding
A lossless compression method that treats the entire data stream as a series of bits and takes no account of the information being compressed.

Entry Server Offering (See ESO)

envelope delay
An analog line impairment that conditioning is meant to overcome. It is a variation of signal delay with frequency across the data channel bandwidth.

environmental, safety & health (See ES&H)

EO (Enterprise Option — Lotus)

EOC (enterprise operations center)
The concept of managing multitechnology computing platforms. Not necessarily a centralized facility, but rather the organizational and process management of enterprise IT assets and operations.

EOD (end of data)

EOF (end of file)

EOM (end-of-message

EOM (Enterprise Output Management — New Dimension Software)

E-OO4GL (enterprise object-oriented fourth-generation language)

E-OOA/OOD (enterprise object-oriented analysis/object-oriented design)

EOP (end of partition)

EOQ (economic order quantity)

EOS (electronic output strategy)
An enterprise's integrated policies, procedures and infrastructure for printing and publishing electronically generated documents.

EOT (end of tape)

EOT (end of transmission)

EOW (end-of-week)

EPABX (electronic private automatic branch exchange)

EPC (engineer procure construct)
Also referred to as A&E for architectural & engineering, a class of service enterprises.

EPC (event-driven process chain)

EPD (electronic product definition)

EPF (enhanced platform feature)

EPHOS (European Procurement Handbook for Open Systems)
A set of profiles published by the European Commission to aid the buying process of Open Systems Interconnection (OSI) systems.

EPIC (Explicitly Parallel Instruction Computing)
An effort by Intel and Hewlett-Packard (HP) to create an open terminology that the industry would use to represent the latest iteration of wide word technology. It is the core technology used for IA-64.

EPM (Enterprise Production Management — New Dimension Software, formerly known as 4th Dimension Software)

EPMS (Electronic Publishing Management System — Dataware Technologies)
Now called Dataware II.

EPOS (electronic point of sale)

EPP (Enhanced Parallel Port)

EPROM (erasable programmable read-only memory)
Memory chips programmed after manufacture which may be reprogrammed at a later date.

EPS (Encapsulated PostScript)

EOC

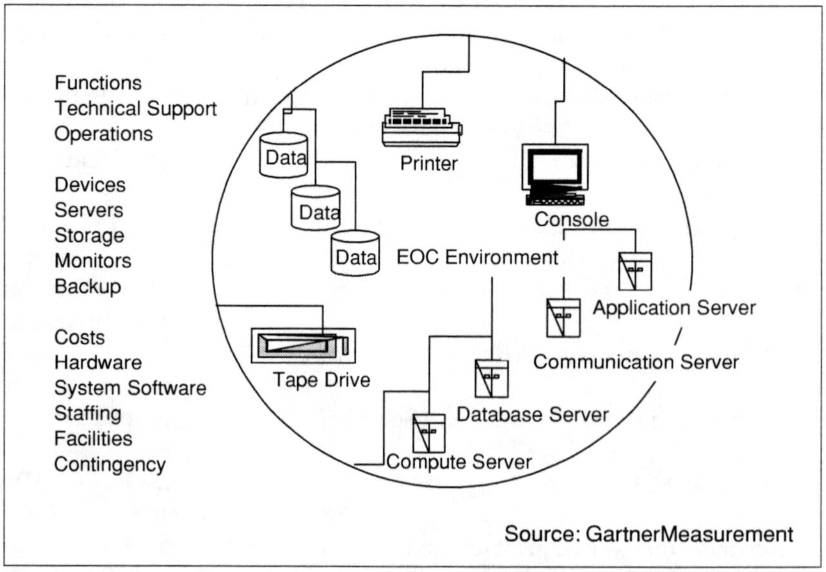

Enterprise Operations Center Cost Model Representative Components

EPSCS (enhanced private shared communications service)
EPSCS is a service designed to provide customized private communications to customers. Switching centers are located on telephone company premises and may be shared with other EPSCS customers or other telephone company services. Private-line channels between switching centers and a customer's premises are dedicated to specific customers.

EPSCS (Enhanced Private Switched Communications Service)
An AT&T Communications service providing a private interLATA electronic tandem tie-line network linking several of a customer's locations together.

EPSO (Enhanced Parallel Sysplex Offering)
An IBM package designed to help users migrate to a Parallel Sysplex environment through the packaging of hardware, maintenance and services. Unlike IBM's Entry Server Offering (ESO), it does not include software.

equal access
The U.S. Department of Justice ruling, effective September 1984, that requires most local telephone companies to offer the same quality of connection, at the same rates, to all common carriers.

equalization
Compensation for the attenuation (signal loss) variation with frequency (attenuation equalization) and propagation time variations with frequency (delay equalization).

equipment asset management (See EAM)

equipment management system (See EMS)

ER (entity relationship)

ER (explicit rate)
In an asynchronous transfer mode (ATM) network, one of two feedback mechanisms used by the available bit rate (ABR) service category to inform the source of the network resources available to it.

erasable optical storage device
An optical storage device on which data can be rewritten, either after bulk erasure or spot erasure.

erasable programmable read-only memory (See EPROM)

ERC (European Radiocommunications Committee)
Established in 1990, in response to concern expressed by the Commission of the European Community (CEC) at the slow progress being made in European frequency harmonization. The ERC brings together the radio regulatory authorities of the European Conference of Postal and Telecommunications Administrations (CEPT) countries.

ERD (entity-relationship diagram)

ERL (Echo Return Loss)
Attenuation of echo currents in one direction caused by telephone circuits operating in the other direction.

Erlang (See E)

ERM (e-mail response management system)

ERMES (European Radio Messaging)
A program sponsored by the Commission of the European Community (CEC) for a Pan-European radio (i.e., paging) message system.

ERMS (e-mail response management system)
A customer service and support (CSS) software feature for handling and managing e-mail from customers. It integrates e-mail and Web forms into

the incoming call flow to ensure that these inquiries and transactions are handled on a timely basis.

ERO (enterprise resource optimization)

ERO (European Radiocommunications Office)
Established in 1991, the ERO is responsible for administrative regulatory radio and spectrum matters. The ERO is a permanent organ of the European Conference of Postal and Telecommunications Administrations (CEPT) and is managed by the European Radiocommunications Committee.

ERP (enterprise resource planning)
A concept developed by GartnerGroup describing the next generation of manufacturing business systems and manufacturing resource planning (MRP II) software. It includes the client/server architecture, uses graphical user interfaces (GUIs) and can be crafted with open systems. Beyond the standard functionality that is offered, other features are included (e.g., quality, process operations management and regulatory reporting). In addition, the base technology used in ERP will give users software and hardware independence as well as an easy upgrade path. Key to ERP is the way in which users can tailor the application so it is intrinsically easy to use.

error
In data communications, any unwanted change in the original contents of a transmission.

error burst
A concentration of errors within a short period of time as compared to the average incidence of errors. Retransmission is the normal correction procedure in the event of an error burst.

error control
An arrangement that detects the presence of errors. In some systems, refinements are added that correct the detected errors, either by operations on the received data or by retransmission from the source.

error-correcting code (See ECC)

error rate
The ratio of the number of bits, elements, characters or blocks incorrectly received to the total number of bits, elements, characters or blocks transmitted.

ERSO (Electronics Research and Service Organization)

ES (Enterprise Server — Netscape)
Netscape's Hypertext Transport Protocol (HTTP) server.

ESA (Enterprise Service Agreement)
IBM umbrella contracts that bundle different services to different customer needs.

ESA (Enterprise Storage Array)
An Ultra Small Computer Systems Interface (SCSI) disk array from Digital Equipment.

ESA (Enterprise Systems Architecture)
ESA/370 is IBM's System/370 extended architecture for the 3090 and 4381 processors, and is supported by MVS/ESA (Multiple Virtual Storage/ESA). The major ESA feature is the support of data spaces in addition to the program-and-data address spaces of System/370.

ESC (escape) key
A control character whose function varies with the software or type of terminal. It generally serves to transfer control to another part of the program or to exit the program.

escape character
A symbol that indicates that the next character is a member of a different character set or a control character.

ESCON (Enterprise Systems Connection)
A high-speed fiber-optic serial channel for IBM's ES/9000 processors announced in September 1990.

ESCON was initially based in part on a fiber-optic link operating at a speed of 200 megabits per second (Mbps) regardless of the driver light source, but has been driven much faster.

ESD (electronic software distribution)
A means of installing software by transmitting it over a network. ESD is designed to help users distribute programs and files in their environments. The development of client/server applications has made ESD a critical requirement. Without an effective means of automating the distribution and installation of software, most applications of client/server technology will not be viable.

ESD (electrostatic discharge)

ESD (End System Designator)

ESDI (Enhanced Small Device Interface)

ESDS (electronic software delivery system)

ESE (Extended Selling Enterprise)

ESF (Extended Super Frame)
AT&T's and Bell Communications Research's (different) framing standards that improve networking performance monitoring. ESF is a T1 format that is comprised of 24 frames of 192 bits each. A 193rd bit is used for link control and error checking.

ES&H (environmental, safety & health)
An application area or class of software used to manage issues related to environmental safety and health topics.

e-sig (electronic signature)

ESIOP (Environment-Specific Inter-ORB Protocol)

ES-IS (End System to Intermediate System)
Open Systems Interconnection (OSI) routing protocol defining the contact between systems at the center (i.e., hosts) and in the middle of the network.

ESM (enterprise support management)
A software tool that can assist in automating basic and advanced e-mail-handling functions.

ESM (European Satellite Multimedia Services)

ESMR (Enhanced Special Mobile Radio)

ESMS (enterprise system managed storage)

ESMTP (Extended Simple Mail Transfer Protocol)
Extensions to the Simple Mail Transfer Protocol (SMTP) that provide faster delivery and message status.

ESO (Entry Server Offering, also called Enterprise Server Offering)
A marketing package for IBM's S/390 complementary metal-oxide semiconductor (CMOS) offering, which combines hardware, software, maintenance and services.

ESP (EMC Enterprise Storage Platform)

ESP (enterprise server platform)
An inherently distributable, multiply interoperable server engineered for use within the context of a larger information technology architecture. It transparently provides services to any authorized client. ESP is a collection of services that enable enterprises to manage and leverage the benefits of personal, workgroup and enterprise information processing resources.

ESP (Enterprise Storage Platform)

ESP (external services provider)
A firm that is a separate legal entity from the contracting company and that provides services such as consulting, software development (including systems integration) and outsourcing. ESPs supplement the skills and resources of an in-house information systems (IS) department. Common functions of ESPs include:

- Outsourcing to reduce costs and improve efficiency.
- System integration to provide programming expertise and supplemental resources.
- Consulting and project management to provide experience and knowledge.

ESPRIT (European Strategic Program for Research and Development of Information Technology)
A research and development (R&D) program, funded by the European Community, that was chartered to create a technology base for the development of products, processes and services for European companies in an effort to gain world information market share.

ESQL (Embedded Structured Query Language)
Statements inserted within a program during its preparation that will not change when the program is run.

ESS (electronic switching system)
A circuit switch environment that has supported delivery of services through telecommunications networks for most of this century. The architecture is now changing over to asynchronous transfer mode (ATM).

ESS (employee self-service)
Once simply defined as employee access to human resources (HR) for review or update of benefits or address information that had previously been in an HR staff-controlled domain. Today, the definition has expanded to include "look up" or edit access to many other areas (e.g., employee time tracking, payroll deductions, training registration and job postings).

ESS (enterprise scheduling system)
A complex system that interacts with enterprise applications such as enterprise master person indi-

ESP

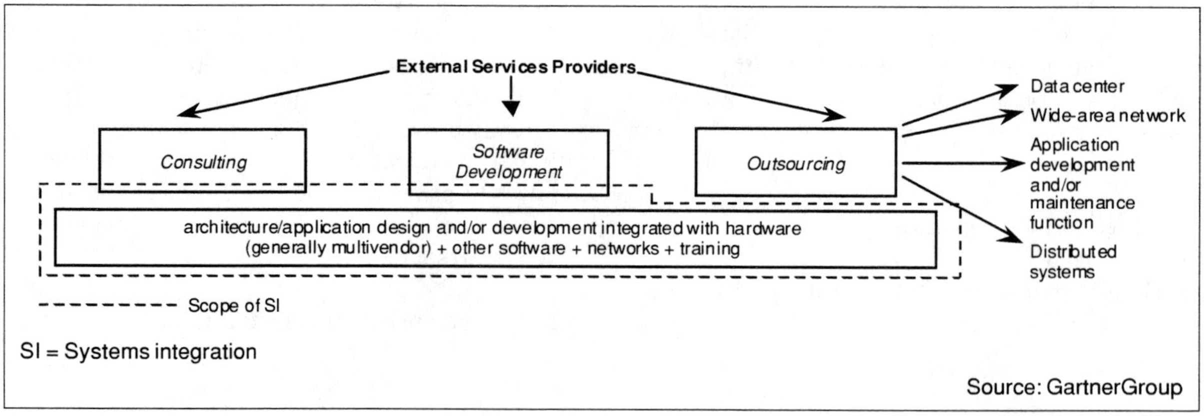

External Services Providers

ces (EMPIs), computer-based patient record systems (CPRs), clinical decision support systems (CDSSs) and departmental scheduling systems. To achieve a successful ESS implementation, a care delivery system (CDO) must consider not only the features that the ESS supports, but also how it interoperates with the CDO's environment.

ESW (externally sourced worker)

ETACS (Extended TACS)
See also TACS.

ETCO (enterprise TCO)
A new Institute of Management Accountants (IMA) workpoint accounting standard that adds direct and indirect costs to the total cost of ownership of information technology infrastructure (IT TCO) from the workpoint framework to include direct and indirect occupancy costs, home office setup, direct and indirect non-IT equipment, and direct and indirect non-IT support costs.

ETG (European Telecommunications Group)

Ethernet
A baseband local-area network (LAN) developed by Xerox and supported by Intel, Digital Equipment and Hewlett-Packard. It has a bus topology with carrier sense multiple access with collision detection (CSMA/CD) access control. Ethernet is not identical to Institute of Electrical and Electronics Engineers (IEEE) 802.3. Related terms include:

1. Ethernet address: 48-bit code for Layer 2 networking maintained by the IEEE and hardwired into network adapters; also called MAC address.
2. Ethernet, thick: Ethernet coaxial cable suitable for networks that are medium/large or with widely spaced nodes.
3. Ethernet, thin: Ethernet coaxial cable suitable only for small networks with closely connected nodes.

Ethernet LAN connect
Connection from a midrange system to Macintoshes via Ethernet protocols.

ETN (electronic tandem network)
A private telecommunications network in which calls are automatically switched over specific trunks.

ETNO (European Public Telecommunications Network Operators' Association)
Established in 1992, by European fixed public telecommunications network operators, ETNO has taken over the operational interests relating to telecommunications, which were formerly the responsibility of the European Conference of Postal and Telecommunications Administrations (CEPT).

ETO (engineer-to-order)
Configurable product offerings that consist of standard and custom-engineered components.

ETS (electronic trading system)

ETS (Engineering and Technical Systems)

ETSI (European Telecommunications Standards Institute)
The European counterpart to the American National Standards Institute (ANSI), chartered to help pave the way for telecommunications integration in the European Union. It is made up of national representatives from the European Conference of Postal and Telecommunications Administrations (CEPT) countries, the composition of which can include public and private telecommunications providers and equipment manufacturers and users, subject to national determination.

ETT (extraction/transformation/transport)
Technology for extracting data and its metadata out of one data store, transforming the record structure and the contents using a language other than the native data manipulation language (DML) or Structured Query Language (SQL), and transporting the results to another data store.

EU (European Union)
See also EC.

EUC (end-user computing)
Computer operations or activities carried out by the end user, often incurring hidden costs.

EULA (End-User License Agreement — Microsoft)

EUNIS (European Universities Information Systems Organization)

Euro
The new pan-European currency of the European monetary union.

European Association of Securities Dealers Automated Quotations (See EASDAQ)

European Committee for Telecommunications Regulatory Affairs (See ECTRA)

European Conference of Postal and Telecommunications Administrations (See CEPT)

European Procurement Handbook for Open Systems (See EPHOS)

European Public Telecommunications Network Operators' Association (See ETNO)

European Radiocommunications Committee (See ERC)

European Radiocommunications Office (See ERO)

European Radio Messaging (See ERMES)

European Strategic Program for Research and Development of Information Technology (See ESPRIT)

European Telecommunications Standards Institute (See ETSI)

European Workshop on Open Systems (See EWOS)

EuroSmart
A method developed by GartnerGroup that provides users with a way of estimating the size of European monetary union (EMU) information technology (IT) needs.

EUT (end-user training)
Classroom, desktop-based or printed manual instruction in the operation of computer technology.

EUTELSAT (European Telecommunications Satellite Organization)

EVA (economic value added)
A methodology developed by Stern Stewart & Co. — a New York management consulting firm — that measures corporate economic performance. It views investments (including IT investments) in terms of their impact on shareholder wealth — that is, the increase (or decrease) in enterprise wealth that results from an investment.

even parity check/odd parity check
A test determining whether the number of digits in a group of binary digits is even (i.e., even parity check) or odd (i.e., odd parity check).

EW (early warning)

EW (electronic warfare)

EW 3 (Easy World Wide Web — AT&T)

EWDP (Enhanced Web Development Package — AT&T)

EWOS (European Workshop on Open Systems)
When fully operational, this will provide a flexible, responsive and open framework for the rapid development of information technology (IT) standards.

EWW (enterprisewide web)
Internal implementations of Web-based system components and standards that support basic intraenterprise publishing, broadcasting and information-sharing capabilities.

exchange
The assembly of equipment in a communications system that controls the connection of incoming and outgoing lines and includes the necessary signaling and supervisory functions. Different exchanges, or switches, can be colocated to perform different functions (e.g., local exchange and trunk exchange). Special types of exchanges that may be installed within an enterprise include:

1. Private exchange (PX): An exchange serving a particular organization and having no means of connection with a public exchange.
2. Private automatic exchange (PAX): A dial telephone exchange that provides private telephone service to an organization and that does not allow calls to be transmitted to or from the public telephone network.
3. Private automatic branch exchange (PABX): private automatic telephone exchange that provides for the transmission of calls internally and to and from the public telephone network. Also called private branch exchange (PBX).
4. Private automatic telex exchange (PATX): Provides telex service within and without an enterprise (largely obsolete).

exchange area
A calling area served by a local telecommunications company central office switch; may be comprised of one or more area code and exchange (NXX) codes.

exchange line socket
A two- or four-wire socket providing physical access to the public switched telephone network (PSTN).

exciter
The transmitter component that modulates and drive a signal. It is used in uplinks.

executive information system (See EIS)

ExHPDM (Extended High Performance Data Mover — Storage Technology)

expandor
A transducer that, for a given amplitude range of input voltages, produces a larger range of output voltages.

expansion card
Circuit boards that can be inserted into the computer to increase its capabilities. Also called expansion board.

expert system
A software system that can learn new procedures by analyzing the outcome of past events, or that contains a knowledge base of rules that can be applied to new data or circumstances not explicitly anticipated by the developer. Applications include network management, database management and data mining, computer vision and image processing, speech recognition, biometrics and software

for complex evaluation in such fields as petroleum geology.

Explicit Forward Congestion Indicator (See EFCI)

explicit input
The definition of model dimensions using explicit numbers as opposed to variables.

Explicitly Parallel Instruction Computing (See EPIC)

explicit rate (See ER)

explicit tagging
A frame is classified as belonging to a particular virtual local-area network (VLAN), based on a VLAN tag value that is included in the frame.

explosion
An extension of a bill of material into the total of each of the components required to manufacture a given quantity of upper-level assembly or subassembly.

Extended Architecture (See XA)

Extended Area Service (See EAS)

Extended Binary-Coded Decimal Interchange Code (See EBCDIC)

extended data output (See EDO)

Extended Industry Standard Architecture (See EISA)

Extended Java VM
A Java virtual machine (VM) certified by Sun Microsystems as conforming to the VM specification but adding functionality or application programming interfaces (APIs) that may be proprietary.

Extended Recovery Facility (See XRF)

extended remote copy (See XRC)

Extended Super Frame (See ESF)

Extensible Form Definition Language (See XFDL)

Extensible Markup Language (See XML)

Extensible Markup Language electronic data interchange (See XML/EDI)

Extensible Style Language (See XSL)

Exterior Gateway Protocol (See EGP)

external function testing
The verification of the specifications and performance of devices located outside of the computer.

external services provider (See ESP)

extraction/transformation/transport (See ETT)

extranet
A collaborative Internet-based technology that creates a network to link businesses with their suppliers, customers or other external business partners and facilitates productive intercompany relationships. An extranet can be constructed as a direct extension of a company's intranet or as a connection to enable companies to collaborate via the Internet. Either way, an extranet is a private, secure environment. Individuals cannot access an extranet without permission.

F

FA (financial administrator)

Face Recognition Technology (See FERET)

facilities administration and control
Enables PBX users to administer the assignment of parameters that determine user calling privileges, such as restriction levels and authorization codes.

facilities assurance reports
Enables PBX users to obtain an audit trail of the data generated by the automatic circuit assurance feature.

facilities management (See FM)

facilities restriction level
The parameter associated with each authorization code, each station at a private branch exchange (PBX), each incoming tie trunk group from subtending PBXs, and attendants as a whole, which determines the types of calls and types of facilities within the privileges of the associated user.

facility
A transmission path between two or more points, provided by a common carrier.

facsimile (See fax)

fading

1. A phenomenon, generally of microwave or radio transmission, where atmospheric, electromagnetic, or gravitational influences cause a signal to be deflected or diverted away from the target receiver.
2. The reduction in intensity of the power of a received signal.

failsafe
Internal circuitry that monitors a system and shuts it down or alerts the operator in the event of a problem.

fail softly
When a piece of equipment fails and the system falls back to a degraded mode of operation rather than shutting down.

failure
Any anomaly of a system that results in an impairment of a mission-critical business process and:

1. A hard stop (abend) of any duration.
2. Incorrect calculations causing incorrect output.

Fairchild Advanced Schottky TTL (See FAST)

fair market value (See FMV)

FAPs (formats and protocols)
Rules that specify format, timing and error checking between clients and servers.

FAQ (frequently-asked questions)
A list of questions with their answers posted regularly over the Internet. Usually applied to Usenet.

far-end crosstalk
Crosstalk that travels along a circuit in the same direction as the signals in that circuit. See also near-end crosstalk.

FAST (Fairchild Advanced Schottky TTL)
A type of integrated circuit.

Fast Ethernet
The Institute of Electrical and Electronics Engineers (IEEE) standard based on 802.3 but running at

100 megabits per second (Mbps) instead of 10 Mbps and using 100Base-T or 100Base-F families of cabling standards.

fast-packet switching
A generic term for improved packet-switching technologies such as frame relay and cell relay. Fast-packet techniques feature less functionality than traditional X.25 packet-switching for higher packet-switching speeds and lower processing costs.

FAT (file allocation table — Microsoft)
An index for mapping logical files to physical locations on a disk storage device.

fault detection and isolation
Online diagnostics that detect and isolate faults in real time, prevent contamination into other areas, and attempt to retry operations.

fault tolerant or fault tolerance (See FT)

fax (facsimile)
The system or equipment used for the transmission of images, usually over the public telephone network. The image is scanned at the transmitter, reconstructed at the receiving station, and duplicated on some form of paper.

FBIA (financial business intelligence applications)

FC (feature code)

FC (Fibre Channel)
A high-speed serial communication protocol developed by IBM and others; usually used for storage subsystems. The transmission medium may be fiber optics or copper.

FC25 (Fibre Channel 25 Mbytes/second — Sun Microsystems)

FC-AL (Fibre Channel-Arbitrated Loop)
A subset of the Fibre Channel Standard that was defined to support network storage. It is an inexpensive technology that supports up to 126 devices that can be configured in a fibre channel ring network and arbitrate for network access. Only one pair of devices can talk at one time on the loop. Each port on the loop sees all messages and ignores those not intended for it.

FCC (Federal Communications Commission)
The U.S. federal agency responsible for regulating interstate telecommunications, as well as international telecommunications, aspects of cellular communications and broadcasting. The FCC was established by the Communications Act of 1934.

FC-EL (Fibre Channel-Enhanced Loop)
An expanded version of FC-AL aimed at extending loop topologies to support additional applications.

FC-IC (Fibre Channel Interconnect)

FCIF (Full Common Intermediate Format)
Part of the H.261 worldwide video code standard, which is designed to accommodate both the North American National TV System Committee (NTSC) and European PAL protocols, that is, the accommodation is accomplished by using the NTSC frame rate and the PAL resolution in a compromise called the Common Intermediate Format (CIF), of which there are two versions: Full CIF (FCIF) and Quarter CIF (QCIF). Full CIF pictures will be sharper in the future, but at the cost of additional processing power requirements.

FCLC (Fibre Channel Loop Community)

FCO (field change order)

FCP (Foundation for Cooperative Processing)

FCS (Fibre Channel Standard)
A definition of Fibre Channel specifications undertaken by the American National Standards Institute (ANSI) Technical Committee, now known as X3T11. The developers wanted to provide an extremely flexible method of information transfer that can support both channel-style and network-style peripheral interconnections.

FCS (first customer shipment)
The stage at which a product is released from development, and ready for beta testing.

FD or FDX (full duplex)
Refers to a communications system or equipment capable of transmitting simultaneously in both directions. See also half duplex.

FDC (financial data control)

FDD (flexible disk drive)
A low-cost, low-capacity (usually 1.4 megabytes or less) removable disk storage device. See also floppy disk.

FDDI (Fiber Distributed Data Interface)
An American National Standards Institute (ANSI) standard for 100 megabits per second (Mbps) fiber-optic local-area networks (LANs). Incorporates token processing and supports circuit-switched voice and packetized data.

FDDI II (Fiber Distributed Data Interface II)
An FDDI that can carry isochronous traffic.

FDDI XTP (Fiber Distributed Data Interface Express Transfer Protocol)
Express Transfer Protocol for use with FDDI.

FDM (frequency division multiplexing)
The division of a transmission frequency range into narrower bands to create two or more channels, enabling each data source to have its own channel.

FDMA (frequency division multiple access)
Communicating devices at different locations sharing a multipoint or broadcast channel by means of a technique that allocates different frequencies to different users.

FD:OCA (Formatted Data: Object Content Architecture)
An architecture, central to Distributed Relational Data Architecture (DRDA), that can exchange field-formatted information — that is, primarily Structured Query Language (SQL) data. It associates tags with data so that heterogeneous database management systems (DBMSs), initially within IBM but potentially beyond, can converse.

FDR (Fast Dump Restore)

FDRSOS (Fast Dump Restore Safeguard Open Storage — EMC)

FE (field engineer)
An engineer who can work on site.

feature-based modeling
A modeling technique that allows the creation of manufacturing form features, e.g., through holes, ribs or slots, when defining mechanical component models.

feature-driven manufacturing
The ability to automatically create optimized process instructions and machine tool paths by utilizing mechanical component form features.

FEC (forward error correction)

FECN (forward explicit congestion notification)

Federal Communications Commission (See FCC)

Federal Information Processing Standard (See FIPS)

FEDI (financial electronic data exchange)
Information that passes between banks and companies that relates directly to payments and bank balances.

feedback
A method of signal regeneration involving a coupling from a high-level point in an amplifier to a lower-level point in the same or previous stage, in such a manner as either to increase or decrease apparent gain of the amplifier.

feed horn
A small antenna, located at the focal point of a reflector antenna, which gathers the signal.

FEMA (Federal Emergency Management Agency)

FENIT (Federation of Netherlands Information Technology Organizations)

FEP (front-end processor)
A dedicated communications system that intercepts and handles activity for the host. It may perform line control, message handling, code conversion, error control, and such application functions as control and operation of special-purpose terminals. See also communication controller.

FEPI (front-end programming interface)

FERET (Face Recognition Technology)
A comprehensive U.S. government face recognition test, used for personnel security.

FERRAM (ferroelectric random-access memory)
An early form of random access memory used in early IBM mainframes. It consisted of tiny ferrite rings that could be magnetized by electric pulses to indicated a binary "1" bit. Also known as core memory.

ferrule
The tip of a fiber optic connector.

FET (field-effect transistor)

FFAPI (File Format Application Programming Interface)
The file format used only by Microsoft Mail is held as proprietary to Microsoft. In order to read or write such a file, the FFAPI utilities provided by Microsoft must be used. The utility creates the message header, or envelope, by writing field tags and data to the file in the Microsoft Mail structured data format. Another utility extracts the data by parsing the data structure.

FFS (fee for service)

FFT (fast Fourier transform)

FFT:DCA (Final Form Text: Document Content Architecture)
The data stream for passing documents in final form (i.e., unrevisable) under IBM's second-generation Document Content Architecture.

FH (Frequency Hop)

FHSS (frequency-hopped spread spectrum)

FIB (Forward Indication Bit)
An Integrated Services Digital Network (ISDN) term.

Fiber Distributed Data Interface (See FDDI)

Fiber Distributed Data Interface Express Transfer Protocol (See FDDI XTP)

Fiber Link Around the Globe (See FLAG)

Fiber Optic 10BASE-F
10 megabits per second (Mbps) over fiber; an Institute of Electrical and Electronics Engineers (IEEE) standard for 802.3.

Fiber Optic Inter-Repeater Link (See FOIRL)

fiber optics
A high-bandwidth transmission technology that uses light to carry digital information. One fiber telephone cable carries hundreds of thousands of voice circuits. These cables, or light guides, replace conventional coaxial cables and wire pairs. Fiber transmission facilities occupy far less physical volume for an equivalent transmission capacity, which is a major advantage in crowded ducts. Optical fiber is also immune to electrical interference.

fiber optic transmission systems (See FOTS)

fiber optic waveguides
Thin filaments of glass through which a light beam can be transmitted for long distances by means of multiple internal reflections. Occasionally, other transparent materials, such as plastic, are used.

fiber to the building (See FTTB)

fiber to the curb (See FTTC)

fiber to the home (See FTTH)

Fibre Channel (See FC)

Fibre Channel-Arbitrated Loop (See FC-AL)

Fibre Channel Connectivity (See FICON)

Fibre Channel-Enhanced Loop (See FC-EL)

Fibre Channel Standard (See FCS)

FICON (Fibre Channel Connectivity)
An IBM channel architecture introduced in 1998.

field engineer (See FE)

FIFO (first in, first out)
A method of transmitting data through a switch to minimize delay.

file
A collection of bytes containing data, text or other information, or software that is stored and accessed as a coherent unit. Examples include: data file or table, spreadsheet, document, image, program, audio and video.

file allocation table (See FAT)

file server
A computer containing files available to all users connected to a local-area network (LAN). In some LANs, a microcomputer is designated as the file server, while in others it is a computer with a large disk drive and specialized software. Some file servers also offer other resources such as gateways and protocol conversion.

File Transfer, Access and Management (See FTAM)

File Transfer Protocol (See FTP)

filter
A circuit designed to transmit signals of frequencies within one or more frequency bands and to attenuate signals of other frequencies.

Final Form Text: Document Content Architecture (See FFT:DCA)

financial footprint
The amount of money paid, monthly or yearly, to a vendor to support a particular system or application. Because most hardware and software is easily upgradable, financial-footprint management involves managing a stream of recurring payments instead of physical assets.

Financial Products Markup Language (See FpML)

finger
A Unix command that traces any user logged onto the system. Widely used on the Internet.

finite loading
Conceptually, the term means putting no more work into a factory than the factory can be expected to execute. The term usually refers to a computer technique that involves automatic shop priority revision to level load operation by operation.

FIPS (Federal Information Processing Standard)
A set of standards produced by the National Institute of Standards and Technology setting forth protocols, encryption, interoperability, hardware, and other specifications for the federal government.

FIRE (Flexible, Intelligent Routing Engine)
A set of application-specific integrated circuits (ASICs) developed by 3Com to add wire speed routing and policy capabilities to its CoreBuilder 3500 and 9000 series and products.

firewall
An application or an entire computer (e.g., an Internet gateway server) that controls access to the network and monitors the flow of network traffic. A firewall can screen and keep out unwanted network traffic and ward off outside intrusion into a private network. This is particularly important when a local network connects to the Internet. Firewalls have become critical applications as use of the Internet has increased.

FireWire
Also known as Institute of Electrical and Electronics Engineers (IEEE) 1394, this is a high-speed serial bus similar to the Universal Serial Bus (USB), but much faster and more expensive to implement. Its primary supporters are Apple Computer and consumer electronics firms such as Fuji, Sony, Hitachi and Nintendo. These firms will use FireWire as the input/output (I/O) bus for next-generation digital products: camcorders, VCRs, TVs, digital cameras and game players.

firm planned order
A planned order that can be frozen in quantity and time. The computer is not allowed to automatically change it; this is the responsibility of the planner in charge of the item that is being planned. This technique can aid planners working with material requirements planning (MRP) systems to respond to material and capacity problems by firming up selected planned orders. Additionally, firm planned

FireWire

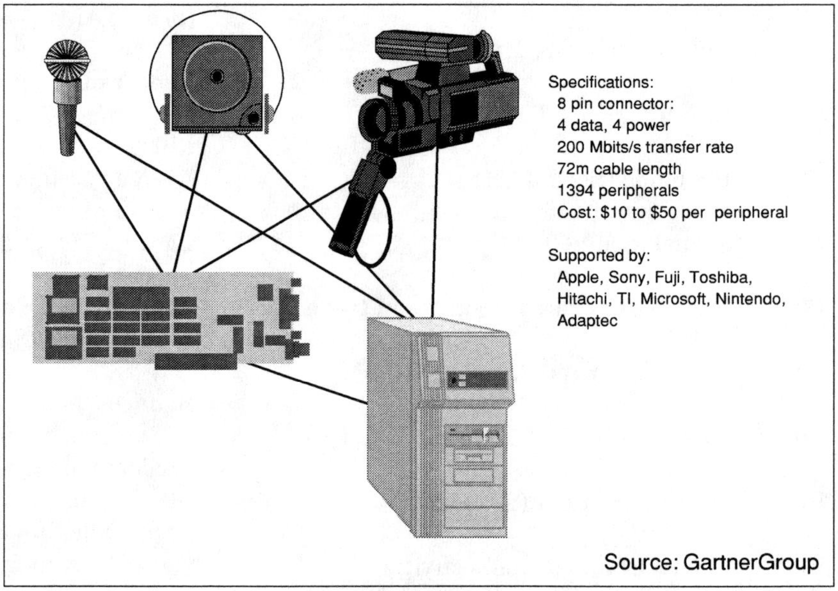

FireWire/Institute of Electrical and Electronics Engineers 1394

orders are the normal method of stating the master production schedule.

firmware
A category of memory chips that hold their content without electrical power and include ROM, PROM, EPROM and EEPROM technologies. Firmware becomes "hard software" when holding program code. The contents are generally permanent or semipermanent control coding implemented at a microinstruction level for an application program, instruction set, operating routine, or similar user-oriented function.

first customer shipment (See FCS)

first generation
The class of office information systems (OIS) products dominated by dedicated word processors, such as Digital Equipment's DECmate, IBM's DisplayWriter and Wang's OIS. The period began with the first word processors (late 1970s) and lasted until the introduction of the first integrated office systems (1983).

first in, first out (See FIFO)

FISU (Fill In Signal Unit) (ISDN term)

FIX (Financial Information Exchange)

FIXML (Financial Information Exchange Markup Language)

flag
A data bit or group of bits that can be set on or off to signal the status of a system or process.

FLAG (Fiber Link Around the Globe)
An undersea fiber optic system using two fiber pairs, each operating at 5 gigabits per second (Gbps), with capacity for 120,000 64-kilobit per second (Kbps) digital circuits.

flame
An insult or angry remark in Internet e-mail or Usenet messages. A flame may contain obscene language, sarcasm or derogatory comments. It may be "shouted" by placing the words in capital letters. Flaming is considered rude and inconsiderate, but it frequently occurs in newsgroups and e-mail.

flash memory
A nonvolatile storage chip developed by Intel that enables easy electrical erasability and reprogramming, often used to remotely update routers or modems with new versions of software.

flat-panel display (See FPD)

flat rate
A fixed payment for service within a defined area, independent of use, with an additional charge for each call outside the area.

Flexible, Intelligent Routing Engine (See FIRE)

flexible route selection (See FRS)

floating-point unit (See FPU)

floppy disk
A reusable, portable storage device that generally holds 1.4 megabytes of data. Floppy disks, sometimes called flexible disks or diskettes, were the primary method of software and data distribution beginning in the 1970s. They were originally eight inches wide and enclosed in a flexible envelope; a 5.25-inch version was later introduced, and finally a 3.5-inch floppy disk encased in rigid plastic became the standard. CD-ROMs have become a popular alternative to floppy disks, especially for larger software and multimedia files, given their higher storage capacity. As network speeds have increased and Internet access has expanded, more software and data is now transmitted directly rather than stored.

FLOPS (floating-point operations per second)

flow control
Management of data transmission; an important part of asynchronous transfer mode (ATM).

Flow Control Layer
Layer 5 of the Systems Network Architecture (SNA) architectural model, which determines and manages interactions between session partners. Corresponds to the Session Layer of the Open Systems Interconnection (OSI) model.

flow manufacturing (See FM)

flyoff
A process used in the procurement of products and services, in which the prospective buyer chooses two or more vendor "finalists" and engages them in a competition. The buyer contracts separately with each of the finalists for a given time period and makes its final selection based on vendor performance information obtained during the flyoff.

FM (facilities management)

1. Entering into an agreement with a service supplier to manage internal company facilities such as telecommunications or data-processing services. Facilities management does not involve the transfer of ownership of facilities to the service provider.

2. For government enterprises, FM is the most prevalent type of contractual relationship where the vendor assumes responsibility for one or more information technology (IT) functions. Unlike outsourcing, it refers to the vendor operating and managing the assets (usually hardware and software), but not taking ownership. In a government-owned, contractor-operated deal, the government owns the equipment and operating systems, and the contractor operates the equipment with its personnel. Usually, the equipment is maintained in a government facility, but it can reside in a vendor-owned facility. In a government-owned, government-operated arrangement, the government owns the equipment and manages the operation using contractor personnel.

FM (financial management)

FM (flow manufacturing)
An alternative to the traditional American Production and Inventory Control Society (APICS) style of material requirements planning (MRP) production. It differs from MRP in that it has a flat bill of materials, more direct routing and a less complex plant or line design. FM is based on operation time or task time and product cycle time vs. a classic scheduled, based bill of materials explosion. Other differences include: pull vs. push operations; single-level bills of materials (BOMs) vs. multiple-level BOMs; orderless production vs. work order production; kanban cards vs. pick lists; sequence of tasks vs. product routings; feeder lines vs. subassemblies; and actual costing vs. standard costing.

FM (frequency modulation)
One of three ways of modifying a sine wave signal to make it carry information. The sine wave or "carrier" has its frequency modified in accordance with the information to be transmitted. The frequency function of the modulated wave can be continuous or discontinuous.

FMV (fair market value)
The price for which equipment could be sold in an arm's-length transaction between unrelated parties.

FNC (Federal Networking Council)

FOCA (Font Object Content Architecture)

Focus
A fourth-generation language (4GL) from Information Builders. It belongs to a class of software called information generators. Focus boasts easy-to-use,

English-language commands with online help and error correction. Focus features "talk" windows, which improve end-user productivity. It also provides integrated reporting, ad hoc queries, graphs, statistics, financial modeling and a spreadsheet for building decision support systems.

FODS (front-office decision support)

FOIRL (Fiber Optic Inter-Repeater Link)
Often known as Ethernet over fiber, FOIRL is made up of dual fiber links (transmit and receive), as defined within Institute of Electrical and Electronics Engineers (IEEE) 802.3.

foreign exchange (See FX)

formal standards
Specifications or styles that are approved by vendor-independent standards bodies, such as the American National Standards Institute (ANSI), the International Organization for Standardization (ISO), the Institute of Electrical and Electronics Engineers (IEEE) and the National Institute for Standards and Technology (NIST).

formats and protocols (See FAPs)

Format Specification Document Participant
A format-specific Linear Tape Open (LTO) license package for vendors that want competitive intelligence on the LTO technology.

Formatted Data: Object Content Architecture (See FD:OCA)

formatting
The preparation of a storage medium with guidance information, synchronization information, and a structure for keeping or collecting information for a directory; this collection of material placed on the disk before user data is written is called a "format," and frequently also includes room for error correction check sums and rewriting of bad or updated sectors.

formatting code
Formatting code (e.g., bold or italic) is rudimentary markup that applications convert to presentation characteristics (e.g., typeface and colors).

form factor
The size and shape of a product. For example, most 5.25-inch Winchester drives have the same dimension so that they can fit interchangeably into computer cabinets. For the same reason, 5.25-inch optical drives are expected to have the same form factor as their predecessor Winchesters.

FORTRAN (Formula Translator)
A programming language developed primarily for numeric computations and chiefly used in mathematics, science and engineering. It was introduced in the 1950s as the first high-level language (i.e., closer to natural language than to machine language).

forward channel
The communications path carrying voice or data from the call initiator to the called party.

forward error correction
A technique for correcting errors incurred in transmission over a communications channel by the receiver, without requiring the retransmission of any information by the transmitter. It typically involves a convolution of the transmitted bits and the appending of extra bits, using a common algorithm by both the receiver and transmitter.

Forward Indication Bit (See FIB)

FOTS (fiber optic transmission systems)
See fiber optic waveguides.

four-wire circuit
A circuit using two pairs of conductors, one pair for the outbound channel and the other pair for the return channel.

FP (FrontPage)
A Hypertext Markup Language editor.

FP (function point)
Function points measure the size of an application system based on the functional view of the system. The size is determined by counting the number of inputs, outputs, queries, internal files and external files in the system and adjusting that total for the functional complexity of the system. Function point analysis, originally developed at IBM, has as an advantage its focus on measuring software produced in terms of functionality delivered to the end user, rather than in terms of development deliverables, which have no direct bearing on the end user.

FPD (flat panel display)
A core component for notebooks, liquid crystal display (LCD) flat panel displays are broadening their applications on the commercial desktops. There are five key FPD technologies available: LCD, gas plasma, electroluminescent (EL) display, field emission display and digital micromirror devices. The most mature is LCD, which includes active-matrix liquid crystal display (AMLCD) and passive-matrix liquid crystal display (PMLCD).

FPDA (focus, plan, define, act)

FPE (FrontPage Extension)
Web server support for certain specific features of Microsoft's Front Page (a Web site editor).

FPGA (field-programmable gate array)

FPLA (field-programmable logic array)

FpML (Financial Products Markup Language)
An Extensible Markup Language (XML)-based computer language introduced by J.P. Morgan and PricewaterhouseCoopers in June 1999.

FPS (frames per second)

FPU (floating-point unit)
A processor specially designed to manipulate floating-point values rather than integer values.

FR (frame relay)
An American National Standards Institute (ANSI) standard (T1S1) for an Integrated Services Digital Network (ISDN) packet-mode bearer service that defines a user-to-network interface. The two main benefits are bandwidth on demand and integrated access. The standard currently addresses data communications speeds up to 2 megabits per second (Mbps) over permanent virtual circuits. Frame relay transmits data packets at high speeds across a digital network encapsulated in a transmission unit called a frame. It requires a dedicated connection during the transmission period. It is used on wide area networks (WANS) and also in private network environments with leased lines over T-1 lines. Frame relay is faster than traditional networks, because it was designed for today's reliable circuits and performs less rigorous error detection. When circuits are less reliable, a great deal of network traffic is dedicated solely to correcting errors.

Fractional T1
Telecommunication service providing permanent leased lines operating at a bit rate between 64 kilobits per second (Kbps) and 1.544 megabits per second (Mbps). (U.S. term.) See also T1.

FRAD (frame relay assembler/disassembler)
A communications device that formats outgoing data into the format required by a frame relay network. It performs a similar function in a frame

relay network to a packet assembler/disassembler (PAD) in a packet switched network, i.e., it converts an asynchronous data stream into data units that can be transmitted over a frame relay network and vice versa. This enables asynchronous devices such as personal computers (PCs) to communicate over a frame relay network.

FRAM (ferroelectric RAM)

frame
1. In High-Level Data-Link Control (HDLC), the sequence of contiguous bits bracketed by and including opening and closing flag (01111110) sequences.
2. In data transmission, the sequence of contiguous bits bracketed by and including beginning and ending flag sequences.
3. A set of consecutive digit time slots in which the position of each time slot can be identified by reference to a frame alignment signal.
4. In a time division multiplexing (TDM) system, a repetitive group of signals resulting from a signal sampling of all channels, including any additional signals for synchronizing and other required system information.

frame check sequence
A checking code used to detect data corruption.

frame relay (See FR)

frame relay assembler/disassembler (See FRAD)

frame relay to ATM service interworking (See FRASI)

Frame Relay User Network Interface (See FUNI)

framework
A style guide that defines the look, feel and interoperability of software applications.

framing
A control procedure used with multiplexed digital channels, whereby bits are inserted so the receiver can identify the time slots allocated to each channel. Framing bits can also carry alarm signals indicating specific alarm conditions.

FRASI (frame relay to ATM service interworking)
A network-based function that enables frame relay traffic to be mapped to asynchronous transfer mode (ATM). This enables customers to have frame relay access services in some locations and ATM in others, while still permitting intercommunication between them.

free MIPS
Excess mainframe capacity.

frequency
An expression of how frequently a periodic wave form or signal repeats itself at a given amplitude. It can be expressed in hertz (Hz), kilohertz (kHz), megahertz (MHz), etc.

frequency coordination
International procedure to prevent interference between new and existing radio communications services. Under International Telecommunication Union (ITU) Radio Regulations, potential operators must consult countries and administrations whose services might be affected.

frequency division multiple access (See FDMA)

frequency division multiplexing (See FDM)

frequency modulation (See FM)

Frequency Shift Keying (See FSK)

frequency-to-voltage (See F/V)

frequently asked questions (See FAQ)

Fresnel zone
Zone of clearance used in calculations during the setting up of a microwave link. Although not directly between the transmitter and receiver, an object near the line-of-sight path can interfere with the propagated signal.

front-end processor (See FEP)

FrontPage (See FP)

FrontPage Extension (See FPE)

frontware
Software that runs on a client workstation to provide better end-user interfaces for application programs running elsewhere.

FRS (flexible route selection)
Used with Centrex service to achieve least-cost routing.

FRU (field-replaceable unit)

FS (Future System)
FS was thought by some factions within IBM to be the successor architecture to S/370. It featured one-level addressing, an object orientation, interactive interfaces for operations and programmers, and high-level input/output (I/O).

FSCC (financial services call center)

FS/D (field service/dispatch)

FSDM (financial services data model)

FSK (Frequency Shift Keying)
A method of modulation that uses two different frequencies to distinguish between a mark (digital 1) and a space (digital 0) when transmitting on an analog line. FSK is used in modems operating at 1200 bits per second (bps) or slower.

FSN (forward sequence number — ISDN term)

FT (fault tolerant or fault tolerance)
Fault tolerancing enables users to maintain continuity if the process they are attached to fails. Once the process fails on the server, another process is launched to resume the user session from where it left off, with little to no loss in productivity.

FTAM (File Transfer, Access and Management)
The Open Systems Interconnection (OSI) protocol for file transfer (i.e., the communication of an entire file between systems), file access (i.e., the ability to remotely access one or more records in a file) and management (e.g., the ability to create/delete or name/rename a file).

FTP (File Transfer Protocol)
A Transmission Control Protocol/Internet Protocol (TCP/IP) standard used to log onto a network, list directories and copy files. That is, it provides authentication of the user and lets users transfer files, list directories, delete and rename files on the foreign host, and perform wild-card transfers.

FTPI (flux transitions per inch)

FTTB (fiber to the building)
Fiber optic access to an individual building for telephony, video, and other multimedia services where several users share the same fiber termination. FTTB access terminates typically in a building basement from which access to multiple end users is implemented through an in-building digital home network (DHN).

FTTC (fiber to the curb)
Fiber optic distribution of telephony, telecommunications, and multimedia and media services, such as cable TV, to a point outside the customer's premises.

FTTH (fiber to the home)
Fiber optic access to users' homes for telephony, video, and other multimedia services where each home has a direct fiber connection.

Full Common Intermediate Format (See FCIF)

full duplex (See FD, FDX)

functional profile
A defined protocol, together with options applicable to specific functions, which can be implemented as a product. Also known as a functional standard or protocol stack.

functional split
A division within an automatic call distributor (ACD) that allows incoming calls to be directed from a specific group of trunks to a specific group of agents.

functional standard
See functional profile.

functional test
A test carried out under normal working conditions to verify that a circuit or a particular part of the equipment functions correctly.

function point (See FP)

FUNI (Frame Relay User Network Interface)
A variable frame length version of asynchronous transfer mode (ATM).

FURPS (functionality, usability, reliability, performance and support)

Future System (See FS)

fuzzy logic
This reasoning paradigm deals with approximate or imprecise information by enabling variables to be described (often linguistically) and acted upon in terms of their degree of membership in predetermined sets. Control systems in electronic equipment and consumer products and other embedded control systems are among the most popular applications.

F/V (frequency-to-voltage)
A signal-conversion process wherein frequency variations are converted to amplitude variations.

FX (foreign exchange)
U.S. term that connects a customer's location to a remote exchange. This service provides the equivalent of local service from the distant exchange.

G

G3 (Generation 3 — IBM)
IBM's third generation of complementary metal-oxide semiconductor (CMOS) 9672 mainframe models — Rn4.

G4 (Generation 4 — IBM)
IBM's fourth generation of complementary metal-oxide semiconductor (CMOS) 9672 mainframe models — Rn5.

G5 (Generation 5 — IBM)
IBM's fifth generation of complementary metal-oxide semiconductor (CMOS) 9672 mainframe models — Rn6.

G6 (Generation 6 — IBM)
IBM's sixth generation of complementary metal-oxide semiconductor (CMOS) 9672 mainframe models, introduced in May 1999.

G.700 series
A series of standards set by the International Telecommunication Union (ITU) for telecommunications and data communications, as used in Europe. Includes:

1. G.703: Standard specifying plesionchronous digital hierarchy (PDH).
2. G.709: Standard specifying synchronous digital hierarchy (SDH).
3. G.711: Standard specifying the encoding of digital speech based on a pulse code modulation (PCM) digitizing algorithm using logarithmic encoding.
4. G.721: Standard specifying the encoding of digital speech based on a subband adaptive differential pulse code modulation (ADPCM) technique.
5. G.723: The voice component of the H.323 videoconferencing suite.
6. G.728: Standard specifying the encoding of digital speech using low bit rates based on a sector generalization scheme. Gives poorer sound quality than G.711.
7. G.804: ITU framing standard defining the way that asynchronous transfer mode (ATM) cells are mapped onto the physical medium.

GA (general availability)
The point at which a new product is available on the open market.

GA (genetic algorithm)
Genetic algorithms optimize code by using the principles of natural selection and genetics, generating variations of code structures by random "mutation." Successful code survives iterations of the algorithm. They are used to optimize plans and neural networks.

GaAs (Gallium Arsenide)
A semiconductor material.

gain
Denotes an increase in signal power in transmission from one point to another, usually expressed in decibels (dB).

gain-sharing
Describes a contract that defines the vendor's contribution to the customer in terms of specific benefits to the customer's business. Such a contract also defines the payment the customer will make accord-

ing to the vendor's performance in delivering those business benefits. Gain-sharing contracts require the development of a delivery paradigm that links a customer's business metrics to a vendor's IT solution. The key elements of this paradigm, in order, are:

1. Business metric definition and selection
2. Client metric benchmarking
3. Development of key performance indicators
4. Investment options evaluation
5. Gain-sharing contract development
6. Financial engineering
7. Delivery of services
8. Re-evaluation and adjustment of metrics

Gallium Arsenide (See GaAs)

GAP (Groupe d'Analyse et Prévision)
An ad hoc working group, made up of industrial, member state and commission representatives in the European Community for the study and proposal of common approaches to various communication issues. GAP reports to a Senior Officials Group for Telecommunications (SOG-T) made up of senior commission and member state officials. Reports by the group have covered Integrated Services Digital Network (ISDN), broadband technologies and networks, mobile communications and Open Network Provision (ONP).

GARP (Generic Attribute Registration Protocol)
Part of the Institute of Electrical and Electronics Engineers (IEEE) 802.1p extension to 802.1d (spanning tree). Includes:

1. GARP Information Declaration (GID): The part of GARP that generates data.

2. GARP Information Propagation (GIP): The part of GARP that distributes data.

3. GARP Multicast Registration Protocol (GMRP): Provides a mechanism that allows participants to dynamically register and deregister information with the Media Access Control (MAC) Bridges attached to the same local-area network (LAN) segment.

GARP Information Declaration (GID) (See GARP)

GARP Multicast Registration Protocol (GMRP) (See GARP)

gate assignments
Used in the context of automated call distribution (ACD) equipment. Gates are made up of trunks that require similar agent processing. Individual agents can be reassigned from one gate to another gate by the customer via the supervisory control and display station. Also called splits.

gatekeeper (See firewall)

gateway
1. A computer that sits between different networks or applications. The gateway converts information, data or other communications from one protocol or format to another. A router may perform some of the functions of a gateway. An Internet gateway can transfer communications between a corporate network and the Internet. Because organizations often use protocols on their local-area networks (LANs) that differ from those of the Internet, a gateway will often act as a protocol converter so that users can send and receive communications over the Internet.

2. A physical or logical network station that interconnects two otherwise incompatible networks, network nodes, subnetworks or devices. Gateways perform protocol conversion operations across a wide spectrum of communications functions or layers. A product or feature that uses proprietary techniques to link heterogeneous systems.

Gb (gigabit)
See Gbit.

GB (gigabyte)
See Gbyte.

Gbit or Gb (gigabit)
Approximately one billion bits (abbreviated to Gbit); more precisely 1,024x1,024x1,024 or 1,073,741,824 bits.

Gbps (gigabits per second)

Gbyte or GB (gigabyte)
One billion (actually 1,073,741,824) bytes.

GCOS (Groupe Bull Operating System for Mainframe and Midrange Server)

GCR (group code recording)

GDDM (Graphical Data Display Manager)
A format manager that handles both graphics and alphanumerics on display devices and printers. Its major component is a set of functions for drawing pictures and handling text. The GDDM application programming interface (API) is the basis for IBM's Systems Application Architecture (SAA) Presentation Manager (PM).

GDI (graphics device interface)

GDMO (Guidelines for the Definition of Managed Objects)
An International Organization for Standardization (ISO) common object modeling technology standard, part of the Open Systems Interconnection (OSI) Common Management Information Protocol (CMIP). A quasi-object database that "abstracts" objects but does not embed procedures (i.e., the objects have persistence and class, but not inheritance). It is endorsed by the Network Management Forum (NMF) of independent vendors and users.

GDPS (Geographically Dispersed Parallel Sysplex)
Previously known as a "Geoplex," a GDPS is designed to enable users to survive catastrophic events, such as a complete site failure, by enabling a Parallel Sysplex to be installed.

GDS (Global Directory Service)
The part of the Distributed Computing Environment (DCE) directory services, based on Siemens Nixdorf's X.500 directory, that provides a pointer to resources between cells.

Gearbox
An industrialized personal computer developed by IBM that is configured much like a programmable logic controller.

GEM (global electronic marketplace)

GEMMS (Global Enterprise Manufacturing Management System)
A manufacturing product for the process industries from Datalogix, with a niche-oriented process-manufacturing application.

GEMS (Global Enterprise Management of Storage)
A Legato NetWorker product that establishes a Web-server-based global control zone, which enables the administration of multiple NetWorker servers (data zones) as a single image.

general availability (See GA)

General Inter-ORB Protocol (See GIOP)

General Public License (See GNU)

General Security Services Application Programming Interface (See GSS-API)

Generic Attribute Registration Protocol (See GARP)

Generic Top-Level Domain Memorandum of Understanding (See gTLD-MoU)

Generic Top-Level Domain Name (See gTLD)

genetic algorithm (See GA)

GEO (geosynchronous orbit)
The altitude, about 23,000 miles, at which an orbiting satellite will remain over the same location on the earth's surface. Such a satellite, called geostationary, can be used as part of a permanent communications or navigational system.

Geographically Dispersed Parallel Sysplex (See GDPS)

Geoplex (See GDPS)

geostationary
An orbit that permits a satellite to appear stationary relative to the Earth. It is a circular, 35,786-kilometer-high orbit in the plane of the equator. A satellite moving from west to east in this orbit has no apparent motion with respect to the surface of the Earth.

geosynchronous orbit (See GEO)

GFLOPS (gigaFLOPS)
One billion floating-point operations per second (if used with a specific amount, e.g., 50 GFLOPS).

GHz (gigahertz)
A frequency unit equal to one billion cycles per second.

GID (GARP Information Declaration)

GIF (Graphics Interchange Format)
An integrated Web component of Hypertext Markup Language (HTML) into which graphics files can be converted so that programs can read and write them.

gigabit (See Gbit)

Gigabit Ethernet
The Institute of Electrical and Electronics Engineers (IEEE) standard (802.3z) for transmission of standard Ethernet traffic at 1 gigabits per second (Gbps) speeds.

gigabyte (See Gbyte)

gigaFLOPS (See GFLOPS)

gigahertz (See GHz)

giga-point-of-presence (See gigaPOP)

gigaPOP (giga-point-of-presence)
A concept developed by the Internet 2 Architecture Planning Group. A gigaPOP has lower-speed Internet Protocol (IP) routing capabilities similar to today's Internet service provider (ISP) environments at the fringes of the backbone networks, and an asynchronous transfer mode (ATM) switching core that should be able to scale to 2.4 gigabits per second (Gbps) by 2000 and much higher than that by 2004. The gigaPOP is the linchpin of the future network because, with an ATM core, it can carry everything from IP, X.25, frame relay and ATM traffic, eliminating the need for separate and costly networks to support a particular traffic type.

GIOP (General Inter-ORB Protocol)
A protocol that defines a small set of messages and data formats. It enables a client-side object request broker (ORB) to forward object method invocations to another, server-side ORB and receive back replies and error messages.

GIP (GARP Information Propagation) (See GARP)

GIPS (billion instructions per second)

GIS (geographic information system)

GL (graphics library)
A component of a graphical user interface (GUI) that provides a high-level graphics programming interface.

G.Lite
An International Telecommunication Union (ITU) specification (G.992.2) for a reduced-speed, splitterless version of asymmetric digital subscriber line (ADSL) that has been proposed as less technically challenging to deliver on voice-grade copper pairs. Various groups, including the vendor consortium UAWG (Universal ADSL Working Group) are working on compatibility and plug-and-play issues for G.Lite.

Global Directory Service (See GDS)

Global Enterprise Management of Storage (See GEMS)

Global Enterprise Manufacturing Management System (See GEMMS)

Global Positioning System (See GPS)

Global, Site, and End-System (See GSE)

global supply chain model (GSCM)

Global System for Mobile Communications (See GSM)

GloBanD
The name given to a set of European network services that offer digital dial-up bandwidth on demand in 64 kilobit per second (Kbps) increments, accessed from customer premises over Primary Rate Interface (PRI) lines. These services are offered under different names in each participating country.

GMLC (Graduated Monthly License Charge)
The traditional S/390 software pricing structure offered by IBM.

GMR (giant magnetoresistor)

GMRP (GARP Multicast Registration Protocol)

GN (global network)

GNS (Global Network Services)

GIOP

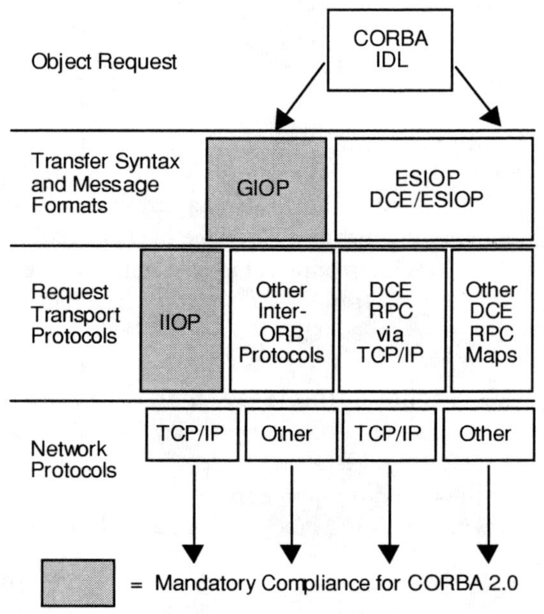

CORBA = Common Object Request Broker Architecture
DCE = Distributed Computing Environment
ESIOP = Environment-Specific Inter-ORB Protocol
GIOP = General Inter-ORB Protocol
IDL = Interface definition language
IIOP = Internet Inter-ORB Protocol
ORB = Object request broker
RPC = Remote procedure call
TCP/IP = Transmission Control Protocol/Internet Protocol

Source: GartnerGroup

General Inter-ORB Protocol Example

GNU (General Public License)
An open-source software (OSS) licensing model.

GOCA (Graphics Object Content Architecture)
IBM's Object Content Architecture format for vector graphic objects. Describes complex pictures to interchange within or across environments.

GOCA Extended (Graphics Object Content Architecture Extended)
An extension to GOCA that can describe complex pictures that contain advanced text, image and graphics.

GOLD
Integrion's GOLD specification encompasses a range of messages and transactions used by financial institutions to communicate with end users. It supports online services and batch protocol.

gopher
A text-based distributed document delivery and retrieval system used over the Internet. It predates, and has been largely superseded by, hypertext documents on the World Wide Web (WWW). It can be accessed via the WWW.

GOSIP (Government Open Systems Interconnection Procurement specifications)
Open Systems Interconnection (OSI) specifications mandated by various governments for open systems procurement.

GPC (general-purpose computer)

GPRS (general packet radio service)

GPS (Global Positioning System)
A satellite-based system for calculating a precise location on the planet. A transceiver based on the ground or in an aircraft detects signals from multiple geostationary satellites to calculate its latitude and longitude.

GPWW (group practice without walls)

grade of service
Quality of telephone service provided by a system. It is described in terms of the probability that a call will encounter a busy signal during the busiest hour of the day.

Graduated Monthly License Charge (See GMLC)

granularity
The ability to increase a system's capacity and performance through incremental processor expansion.

Graphical Data Display Manager (See GDDM)

graphical shell
A graphical-user-interface-based "desktop manager" enabling the majority of end-user operations (e.g., running applications and manipulating files) to be performed in a "point and click" manner without use of a traditional, character-oriented command language. Examples include Hewlett-Packard's Visual User Environment, IXI X.desktop, Visix Looking Glass and TeleSoft TeleUSE.

graphical user interface (See GUI)

Graphics Interchange Format (See GIF)

graphics library (See GL)

Graphics Object Content Architecture (See GOCA)

Graphics Object Content Architecture Extended (See GOCA Extended)

gray scale
A range of gray tones from black to white used to create an image.

ground circuit

1. A circuit in which energy is carried one way over a metallic path and returned through the earth.
2. A circuit connected to the earth at one or more points.

ground start

A telephony term describing a signaling method whereby one station detects that a circuit is grounded at the other end.

ground station

An assemblage of communications equipment, including a signal generator, transmitter, receiver and antenna, that receives (and usually transmits) signals to and from a communications satellite. Also called earth station.

group band modem

A modem designed for ITU V.35, V.36, or V.37 standard for transmission over group band (60 to 108 kHz) circuits.

Groupe d'Analyse et Prévision (See GAP)

Groupe Speciale Mobile (See GSM)

group technology

An engineering and manufacturing philosophy which identifies the "sameness" of parts, equipment or processes. It provides for rapid retrieval of existing designs.

groupware

Software that supports nonstructured, nondeterministic interpersonal processes and the objects with which people commonly work. Groupware was originally coined to describe a new class of applications designed to provide electronic support for groups of individuals working together toward a common goal. The term has been applied to applications ranging from unstructured electronic mail to rigorously structured workflow systems. Groupware is more useful as a concept when it is broken down into three major stages: communication, coordination and cooperation. In this light, groupware applications can be viewed in terms of the degree of structure in the group interaction and in the complexity of that structure, and the rigor with which the activity itself is monitored. This categorization of the groupware concept into stages provides meaningful differentiation and definition of the categories of applications it addresses.

GRS (Global Resource Serialization)

GSCM (global supply chain model)

GSE (Global, Site, and End-System)

Alternate addressing architecture for Internet Protocol IPv6.

GSIC (graphics-specific integrated circuit)

GSM (Global System for Mobile Communications — formerly Groupe Speciale Mobile)

A pan-European digital mobile telephone network based on digital technology utilizing the 905-915 megahertz (MHz)/950-960 MHz reserved spectrum to provide the capability of roaming over 18 countries with competition both within and between countries. The digital GSM cellular system was implemented as the one compatible system across Europe, but calling a roaming station requires signaling on the digital terrestrial networks, which is not scheduled in some European networks until beyond the year 2000. GSM also refers to the working party, now a Technical Committee responsible to the European Telecommunications Standards Institute (ETSI), which is elaborating the standard.

GSM 1900

The North American version of Global System for Mobile Communications (GSM). It is a modification of the European specification that allows use of the standard in the 1,900-megahertz (MHz) frequency band, which the Federal Communications Commission (FCC) and Industry Canada have allocated for personal communications services (PCS). (GSM in Europe operates at 900 MHz.)

GSP (graphics system processor)

GSR (Gigabit Speed Router)

GSS-API (General Security Services Application Programming Interface)
An information security standard described in Internet Engineering Task Force (IETF) Request for Comment (RFC) 1508 that defines the formats for access control, user identification, etc.

gTLD (Generic Top-Level Domain Name)
A generic name such as .firm, .store, .web, .arts or rec.

Guardian
Tandem's operating system, which resides in each processor of a multiprocessor complex and manages the system resources as a single image.

GUI (graphical user interface)
A graphics-based operating system interface that uses icons, menus and a mouse (to click on the icon or pull down the menus) to manage interaction with the system. Developed by Xerox, the GUI was popularized by the Apple Macintosh in the 1980s. At the time, Microsoft's operating system, MS-DOS, required the user to type specific commands, but the company's GUI, Microsoft Windows, is now the dominant user interface for personal computers (PCs). A comprehensive GUI environment includes four components: a graphics library, a user interface toolkit, a user interface style guide and consistent applications. The graphics library provides a high-level graphics programming interface. The user interface toolkit, built on top of the graphics library, provides application programs with mechanisms for creating and managing the dialog elements of the windows, icons, menus, pointers and scroll bars (WIMPS) interface. The user interface style guide specifies how applications should employ the dialog elements to present a consistent, easy-to-use environment (i.e., "look and feel") to the user. Application program conformance with a single user interface style is the primary determinant of ease of learning and use, and thus, of application effectiveness and user productivity.

GUI applications development tools
Graphical, interactive tools for the nonprocedural development of application user interfaces compliant with the system's user interface style guide. Examples include Digital Equipment's Visual User Interface Tool and NeXT's Interface Builder.

Guidelines for the Definition of Managed Objects (See GDMO)

Gunn diode
Named for IBM scientist John Gunn. Until recently, it was the standard form for generating microwave energy. It produces only a single fixed frequency.

GVP (gross vendor product)

GWAC (governmentwide agency contract)

H

H.100
A hardware standard that will merge Signal Computing System Architecture (SCSA) and Multivendor Integration Protocol.

H.221
A standard describing a method of inverse multiplexing for videoconferencing terminals, to be used with Px64 videoconferencing.

H.261
An International Telecommunication Union (ITU) standard for video compression (also known as px64). H.261 will be the worldwide standard and therefore must accommodate both the North American National Television System Committee (NTSC) and European Phase Alternate Line (PAL) protocols.

H.263
The video component of the H.323 videoconferencing suite.

H.320
An international standard specification for audioconferencing and videoconferencing that comprises many standards, including H.261 standard, the compression schema for video transmissions.

H.323
A key standard for audio- and videoconferencing, ratified by the International Telecommunication Union (ITU). It is a videoconferencing suite that has G.723 voice, T.120 collaborative and H.263 video components in a single session.

H.324
An international standard protocol for "plain old telephone service" (POTS).

HA (high availability)
A high probability that a system at any given time will be operational for useful work and has the ability to recover quickly and with minimum disruption to the user in case of failure. Those characteristics of a data processing system that reduce or eliminate its vulnerability to unscheduled outages, such as power failures, code defects or hardware failures. One element of 24x7.

HACMP (High Availability Clustered Multiprocessing)
An IBM RS/6000 product originally designed to provide a high-availability configuration (by enabling automated failover from one RS/6000 to another). HACMP comprises:

1. Cluster management software to restart an application or subsystem on an alternate RS/6000 processor after a failure of the primary processor.
2. Distributed lock manager software to coordinate and synchronize process execution on multiple processors in a cluster.
3. Configuration and topology software management tools to enable developers to build cluster-aware applications.

HADA (high-availability disk array)

HAL (hardware abstraction layer)
Operating-system protection that prevents unauthorized access to the operating-system kernel.

half duplex (See HD)

Handheld Device Markup Language (See HDML)

handler
A program with the sole function of controlling a particular input, output, storage device, file or interrupt facility.

handoff
The transfer of duplex signaling as a mobile terminal passes to an adjacent cell in a cellular radio network.

handset
The portion of the telephone containing the transmitter and receiver.

handshaking
The exchange of predetermined signals for control when a connection is established between two modems or two other devices.

handwriting recognition
Systems using pattern matching to convert handwritten letters into corresponding American Standard Code for Information Interchange (ASCII) values. The two subfields are static recognition of handwritten documents such as forms, and dynamic recognition of real-time handwriting (e.g., for personal digital assistants — PDAs).

hard disk
The main data storage area of computing devices. The hard disk is where the operating system and other software are permanently stored on a computer (PC). Hard disks typically have a larger storage capacity and faster data retrieval capabilities than floppy disks.

hardware
Machinery and equipment associated with computing devices. A computer is composed of both hardware and software. The software provides the instructions, and the hardware performs the processing.

hardware abstraction layer (See HAL)

hardware device module (See HDM)

hardware RAID
All hardware redundant array of independent disks (RAID) products employ software instructions that specify the required data movements and parity computations. The term "hardware RAID" generally implies a dedicated disk array controller board — with its own microprocessor, memory and microcode — that implements the RAID functions and computations. However, the concept can be extended to storage servers that perform the RAID operations using standard computer hardware and operating system software. The crucial point is that a hardware RAID solution performs its RAID operations in a processor that is separate from the application processor, and that provides nonvolatile memory for the data and instructions it receives from the host system.

hardwired
1. A communications link, whether remote phone line or local cable, that permanently connects two nodes, stations, or devices.
2. Electronic circuitry that performs fixed logical operations by virtue of unalterable circuit layout, rather than under computer or stored-program control.

harmonic distortion
The presence of harmonic frequencies in a received signal due to nonlinear characteristics of a transmission line.

HASP (Houston Automatic Spooling Program)
Batch-oriented IBM software that provides supplementary job management, such as job spooling, and controls communications between local and remote processors and Remote Job Entry (RJE) stations.

HBA (host bus adapter)

HBT (heterojunction bipolar transistor)

HCF (high-cost fund)
An access charge paid by interexchange carriers (IXCs), HCF was developed by the Federal Communications Commission (FCC) to help local exchange carriers (LECs) pay for their installed network infrastructures and for new network developments after the splitting up of AT&T in 1984.

HCFA1500 (Healthcare Financing Administration Codes, labeled 1500)
This Uniform Billing scheme for physician practices consists of information with uniform, prescribed content and formats used by virtually every payer for purposes of reimbursement and historical documentation. It includes details regarding procedures, tests and treatments from every point of care within the scope of the organization that owns the data.

H channel
A transmission channel, defined in the Integrated Services Digital Network (ISDN) standards, made up of multiple B channels. Currently defined H channels include:

1. H0: Comprised of 6 B channels to create a 384 kilobit per second (Kbps) ISDN channel.
2. H10: Comprised of 23 B channels to create a 1472 Kbps ISDN channel.
3. H11: Comprised of 24 B channels to create a 1536 Kbps ISDN channel.
4. H12: Comprised of 30 B channels to create a 1920 Kbps ISDN channel.

HCIS (healthcare information system)

HCPCS (Healthcare Procedural Classification System)
One of the standard code formats and definitions included in the Uniform Billing Codes.

HD or HDX (half duplex)
A circuit designed for transmission alternately in either direction but not in both directions simultaneously. See also full duplex.

HDA (head disk assembly)
A sealed assembly containing magnetic disks, head and access arms. By reducing contamination, a sealed HDA enables the head to fly closer to the disk surface, increasing the areal density that can be obtained.

HDCD (high-density CD)

HDD (hard disk drive)

HDL (hardware description language)

HDLC (High-Level Data Link Control)
A bit-oriented data link protocol developed by the International Organization for Standardization (ISO) and used in Open Systems Interconnection (OSI).

HDM (hardware device module)
Processes most of the input/output (I/O) request locally with direct memory access, and notifies the operating-system module when the operation is complete.

HDML (Handheld Device Markup Language)
A device- and network-independent application language developed by Unwired Planet for Web programming on a handheld device with limited memory and display such as a cellular phone or an organizer.

HDO (help desk outsourcing)

HD-ROM (high-density read-only memory)

HDS (Hitachi Data Systems)

HDSL (high-speed digital subscriber line)
One of a group known as digital subscriber line (DSL) technologies, HDSL gives network or Inter-

net access over voice lines at 1.5 megabits per second (Mbps) on T1 lines with two pairs combined.

HDTV (high-definition television)

HDX (half duplex) (See HD)

head disk assembly (See HDA)

head end
The originating point in a one-to-many system such as a TV cable network or a central information-gathering point of an Internet service provider (ISP).

header
The initial portion of a message, which contains any information and control codes that are not part of the text (e.g., routine, priority, message type, destination addressee and time of origination).

header record
Data containing common, constant or identifying information for a group of records that follow.

head-mounted display (See HMD)

Healthcare Financing Administration Codes, labeled 1500 (See HCFA1500)

Healthcare Procedural Classification System (See HCPCS)

Health Information Management and Systems Society (See HIMSS)

Health Insurance Portability and Accountability Act (See HIPAA)

Health Level 7 (See HL7)

Health Plan Employer Data and Information Set (See HEDIS)

HEDIS (Health Plan Employer Data and Information Set)
In 1992, the National Committee on Quality Assurance (NCQA) accepted accountability for the creation of a standardized set of measures for comparing and subsequently accrediting health plans. The initial intent was employer, not practitioner, focused. This set of measures, which became HEDIS, has undergone improvements through several versions since 1993, leading up to HEDIS 3.0. NCQA states that nearly 90 percent of all health plans — more than 300 — collect and report some subset of the HEDIS measures, representing over 37 million Americans.

helical-scan recording
In tape recording, when the tape is wrapped around a transport drum at an angle, track length is created that is nearly 10 times longer than the tape width. These diagonal tracks can increase track density and data transfer rates.

help desk
The first point of contact for all technical and end-user support issues, it includes Tier 1 and Tier 2 support levels. Tier 1 is the first point of contact. Tier 2 help desk analysts have more in-depth technical knowledge or specialized expertise.

help system
A consistent, system-supplied mechanism for system and application programs to offer online, context-sensitive help to end users.

Henderson Strategic Alignment Model
Developed by John Henderson of Boston University, this model provides a helpful framework for the CIO to understand the transition to a new management approach appropriate for the times. In this model, business strategy serves as a demarcation between current and future business platforms. The process of developing business strategy, including the requisite dialog between the IS organi-

zation and business units, leads to derivation of future business and IT architectures that will serve the enterprise.

hertz (See Hz)

heterogeneous
A system composed of hardware, operating systems, middleware or applications from several different vendors.

heterogeneous (computer) network
A system of different host computers, such as those of different manufacturers. See also homogeneous (computer) network.

Heterogeneous LAN Management (See HLM) Specification

heterogeneous multiprocessing (See HMP)

hexadecimal
A number system with 16 members represented by 0 through 9 followed by A through F. Used to identify the 16 possible bit patterns of a half byte; two hex digits represent one byte. Synonymous with hex.

HF (high frequency)
The portion of the electromagnetic spectrum typically used in shortwave radio applications — frequencies approximately in the 3 to 30 megahertz (MHz) range.

HFC (hybrid fiber coaxial)
Network architecture that consists of fiber in the backbone and coax as the access. This type of architecture permits very-high-speed services into the home for applications such as video.

HFC (hybrid fiber-coaxial cable)

HHIS (home-health information system)

hierarchical database
A database that is organized in a tree structure in which each record has one owner. Navigation to individual records takes place through predetermined access paths.

hierarchical storage management (See HSM)

high availability (See HA)

High Availability Cluster Multiprocessing (See HACMP)

high-cost fund (See HCF)

High Frequency (See HF)

High-Level Data Link Control (See HDLC)

high-level language (See HLL)

High-Level Language Application Program Interface (See HLLAPI)

Henderson Strategic Alignment Model

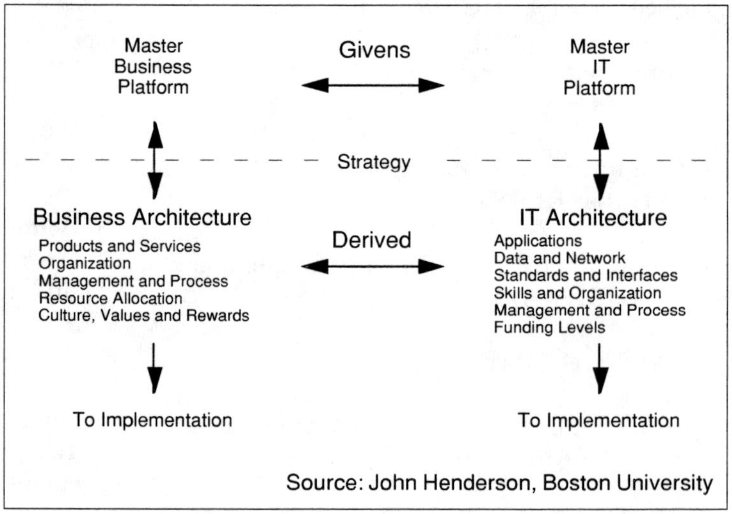

A Strategic Alignment Model

highly parallel systems (See HPS)

High-Performance File System (See HPFS)

High-Performance Parallel Interface (See HIPPI)

High-Performance Routing (See HPR)

High-Performance Space (See Hiperspace)

high-speed digital subscriber line (See HDSL)

high-speed local-area network (See HS/LAN)

High-Speed Serial Interface (See HSSI)

high-speed subscriber data line (See HSDL)

High-Speed Token-Ring Alliance (See HSTRA)

HIM (health information management)

HIMSS (Health Information Management and Systems Society)
A healthcare industry association.

HIPAA (Health Insurance Portability and Accountability Act)
HIPAA, which became effective in August 1997, calls for electronic data interchange (EDI) use in medical transactions and also calls for protecting patient healthcare information. Enterprises face fines of up to $250,000 and 10 years imprisonment for wrongfully disclosing patient information.

Hiperspace (High-Performance Space)
Introduced with Enterprise Systems Architecture (ESA)/370, Hiperspace refers to an address space occupied only by data and to which access is controlled by hardware via special instructions.

HIPPI (High-Performance Parallel Interface)
An American National Standards Institute (ANSI) standard for high-speed channels used in I/O-intensive systems, including supercomputers.

HIS (healthcare information system)

HIS (hospital information system)

Hitachi Online Data Migration (See HODM)

Hitachi Remote Copy (See HRC)

HL7 (Health Level 7)
An application-level standard for community health information network (CHIN) initiatives, widely used in hospitals.

HLL (high-level language)
A procedural programming language that offers a higher level of abstraction than assembly language. Examples of HLLs include COBOL, FORTRAN, PL/I, C, Pascal and Ada. The term is interchangeable with "3GL."

HLLAPI (High-Level Language Application Programming Interface)
IBM's high-level language multiprotocol applications interface.

HLM (Heterogeneous LAN Management) Specification
A proprietary network management draft developed jointly by 3Com and IBM that specifies using Common Management Information Protocol (CMIP) over Logical Link Control (LLC) to provide network management of devices on mixed-media local-area networks (LANs). Also known as CMOL.

HMBR (Hitachi Multihost Backup/Restore)

HMD (head-mounted display)
A display mounted close to the eye on a headset or goggles typically uses optics to create the illusion of

H

a larger screen further away from the eye. Most techniques involve a small liquid crystal display (LCD), usually monochrome and low resolution (other approaches include light-emitting diode — LED — or electroluminescent technologies). Applications include industrial inspection and maintenance. The 3-D head-mounted displays used in immersive virtual reality systems are typically based on dual LCDs with a distinct image for each eye (offset to provide depth perception), updated at 30 frames per second. This is coupled with head tracking so that the image changes appropriately in response to head movement.

HMDE (Hitachi Multiplatform Data Exchange)

HMI (human machine interface)

HMMP (Hypermedia Management Protocol)
This protocol is a part of the Web-Based Enterprise Management (WBEM) proposal. It operates over the Hypertext Transport Protocol (HTTP) standard, collecting and transporting device management data to populate a management database. Initially, HMMP will complement Simple Network Management Protocol (SNMP), not replace it, although that is the long-term objective.

HMMS (Hypermedia Management Schema)
A schema that was a part of the Web-Based Enterprise Management (WBEM) proposal. It describes what is to be contained in an object model, outlining a data model for representing the relationship between network elements, not just the elements themselves. The schema relies on basic object-oriented constructs, establishing classifications of managed elements in the network environment. The four classes are: system elements, application components, resource components and network components. HMMS has since been renamed Common Information Mode (CIM) by the Desktop Management Task Force (DMTF).

HMOM (Hypermedia Object Manager)
Included within the Web-Based Enterprise Management (WBEM) proposal, HMOM is an example of a specification designed to use the data model — as described by Hypermedia Management Schema (HMMS) — in developing a repository of object instances, each representing network elements. HMOM serves as a controller to management data (allowing network managers and management applications to observe and manipulate this data) through a series of management protocols and interfaces.

HMP (heterogeneous multiprocessing)
An operating-system (OS) shell that runs the mainframe OS as a mandatory partition with the optional ability to run Unix or NT.

HMP (Hierarchical Multiprocessing)

HMRS (Hitachi Multihost Resource Sharing)

HODM (Hitachi Online Data Migration)
A controller-based feature that requires the target volume(s) to be contained within a Symmetrix or 7700 subsystem. Depending on customer configuration, the recabling required to support data migration may or may not be disruptive.

holddown
Used to flush bad routing information from all routers on a network; it stops routers from advertising for or accepting information about routes for a specified length of time.

holding time
The length of time a communications channel is in use for each transmission. It includes message time and operating time. Also called connect time.

home page
The top-level page or entry point into a Web site.

homogeneous (computer) network
A system of similar computers, such as those of one model by the same manufacturer, See also heterogeneous computer network.

homologation
Conformity of a product to international standards.

hop count
Measures the number of stops a packet makes from source to destination.

HOPS (HTTP operations per second)

host
Any computer connected to the Internet that has a domain name associated with it. It provides the services and facilities used by the other computers and terminals.

HOST (Healthcare Open Systems and Trials)

host computer
The primary or controlling system in a multiple computer network operation.

hosting
Storage of data on a server for later access. Typically, the hosting server provides services and tools that expedite access by individuals or other servers. The popularity of the World Wide Web has given rise to an industry of hosting services that store large amounts of data that can be accessed from the Internet 24 hours a day, seven days a week.

host interface
The link between a communications processor or network and a host computer.

host processor
A mainframe attached to a network for network users' access.

hot links and links
Areas on a Web page that when "clicked on" will transport the user to another Web page. These are analogous to hypertext.

hot standby
Alternate equipment ready to take over an operation quickly if the equipment on which it is being performed fails.

hot swap
To exchange a component or a module in a networking device without powering down.

HOTT (Hands On Technology Transfer)

Houston Automatic Spooling Program (See HASP)

HPC (handheld PC)

HPC (high-performance computing)

HPCC (High-Performance Computing and Communications-federal program)

HPFS (High-Performance File System)
The data-mapping protocol used for disk storage by IBM's OS/2 operating system. It replaces the file allocation table (FAT) system used in PC-DOS.

HPPA (Hewlett-Packard precision architecture)

HPPD (hours per patient day — healthcare)

HPR (High-Performance Routing)
IBM's technology to enable users to send Systems Network Architecture (SNA) traffic over frame and cell-based networks, making for more efficient communications. For example, the HPR version of Advanced Peer-to-Peer Networking (APPN) is generally superior to Transmission Control Protocol/ Internet Protocol (TCP/IP), which uses reactive

congestion control, while APPN is predictive, resulting in higher network utilization and throughput for APPN. Because it is newer, APPN can better take advantage of increasingly error-free, high-speed digital transmission facilities. TCP/IP's domain name service and limited (now insufficient) addressing capacity are inferior in performance to APPN's topology database and use of logical unit names. APPN supports a prioritization/class-of-service mechanism for different types of network applications, while individual router vendors have been forced to add their own nonstandard prioritization capabilities to TCP/IP.

HPS (highly parallel systems)
Hardware configurations having from 10 to 99 central processing units (CPUs).

HP-UX
Hewlett-Packard's System V-based Unix implementation, with real-time extensions added.

HRC (Hitachi Remote Copy)
A controller-based remote-copy capability that Hitachi Data Systems (HDS) is evolving into a competitive alternative to Symmetrix Remote Data Facility (SRDF).

HRE (Hardware Routing Engine — Xylan)

HREF (Hypertext Reference)
In Hypertext Markup Language (HTML), HREF is used to assign a hypertext address to a link.

HRIS (human resources information system)

HRMS (Human Resource Management System — PeopleSoft)
Also used as a generic term.

HSC (High-Speed Connect)

HSCSD (high-speed circuit switched data)

HSDL (high-speed subscriber data line)
A local phone line with full-duplex TI capabilities. As corporate intranets grow, bigger "pipes" are needed to maintain network performance. The use of inverse multiplexers that combine multiple E1 circuits will be the best way to deliver that bandwidth between the user site and the carrier's central office. But the use of HSDL technology, as an alternative to inverse multiplexing of E1 circuits, will be a "dark horse" alternative to inverse multiplexing. Unlike inverse multiplexing, HSDL would require new support systems and maintenance procedures.

HS LAN (high-speed local-area network)
A LAN operating at four megabits (Mbps) per second or more to facilitate rapid exchange of files and mail within a broader departmental or divisional environment.

HSM (hierarchical storage management)
A storage management technology that can be used to identify inactive data and move it to near-line storage, automate the retrieval process, and migrate the data back to the primary storage medium and provide access for the user.

HSSI (High-Speed Serial Interface)
Standard for a serial interface used to connect to T3 lines. HSSI operates over a shielded cable at speeds of up to 52 megabits per second (Mbps) and distances of up to 50 feet. Functionally, it serves the same purpose as lower-speed serial interfaces such as V.35 and RS232, in that it provides the interface to DCE for wide-area-network (WAN) communications.

HSTR (High-Speed Token Ring — IBM)

HSTRA (High-Speed Token Ring Alliance)
A consortium of vendors formed in 1997 as a re-creation of the Alliance for Strategic Token Ring Advancement and Leadership (ASTRAL). HSTRA plans to develop draft standards for 100 megabits

per second (Mbps) Token Ring and Gigabit Token Ring and present them to the Institute of Electrical and Electronics Engineers (IEEE) 802.5 committee.

HTML (Hypertext Markup Language)
A document-formatting language derived from the Standard Generalized Markup Language (SGML), predominately used to create World Wide Web pages. The user's browser interprets HTML commands and formats the page layout, fonts and graphics on the screen. One of the more powerful features of HTML is its ability to create hyperlinks that enable the user to navigate between documents and files with a single click. HTTP is also sometimes used for messaging attachments as a way of supporting rich text formatting across product boundaries.

HTML that is generated by a program or service is considered "dynamically generated HTML," which has been confused with the Netscape and Microsoft technology called dynamic HTML (DHTML). These technologies offer client-side mechanisms for enhancing the capabilities of the Web browser and HTML documents. Dynamically generated HTML might contain DHTML, but they are not the same thing.

HTTP (Hypertext Transport Protocol)
The Internet standard for accessing and exchanging documents on the World Wide Web. It is a client/server protocol used to connect to Web servers.

hub
A central device, usually in a star topology local-area network (LAN), to which each station's wiring is attached. Also called wiring concentrator. See also intelligent hub.

Huffman Code
A code used for one-dimensional data compression in the International Telecommunication Union Telecommunications Standards Sector (ITU) Group III digital facsimile standard.

hum
Spurious electrical interference, usually picked up from a conventional alternating current power supply.

HW (hardware)

HXRC (Hitachi Extended Remote Copy)

HTML

```
<HTML>
<HEAD>
<TITLE>Welcome to Gartner Group</TITLE>
<SCRIPT LANGUAGE="JavaScript">
<!--
function makearray( n )
{
 this.length = n;
 for( var i = 1; i <= n; i++ )
   this[ i ] = 0;
 return this;
}
function other( img, len )
---------  [snip, snip]  -------------
//-->
</SCRIPT>
</HEAD>
```

HTML, a derived subset of SGML, defines a series of tags or codes that tell a Web browser how to interpret the text or image enclosed in the tags (see <TITLE> Welcome to Gartner Group</ TITLE>). Based on the simple ASCII text-based tags, the browser can adjust font size, display tables, or tell HTTP and other Web-related protocols to take an action (e.g., link to a given URL, send E-mail, or download a file). The benefits are HTML's relative simplicity and independence from operating-system, server or client platform. Since the browser is simply interpreting strings of ASCII characters, pages and basic form-based applications are inherently cross-platform.

The introduction of JavaScript (see <SCRIPT LANGUAGE= "JavaScript"> code </SCRIPT>) enables dynamic functionality, form and table manipulation, and interactive multimedia effects, as well as applet-based functionality.

ASCII = American Standard Code for Information Interchange
HTML = Hypertext Markup Language
HTTP = Hypertext Transport Protocol
SGML = Standard Generalized Markup Language
URL = Uniform resource locator

Source: GartnerGroup

H

H.x series
Any of several standards associated with videoconferencing (see individual listings at the beginning of this section).

hybrid circuit
A circuit having four sets of terminals arranged in two pairs. It is designed so that there is high loss between the two sets of terminals of a pair when the terminals of the other pair are suitably terminated. Hybrid circuits are commonly used to couple four-wire circuits to two-wire circuits.

hybrid fiber coaxial (See HFC)

hybrid modeling
A term, coined by GartnerGroup, that is used to signify second-generation, dimension-driven, constraint-based solids modeling technology beyond first-generation parametric modeling. Hybrid modelers offer multiple design input mechanisms, flexible constraint management, and robust interoperability with legacy computer-aided design (CAD) data.

hybrid private/public networking
The creation of a network using both private leased lines and public switched facilities (digital dial-up bandwidth).

hype cycle
GartnerGroup's hype cycle is designed to help clients make intelligent decisions about when to implement emerging technologies. Like all technology investments, there is no simple answer for each technology, rather the business needs should determine when it makes sense to invest in a particular new technology. The annually updated GartnerGroup hype cycle provides not only a scorecard to separate hype from reality, but also a model that can be used to decide when it makes sense for an enterprise to move forward with a new technology. The five distinct phases in the hype cycle are: technology trigger; peak of inflated expectations; trough of disillusionment; slope of enlightenment; and plateau of productivity.

hyperlink
A predefined link from one location to another. The link can jump within a particular location, to another location with the same computer or network site or even to a location at a completely different physical site. Hyperlinks are commonly used on the World Wide Web to provide navigation, reference and depth where published text cannot. A hyperlink can be created from text (which typically appears as blue underlined text within a Hypertext Markup Language/HTML page) or from a graphic.

hypermedia
Hypertext for multimedia documents. Can include audio and video as well as text and graphics.

Hypermedia Management Protocol (See HMMP)

Hypermedia Management Schema (See HMMS)

Hypermedia Object Manager (See HMOM)

Hypermedia/Time-Based Structuring Language (See HYTime)

hyperprotocol
A file transfer protocol that sends data in a steady stream, rather than in packets, with built-in error correction and data compression.

hypertext
Software technology used to create and store simple and complex navigational paths across computerized data. When the text is "clicked on," it can enable a user to navigate within or between Web pages.

Hypertext Markup Language (See HTML)

Hypertext Reference (See HREF)

Hypertext Transport Protocol (See HTTP)

HyTime (Hypermedia/Time-Based Structuring Language)
An extension to Standard Generalized Markup Language (SGML) providing structure for multimedia documents. It facilitates the creation of pointers and the description of spatial and temporal relationships between parts of the document. Developed by the American National Standards Institute (ANSI), now owned by the International Organization for Standardization (ISO). See SGML.

Hz (hertz)
A unit of frequency equal to one cycle per second.

H

I

IA-32
Intel proprietary complex instruction set computer (CISC) architecture.

IA-64
Explicitly Parallel Instruction Computing (EPIC)-based architecture by Intel, code named Merced.

IAA (insurance application architecture)

IAAI (Innovative Applications of Artificial Intelligence)
A yearly conference focused on deployed applications of artificial intelligence (AI) technology. It runs in conjunction with the American Association of Artificial Intelligence conference.

IAB (Internet Activities Board)
The technical policy- and standards-setting body for the Internet, Transmission Control Protocol/Internet Protocol (TCP/IP), and connected protocols. It consists of two task forces: Internet Engineering Task Force (IETF) and Internet Research Task Force (IRTF).

IAC (interapplication communication)

IAD (integrated access device)

IAE (integrated applications environment)
An environment with a strong integrated development environment (IDE), application server, middleware, and the "glue" (or framework) to provide for integrating all applications development (AD) facilities.

IAF (Internet Administration Framework)
An electronic-commerce-based, technology-enabled relationship management (TERM)-oriented suite — from Solect Technology Group — that provides a sales, marketing, customer care, service management and billing solution for Internet service providers (ISPs). IAF provides tools that enable ISPs to define and offer new services, provision and rate services online, and meter and bill.

IANA (Internet Assigned Numbers Authority)
The part of the Internet Activities Board (IAB) that delegates Internet Protocol (IP) address allocation and maintains a database of assigned protocol identifiers in the Internet, Transmission Control Protocol/Internet Protocol (TCP/IP) stack.

IBG (interblock gap)
Space left unused between consecutive data blocks.

IBM 3270 Pass-Through
A facility that enables attached terminals or PCs to connect to an IBM mainframe system through the midrange system and appear to the IBM system as 3278-type terminals.

IBSTPI (International Board of Standards for Training, Performance and Instruction)

IC (integrated circuit)
An assembly of electronic circuits contained on a single piece of semiconductor material.

ICA (Independent Computing Architecture)
A protocol that provides users with integrated access to the local hard drive, printer and serial port resources.

ICA (International Communications Association)

iCAL (Internet calendar specification)

I-CASE (integrated-computer-aided software engineering)
Refers to the integration of lower-CASE (computer-aided software engineering) tools with upper-CASE tools. (Upper-CASE tools are used in the analysis and design phases of a system's life cycle. Lower-CASE tools take the information contained in the upper-CASE tools and rapidly generate whole applications, or parts of an application.) I-CASE creates a bidirectional link that transfers information back and forth.

ICB (Integrated Cluster Bus)

ICC (Internal Coupling Channel)

ICD (International Code Designator)
One of two formats from the Asynchronous Transfer Mode (ATM) Forum for address usage. See also DCC.

ICD-9 (International Classification of Diseases, Ninth Revision)

ICDA (Integrated Cached Disk Array)
A family of storage products for the IBM AS/400 from EMC. The ICDA Symmetrix product line provides three key benefits: 1) a high-performance read/write cache, 2) a "Perma Cache" (solid-state disk) option for ultra-high-performance data sets, and 3) a mirroring option for critical data sets requiring high availability.

ICE (information and content exchange)

ICE (Information Context Exchange)
An initiative under development in the World Wide Web Coalition (W3C) that provides a common protocol, vocabulary and management model for information providers and recipients (other organizations) to use when sharing and reusing information. ICE components include:

- Subscription management (including start and stop dates)
- Time and frequency of delivery
- Delivery method (push or pull)
- Data delivery, detailing what items must be sent to fulfill a subscription
- Event logs diagnosing problems
- Miscellaneous functions, including sending messages destined for system administrators and troubleshooting

ICE (integrated computing environment)

ICF (internal coupling facility)

ICMF (Integrated Coupling Migration Facility)
IBM's internal Coupling Facility product for Parallel Sysplex support.

ICMP (Internet Control Message Protocol)
A route management protocol that is part of the Internet Protocol (IP), handling error and control messages.

ICMP Router Discovery Protocol (see IRDP)

iCOMP (Intel Comparative Microprocessor Performance)
A proprietary Intel test suite and performance measurement that is applicable only to Intel processors.

icon
A symbol or pictorial representation of an object or idea in graphic interfaces, used to represent the different functions or applications available to the user. A mouse is typically used to select the desired operation by pointing to one of the icons on the screen.

ICP (Internet Cache Protocol)

ICPR (Internet commercial publishing revenue)
The sum of advertising revenue generated from classified ads, display ads, banner ads and cooperative marketing sources, and subscription revenue generated for a multiple-issue schedule or on a per

content use basis from Internet publications and directory sources.

ICR (intelligent character recognition)
A technology that employs either software alone or software and hardware to automatically recognize and translate raster images into structured data.

ICX (Intercartridge Exchange)

IDA (integrated digital access)
A British Telecom ISDN precursor.

IDA (intelligent drive array)

IDAPI (Integrated Database Application Programming Interface)
An application programming interface (API) for data integration first promoted by Borland, IBM, Novell and WordPerfect in November 1992 to counter Microsoft's Open Database Connectivity.

IDARS (integrated document archive and retrieval system)
A GartnerGroup term and concept for the emerging market that is subsuming and transforming the common output to laserdisc (COLD), computer output microfiche (COM), computer output microfiche replacement (COM-R) and report distribution systems (RDS) markets. At the heart of IDARS is consolidated storage, access, management and viewing of data that is often print stream originated.

IDE (integrated development environment)
Environments for writing application logic and designing application interfaces. They differ from integrated applications environments (IAEs) in that they lack solutions that include application servers and a framework (or glue) to assist developers with applications development (AD).

IDEA (International Data Encryption Algorithm)

IDEF1 (Integrated Definition Methodology)
The most commonly used representation standard for data models.

IDH (integrated data hub)

IDIQ (indefinite delivery/indefinite quantity)
Contracts that enable government customers to buy information technology (IT) services from preselected vendors at prenegotiated rates. These contracts, developed and administered by individual government organizations to meet their own IT service requirements, are usually available to all federal agencies for a small (1 percent) administrative fee. The contracts typically cover a broad scope of IT services, and are awarded to several "prime" contractors. Each prime contractor team includes a group of subcontractors that enable it to provide the full suite of required services.

IDL (interface definition language)
A standard language for defining objects' abstract descriptions in terms of their external interfaces (i.e., methods and parameters). The IDL compiler will create relevant runtime static and dynamic interface binding information.

IDL (Interface Description Language)

IDM (integrated document management)
A vital class of middleware services that integrates library services, document-manufacturing and document-interchange technologies with critical business-process applications. The term "integrated" describes the transformation of document management from an end-user application to a network-based service integrated with a full complement of end-user personal-productivity and custom-developed applications.

IDMS or CA-IDMS (Integrated Database Management System — Computer Associates)
The database management system introduced by Cullinet in 1973, based on technology acquired

from B.F. Goodrich. Computer Associates (CA) acquired Cullinet and has maintained the product line since 1989.

IDN (Integrated Digital Network)
A network employing both digital switches and digital transmission.

IDNX (Integrated Digital Network Exchange)

IDOM (Integrated Document and Output Management — GartnerGroup)
A collection of technologies, architectures and services aimed at applying the value of information in documents to business practices. IDOM takes a digital approach to reducing the burden and cost of paper-based documents.

IDOM suite
A GartnerGroup concept that describes the convergence of digital document-processing technologies into integrated product portfolios. An IDOM suite is an aggregation of "point" technologies, but it is also a product architectural foundation built on a core set of backbone services providing the basics of cross repository query, common administration, unified system management and integrated applications development environments.

IDRC (Improved Data Recording Capability)
A 3480 feature announced in 1989 that improves the effective capacity of the cartridge.

IDRP (Interdomain Routing Protocol)

IDS (integrated delivery system)
A system typically built around a health maintenance organization (HMO), a group practice, one or more hospitals, or a corporation that owns and operates several different healthcare delivery organizations. Many IDSs deliver a vertical array of healthcare services, including physician, inpatient, laboratory, home care and radiological services, through owned or contracted resources.

IDSL (ISDN digital subscriber line)

IE (information engineering)
A methodology for developing an integrated information system based on the sharing of common data, with emphasis on decision support needs as well as transaction-processing (TP) requirements. It assumes logical data representations are relatively stable, as opposed to the frequently changing processes that use the data. Therefore, the logical data model, which reflects an organization's rules and policies, should be the basis for systems development.

IE (Internet Explorer — Microsoft)
Microsoft's World Wide Web browser, now partially integrated into Windows.

IEC (interexchange carrier)

IEC (International Electrotechnical Commission)
A standards-setting body, often jointly responsible with the International Organization for Standardization (ISO) for Open Systems Interconnection (OSI) standards.

IEEE (Institute of Electrical and Electronics Engineers)
An organization of engineers, scientists and students involved in electrical, electronics and related fields. IEEE also functions as a publishing house and standards body.

IEEE 802
An Institute of Electrical and Electronics Engineers standard for interconnection of local-area networking equipment dealing with the physical and link layers of the International Organization for Standardization (ISO) model for Open Systems Interconnection (OSI).

IEEE 802.1p (priority queues)
A standard that provides for up to eight distinct priority queues within local-area network (LAN) switches.

IEEE 802.1Q or IEEE 802.1q (bridged virtual local-area networks)
A standard for the identification of virtual local-area networks (LANs), to increase the interoperability between different vendors for switch trunking and server connections.

IEEE 802.3
The physical and medium-access control standards for CSMA/CD (carrier sense multiple access with collision detection) local-area networks (LANs) such as Ethernet.

IEEE 802.4
The physical and medium-access control standard for token bus local-area networks (LANs).

IEEE 802.5
The physical and medium-access control standard for Token Ring local-area networks (LANs).

IEEE 802.6
The physical and medium-access control standard for metropolitan-area networking.

IEEE 1394 (See FireWire)

IEF (Information Engineering Facility — Texas Instruments)
A life-cycle management computer-aided software engineering (CASE) product offered by Texas Instruments (TI) that focuses on Customer Information Control System/Database-2 (CICS/DB2) applications.

IEFM (integrated e-form management)
A GartnerGroup concept that describes a system designed for creating and administering e-form applications using installed databases, messaging, document management and workflow infrastructures.

IESG (Internet Engineering Steering Group)
An organization appointed by the Internet Activities Board (IAB) to manage the operation of the Internet Engineering Task Force (IETF).

IETF (Internet Engineering Task Force)
A subgroup of the Internet Society responsible for recommending protocols and procedures used over the Internet. It is composed of representatives from vendor, government, and academic communities, and is divided into six subcommittees (with further divisions into working parties). The chairperson sits on the Internet Activities Board (IAB). IETF working group meetings are open to the public.

IEW (Information Engineering Workbench)
KnowledgeWare's upper-CASE (computer-aided software engineering) product that includes planning, analysis and design functions.

IFPUG (International Function Point Users Group)

IFRB (International Frequency Registration Board)
Within the International Telecommunication Union (ITU), the IFRB is responsible for the maintenance of an international list of radio frequency usage and the allocation of new frequencies.

IFX (Interactive Financial Exchange)

IGBT (insulated-gate bipolar transistor)

IGES (Initial Graphics Exchange Specification)
A standard for the exchange of computer-aided design (CAD) geometry. IGES is largely superseded by STEP (Standard for the Exchange of Product Model Data) and PDES (Product Design Exchange using STEP). A vendor-neutral method

of representing parts, geometrics and product dimensions, used as an intermediate system for transfer between specific computer-aided design (CAD) products.

IGFET (insulated-gate field-effect transistor)

IGP (Interior Gateway Protocol)
A Transmission Control Protocol/Internet Protocol (TCP/IP) used by interior routers to move information within an autonomous system or group of networks under the control and authority of a single entity. IGPs transfer packets from one network to an adjacent one. Examples are: Enhanced Interior Gateway Routing Protocol (EIGRP), open shortest path first (OSPF) and Routing Information Protocol (RIP).

IGRP (Interior Gateway Routing Protocol)
Cisco Systems proprietary routing algorithm.

IHV (independent hardware vendor)

IIA (Information Industry Association)

IIN (IBM Information Network)

IIOP (Internet Inter-ORB Protocol)

IIS (Internet Information Server)
Microsoft's Hypertext Transport Protocol (HTTP) server, packaged with the NT Operating System.

IKE (Internet key exchange)

ILEC (incumbent local-exchange carrier)

ILPT (instructor-led practical training)
A training method that has some lectures and discussions, but concentrates on giving trainees many chances to practice what they are learning in a risk-free situation.

ILS (Integrated Logistics Strategies)

ILTC (instructor-led training in the classroom)
The most common form of training. It uses lecture sessions and discussions to convey information. It is most commonly used for briefings and high-level education, but many commercial training courses also use this method.

IM (information management)
A method of using technology to collect, process and condense information with a goal of efficient management. Most large enterprises have a central IM function to facilitate this coordination. The primary technologies needed are contained in a set of modeling tools that either have or interface to a production-worthy repository where the information is stored and managed. The repository and tools must be capable of receiving information in a "top-down," "bottom-up," or "middle-out" evolutionary manner.

ILPT and ILTC

	ILTC	ILPT	CBT	MM	Internet
Degree of retention	Low	High	Med. /High	High	Med.
Opportunity to practice	Low	High	Med.	Med.	Med.
Chance to exchange experiences	High	High	Low	Low	Med.
Ability to evaluate results	Med.	Med.	Low	Med.	Med.
Formal structure	High	Low	High	Med.	Med.
Speed of delivery	Med.	High	Low	Low	Med.

CBT = Computer-based training
ILPT = Instructor-led practical training
ILTC = Instructor-led training in the classroom
MM = Multimedia

Source: GartnerGroup

Comparison of ILTC and ILPT with Other Training Methods

I

IM (interactive marketing)
Integrated IM systems consist of two or more of the following functions: personalization, ad management, Web measurement, content management and commerce transaction management.

IMA (Institute of Management Accountants)

IMA (inverse multiplexing over asynchronous transfer mode)

Image and Scanner Interface Specification (See ISIS)

Image Object Content Architecture (See IOCA)

ImagePlus
A document image package, introduced by IBM in 1988, that represented the commercial versions of image systems developed jointly by IBM and two customer "partners," USAA and Citibank. ImagePlus provided generic application software for using document images in common user environments.

image support
Hardware (scanner, workstation, printer) and software support for image as a system-recognized information type. Typically, although not necessarily, support for optical storage devices is included.

image understanding
Image understanding systems analyze captured still video images and extract their content (e.g., color, texture, shape) for indexing or other action. Image understanding is used for content-based retrieval of image archives.

IMAP (Internet Message Access Protocol)
A standard mail server that holds incoming e-mail messages until users log on and download them. It is more sophisticated and has more functionality than Post Office Protocol (POP), which only downloads messages to the client device. The IMAP protocol enables the user to read messages in place, file them into public or private named folders on the server, and synchronizes the client file cabinet with the server file cabinet after an offline session.

IMAP4 (Internet Message Access Protocol 4)
Version 4 of the message-fetching protocol for client/server access to messages stored in an IMAP4 message store on a Simple Mail Transfer Protocol (SMTP) system. This is a superset of the

IM

IM Characteristics	KM Characteristics
Focus on recording and processing explicit information	Focus on capturing tacit and explicit information
Takes information from multiple sources and organizes into database system	Takes information from one source and promotes reuse in other situations
Designed for centralized information storage and control (IS empowerment)	Designed for distributed access, storage and control (end-user empowerment)
Emphasizes inquiries to highly structured repositories	Emphasizes collaboration and sharing
Concerned with information collection, classification and distribution	Enables end-user-defined information relationships and needs
Dependent on well-defined inquiries for retrieval	Employs technologies (i.e., visualization) for knowledge discovery
Required to maintain mission-critical enterprise data	Adds value for growth, innovation and leverage
Productivity for efficiency	Productivity for innovation

IM = Information management
IS = Information systems
KM = Knowledge management

Source: GartnerGroup

Information Management vs. Knowledge Management

services provided by version 3 of the Post Office Protocol (POP3).

IML (initial microprogram load)

IMLC (Indexed Monthly License Charge)
An S/390 software licensing arrangement offered by IBM. It yields charges based on the machine capacity in millions of service units (MSUs), if the machine was not previously available, and has capacity greater than the newly defined upper limit to the Graduated Monthly License Charge (GMLC) Group 80 — approximately 480 million instructions per second (MIPS).

IModem
A data transmission protocol with no error correction; intended for high-speed modems with inbuilt error correction.

impedence
A measure of the electrical property of resistance, expressed in ohms.

IMPL (initial microcode program load)

implementation inheritance
A relationship among classes in which a subclass shares, overrides or supplements operations or data values from one or more superclasses. A subclass is a specialization of one or more superclasses.

implicit tagging
A frame is classified as belonging to a particular virtual local-area network (VLAN) based on the data content of the frame and/or the receiving port.

implode
Compression of detailed data into a summary-level record or report.

Improved Data Recording Capability (See IDRC)

IMS (Information Management System)
The name for two IBM Multiple Virtual Storage (MVS) products, a database management system (IMS/DB) and a transaction-processing monitor (IMS/TM), which are capable of accessing either Database-2 (DB2) or IMS/DB or both. IMS applications run in what are called message-processing regions, each in its own address space. They communicate as needed with the IMS control region, which can be located in a separate MVS address space.

IMS/DB (Information Management System/ Database Manager)
A Multiple Virtual Storage (MVS) database management system (DBMS) that supports the hierarchical data model (with optional extensions for some network data model features). IMS/DB may be used with either Information Management System/Transaction Monitor (IMS/TM) or Customer Information Control System (CICS) to provide online access to the database, or it may be used without a monitor for batch processing.

IMS/DC (Information Management System/ Data Communication)
IMS/DC is the part of Information Management System (IMS) that is used to create online transaction processing (OLTP) applications. Roughly comparable to Customer Information Control System/ Virtual Storage (CICS/VS), IMS/DC became known as IMS/ESA TM (Information Management System/Enterprise Systems Architecture Transaction Manager) when ESA was introduced (see IMS/ ESA TM). IMS/DC has a multiaddress space architecture and is quite fast-which explains why IBM tends to run its DB2 benchmarks with IMS/ DC rather than CICS.

IMS/ESA DM (Information Management System/Enterprise Systems Architecture Database Manager)
IMS/ESA may be used with either IMS/DC (Information Management System/Data Communication)

or CICS/VS (Customer Information and Control System/Virtual Storage) to provide online access to the database.

IMS/ESA TM (Information Management System/Enterprise Systems Architecture Transaction Manager)
The part of Information Management System (IMS) needed to create online transaction processing (OLTP) applications. Until the announcement of Information Management System/Enterprise Systems Architecture (IMS/ESA), IMS/TM was a feature of IMS, not a product separate from Information Management System/Database Manager (IMS/DB). IMS/TM, once called Information Management System/Data Communication (IMS/DC), has a multiaddress-space architecture. It is quite fast, which is why IBM runs its Database-2 (DB2) benchmarks with IMS/DC rather than Customer Information Control System (CICS).

IMS/FP (Information Management System/FastPath)
A functional extension to IBM's Information Management System (IMS) that improves performance for specific transactions, and features high data availability and specialized facilities for very large databases. It was introduced as a separately priced feature of IMS v.1.1.4. With IMS v.1.1.3, FastPath became part of Information Management System/Data Communication (IMS/DC).

IMS/VS (Information Management System/Virtual Storage)
A common IBM host operating environment, usually under the IBM Multiple Virtual Storage (MVS) operating system, oriented toward batch processing and telecommunications-based transaction processing.

IMTS (international message telephone service)

IN (intelligent network)
A telecommunications network offering enhanced facilities such as freephone, premium rate information services, call distribution services (e.g., according to the geographical origin of a call), alternate call billing (sometimes provided through the use of personal calling cards), and virtual private network services. The intelligence to support these facilities is normally provided through specialized network nodes in addition to the normal telecommunications switches.

indefinite delivery/indefinite quantity (See IDIQ)

Independent Computing Architecture (See ICA)

independent software vendor (See ISV)

Indexed Monthly License Charge (See IMLC)

Indexed Sequential Access Method (See ISAM)

industrial computer
A personal or process control computer that is designed to withstand the rigors of the factory floor. Some industrial computers are configured so that maintenance and cold start-up are relatively simple. These devices are used for applications such as data collection, monitoring and programming.

Industry Standard Architecture (See ISA)

INEWS (integrated electronic warfare system)

information architecture
All the sources of information — including paper, graphics, video, speech and thought — that define the enterprise are represented by this layer of applications architecture. It also defines the sources and destinations of information, its flow through the enterprise, as well as the rules for persistence, security and ownership.

Information Context Exchange (See ICE)

information engineering (See IE)

Information Engineering Facility — Texas Instruments (See IEF)

Information Engineering Workbench — KnowledgeWare (See IEW)

information (knowledge) assets
Information relevant to an enterprise's business function, including captured and tacit knowledge of employees, customers or business partners; data and information stored in highly structured databases; data and information stored in textual form and in less-structured databases such as messages, e-mail, workflow content and spreadsheets; information stored in digital and paper documents; purchased content; and public content from the Internet or other sources. See also knowledge management (KM).

information management (See IM)

Information Management System (See IMS)

Information Management System/Database Manager (See IMS/DB)

Information Management System/Data Communication (See IMS/DC)

Information Management System/Enterprise Systems Architecture Database Manager (See IMS/ESA DM)

Information Management System/Enterprise Systems Architecture Transaction Manager (See IMS/ESA TM)

Information Management System/FastPath (See IMS/FP)

Information Management System/Virtual Storage (See IMS/VS)

information path
The functional route by which information is transferred.

Information Architecture

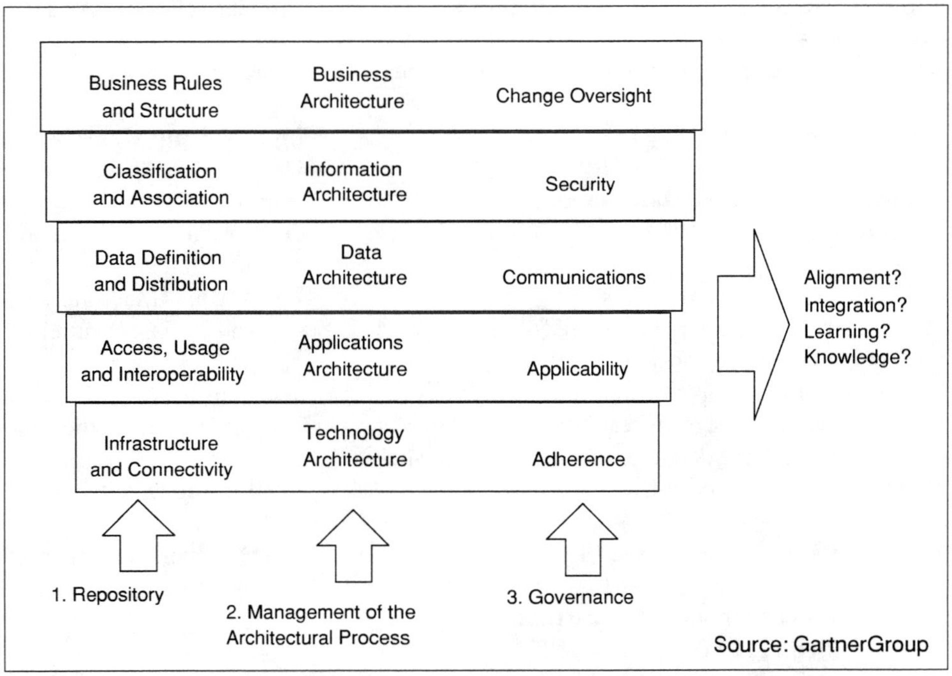

The Role of Information Architecture Within the Overall IT Architecture

information repository
Holds all the information needed to create, modify and evolve a software system, including information on the problem to be solved, problem domain, emerging solution, software process being used, project resources and history, and organizational context.

information resource center (See IRC)

Information Resource Dictionary System (See IRDS)

information retrieval (See IR)

information superhighway
A proposed high-speed computing and communications network to deliver ubiquitous voice, telephony data, video graphics, and more. The Internet itself was originally only cited as a model for the information superhighway, though the popularity of the World Wide Web made it the default successor to the concept. The Web currently falls short in comparison to the initial vision of the information superhighway due to the speed of communications.

information systems (See IS)

Information Systems Management Architecture (See ISMA)

information systems network
A network of multiple operational-level systems and one management-oriented system (centered around planning, control and measurement processes). The network retrieves data from databases and synthesizes that data into meaningful information to support the enterprise.

information technology (See IT)

Information Technology Infrastructure Library (See ITIL)

Information Technology Steering Committee (See ITSTC)

infrared
The portion of the electromagnetic spectrum above radio frequencies but below visible light, with wavelengths between 10 and 780 nanometers. Many lasers emit infrared light.

Initial Graphics Exchange Specification (See IGES)

INMARSAT (International Maritime Satellite Organization)
INMARSAT's work now increasingly covers aeronautical and mobile as well as maritime satellite communications.

INMS (integrated network management system)

Innovative Applications of Artificial Intelligence (See IAAI)

input/output (See I/O)

Input/Output Control System (See IOCS)

Inquire/Text
Content-based retrieval and document management product for IBM Multiple Virtual Storage (MVS) and Virtual Machine (VM) environments from Infodata of Falls Church, Va.

insertion loss
The difference in the amount of power received before and after a device is inserted into a circuit or a call is connected.

INSM (integrated network and systems management)

INSPECT
GartnerGroup's iterative framework for planning and executing application change. The letters stand for: Inventory, Scope, Parse, Examine, Consider options, Tactical solutions.

Institute of Electrical and Electronics Engineers (See IEEE)

instructor-led practical training (See ILPT)

instructor-led training in the classroom (See ILTC)

Insured Rate
In an asynchronous transfer mode (ATM) network, the long-term agreed rate of data throughput.

INTA (International Trademark Association)

INTAP (Interoperability Technology Association for Information Processing)
The Japanese organization concerned with conformance testing for Open Systems Interconnectivity (OSI) products.

integrated applications environment (See IAE)

Integrated Cached Disk Array (See ICDA)

integrated circuit (See IC)

integrated computer-aided software engineering (See I-CASE)

Integrated Coupling Migration Facility (See ICMF)

Integrated Database Application Programming Interface (See IDAPI)

Integrated Database Management System — Computer Associates (See IDMS)

Integrated Definition Methodology (See IDEF1)

integrated delivery system (See IDS)

integrated development environment (See IDE)

integrated digital access (See IDA)

Integrated Digital Network (See IDN)

Integrated Document and Output Management (See IDOM)

INSPECT

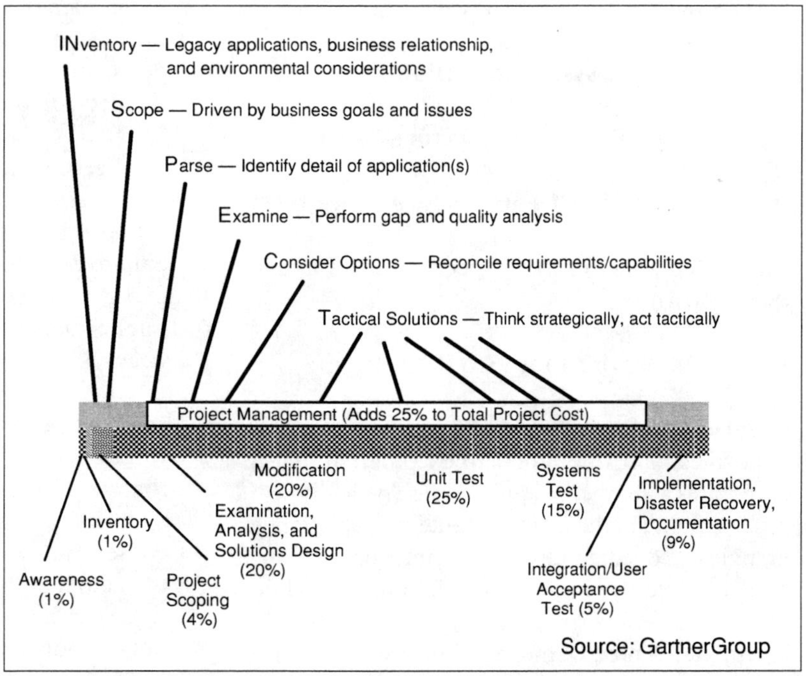

The INSPECT Process

integrated document archive and retrieval system (See IDARS)

integrated document management (See IDM)

integrated e-form management (See IEFM)

integrated e-mail
A facility that enables PC users to create, send, receive, read, forward and file mail through the midrange system mail system directly from an application, without explicitly invoking the mail system.

Integrated IS-IS
A routing protocol based on Intermediate System to Intermediate System (IS-IS) but with support for Internet Protocol (IP) and other protocols. Formerly known as Dual IS-IS.

integrated office system (See IOS)

Integrated On-Demand Network (See ION)

integrated plant system (See IPS)

integrated publishing architecture (See IPA)

Integrated Services Digital Network (See ISDN)

Integrated Services over Specific Link Layers (See ISSLL)

Integrated Service Unit (See ISU)

integrated software
A business software productivity program that incorporates a number of applications (typically word processing, database management, spreadsheet, graphics and communications) into one product, allowing data sharing between all or most modules.

Integrated Voice/Data Terminal (See IVDT)

integrative policy group (See IPG)

Integrion
A private company owned by 18 banks and IBM. Its purpose is to develop and maintain highly scalable and secure online banking solutions for the large-bank marketplace.

integrity
An operating system's ability to ensure that only authorized users can enter a privileged state (supervisor mode, protect key zero, superuser or root). Integrity is a prerequisite for security in an operating system. In Multiple Virtual Storage (MVS), it is the ability to ensure that only authorized users can enter a privileged state (e.g., protect key zero). The term is not synonymous with security, but security requires it. In database technology, it is a broad term denoting the correct state of the database.

intellectual assets
The intellectual assets of an enterprise include its brand names and image; the knowledge of its employees; data and information about processes, experts, products, customers and competitors; and intellectual property.

intellectual (knowledge) capital
Intangible assets of an enterprise that are required to achieve business goals, including knowledge of employees; data and information about processes, experts, products, customers and competitors; and intellectual property such as patents or regulatory licenses. See also knowledge management (KM).

intellectual property
Intellectual property traditionally includes assets that are protected through regulatory methods such as patents, copyrights and regulatory licenses; however, this protection is being expanded to include software and business processes when these can be demonstrated to be original, novel and non-obvious. Customer intelligence and business intelligence may be considered intellectual "prop-

erty" by its owner, depending on its value to enterprise competitiveness and its integration into business processes.

intelligent agents
Dynamic software entities that are self-contained and perform tasks proactively on behalf of a user-initiated process. Uses include World Wide Web and document search and filtering, and network management.

intelligent character recognition (See ICR)

intelligent hub
An evolution of the wiring concentrator, an intelligent hub can also act as a platform for chassis-mounted bridges, routers, terminal servers, gateways, and print servers, and can be fully managed.

Intelligent Input/Output (See I_2O)

intelligent network (See IN)

Intelligent Printer Data Stream (See IPDS)

intelligent terminal
A terminal with some logical capability; a remote device that is capable of performing some editing or other function upon input or output data.

intelligent workstation (See IWS)

interactive
In communications, a term describing time-dependent data communications, typically where a user enters data and then awaits a response message from the destination before continuing.

interactive marketing (See IM)

interactive selling system (See ISS)

Interactive System Productivity Facility (See ISPF)

interactive television (See ITV)

Interactive Terminal Interface (See ITI)

interactive TV/Web TV
Provides two-way access to entertainment, communication, information and transaction services through cable, telephone or wireless networks using a low-cost addition to a television set.

interactive voice response (See IVR)

interactive voice response/voice response unit (See IVR/VRU)

interblock gap (See IBG)

interchange point
A location where interface signals are transmitted.

intercom
An internal communications system that enables calling within the same building, but not outside the system.

interexchange carrier (See IXC)

interexchange channel (See IXT)

interface
The boundary between two pieces of equipment across which all the signals that pass are carefully defined. The definition includes the connector signal levels, impedance, timing, sequence of operation and the meaning of signals.

interface definition language (See IDL)

interface inheritance
An object request broker (ORB) technique for reusing the interface definition language (IDL) from another object implementation (program) in a new one. Unlike implementation inheritance, this does

not make data and code visible and usable by another object.

Interior Gateway Protocol (See IGP)

Interior Gateway Routing Protocol (See IGRP)

InterLATA
A United States term meaning between different local access and transport areas.

interleaving
A multiprogramming technique in which segments of one program are inserted into other programming so that during delays in the processing of one of the programs, the other program can be processed.

Intermediate-System-to-Intermediate-System (IS-IS) Routing
A routing method among Intermediate Systems that requires the end systems, rather than the intermediate systems, to be responsible for providing error correction. IT reduces complexity and overhead of routing protocols.

internal rate of return (See IRR)

International Code Designator (See ICD)

International Electrotechnical Commission (See IEC)

International Frequency Registration Board (See IFRB)

International Maritime Satellite Organization (See INMARSAT)

International Organization for Standardization (See ISO)

International Organization for Standardization/International Electrotechnical Commission (See ISO/IEC)

International Telecommunication Union (See ITU)

International Telecommunication Union-T (See ITU)

International Telecommunications Users Group (See INTUG)

Internet
A loose confederation of independent yet interconnected networks that use the Transmission Control Protocol/Internet Protocol (TCP/IP) protocols for communications. The Internet evolved from research done during the 1960s on a network called the ARPANet. It provides universal connectivity and three levels of network services: connectionless packet delivery, full-duplex stream delivery, and application-level services (mainly electronic mail/e-mail).

Internet 2
An initiative by the research and academic community to build a 2.4-gigabit-per-second (Gbps) network. It outlines a plan for network service providers (NSPs) to converge their data networks and then, much later, their voice and data networks. It has specific plans for creating a closed user group of research and academic institutions that is connected via a high-speed network offering varying classes of services as well as guaranteed quality of service.

Internet Activities Board (See IAB)

Internet address (See IP address)

Internet Administration Framework (See IAF)

Internet Assigned Numbers Authority (See IANA)

Internet-based digital stamping
A technology that will let users download postage from the Internet, then print it on envelopes. It requires an Internet connection and the stamping application, and may require an optional hardware component that resides between the PC and printer and contains the downloaded postage. Enterprises can also access postage directly from vendors' Web sites during the stamping process, so the postage is never stored locally.

Internet commercial publishing revenue (See ICPR)

Internet Control Message Protocol (See ICMP)

Internet Engineering Steering Group (See IESG)

Internet Engineering Task Force (See IETF)

Internet Explorer (See IE)

Internet Information Server (See IIS)

Internet Message Access Protocol (See IMAP)

Internet Message Access Protocol 4 (See IMAP4)

Internet Protocol (See IP)

Internet Relay Chat (See IRC)

Internet Research Steering Group (See IRSG)

Internet Research Task Force (See IRTF)

Internet sales outlet (See ISO)

Internet Server API (See ISAPI)

Internet service provider (See ISP)

Internet Society (See ISOC)

Internet telephony
Use of Internet protocols for transmitting two-way audio signals in real time, as an alternative to traditional telephone carriers.

internet(work)
Two or more networks linked together. A local internet is confined within a single building; a campus internet includes two or more nearby buildings.

Internetworking Operating System — Cisco Systems (See IOS)

Internetwork Packet Exchange (See IPX)

Internetwork Protocol address (See IP address)

interoperability
The ability for a device from one manufacturer to work with one from another.

Interoperability Technology Association for Information Processing (See INTAP)

interpreter
A computer program that translates and executes each source language statement before translating and executing the next one. Also known as incremental coupler.

interprocess communications (See IPC)

interrupt
A jump out of one software program into another due to an external event. A mechanism is usually provided to store the information needed for a return to the interrupted program.

Interswitching System Interface (See ISSI)

IntraLATA
United States term meaning within a single local access and transport area (LATA).

intranet
A network internal to an enterprise that uses the same methodology and techniques as the Internet. It is not necessarily connected to the Internet and is commonly secured from it using firewalls. Intranets often use an organization's local-area networks (LANs) or wide-area networks (WANs). Services include Web sites, collaboration, workflow and messaging services, and applications development.

INTUG (International Telecommunications Users Group)
Formed in 1974, INTUG coordinates users' views and exerts influence at the policy-making level.

inverse multiplexing
Several combined, lower-speed circuits that make up one circuit for greater bandwidth. Inverse multiplexing also pulls together and synchronizes multiple channels at the receiving end of data, voice, or video transmission.

I/O (input/output)
The activity of sending information to or from peripheral devices, terminals, direct-access storage devices (DASDs), tape drives and printers. Physical I/O performance lags behind that of memory and logical technologies.

I/O bound
Refers to programs with a large number of I/O (input/output) operations, which slow the central processing unit (CPU).

I/O channel
Equipment forming part of the input/output system of a computer. Under the control of input/output (I/O) commands, the channel transfers blocks of data between main storage and peripherals.

I_2O (Intelligent Input/Output)
The I_2O initiative seeks to change server input/output (I/O) from a tightly related driver-device structure to a more abstract, layered, message-oriented structure. It is being fostered by the I_2O Special Interest Group (I_2O SIG). The I_2O architecture is designed to facilitate the introduction of new I/O devices while offloading most I/O processing to intelligent I/O processors.

IOCA (Image Object Content Architecture)
A standard definition for the representation of images for interchange between environments. An element of Mixed Object: Document Content Architecture (MO:DCA), IOCA is used in ImagePlus and OS/2 Image Support.

IOCS (Input/Output Control System)
A set of programs used in an operating system that handles all data transfers including opening and closing files.

ION (Integrated On-Demand Network)
The enterprise-oriented part of Sprint's overall strategy to migrate from various transmission, access and switching systems to a Synchronous Optical Network (SONET)/dense wave-division multiplexing (DWDM) enhanced-transmission platform and an asynchronous transfer mode (ATM) core-switching fabric. It is intended to ultimately deliver all local service, local access and long-distance voice and data network services.

IOP (input/output processor)

IOS (integrated office system)
The label applied to second-generation office information systems (OISs) originating from the tight integration between the bundled applications, usually word processing, filing, e-mail, calendars, scheduling and basic decision support.

IOS (Internetworking Operating System — Cisco Systems)
The proprietary software run by Cisco routers and access servers. It supports both local-area network (LAN) and wide-area network (WAN) protocols. It

originated from code developed at Stanford University in the mid-1980s.

IP (Internet Protocol)
Transmission Control Protocol/Internet Protocol (TCP/IP) tracks the address of nodes, routes outgoing messages, and recognizes incoming messages. Current networks consist of several protocols, including IP, Internetwork Packet Exchange (IPX), DECnet, AppleTalk, Open Systems Interconnection (OSI) and LLC2. This wide diversity of protocols results from application suites that assume their own particular protocols. Collapse from this wide variety is inevitable, but users will only be able to reduce this diversity, not eliminate it. Most users will collapse networks into two main protocols: IP and IPX. Installed-base applications and the pain of change will prevent a total reduction to a single backbone protocol.

IPA (integrated publishing architecture)
A GartnerGroup concept that defines the creation, assembly and production functions to support the complete document life cycle. Creation includes document component modeling, authoring, content identification, revision, review and approval; assembly includes document aggregation modeling, on-demand document construction and database interchange; and production includes composition, layout and file formatting for multiple communication channels.

IP address (Internetwork Protocol address or Internet address)
A unique number assigned by an Internet authority that identifies a computer on the Internet. The number consists of four groups of numbers between 0 and 255, separated by periods (dots). For example, 195.112.56.75 is an IP address.

IPC (interprocess communications)
A system that lets threads and processes transfer data and messages among themselves; used to offer services to, and receive them from, other programs.

I_2O

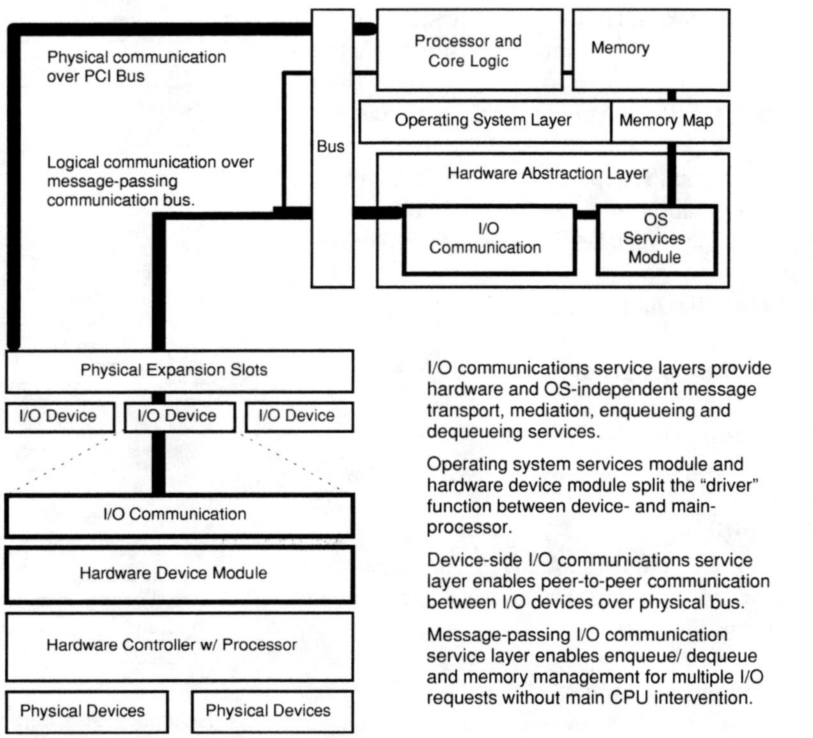

CPU = Central processing unit OS = Operating system
I/O = Input/output PCI = Peripheral Component Interconnect

Source: GartnerGroup

Intelligent Input/Output Architecture

IPDS (Intelligent Printer Data Stream)
IBM format for sending files to a laser printer. It provides an interface to all-points-addressable printers that make possible the presentation of pages containing a mix of different types of data, such as high-quality text, raster image, vector graphics and bar codes. In addition, IPDS provides commands for the management of printing resources such as fonts and overlays; for the control of device functions such as paper sourcing and stacking; for the comprehensive handling of exception functions; and for a complete acknowledgment protocol at the data stream level. IBM has positioned IPDS as the ubiquitous enterprise data stream.

IPG (integrative policy group)
IPGs are responsible for the formulation and maintenance of all policy and procedures regarding an enterprise's intranet. Cross-functional representation on this team is critical and should include the IS department, business units and corporate communications. While the information systems (IS) department should play a major role, facilitation of the team should be provided by someone from a key business unit, if possible.

IPI (Intelligent Peripheral Interface)

IPL (initial program load)

IPM (Impulses Per Minute)
The interruption rate for call progress tones.

IP multicast
A routing technique that enables propagation of Internet Protocol (IP) traffic from one source to many destinations.

IP next generation (See IPng)

IPng (IP next generation)
A new standard intended to replace Internet Protocol (IP) under the auspices of the Internet Engineering Task Force (IETF) under RFC 1752. It offers 128-bit addressing to overcome the limitations of the numbers of IP addresses. It also has facilities for mobile logins and includes authentication.

IPNS (ISDN Private Networking Specification IPNS Forum)
A forum established by major European vendors with the aim of contributing to European and world standards organizations in the area of Integrated Services Digital Network (ISDN) private automatic branch exchange (PABX) networking.

IPS (integrated plant system)
A GartnerGroup-defined architectural model for information technology (IT) and process control

IPA

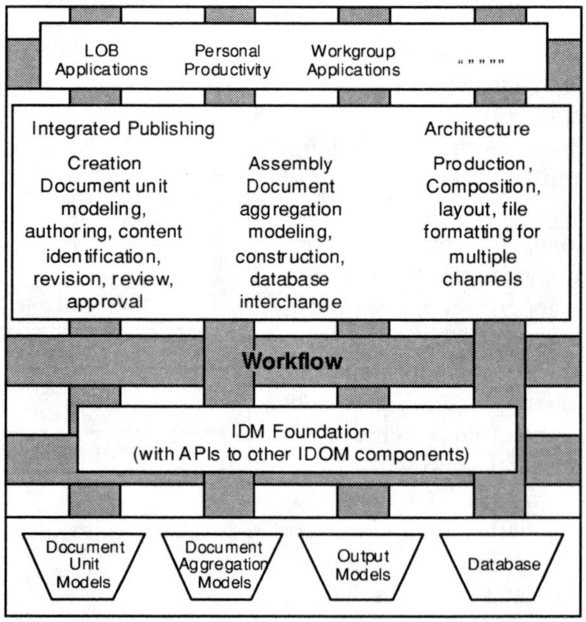

API = Application programming interface
IDM = Integrated document management
IDOM = Integrated Document and Output Management
LOB = Line of business

Source: GartnerGroup

Integrated Publishing Architecture

systems used in manufacturing plants to manage the control and execution of production processes. It differs from other industry models in that it is not hierarchical but rather defines an integrated homogenous collection of cooperating systems.

IPsec (IP Security)
A working group of the Internet Engineering Task Force (IETF) that is developing a security standard for Internet Protocol (IP). Also, the security standard developed by a workgroup of the Internet Engineering Task Force (IETF). It defines protocols for authentication, privacy and data integrity based on encryption and X.509 digital certificates.

IP Security Option (See IPSO)

IP subnet
An Internet Protocol (IP) subnet or subnet mask is a way to subdivide a network into smaller networks to allow a large number of computers on a network with a single IP address.

IPSO (IP Security Option)
A U.S. Government specification defining an optional field in the Internet Protocol (IP) packet header for hierarchical packet security levels on a per-interface basis.

IP Telephony
Voice traffic or data traffic that has traditionally been treated like voice traffic — it is transmitted over an Internet Protocol (IP) network. Three distinct types of IP telephony traffic exist: real-time voice, non-real-time voice and fax.

IPV (in-place value)

IPv4
The current version of Internet Protocol (IP), now informally redesignated to distinguish it from IPv6.

IPX (Internetwork Packet Exchange)
A very widely used routing protocol, based on Xerox's XNS, developed by Novell and implemented in Novell's NetWare. From a user perspective, an IPX implementation allows concurrent dual access to both an application server and a native NetWare file server without imposing memory overhead on client workstations.

IR (information retrieval)
IR products index documents based on the textual content, predominantly through a statistical analysis of words. IR vendors can add collaborative functionality by developing or acquiring it. Traditional collaborative software — groupware — has not effectively integrated IR, relegating content retrieval to searching a single application at a time.

IR (infrared)

IRC (information resource center)
A service organization whose primary mission has been to respond to requests for specific information and to organize and maintain content collections. More recently, its role has expanded to the delivery of desktop content resources.

IRC (Internet Relay Chat)
Real-time conferencing service, organized in channels, on the Internet.

IRDA (Infrared Data Association)

IRDP (ICMP Router Discovery Protocol)
Similar to End System to Intermediate System (ES-IS) but used with Internet Protocol (IP). IRDP enables a host to determine the address of a router it can use as a gateway.

IRDS (Information Resource Dictionary System)
A standard data dictionary specification from the American National Standards Institute (ANSI) X3H4 Committee.

IRLM (IMS Resource Lock Manager)

IRR (internal rate of return)
IRR analysis determines the interest rate and then compares this rate to the "risk-adjusted rate of return."

IRSG (Internet Research Steering Group)

IRTF (Internet Research Task Force)
A committee of network experts concerned with long-term research into Transmission Control Protocol/Internet Protocol (TCP/IP) and the Internet. It is further divided into research groups. The chairperson sits on the Internet Activities Board (IAB).

IS (information systems)
The use of and investment in computer technology by the principal or centralized organization formally charged with the responsibility for computer technology. Often the IS organization is led by a chief information officer (CIO), vice president of the IS organization or director of data processing. IS is also often the formal name of the department within an enterprise that is responsible for information technology. Other common names for the IS department are:

- Management information systems (MIS)
- Data processing (DP)
- Information processing (IP)

ISA (Industry Standard Architecture)
Bus architecture originally developed and evolved by IBM for personal computers, now in the public domain. Now largely superseded by the Peripheral Connect Interface (PCI).

ISA (Instrument Society of America)

ISAM (Indexed Sequential Access Method)
Disk access method that stores data sequentially, maintaining an index of key fields to all the records in the file.

ISAPI (Internet Server API)
A proprietary Web server application programming interface (API) from Microsoft. It is geared to provide direct function-level access to its Internet Information Server.

ISDN (Integrated Services Digital Network)
As a technical standard and design philosophy for digital networks, ISDN provides high-speed, high-bandwidth channels to every subscriber on the public switched telephone network (PSTN), achieving end-to-end digital functions with standard equipment interface devices. ISDN networks enable a variety of mixed digital transmission services to be accommodated at a single interface (including voice, circuit-switched and packet-switched data). Standards for this service are set by the International Telecommunication Union (ITU). Access to the service is at one of two rates: the basic rate of 144 kilobits per second (Kbps) is provided as two B data channels of 64 Kbps and one D control channel of 16 Kbps; the second primary rate is DS1 or 2.048 megabits per second (Mbps) in Europe and 1.544

IR

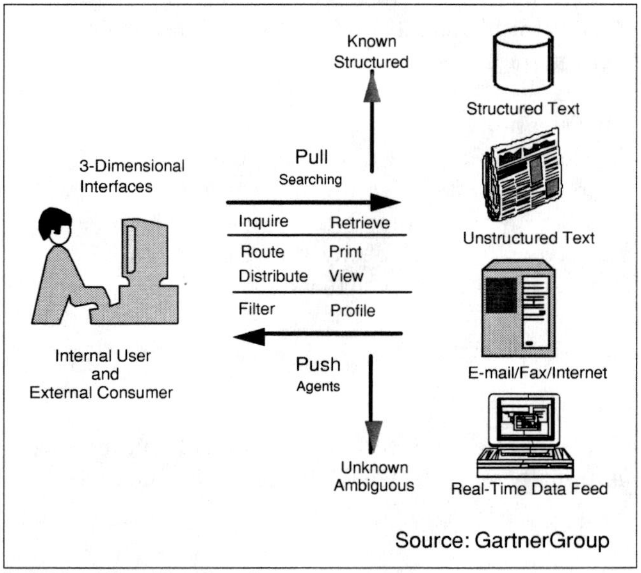

Information Retrieval

Mbps in the United States, Japan, and Canada, and is often referred to as 30BD. Signaling System 7 (SS7), an out-of-band signaling scheme, is key to ISDN implementation.

ISDN PABX Networking Specification Forum
A forum established by major European vendors with the aim of contributing to European and world standards organizations in the area of Integrated Services Digital Network (ISDN) private automatic branch exchange (PABX) networking.

ISDN Private Networking Specification IPNS Forum (See IPNS)

ISDN user part (See ISUP)

I series
International Telecommunication Union (ITU) recommendations for Integrated Services Digital Network (ISDN).

ISIS (Image and Scanner Interface Specification)
A common interface standard that allows consistent scanner control dialogue.

ISL (Integrated Services Layer)

ISMA (Information Systems Management Architecture)
An IBM process model introduced in 1979 that identified 11 key process groups and 42 subprocesses for information technology (IT) management.

ISO (International Organization for Standardization)
A voluntary, nontreaty organization established in 1949, as a technical agency of the United Nations, to promote international standardization in a broad range of industries. ISO's Open Systems Interconnection (OSI) Reference Model establishes guidelines for network architectures.

ISO (Internet sales outlet)
A third-party Web site that attracts visitors looking to buy goods or services. ISOs make money by selling links or ads that lead directly to Web merchant sites or by selling products or services on behalf of Web merchants.

ISO 9000
The international standard for quality control. It is also known as BS5750 and EN29001. The three standards are identical, but they are numbered and published differently by different standards bodies. The worldwide standard is published by the International Organization for Standardization (ISO), and is the one generally referenced. ISO 9000 is a generic standard that any enterprise or individual department can use. It is not specific to the IT industry. The standard is subdivided into three — ISO 9001, ISO 9002 and ISO 9003. Enterprises use some or all of the parts, depending on the nature of their business. Any enterprise can claim that it complies with ISO 9000. To make the claim credible, an external assessor from an accreditation body must evaluate the enterprise's Quality system. ISO 9000 certification does not guarantee quality; it guarantees consistency of approach.

ISOC (Internet Society)
Originating from the U.S. academic community, that ISOC is now a body dedicated to the development of Internet standards via its subgroup, the Internet Engineering Task Force (IETF).

isochronous
A transmission technique characterized by synchronization of the transmitter and receiver, so that packets are delivered to the destination at regular intervals, such as that required by voice or video.

isochronous Ethernet
An extension to the Ethernet standard combining a standard Ethernet channel with 96 64 kilobit per second (Kbps) voice grade channels. It is intended for multimedia applications.

isochronous transmission
A transmission where the signal recurs at known, equally spaced time intervals relative to a single time reference. It is a form of periodic transmission.

ISODE (ISO Development Environment)
A software package that allows the use of TP4 (Transaction Processing Facility 4) and high-layer International Organization for Standardization/Open Systems Interconnection (ISO/OSI) protocols over Transmission Control Protocol/ Internet Protocol (TCP/IP).

ISO/IEC (International Organization for Standardization/International Electrotechnical Commission)
The international body that controls cabling and wiring standards.

ISP (Internet service provider)
A company that provides Internet access to its customers. The majority of ISPs are too small to purchase access directly from the network access point (NAP), and instead buy pieces of bandwidth that are available from larger ISPs. Access to the Internet can be provided either via modem or by direct connection, which offers far higher speeds.
Internet service providers are different from online services, although these services sometimes also provide access to the Internet. Online services provide access to exclusive content, databases and online discussion forums that are not available outside the service.

ISPBX (integrated services private branch exchange)

ISPF (Interactive System Productivity Facility)
ISPF is an IBM-licensed program that is used for writing application programs. It serves as a full-screen editor and dialogue manager and provides a means of generating standard screen panels and interactive dialogues between the application programmer and the terminal user.

ISPF/PDF (ISPF/Program Development Facility)

ISS (interactive selling system)
An ISS is the integration of a marketing encyclopedia system (MES), a sales configuration system, a proposal generation system and an order management system under a common user interface. It is used by organizations to streamline and enhance the selling process. The ISS effectively combines the application functionality that helps enterprises to configure solutions that meet customer needs, while avoiding data entry and business process errors. With an ISS, the salesperson can sit in front of the customer and pull up data to prove value, configure an order, create a proposal, and then turn the proposal into an order and book the order.

ISSI (Interswitching System Interface)
The standard interface between Switched Multimegabit Data Service (SMDS) switches.

ISSLL (Integrated Services over Specific Link Layers)
A working group given the task of providing mappings and interfaces between the advanced services that are available with a number of technologies. Two specific tasks are: looking to negotiate between Resource Reservation Protocol (RSVP) and asynchronous transfer mode (ATM) class-of-service queues, and between Institute of Electrical and Electronics Engineers (IEEE) 802.1p priority queues and asynchronous transfer mode (ATM).

ISSS (Information Society Standardization System)

ISU (Integrated Service Unit)
A single device combining the functions of a channel service unit (CSU) and a data service unit (DSU).

ISUP (ISDN user part)
Provides Integrated Services Digital Network (ISDN) call setup and control and is harmonized to work with ISDN access protocol (ISDN term).

ISV (independent software vendor)
A software producer that is not owned or controlled by a hardware manufacturer; a company whose primary function is to distribute software. Hardware manufacturers that distribute software (such as IBM and Unisys) are not ISVs, nor are users (such as banks) that may also sell software products.

ISVs typically offer products that the primary vendor (i.e., IBM) does not offer, allowing clients of that vendor to round out their software needs. ISVs create price competition and also increase the pace of technology innovation in their markets.

IT (information technology)
This is the common title for the entire spectrum of technologies for information processing, including software, hardware, communications technologies and related services. In general, IT does not include embedded technologies that do not generate data for enterprise use.

ITAA (Information Technology Association of America)

IT asset management
A systematic approach to managing IT assets, including information systems (IS) department staff, end users performing IT support, technology procurement teams, suppliers, facilities, hardware and software.

IT consulting
An area of consulting that includes systems architecture design/development and IS organizational planning, as well as technical consulting — including technology assessment, and hardware and software tuning.

item master file
Typically, this computer file contains identifying and descriptive data, and control values (e.g., dead time and lot sizes). It may also contain data on inventory status, requirements and planned orders. There is normally one record in this file for each stock-keeping unit. Item master records are linked together by product structure records, thus defining the bill of material.

ITEP (Information Technology Executive Program)
A GartnerGroup service.

ITI (Interactive Terminal Interface)
A packet assembler/dissembler (PAD) supporting network access by means of asynchronous terminals.

ITIL (Information Technology Infrastructure Library)
An initiative developed by the Central Computing and Telecommunications Agency consultancy for the government of the United Kingdom. It offers a set of best practices in 24 service delivery and IT service support areas, including help desk, problem management, change management, software distribution and cost control.

ITIL security management
The part of the Information Technology Infrastructure Library (ITIL) designed to guarantee continuity of the IT organization (internal scope) and the quality of IT services (external scope) though service-level agreements (SLAs).

IT infrastructure
The underlying technological components that constitute an organization's systems architecture. The seven components of IT infrastructure are hardware, operating system, network, database, development environment, user interface and application.

ITIS (information technology integration services)

ITO (IT outsourcing)
The contractual vehicle through which end users externalize life cycle service and support operations for their IT infrastructure. Outsourcing can be par-

tial (i.e., modular or selective) or total, and can involve not only operations but also the acquisition of customer assets and personnel. IT outsourcing is divided into five primary market segments: data center operations, network operations, client/server operations, application management and desktop management.

ITOA (IT Overview Analysis)
A GartnerGroup service. Using multiple key metrics, ITOA integrates data from across several IT functional areas to provide a management-level, integrated overview of IT performance and cost.

IT outsourcing (See ITO)

IT Overview Analysis (See ITOA)

ITSEC (Information Technology Security Evaluation and Certification)

ITSTC (Information Technology Steering Committee)
The committee that administers the European Standards Institute/European Electrical Standards Institute's (CEN/CENELEC's) information technology (IT) program. It uses ad hoc expert groups.

IT strategy
Setting or executing corporate business strategy or vision and assistance for the analysis of business processes (re-engineering) or change management.

IT TCO (total cost of ownership for IT infrastructure)

ITU (International Telecommunication Union)
Formerly the International Telegraph and Telephone Consultative Committee (Comité Consultatif International Telegraphique et Telephonique). In March 1993, the name was changed to the International Telecommunication Union or ITU. The ITU is a specialized agency of the United Nations based in Geneva and coordinates and fosters cooperation in the use of international telecommunications systems. It provides communications procedures and practices, including frequency allocation and radio regulations, on a worldwide basis.

Specialized ITU functions include the ITU Telecommunications Standards Sector (ITU-T or ITU-TSS) and the ITU-R (for radio), formerly the Comité Consultatif International de Radio Communications (CCIR), which produces standards and recommendations for radio, television and frequency assignments.

ITV (interactive television)
Devices that allow for the passing of information back and forth through standard television delivery mediums like cable and satellites, using a TV-compatible interface.

IVDT (Integrated Voice/Data Terminal)
A device that features a keyboard/display and a voice telephone instrument. Many contain varying degrees of local processing power, ranging from full personal computer (PC) capacity to directory storage for automatic telephone dialing. They may be designed to work with a specific customer-premises private branch exchange (PBX) or to be PBX independent.

IVDW (intelligent voice/data workstation)

IVR (interactive voice response)
A voice/call-processing option for improving call center functionality and integration. It enables callers to have more flexibility to access information or leave messages. Use of this option can "offload" call volume from agents to the IVR or improve load balancing by having agents handle recorded messages during slow periods. A slowly growing number of IVR developers are now using speech recognition in their applications.

IVR/VRU (interactive voice response/voice response unit)
A technology tool for taking voice queues from callers to progress a request.

IV&V (independent verification and validation)

IWS (intelligent workstation)
A term synonymous with programmable workstation (e.g., a personal computer).

IXC (interexchange carrier)
A long-distance telephone company in the United States that provides service between local access and transport areas (LATAs).

IXSD (international telex subscriber dialing)

IXT (interexchange channel)
A direct circuit between telephone exchanges.

J

Jabber
An Ethernet data packet with more than 1518 bytes and a faulty Frame Check Sequence (FCS).

jack
A device used generally for terminating the permanent wiring of a circuit, access to which is obtained by the insertion of a plug.

JAD (joint applications development)
An effective process for ensuring high levels of functional quality, since it requires participation of the prospective end user. It is especially effective in developing graphical user interface (GUI) requirements.

JAR (Java Archive)

Java
The term "Java" can be applied to the Java platform or to the Java programming language. The Java platform is made up of a set of technologies that provide cross-platform, network-centric computing solutions. The programming language is simply one aspect of the Java platform. The elements of the Java platform are: the Java virtual machine (JVM), which provides a uniform Java byte code emulator for Java's cross-platform runtime environment; the Java programming language, which provides a robust, object-oriented language for constructing Java components and applications; and the standard Java class library packages, which provide sets of reusable services that promote consistency among components and applications.

The Java programming language, which is based on C, was developed by Sun Microsystems. It extends and complements the basic capabilities of Hypertext Markup Language (HTML). Originally developed as a language for consumer-oriented devices such as TV set top boxes, Java became a viable alternative to other programming languages with the rapid growth of the Internet, as it has the potential to work on an unlimited number of computing devices and operating systems. Java permits the creation of applications and application modules ("applets") that run in the Java virtual machine (JVM) on the browser, either as software on a PC or on the Sun picoJava chip, a piece of dedicated hardware. Browsers from both Netscape and Microsoft have a JVM. Java's platform independence and security are designed in, rather than added on, so applications can run on a wide variety of desktop platforms as long as they can run a Java-enabled browser.

Java applet
A small piece of Java code that implements a specific function. Applets may run on a server or be downloaded and run on the client's machine.

JavaBeans
Similar to ActiveX, this Sun Microsystems product lets external applications access each other's services.

Java Native Interface (See JNI)

Java Server Pages (See JSP)

Java servlet
A Java program that operates in conjunction with a Web server, and can output Hypertext Markup Language (HTML) to a browser or even communicate with Java applets. Servlets offer an alternative to using Common Gateway Interface (CGI) and server application programming interfaces (SAPIs) to communicate with Web server processes.

Java Telephony Application Programming Interface (See JTAPI)

Java virtual machine (See Java)

JBIG (Joint Bitonal Image Group)
An emerging standard for black-and-white and gray-scale compression.

JC (Java computer)

JCAHO (Joint Commission on Accreditation of Healthcare Organizations)

JCALS (Joint Continuous Acquisition and Life-Cycle Support)

JCL (Job Control Language — part of MVS)
A language used to communicate with the operating system. JCL is used to tell the system who a user is, what program(s) are being invoked and what resources will be needed.

This specification approximates the Open Database Connectivity (ODBC) functionality for data access and is usable in cross-platform efforts.

JDBC (Java Database Connectivity)

Jdirect
Microsoft's application programming interface (API) for directly accessing Win32 API functions.

JDK (Java Development Kit)

JEDEC (Joint Electronics Device Engineering Council)

JEIDA (Japan Electronic Industry Development Association)

JES (Job Entry Subsystem — part of MVS)
The generic name for the operating system component that reads in jobs, interprets their Job Control Language, schedules their execution, spools the print, and produces the output at the appropriate destination.

JFC (Java Foundation Classes)

JFlow
Officially called Workflow Management Facility (WMF), JFlow was designed to provide a workflow framework and interfaces for the interaction with the workflow process execution environment. In the JFlow model, a workflow system appears externally as a number of different "objects" that must be implemented or simulated. Each invocation of a service creates a "performer object" that knows a reference to a "request object" it must communicate with when it is finished.

JIDL (Java IDL)

Jini
The first distributed-computing product for the consumer market, introduced by Sun Microsystems in July 1998. The system enables any devices that use Sun's Java programming language to communicate and work with one another.

JIT (just in time)
A method of controlling and reducing direct and work-in-process inventory by having suppliers deliver material "just in time" to manufacturing.

JITT (just-in-time training)
A training methodology in which users are trained in a technology just when they begin using it.

jitter
The slight movement of a transmission signal in time or phase that can introduce errors and loss of synchronization for high-speed synchronous communications. See phase jitter.

JMAPI (Java Management API)

JNDI (Java Naming and Directory Interface)

J

JNI (Java Native Interface)
An application programming interface (API) developed by Sun Microsystems that defines a standardized way of naming and calling native functions created in a non-Java language. This is necessary for Java to access pre-existing functionality created with more-historical language environments and languages tuned to specialized purposes. With the JNI, the Java virtual machine (JVM) can locate and invoke native methods, or those native methods can perform Java-specific functions such as creating Java objects, calling Java methods, and even processing Java objects.

Job Control Language (See JCL)

Job Entry Subsystem (See JES)

joint applications development (See JAD)

Joint Bitonal Image Group (See JBIG)

Joint European Standards Institute
The European Standards Institute (CEN) and the European Electrical Standards Institute (CENELEC) combined.

Joint Photographic Experts Group (See JPEG)

Josephson junction
A type of circuit capable of switching at very high speeds when operated at a temperature approaching absolute zero.

JPEG (Joint Photographic Experts Group)
A joint International Organization for Standardization/International Telecommunication Union (ISO/ITU) standard for still-image compression.

JSP (Java Server Pages)
A mechanism that allows Java source code to be embedded into Hypertext Markup Language (HTML) files. This source code is executed on the Web server (by servlets), and the resulting HTML is output to a Web browser. JSP allows many types of developers to interact with both HTML and Java in designing the interface to Java applications.

JTAPI (Java Telephony Application Programming Interface)
A software application programming interface (API) for developing Java-based telephony applications.

JTS (Java Transaction Service)

jukebox
An automatic media handler for an optical disk drive, also called a library. An optical jukebox is designed to move optical platters, of which there are many, in and out of optical drives, of which there are fewer. The intent is to provide a large amount of easily accessed storage in a "near-line" fashion. Jukeboxes use robotics. Similar in concept to music jukeboxes, the robot arm locates the appropriate disk and, if it is not already mounted in a drive, clears the drive and loads the selected disk.

jumper
A patch cable or wire used to establish a circuit, often temporarily, for testing or diagnostics.

junctor
In crossbar systems, a circuit extending between frames of a switching unit and terminating in a switching device on each frame.

junk mail
Unwanted e-mail.

Jupiter
The code name for IBM's system-managed storage project.

just in time (See JIT)

just-in-time training (See JITT)

JVM (Java virtual machine) (See Java)

K

Ka-band
A portion of the electromagnetic spectrum allotted for satellite transmission; frequencies are approximately in the 20 to 30 gigahertz (GHz) range.

Kb or Kbit (kilobit)
One thousand (actually 1,024) bits.

KB or Kbyte (kilobyte)
One thousand (actually 1,024) bytes. Each byte contains eight bits.

KBE (knowledge-based engineering)
A system that encapsulates design knowledge that can be recalled, reused and extended to create product designs.

Kbit (See Kb)

KBMS (Knowledge Base Management System — Trinzic)

Kbps (kilobits per second)
A measure of data transmission rate — one thousand bits of information per second.

KBS (knowledge-based system) (See expert system)

KBTU (one thousand British thermal units)
A unit of measure used to calculate heat.

Kbyte (See KB)

Kerberos
An authentication system used in the Distributed Computing Environment (DCE) to support trust in dial-up, remote or Internet connections. An Internet Engineering Task Force (IETF) standard, Kerberos works by having a central server grant a "ticket" honored by all networked nodes running Kerberos.

Kermit
A packet-oriented public-domain file transfer protocol designed at Columbia University. Kermit uses eight data bits per byte and supports sliding windows and data compression.

kernel
The heart of an operating system, a kernel is the part of the operating system that interconnects with the hardware. With Open Systems Interconnection (OSI) software intended for use in Unix environments, the kernel's functional units are often included as a function library.

key generation unit
A portable, plug-in unit that generates a key for insertion into the encryption device.

key performance indicator (See KPI)

KHz (kilohertz)
A unit equal to 1,000 hertz (one thousand cycles per second).

KIF (Knowledge Interchange Format)

kilobit (See Kb)

kilobits per second (See Kbps)

kilobyte (See KB)

kilohertz (See KHz)

kilovolt ampere (See KVA)

Kinetics Internet Protocol (See KIP)

KIP (Kinetics Internet Protocol)
Allocates Internet Protocol (IP) addresses to AppleTalk computers.

KLOC (one thousand lines of code)

KM (knowledge management)
A discipline that promotes a collaborative and integrated approach to the creation, capture, organization, access and use of an enterprise's information assets. This includes databases, documents and, most important, the uncaptured, tacit expertise and experience of individual workers.

The GartnerGroup KM Process Framework defines five KM activities:

- Create: The activities that result in new knowledge.
- Capture: The activities that enable capture and representation of tacit knowledge in explicit form, thereby moving knowledge from the individual and making it available across the enterprise.
- Organize: The activities that classify and categorize knowledge for storage and retrieval purposes. This includes maintenance of knowledge data as well as the indices, maps and processes that manage it.
- Access: The activities through which knowledge is disseminated to or requested by users
- Use: The application of knowledge to work activities, decisions and opportunities. Use is recursive, i.e., it generates feedback that affects the other activities, and this feedback may be injected into the KM process through any of the other four activities.

KM (Knowledge Module)

K-map (knowledge map)
A representation of concepts and their relationships (e.g., a hierarchy, a taxonomy and a network) that is a navigational aid to enable users to hone in rapidly on the desired concept, and then follow links to relevant knowledge sources (information or people). K-maps model explicit information about people, processes and their information objects, plus the relationships among these elements.

KN (knowledge network)

knowledge access
One of the five activities of the knowledge management process framework. Knowledge access is the retrieval or dissemination of knowledge to users. See also knowledge management (KM).

knowledge architect
The individual who oversees the enterprise architecture implementation; leads the "knowledge architecture team" to identify, organize and provide access to scattered, heterogeneous information in digital and paper form, and leads the knowledge audit to determine and continually re-evaluate the

K-Map

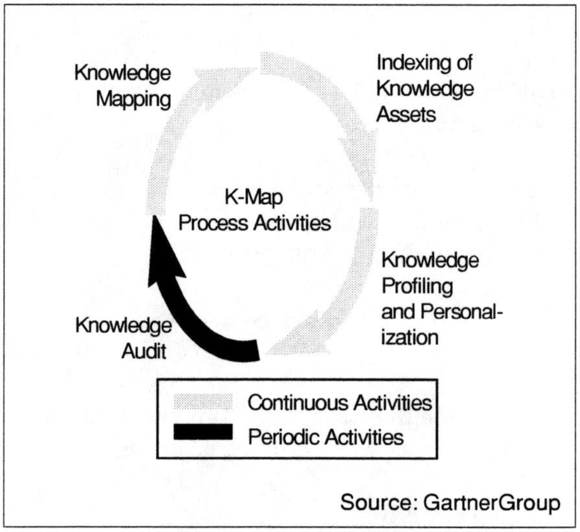

Knowledge-Map Process Activities

specific knowledge needs of users and their business processes. The architect defines knowledge processes and identifies the technology requirements for creating, capturing, organizing, accessing and using knowledge assets. See also knowledge management (KM).

knowledge assets
Information relevant to an enterprise's business function, including captured and tacit knowledge of employees, customers or business partners; data and information stored in highly-structured databases; data and information stored in textual form and in less-structured databases such as messages, e-mail, workflow content and spreadsheets; information stored in digital and paper documents; purchased content; and public content from the Internet or other sources.

knowledge audit
A formal determination and evaluation of how and where knowledge is used in business processes. The audit identifies implicit user needs, as well as explicit information stores. With the audit, enterprises can identify and evaluate all information resources and workflows, and determine enterprise user access requirements. Access requirements will vary widely, from wide access (e.g., policies and procedures) to extremely limited access (e.g., payroll processing). The knowledge audit is a rigorous process using questionnaires, interviews and resource descriptions. See also knowledge management (KM).

knowledge base
The knowledge, which may include assertion, rules, objects and constraints, used by the expert or knowledge-based system. Its organization is based on knowledge representations. The developer of the system or user may be unaware of the underlying knowledge representations, seeing only the domain knowledge representations.

knowledge-based engineering (See KBE)

knowledge-based system (KBS) (See expert system)

knowledge capital
Intangible assets of an enterprise that are required to achieve business goals, including knowledge of employees; data and information about processes, experts, products, customers and competitors; and intellectual property such as patents or regulatory licenses.

knowledge capture
One of the five activities of the knowledge management process framework. Knowledge capture makes tacit knowledge explicit, i.e., it turns knowledge that is resident in the mind of the individual into an explicit representation available to the enterprise. See also knowledge management (KM).

knowledge content owners
Individuals who oversee the definition and delivery of knowledge content for their business processes to the knowledge management environment, and define access privileges to their knowledge resources.

Knowledge Capital

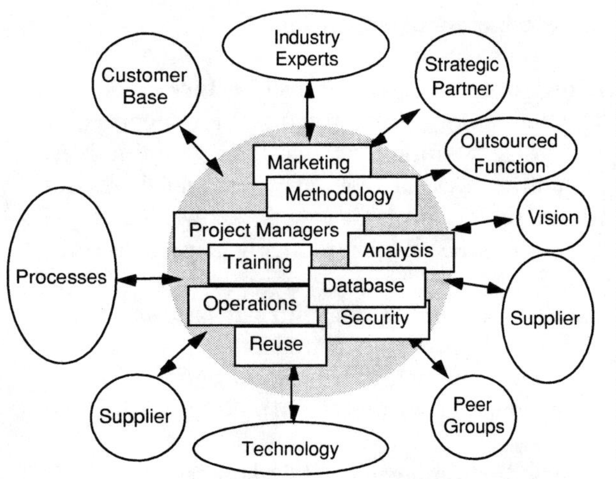

Source: GartnerGroup

Knowledge Capital Structure

K

The human resources executive is an example of a knowledge content owner for benefits information resources, and, as such, is responsible for ensuring that appropriate benefits content is available to support knowledge user and resource requirements, and that appropriate users are granted or denied access to it. See also knowledge management (KM).

knowledge content specialist
A specialist who refines knowledge content from the originating owner into the specific product that the knowledge users require. These specialists have strong skills in the business process and its knowledge resources, as well as in organizing and filtering knowledge into a highly accessible and usable form. As extensions to this definition, external knowledge content specialists manage access to external purchased or subscribed content. See also knowledge management (KM).

knowledge creation
One of the five activities of the knowledge management process framework. Knowledge creation results in new knowledge, or new assemblies of existing knowledge. See also knowledge management (KM).

knowledge management (See KM)

knowledge management architecture
The technology infrastructure that supports an enterprise's knowledge management initiatives, including physical (e.g., intranet, knowledge retrieval tools) and logical (e.g., knowledge maps) dimensions. See also knowledge management (KM).

knowledge management infrastructure
The people, processes and automated systems required to support knowledge management. See also knowledge management (KM).

knowledge management IT manager
An individual who implements and oversees the technology that supports the enterprise knowledge architecture, and ensures the technical integrity of knowledge content and automated processes. See also knowledge management (KM).

knowledge management strategy
A declaration of how the enterprise will use knowledge to compete, and how knowledge management will support its business strategies. A knowledge management strategy may be knowledge-focused if the enterprise's market value is predominantly comprised of intellectual capital, or knowledge-enabled if the enterprise has other equally valuable assets in addition to intellectual capital. See also knowledge management (KM).

knowledge map (See K-map)

knowledge organization
One of the five activities of the knowledge management process framework. Knowledge organization is the classification and categorization of knowledge for navigation, storage and retrieval. This includes knowledge maintenance. See also knowledge management (KM).

knowledge representation
Structures used to store knowledge in a way that relates items of knowledge and permits an inference engine to manipulate the knowledge and the relationships.

knowledge sharing
One of the subprocesses of the knowledge management process framework that incorporates three activities: knowledge capture, knowledge organization and knowledge access. These three activities employ technology, cultural attitudes and business processes to enable people to share knowledge across the boundaries of geography and time. See also knowledge management (KM).

Knowledge Sharing Effort (See KSE)

knowledge use
One of the five activities of the knowledge management process framework. Knowledge use is the application of knowledge to business decisions or opportunities. Use is also recursive, and continually generates feedback that affects and is integrated into the other knowledge activities. See also knowledge management (KM).

knowledge users
Participants in knowledge management programs. They fill the dual roles of applying knowledge in their work tasks and contributing their own knowledge and insight to the enterprise knowledge content. See also knowledge management (KM).

knowledge work management
A discipline that promotes an integrated approach to identifying, managing and sharing all of an enterprise's information assets. Knowledge work management focuses on extending knowledge management to business processes (i.e., policies and procedures as well as unwritten rules).

KPA (key process area)

KPF (knowledge presentation format)

KPI (key performance indicator)
A high-level measure of system output, traffic or other usage, simplified for gathering and review on a weekly, monthly, or quarterly basis. Typical examples are bandwidth availability, transactions per second and calls per user. Often combined with cost measures to build key operating measures of overall system (cost per transaction, cost per user).

KSE (Knowledge Sharing Effort)
An initiative for building standard knowledge representation frameworks, led by a consortium of 18 university and industry research centers. It addresses the entire issues of standard knowledge representation schemes, standard interfaces between objects, the definition of a language that will map between various knowledge representation schemes, and work on standard application-specific ontologies.

KS/NLS (keyword search/natural language search)

KTS (key telephone system)

Ku-band
A portion of the electromagnetic spectrum used increasingly for satellite communications. Frequencies are approximately in the 12 to 14 gigahertz (GHz) range.

KVA (kilovolt ampere)

KW (kilowatt)

KWH (kilowatt hour)

K

L

L2F (Layer 2 Forwarding — Cisco)
A virtual private network.

L2TP (Layer 2 Tunneling Protocol)
The merged virtual private network (VPN) tunneling protocols of Microsoft (Point-to-Point Tunneling Protocol — PPTP) and Cisco (Layer 2 Forwarding — L2F).

laboratory information management system (See LIMS)

labor management system (See LMS)

LAMA (Local Automatic Message Accounting)
The combination of automatic message accounting equipment, automatic number accounting equipment, and automatic number identification equipment in the same office. In such a system, a subscriber-dialed call can automatically be processed without operator assistance.

LAN (local-area network)
A geographically limited communication network that connects users within a defined area. A LAN is generally within a building or small group of buildings and is managed and owned by a single enterprise. The shorter distances within a building or campus enable faster communications at a lower cost than wide-area networks (WANs). Although an increasing number of LANs use Internet standards and protocols, they are normally protected from the public Internet by firewalls.

LANs are generally used to perform the following functions:

- Print on printers attached to the network.
- Transfer data or software to or from other systems attached to the network.
- Send e-mail to other users on the network.
- Access wider-area networks, including the Internet, via a direct connection from the network, for external file transfer, e-mail, facsimile, group collaboration and video-conferencing.

LAN bridging
Multiple physical local-area networks (LANs) can be connected with local-or wide-area connections to support a single logical LAN environment.

LANDA (Local Area Networks Dealers Association)

LANDesk Configuration Manager (See LCM)

LANDesk Management Suite (See LDMS)

LANE (LAN emulation)
An important feature for the wide acceptance of asynchronous transfer mode (ATM) proposed as a standard by the ATM Forum. It makes (ATM) resemble Ethernet or Token Ring — but not Fiber Distributed Data Interface (FDDI) — to the local network. It allows broadcast and multicast messages. Sitting at the Media Access Control (MAC) layer, it is protocol-independent, not recognizing the Network Layer at all.

LANE 2.0 (LAN emulation 2.0)
In July 1997, the Asynchronous Transfer Mode (ATM) Forum ratified a standard that split the local-area network emulation (LANE) standard into two sections — LAN user-to-network interface (LUNI) and LAN network-to-network interface (LNNI). This added considerable functionality to campus

networks while maintaining interoperability with traditional routed networks and LANE 1.0. LANE 2.0 must be implemented to run Multiprotocol over ATM (MPOA). While most of the market's attention has been placed on the LNNI features of redundancy and scalability, only the LUNI portion of LANE 2.0 was ratified at this time. Most vendors already provide LNNI features in their campus products.

LAN emulation (See LANE)

LAN emulation 2.0 (See LANE 2.0)

LAN emulation client (See LEC)

LAN emulation server (See LES)

LAN performance monitor
A tool or toolset (hardware/software) to allow local or remote monitoring of local-area network (LAN) traffic and problems.

LAN switching (See Layer 2 switching)

LAN user-to-network interface (See LUNI)

LAP (Link Access Procedure)

LAP-B or LAPB (Link Access Procedure — Balanced)
A subset of High-Level Data Link Control (HDLC) used in Open Systems Interconnection (OSI) to control Layer 2 functions.

LAP-D or LAPD (Link Access Procedure — D Channel)
A data link layer procedure using D Channel communications, typical of Integrated Services Digital Network (ISDN).

LAPM (Link Access Procedure for Modems)
The Automatic Repeat Request (ARQ) used by modems implementing V.42 error correction.

laptop computer
A portable personal computer (PC) that can be easily used in multiple environments. The portability of the laptop enables individuals to take all of their software, files and applications with them, whether they are in the office, at home or on an airplane. At minimum, laptops include a keyboard, a flat display screen, a central processing unit (CPU), a battery and AC adapter, and a hard disk drive. They are frequently also equipped with compact disc read-only memory (CD-ROM) or floppy disk drives, modems and a variety of communication ports.

Given their small size, laptop computers generally do not have the same performance levels as desktop PCs. For example, laptops usually have smaller keyboards and display screens than those used on larger desktop computers. To compensate for this sacrifice, laptop computers usually have ports to connect external devices such as monitors or keyboards.

LAR (large-account reseller)

large object (See LOB)

large-scale integration (See LSI)

laser
A device that emits a highly coherent beam of light. The term stands for "light amplification by stimulated emission of radiation." A typical laser has an active medium, which emits light, and a cavity structure, which selects certain wavelengths and directions for the emitted light. Lasers convert electrical energy into radiant energy in the visible or infrared parts of the spectrum, emitting light with a small spectral bandwidth. For this reason, they are widely used in fiber optic communications, particularly as sources for long-haul links.

laser disk
An analog or digital storage medium written and read by laser.

LAT (Local Area Transport)
A protocol within Digital Equipment's DECnet for the exchange of small packets of data between Digital Equipment hosts and terminal servers in a local-area network (LAN) environment.

LATA (local access and transport area)
A local telephone network area controlled and operated by a local-exchange carrier (LEC), e.g., one of the Bell operating companies (BOCs). A LATA is one of approximately 200 local telephone companies serving areas generally encompassing the largest standard metropolitan statistical areas. Circuits and calls within a LATA (intra-LATA) are generally the sole responsibility of the LEC, while interexchange carriers (IXCs), such as AT&T or MCI, handle circuits and calls that cross LATA boundaries (inter-LATA).

latency
The time interval during which a network station seeks access to a transmission channel and access is granted or received.

LAWN (local area wireless network)

layer
In the Open Systems Interconnection (OSI) reference model, refers to a collection of related network-processing functions that constitute one level of a hierarchy of functions.

Layer 2
The term used to describe the Media Access Control layer of the International Organization for Standardization (ISO) model where Ethernet, Token Ring, and Fiber Distributed Data Interface (FDDI) reside.

Layer 2 Forwarding — Cisco (See L2F)

Layer 2 switching
Layer 2 switching, commonly called LAN (local-area network) switching, is the transparent wire speed connection of at least two LAN segments to form a single, logical LAN. In this type of switching, application-specific integrated circuits (ASICs) or switching integrated circuits (ICs) provide wire speed performance to link LANs together. Local traffic stays on each segment, and only traffic destined off the segment will be transmitted by the switch. Common switching protocols include Institute of Electrical and Electronics Engineers (IEEE) 802.1D Spanning Tree, IEEE 802.1Q, and IEEE 802.1P.

Layer 2 Tunneling Protocol (See L2TP)

Layer 3
The term used to describe the network layer or Layer 3 of the International Organization for Standardization (ISO) model where protocols such as Internet Protocol (IP) reside.

Layer 3 switching

1. Application-specific integrated circuit (ASIC) or hardware-based routing: Routing technology has been modified for performance with the support of many routing functions performed within the hardware. This provides network-layer routing of such protocols as Internet Protocol (IP) and Internetwork Packet Exchange (IPX) at wire speed performance of more than one gigabit per second full duplex per port.

2. Route once, switch many: This is a tactical technology that was implemented by local-area network (LAN) vendors to use switches to offset performance and latency problems with older routers. With the switch "front ending" a router, the packets go through the switch and the switch allows the first packet to go to the router, which performs address resolution and frame regeneration, and then forwards the packet back to the switch toward the destination. Subsequent packets in a flow are handled by the switch, with no help from the router, by using the information that was learned by the switch from the first routed packet.

3. Fully proprietary implementations: These implementations are numerous, but are falling by the wayside in campus LANs due to their complexity, their need for constant management and their divergence from industry direction. Examples of such implementations include switching between virtual local-area networks (VLANs) at Layer 2 and desktop software for shortcuts between VLANs or subnets.

Layer 4
The transport layer of the International Organization for Standardization (ISO) model where such protocols as Transmission Control Protocol (TCP) and User Datagram Protocol (UDP) reside.

Layer 4 switching
An industry term that is misleading and incorrect. While it is physically impossible to switch in Layer 4, Layer 4 "switching" is, by definition, the control of traffic through the use of policies or filters using Layer 4 or transport layer protocol port IDs to differentiate and act upon application-specific traffic.

LBO (Line Build Out)
A feature of some channel service units (CSUs). Switchable attenuators adjust signal strength; needed when the CSU is too close to a T1 repeater.

LCC (leadless chip carrier)

LCCM (LAN Client Control Manager)

LCD (liquid crystal display)
A low-powered flat-panel device that displays characters created from liquid crystal molecules that are controlled by an electrical field.

LCD (lowest common denominator)
One way to build portable applications is to support only those functions that are provided on all of the target platforms. This "lowest common denominator" approach enables the resulting program to run on any of the required platforms at the expense of not employing the special added-value features offered on those platforms.

LCF (Lightweight Client Framework — Tivoli)

LCM (LANDesk Configuration Manager)
A desktop management tool from Intel intended to facilitate desktop operating system and application upgrades.

LCO (lower cost of ownership)

LCR (least-cost routing)
See ARS (automatic route selection).

LCU (line control unit)
In data communications, a special-purpose processor that controls input/output of communication lines not directly accessed by the computer.

LDAP (Lightweight Directory Access Protocol)
A server-to-server interface for directory information exchange among directories, devised as a low-cost, simpler implementation of the X.500 protocol DAP. It facilitates the implementation of replication and chaining among dissimilar directories. Proposed by the University of Michigan, it was adopted by Netscape in 1996 for directory lookup, and has become the preferred access path for looking up directory information not only in X.500 directories, but also in many other directory structures on the Internet. Version 2 adds services, and version 3 enhances services that can be used to download sets of records from one directory to another, and permits a certain amount of update. Security is weak in v.2, but is improving in v.3. Vendor enhancements and implementation of chaining and referral are strengthening LDAP back-end services.

LDMS (LANDesk Management Suite)
A desktop management tool for software distribution, inventory and remote control from Intel.

LDO (low dropout)

leaky PBX
A private branch exchange (PBX) that allows incoming private-line (tie line) traffic to access the local exchange.

leased line
A dedicated circuit, typically supplied by the telephone company or transmission authority, that permanently connects two or more user locations and is for the sole use of the subscriber. Such circuits are generally voice grade in capacity and in range of frequencies supported, are typically analog, are used for voice or data, can be point-to-point or multipoint, and can be enhanced with line conditioning. Also called a private line, tie line (TL) or dedicated facility.

least-cost routing (See ARS)

least total cost
A dynamic lot-sizing technique that calculates the order quantity by comparing the carrying cost and the setup (or ordering) costs for various lot sizes and selects the lot where comparisons are not nearly equal.

LEC (LAN emulation client)
The end-station part of local-area network emulation (LANE) under asynchronous transfer mode (ATM).

LEC (local-exchange carrier)
The carrier or local telephone company that handles local access and transport area (LATA) traffic, e.g., one of the Bell operating companies (BOCs) or any of the independent telephone companies.

LED (light-emitting diode)
A semiconductor that produces light when activated.

legacy application or system
An information system that may be based on outdated technologies, but is critical to day-to-day operations. Replacing legacy applications and systems with systems based on new and different technologies is one of the information systems (IS) professional's most significant challenges and a big opportunity for IS consultants. As enterprises upgrade or change their technologies, they must ensure compatibility with old systems and electronic data formats that are still in use.

Lempel-Ziv
A compression algorithm developed in the 1970s and selected as the basis for the International Telecommunication Union's (ITU) V.42 bis compression standard.

LANE network-to-network interface (See LNNI)

LEN (Low-Entry Networking)
An IBM networking architecture introduced in 1986. It is an Advanced Program-to-Program Communications (APPC) application and a potential low-end alternative to Systems Network Architecture (SNA). SNA is complex and, for department environments, difficult to manage. LEN uses Synchronous Data Link Control (SDLC) as the backbone protocol and possesses a self-contained network management capability that is less comprehensive than IBM's traditional methods but is much easier to set up and operate.

LEO (low earth orbit or low earth orbiting)

LES (LAN emulation server)
The part of local-area network emulation (LANE) under asynchronous transfer mode (ATM) that resides on the server.

lessee
An entity that contractually obtains use of equipment in return for payments over a specified time.

lessor
An entity that conveys a possession of specified property to a lessee for a period of time.

level
1. In data management structures or communication protocols, the degree of subordination in a hierarchy.
2. Measurement of signal power at a specific point in a circuit.

LEW (logical early warning)

LF (low frequency)
Generally indicates frequencies between 3 and 300 kilohertz (kHz).

library
A data management system for documents frequently, though not necessarily, organized in a hierarchy of folders and drawers. Also called a file cabinet.

LIDM (line impact dot matrix)
A printing technology using a ribbon and an array of impact elements; suitable for making carbon copies.

LIFF (line impact fully formed)
A printing technology using a ribbon and an array of character wheels; suitable for making carbon copies.

LIFO (last in, first out)

light-emitting diode (See LED)

lightwave communications
A term sometimes used in place of "optical communications" to avoid confusion with visual information and image transmission such as facsimile or television. See also fiber optics.

Lightweight Directory Access Protocol (See LDAP)

limited distance modem
A device that translates digital signals into analog signals (and vice versa) for transfers over limited distances. Some operate at higher speeds than modems that are designed for use over analog telephone facilities.

LIMS (laboratory information management system)
Application software used to manage a collection of samples, the testing of those samples in a laboratory, and the reporting of test results. LIMSs can be found in multiple industries and are used within manufacturing as well as environmental and medical practices.

line
1. A communications path between two or more points, including a satellite or microwave channel.
2. In data communications, a circuit connecting two or more devices.
3. Transmission path from a nonswitching subscriber terminal to a switching system.

Linear Tape Open (See LTO)

line balancing
The assignment of tasks to multiple workstations so as to minimize the number of workstations and the total amount of unassigned time at all stations.

Line Build Out (See LBO)

line conditioning (See conditioning)

line control unit (See LCU)

line driver
A communications transmitter/receiver used to extend the transmission distance between terminals and computers that are directly connected; it acts as

an interface between logic circuits and a two-wire transmission line.

line hit
Electrical interference causing the introduction of undesirable signals on a circuit.

line impact dot matrix (See LIDM)

line impact fully formed (See LIFF)

line level
Signal strength on a transmission channel.

line load control
Equipment in a telephone system that provides a means by which essential paths may be ensured continuity of service under overloaded conditions. This is generally accomplished by temporarily denying originating service to some or all of the nonessential lines.

line loading
The process of installing loading coils in series with each conductor on a transmission line, usually 88 millihenry coils installed at 6,000-foot intervals.

line of business (See LOB)

line of sight (See LOS)

line processing
The processing of transactions as they occur, with no preliminary editing or sorting before they enter the system. See also batch processing.

line speed
The maximum data rate that can be reliably transmitted over a line.

line switching
See circuit switching.

line terminating equipment (See LTE)

line turnaround
The time between transmission of one block and the time the next one is sent.

link

1. Physical circuit between two points.
2. Conceptual (or virtual) circuit between two users of a packet switched (or other) network that enables them to communicate, even when different physical paths are used.

Link Access Procedure — Balanced (See LAP-B)

Link Access Procedure — D Channel (See LAP-D)

Link Access Procedure for Modems (See LAPM)

link layer
Layer 2 of the Open Systems Interconnection (OSI) Reference Model, between the physical and network layers, concerned with the transmission of data between adjacent network nodes.

Link Problem Determination Aid (See LPDA)

link redundancy level
The ratio of actual number of paths to the minimum number of paths required to connect all nodes of a network.

links (See hot links)

Link State Protocol
Any routing protocol derived from the Dijkstra algorithm such as Shortest Path First (SPF), Open Shortest Path First (OSPF), and intermediate system to intermediate system (IS-IS). The routers using this protocol update each other and learn network topology by periodically broadcasting link state data across the network. The data from each router

includes only the cost and identification of those networks directly connected to that router. All routers on a network compile tables of routers and connections and can then calculate optimal paths from themselves to each link.

Linpack
An early benchmark for scientific applications, now replaced by the SPECmark.

Linux
A version of Unix developed by Linus Torvalds, who sought to champion openness and counter the closed nature of vendor-proprietary operating systems (OSs). The Linux credo says that the software must be made available as open-source code, enabling anyone to read the coding rules and submit improvements. The source code is accessible free on the Web or else it is virtually given away and vendors derive their revenue from utilities and support.

liquid crystal display (See LCD)

LIS (laboratory information system)

LISP (List Processing)
An object-oriented programming language.

little-endian
A method of storing or transmitting data where the most significant bit or byte is presented last. See big-endian.

LLC (Logical Link Control)
A protocol developed by the Institute of Electrical and Electronics Engineers (IEEE) 802 standard, common to all of its local network standards, for data link-level transmission control. It is the upper sublayer of the IEEE layer 2 — Open Systems Interconnection (OSI) — protocol that complements the Media Access Control (MAC) protocol (IEEE 802.2).

LMCS (Local Multipoint Communications Systems)

LMDS (local multipoint distribution service)

LMI (Link Management Interface)

LMI (Local Management Interface)

LMM (local modifications memory)
A technology that remembers manual changes to the graphical user interface (GUI) design and reapplies them should the screen need to be reconverted and generated.

LMS (labor management system)
A system that provides labor productivity reporting and labor planning capabilities. Labor planning provides the ability to analyze workforce requirements given a certain amount of work to be performed and a standard unit of time to perform each element of work. Labor productivity provide the ability to measure and report the performance of individuals, groups, or facilities vs. a pre-defined standard for performing each defined element of work.

LNA (low-noise amplifier)

LN/AM (learning network/association model)

LN:DI (Lotus Notes: Document Imaging)

LNNI (LAN emulation (LANE) network-to-network interface)
The interface between two local-area network emulation (LANE) servers. It is part of the LANE 2.0 specification.

LNP (local number portability)
The ability to change local phone service provider while retaining the same phone number.

LNP (logistics network planning)
The class of tools required to analyze the trade-offs among inventory quantities, number of warehouses and their locations, and transportation costs to most profitably support a desired level of customer service. LNP is a proven scientific method for analyzing the required cost and service levels that warehouses need to meet specified customer service objectives.

LNTT (line nonimpact thermal transfer)

load
To copy a program into the memory of a computing device so that it can later be used for processing.

load balancing
The ability of processors to schedule themselves to ensure that all are kept busy while instruction streams are available.

load balancing for station/trunk lines
Traffic balancing may be required when system traffic limits are approached. This feature provides the capability, during installation or on an in-service system, to change specific station and trunk terminations on the private branch exchange (PBX) system switching network with minimum installer effort and without requiring number changes for the purpose of balancing the traffic load on the switch network.

loading
Adding inductance (load coils) to a transmission line to minimize amplitude distortion.

loading coil
An induction device employed in local loops, generally those exceeding 5,500 meters in length, that compensates for the wire capacitance and serves to boost voice grade frequencies. They are often removed for new-generation, high-speed, local-loop data services as they can distort data signals at higher frequencies than those used for voice.

LOB (large object)
A data type in the Oracle database architecture.

LOB (line of business)
A corporate subdivision focused on a single product or family of products.

LOC (line of code)

local access and transport area (See LATA)

local area network (See LAN)

Local Area Transport (See LAT)

Local Automatic Message Accounting (See LAMA)

local central office (See local exchange)

local-exchange carrier (See LEC)

local line (See loop)

local modifications memory (See LMM)

local number portability (See LNP)

local telephone exchange (See LTE)

local systems environment
Those resources that exist in a real, open system but that are outside the scope of the Open System Interconnection (OSI) environment.

local trunk
Trunks between local exchanges.

location broker
Middleware that automatically matches a client query with whichever server has the most suitable services, data and computing resources to accomplish the task.

lock
A means of preventing two users from trying to update the same data simultaneously.

LOCT (Layered Open CryptoToolkit)

logical channel number
The number assigned to a virtual call on a packet-switched network.

Logical Link Control (See LLC)

logical terminal
A device addressable by its logical function rather than its physical address. Translation from logical to physical addresses is achieved by a common routine using a table.

Logical Unit (See LU)

Logical Unit 6.2 (See LU 6.2)

login or logon
The procedure by which a user begins a terminal session.

logistics network planning (See LNP)

logistics networks
Logistics networks are like computer networks that can be configured by different hubs, routers and transmission lines. (The logistics network corollaries are warehouses, replenishment rules and trucking companies.) Tools exist to model and optimize the performance of the network. These systems rationalize and quantify the role of each warehouse in satisfying corporate objectives. These systems run on desktops or workstations and should be considered end-user power tools.

logoff or logout
The procedure by which a user ends a terminal session.

LOINC (Logical Observation Identifiers, Names and Codes)

long-haul
Long distance — telephone circuits that cross out of the local exchange.

longitudinal balance
A measure of the electrical balance between the two conductors (tip and ring) of a telephone circuit. Specifically, it is the difference between the tip-to-ground and ring-to-ground AC signal voltages, expressed in decibels.

Longitudinal Redundancy Check (See LRC)

look and feel
The appearance and behavior of a graphical user interface (GUI) to the end user (who sees it as part of an application), determined by the tools and style guide provided by the vendor (and by whether the software developer obeys these guidelines).

loop
A local circuit between an exchange and a subscriber telephone station. Also called subscriber loop and local line.

loopback
A test of the performance and quality of a line and/or terminating equipment. See analog loopback and digital loopback.

loosely coupled multiprocessing
A configuration of several processors, each with its own memory, that execute user and operating system code independently.

LOS (line of sight)
A characteristic of some open-air transmission technologies where the area between a transmitter and a receiver must be clear and unobstructed. This applies to microwave, infrared and open-air laser-type transmissions that operate at frequencies which

transmit through the air in a perfectly straight line. A clear, open-air, direct transmission path is one that is free of obstructions such as buildings but is in some cases, impeded by adverse weather or environmental conditions.

loss (transmission)
The decrease in the energy of signal power in transmission along a circuit due to the resistance or impedance of the circuit or equipment.

lossless compression
A data compression technique where the recovered data after decompression is precisely the same as before compression.

lossy compression
A data compression technique where the recovered data after decompression is different from the data that was compressed, though it will not be perceived as such by an observer.

Low-Entry Networking (See LEN)

lower-CASE tool
A computer-aided software engineering (CASE) tool for application generation rather than application modeling.

lowest common denominator (See LCD)

low frequency (See LF)

LP (load point)

LPAR (logical partition)

LPD (line printer daemon)

LPDA (Link Problem Determination Aid)
IBM's de facto standard for modem management in NetView environments.

LRC (Longitudinal Redundancy Check)
A data communications error-trapping technique in which a character is accumulated at both the sending and receiving stations during the transmission and is compared for an equal condition, which indicates a good transmission of the previous block.

LRU (least recently used)

LSB (least-significant bit)

LSI (large-scale integration)
Between 3,000 and 100,000 transistors on a chip.

LSPR (Large System Performance Reference)

LSSU (Link Status Signal Unit — ISDN term)

LSW (least-significant word)

LTE (line terminating equipment)
Devices that originate or terminate signals.

LTE (local telephone exchange)
The exchange in which subscribers' lines terminate. It has access to other exchanges and to national trunk networks. Also called local central office and end office.

LTL (less than truckload)

LTO (Linear Tape Open)
Technology from Hewlett-Packard, IBM and Seagate Technology, designed to establish an open tape architecture with road maps extending out four generations of drives. The consortium developed two formats to address the needs of read-intensive applications, which require fast data access as well as write-intensive applications, which require high capacity.

LU (Logical Unit — part of SNA)
IBM's term for a logical node that is the user's "port" into a Systems Network Architecture (SNA)

network. LU 1 is a high-performance print data stream and a 3270 data stream. LU 6 enables host-to-host data exchange, and provides a peer-to-peer data stream.

LU 6.2 (Logical Unit 6.2)
An IBM Systems Network Architecture (SNA) protocol. LU 6.2 is a strategic device-independent process-to-process protocol; it also supports asynchronous (store-and-forward) networking. It provides the facilities for peer-to-peer communications between two programs. Among other things, this means that programs and small/midrange computer systems can use LU 6.2 (along with PU 2.1) to establish and control sessions with each other, without host mainframe participation. When LU 6.2 is installed in devices such as PCs and cluster controllers, required functionality, such as multiple sessions among those devices and System/370 hosts, becomes available.

LUN (logical unit number)

LUNI (LAN user-to-network interface)
The section of local-area network emulation (LANE) 2.0 that provides support for a new multicast function in the Broadcast and Unknown Server (BUS) and the multiplexing of extended local-area networks (ELANs) within a single virtual circuit (VC).

lurker
A user who does not participate in a discussion, chat conversation or video gathering, but observes the activity.

LVI (Logical Volume Image)

LVS (Logical Volume Series — Amdahl)

LZS (Lempel-Ziv-Stac)

M

MAC (Media Access Control — IEEE)
The methods used to gain access to the physical layer of a local-area network (LAN).

MAC (message authentication code)
A way of confirming that a message has not been tampered with.

MAC (moves, adds and changes)

MAC address
The 48-bit code for layer 2 networking maintained by the Institute of Electrical and Electronics Engineers (IEEE) and hardwired into network adapters. Also called Ethernet address.

MAC/R (moves, adds, changes and remove)
A component of IBM Asset Services. It provides a single point of contact for all requests and implements a standard process including real-time tracking, scheduling, performing, customer sign-off and updating the asset repository.

MACRS (Modified Accelerated Cost Recovery System)
The current tax depreciation system introduced by the Tax Reform Act of 1986. It is generally effective for all servers placed in service after year-end 1986.

MAD (mass-access device)

MAD or MA&D (mergers, acquisitions and divestitures)

MAED (Model Architecture Environment Design — Manager Software Products)

Magic Quadrant
A two-dimensional graphical framework developed by GartnerGroup that places a particular set of vendors from a specific technology industry sector into a strategic matrix. GartnerGroup analysts use multiple objective and subjective criteria to evaluate individual vendors, presented on two axes:

- Completeness of vision (x-axis). Measures the depth and breadth of a vendor's goals, its knowledge of the markets and customers it serves, and how it is positioned to address future industry scenarios.
- Ability to execute (y-axis). Measures the ability of the vendor to execute its vision. Focuses on the firm's management team and financial stability; sales channels; quality of research and development; its installed product base in the market; its service and support reputation; and its track record in delivering products on time.

magnetic-ink character recognition (See MICR)

magneto-optic (See MO)

mail API (See MAPI)

mail-aware application
A mail-enabled application that is complete without mail but can use messaging services.

mail-enabled application
An application that uses messaging services.

mail-reliant application
A mail-enabled product that is incomplete without mail.

Main Distribution Frame (See MDF)

mainframe
A large-capacity computer system with processing power that is significantly superior to PCs or midrange computers. Traditionally, mainframes have been associated with centralized, rather than distributed, computing environments. Skilled technicians are required to program and maintain mainframes, although client/server technology has made mainframes easier to operate from the user's and programmer's perspectives. They are generally used by large organizations to handle data processing for companywide administrative tasks like payroll or accounts payable.

mainframe data center (See MDC)

maintenance, repair and operations (See MRO)

MAN (metropolitan-area network)
A technology that evolved from local-area network (LAN) designs, but is optimized for longer distances (more than 50 kilometers), greater speeds (more than 100 megabits per second) and diverse forms of information (e.g., voice, data, image and video).

managed network services (See MNS)

managed object
A data processing or data communications resource that may be managed through the use of an Open Systems Interconnection (OSI) management protocol. The resource itself need not be an OSI resource. A managed object may be a physical item of equipment, a software component, some abstract collection of information, or any combination of all three.

management consulting (Tier 1 segmentation)

- Strategic consulting (enterprise): high-level corporate or business unit strategy, e.g., deciding what businesses to participate in or whether to make an acquisition.
- Strategic consulting (operations improvement): targeted business issue analysis, e.g., an airline deciding how to improve customer service, or a bank deciding on the most effective type of retail delivery system.

Management Information Base — part of SNMP (See MIB)

management information systems (See MIS)

Manchester encoding
A method of coding that alters the binary signal by dividing the bit period into halves and using a change in voltage to differentiate the two halves. A binary "1" is indicated by having a high voltage during the first interval and low voltage during the second. A binary "0" is the reverse.

mandatory security controls
An operating system security rating of B1 or higher based on U.S. Department of Defense trusted-computer-system evaluation criteria.

man-machine interface (See MMI)

Manufacturing Accounting and Production Information Control System (See MAPICS)

Manufacturing Automation Protocol (See MAP)

manufacturing execution systems (see MES)

Manufacturing Execution Systems Association (See MESA)

manufacturing lead time
The total time required to manufacture an item. Included are order preparation time, queue time, setup time, runtime, move time, inspection time and put-away time.

Manufacturing Message Service (See MMS)

manufacturing resource planning (See MRP II)

MAP (Manufacturing Automation Protocol)
An application-specific protocol based on Open Systems Interconnection (OSI) standards. It is designed to allow communication among competing vendors' digital products in the factory.

MAPI (mail API)
An application programming interface (API) published by Microsoft to permit access to an e-mail system (in Microsoft's case, Exchange) from another program.

MAPI (Messaging Application Programming Interface)
The programming interface specification that enables an application to send and receive mail over a Microsoft Mail messaging system. It was designed to separate the mail engine from the mail client.

MAPICS (Manufacturing Accounting and Production Information Control System)
IBM's material requirements planning software for the AS/400 and earlier System/36 and System/38 systems. The newest version, MAPICS/DDB, uses the relational-database capability of the AS/400.

MAPI-WF (MAPI Workflow Framework)
A Microsoft framework originally intended to provide a standardized way for any Messaging Application Programming Interface (MAPI)-capable application to be workflow-enabled and to support work item interchange between various workflow engines. It is now expected to be merged with standards based on Multipurpose Internet Mail Extensions (MIME)-based standards.

Mapping
The transcription of functions into terms that make them equivalent on two different systems. In network operations, it is the logical association of one set of values, such as addresses, on one network, with quantities or values of another set, such as devices, on a second network (e.g., name-address mapping, internetwork-route mapping).

MAP/TOP (Manufacturing Automation Protocol/Technical Office Protocol)

MARECS (European maritime satellite system)

MARISAT (maritime satellite service)

mark
A signal condition corresponding to the "on" state (binary 1), usually when current flows or when the voltage exceeds a specified value.

MAPI-WF

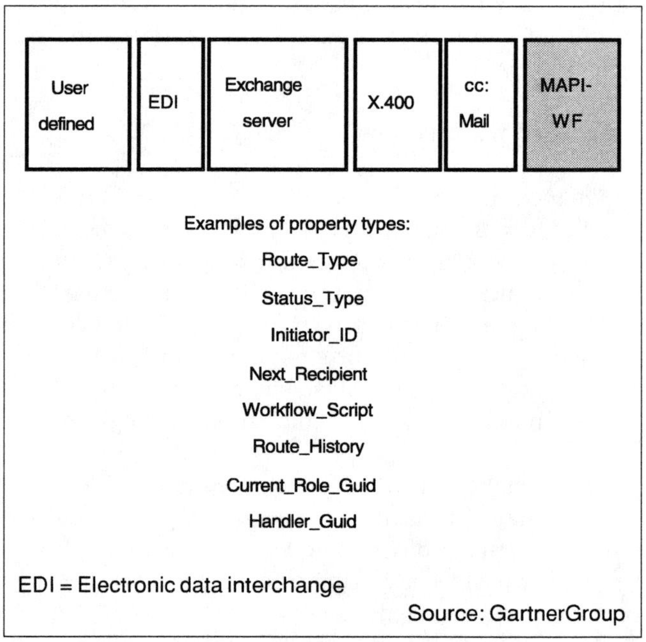

MAPI Message With Workflow Extensions

marketing automation systems or marketing automation software (See MAS)

marketing content management (See MCM)

marketing customer information file (See MCIF)

marketing encyclopedia system (See MES)

MAS (marketing automation systems or marketing automation software)
Systems that help marketers execute multichannel marketing campaigns by providing a scripting environment for authoring business rules and interfaces to a variety of third-party applications.

massively parallel processing (See MPP)

master enterprise identifier (See MEI)

Master License Agreement — Novell (See MLA)

master station
The unit having control of all other terminals on a multipoint circuit for purposes of polling or selection.

master terminal
A reserved workstation used by the system manager that can initiate conversations for network management tasks.

matchmaker
An Internet sales outlet sites that refers a buyer to a Web merchant willing to sell a good or service at the price specified by the buyer (e.g., Priceline.com).

material requirements planning (See MRP)

materials management
A term to describe the grouping of management functions related to the complete cycle of material flow, from the purchase and internal control of production materials, to the planning and control of work in process, to the warehousing, shipping and distribution of the finished product. It differs from materials control in that the latter term, traditionally, is limited to the internal control of production materials.

materials management information system (See MMIS)

MathML (Mathematical Markup Language)

matrix
In switch technology, that portion of the switch architecture where input leads and output leads meet, any pair of which may be connected to establish a through circuit. Also called switching matrix.

MAU (media access unit)
A network device that, along with the cable, forms the Physical Level (1) of the International Organization for Standardization (ISO)/Open Systems Interconnection (OSI) seven-layer reference model. Its functions are signaling, encoding and medium-handling.

MAU (multistation access unit)
A wiring concentrator in the IBM Token Ring Network (TRN) that can connect up to eight lobes to a ring.

MAW (Microsoft at Work)

maximum burst size (See MBS)

Mb (megabit)
See Mbit.

MB (megabyte)
See Mbyte.

MBE (molecular beam epitaxy)
A semiconductor manufacturing technology.

Mbit or Mb (megabit)
One million (actually 1,048,576) bits of stored computer data.

MBO (management by objective)

MBone
Virtual Internet Backbone for Multicast Internet Protocol (IP) — a physical worldwide implementation of IP multicast technology that is application independent.

Mbps (megabits per second)
A measure of data transmission rate meaning one million bits per second.

MBR (mean bit rate)
The number of bits transmitted per time unit averaged over the period of the session.

MBS (maximum burst size)
In asynchronous transfer mode (ATM), the number of cells a source is allowed to send at the peak cell rate (PCR).

Mbyte or MB (megabyte)
One million (actually 1,048,576) bytes . This is the common way in which the size of files or computer random-access memory (RAM) is specified. Megabytes are also used to describe the size of storage space on storage devices such as floppy disks, hard disks or CD-ROMs. The relationship of the size of a file or accumulation of files to the size of the RAM and storage space is critical because it determines the ability of a computing device to process a file.

MC (Memory Channel)
An additional level in the memory hierarchy of certain Encore computers, with an address space shared across clustered nodes. A write from local memory to the MC in one node simultaneously writes to reflective memories in all the other nodes. Each node can be attached to four separate MCs, allowing bandwidth scaling and substantial configuration flexibility. The MC also is used as a fast, low-latency transport for I/O transfer, remote procedure calls (RPCs) and general message passing.

MCA (Micro Channel Architecture)
IBM's bus architecture developed for the Personal System/2 computer. It is now used only in a few of IBM's non-PC products.

MCAD (mechanical computer-aided design)

MCAE (mechanical computer-aided engineering)

MCAP (Managed Care Appropriateness Protocol)

MCIF (marketing customer information file)
A system (or marketing data mart) that may have some or all of the characteristics of a data warehouse, but differs in that it is designed specifically to support marketing activities.

MCIS (Microsoft Commercial Internet System)
The MCIS Membership System provides user management for large hosted Web services. The membership directory is the central repository of user data for MCIS 2.0, including personalization profiles and Internet security information. It can also be used to store user security credentials and permissions that facilitate authentication of users and access to content and applications.

MCM (marketing content management)
A category of applications recently introduced to help enterprises respond rapidly to unfolding business circumstances by applying the optimal combination of marketing content across multiple channels. MCM databases provide enterprises with an overview of all available marketing content.

MCM (multichip module)

MCNS (Multimedia Cable Network System)
Formed by Comcast Cable Communications, Cox Communications, Tele-Communications, Inc. (TCI), and Time Warner Cable.

MCP (Microsoft Certified Professional)
A Microsoft certification that requires passing a single operating system (OS) test. MCPs can further specialize in Internet technologies to attain an MCP with Internet or site-building specialization, or can continue taking the exams necessary to become a Microsoft Certified Systems Engineer (MCSE).

MCR (minimum cell rate)
An asynchronous transfer mode (ATM) parameter used to determine the minimum number of cells permitted in a specific time period.

MC/S (mobile client/server)

MCSD (Microsoft Certified Software Developer)

MCSE (Microsoft Certified Systems Engineer) (See MCP)

MCSS (Mission Critical Server Suites — Hewlett-Packard)

MCU (microcontroller unit)

MCU (multipoint control unit)

MD5
A message digest hash function.

MDA (Monochrome Display Adapter)

MDC (mainframe data center)
The centralized, large-volume processing and storage facilities built around standard mainframe computing platforms.

MDF (main distribution frame)
A wiring arrangement that connects outside lines on one side and internal lines from exchange equipment on the other side.

MDF (Message Development Framework)
A detailed formal methodology for Health Level 7 (HL7) message development, adopted by the HL7 organization in the spring of 1997. MDF, which is explicitly documented, uses Universal Modeling Language (UML), is supported by training classes and trained object modeling facilitators, and employs Rational's Rose as its modeling tool.

MDF (Multiple Domain Facility)

MDF (Multiple Domain Feature — Amdahl)

MDI (multidocument interface)

MDNS (managed data network services)

MDS (multipoint distribution system)

MDT (mobile data terminal)

mean bit rate (See MBR)

mean time between failures (See MTBF)

mean time to repair (See MTTR)

measured usage license charge (See MULC)

Media Access Control — IEEE (See MAC)

Media Access Unit (See MAU)

Media Interface Connector (See MIC)

media objects
Non-Hypertext Markup Language (HTML) files that can be displayed or executed as part of an HTML document or as a stand-alone file. Examples

are Graphics Interchange Format (GIF) or Joint Photographic Experts Group (JPEG) graphic files; audio or video files; and Java applets.

Medical Logic Module (See MLM)

medium

1. The material on which data is recorded. For example, magnetic tape or diskette.
2. Any material substance that is, or can be, used for the propagation of signals, usually in the form of modulated radio, light or acoustic waves, from one point to another, such as optical fiber, cable, wire, dielectric slab, water, air, or free space.

medium frequency (See MF)

medium-scale integration (See MSI)

megabit (See Mbit)

megabits per second (See Mbps)

megabyte (See Mbyte)

megaFLOPS (see MFLOPS)

megahertz (See MHz)

MEI (master enterprise identifier)
An identifier that is unique for each person.

MELP (Microsoft Enterprise License Pak)

Memory Channel (See MC)

MDF

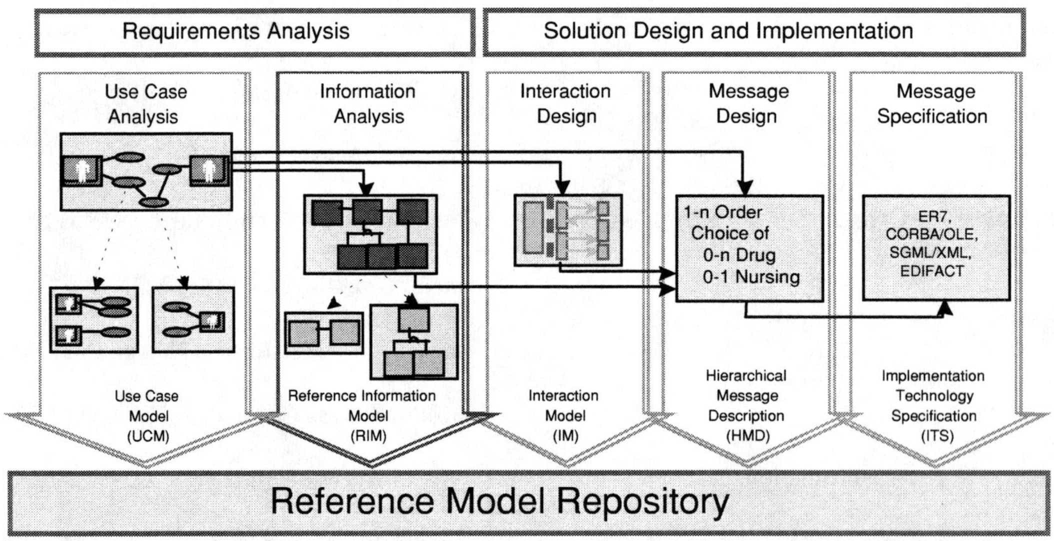

CORBA = Common Object Request Broker Architecture
EDIFACT = Electronic Data Interchange for Administration, Commerce and Transportation
ER7 = Encoding Rules for Health Level 7
OLE = Object Linking and Embedding
SGML = Standard Generalized Markup Language
XML = Extensible Markup Language

Source: Health Level 7

Overview of the Health Level 7 Message Development Framework: Phases, Activities and Models

memory in cassette (See MIC)

Merced
Intel's code name for its first 64-bit (IA-64) processor.

MES (manufacturing execution system)
A category of application software formally defined by the Manufacturing Execution Systems Association (MESA) as any software that is not part of the enterprise resource planning (ERP) suite or used for process control, but is used to manage the execution of manufacturing processes.

MES (marketing encyclopedia system)
Electronically distributes and consolidates up-to-date marketing information into a highly cross-referenced, single-source repository that is easy to use. An MES enables users to quickly locate and display information, thus shortening sales cycles and decreasing printing and distribution costs. An MES contains a database capable of storing all types of information that will be incorporated into the system (e.g., audio, video, sound, text and graphics). The system should have the capability to be used unconnected to a server and should include a remote communications mechanism for electronically downloading and uploading information.

MESA (Manufacturing Execution Systems Association)
A trade association with the mission to define and promote the adoption of manufacturing execution system (MES) application software.

mesh network
A net-like structure where at least two paths exist to all stations.

message
A sequence of characters used to convey information or data. In data communications, messages are usually in an agreed format with a heading, which establishes the destiny of the message, and text, which consists of the data to be sent.

message authentication
A function in which the device determines if the received message arrived from its stated source and in unaltered form. The actual message need not be encrypted, but its authentication code must be.

message authentication code (See MAC)

MES

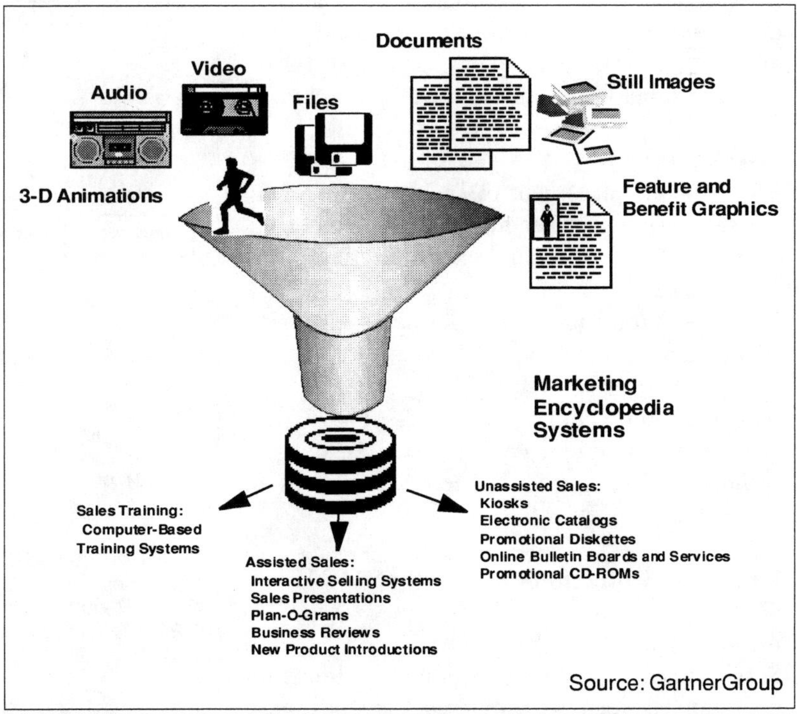

Marketing Encyclopedia Systems

message broker
A logical hub that copies and resends messages to one or more destinations. As a value-adding third party between information sources and information consumers, it can complement a service-oriented architecture.

A message broker, like a service-oriented architecture (SOA), is a design abstraction that may be implemented using component software for some or all of the connections. The interface from a message broker to the application may use an object request broker (ORB) or object transaction monitor (OTM); a request to the message broker may be implemented as a series of method calls to participating components.

Message Development Framework (See MDF)

message feedback
A method of checking the accuracy of data transmission. The received data is returned to the sending end for comparison with the original data, which is stored there for this purpose. Also called information feedback and loop checking.

message format
Rules for the placement of such portions of a message as message heading, address, text, end-of-message indication and error-detecting bits.

Message Handling System/Service — Novell (See MHS)

message numbering
The identification of each message within a communications system by the assignment of a sequential number.

message-oriented middleware (See MOM)

message passing
Services performing a simple, one-way transfer operation between two programs. Like the other one-way messaging models, message passing generally leaves the sending program unblocked. Also, as with all forms of messaging, message passing is usually connectionless, which means that the sending application does not have to explicitly establish and manage a connection with the message's intended recipient. Although message passing is not inherently a two-way communication model, two-way communication can be accomplished by sending the response in a separate message.

message-passing operating system (See MPOS)

message queuing
The message-queuing or store-and-forward model is basically the message-passing model with one additional feature. Message queuing is asynchronous in a manner similar to a traditional postal

Message Broker

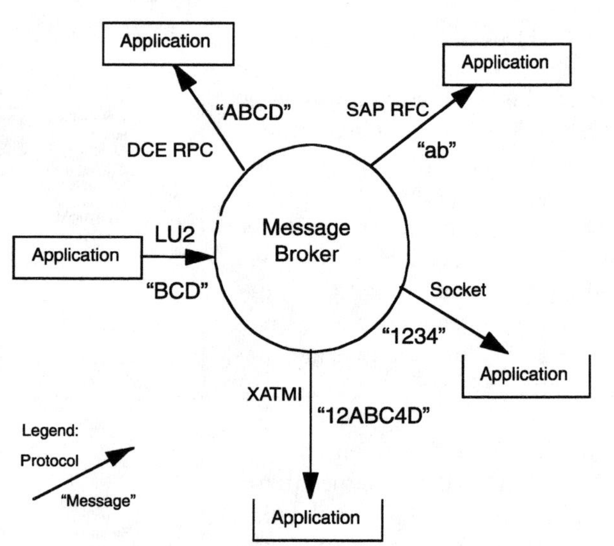

DCE = Distributed Computing Environment
LU2 = Logical Unit 2
RFC = Remote function call
RPC = Remote procedure call
XATMI = X/Open Application Transaction Manager Interface

Source: GartnerGroup

Message Broker Design

system in that the recipient need not be available when the message is sent. Message queuing stores messages at an intermediate node on the network in a queue and then forwards the messages to the intended targets.

message-queuing middleware (See MQM)

Message Security Protocol (See MSP)

message switching
The technique of receiving a message, storing it until the proper outgoing line is available, and then retransmitting. No direct connection between the incoming and outgoing lines is set up as in in-line switching.

message transfer agent (See MTA)

Message Transfer Part — ISDN (See MTP)

message unit (See MU)

message warehouse
A message broker service that temporarily stores messages to be analyzed or retransmitted at a later time.

messaging
In e-mail, messaging consists of moving messages from user to user, application to application, or place to place, providing a service analogous to that of the paper postal service and providing an infrastructure along which many other objects may be moved. The term is sometimes applied, with an entirely different meaning, to real-time interprocess communications in the transaction-processing (TP) environment.

Messaging Application Programming Interface (See MAPI)

Messaging Application Programming Interface-Workflow Framework (See MAPI-WF)

Messaging Hypertext Markup Language (See MHTML)

metadata
Data about data. It consists of identifiers or information about data that explicitly defines things about the data, including what it is, what its purpose is, who can see it, how it can be changed, and how the data should be processed. Metadata is data that is computer-processable, whereas the data itself generally is not.

Metadata Interchange Format (See XMI)

metalanguage
A language used to describe a language. A metalanguage defines the constructs — character sets, syntax, and valid sequences — of a language.

metallic circuit (See loop circuit)

metropolitan-area network (See MAN)

MF (medium frequency)
Frequencies in the range between 300 kilohertz (kHz) and 3 megahertz (MHz).

MF (multifrequency)
See DTMF.

MFC (Microsoft Foundation Class)

MFI (Multifunction Interpreter)
A gateway that handles connectivity between Defense Message System (DMS) and other systems.

MFJ (modified final judgment)
The U.S. District Court judgment under which AT&T began operating in 1984. Agreed to by the U.S. Justice Department and AT&T to settle the department's antitrust suit against AT&T, it divested AT&T of its Bell operating companies (BOCs).

MFLOPS (megaFLOPS)
Millions of floating-point operations per second, if used with a specific amount, e.g. 50 MFLOPS. A measurement for performance on compute-intensive, floating-point-intensive applications. The most commonly cited benchmark is Linpack.

MFM (modified frequency modulation)

MFS (metropolitan fiber system)

MHEG (Multimedia and Hypermedia Information Coding Expert Group)
An International Organization for Standardization (ISO) and International Telecommunication Union (ITU) standard suitable for the interchange of multimedia documents using HyTime.

MHS (Message Handling Service — Novell)
Utility in Novell NetWare platform providing a common format for exchanging information among applications. Used typically for electronic mail.

MHS (Message Handling System/Service)
Electronic mail implemented according to Open Systems Interconnection (OSI) specifications, based on International Telecommunication Union (ITU) X.400 recommendations.

MHS SMF71
The current version of the standard messaging format used in the NetWare Message Handling Service (MHS) is a specification for a message data structure. There is no read/write utility. The application reads and writes the file to a known place on the file server.

MHTML (Messaging Hypertext Markup Language)
A language that is capable of packaging externally referenced image files within an HTML page, potentially increasing the bulk of the page significantly.

MHz (Megahertz)
A unit equal to 1 million hertz (1 million cycles per second).

MIB (Management Information Base — part of SNMP)
A Simple Network Management Protocol (SNMP) flat-file, nonrelational database that describes devices being monitored. Network management platforms (such as Hewlett-Packard's Network Node Manager) monitor nodes by reading the value of the managed resources in the MIB. Management platforms can effect changes in managed resources by altering MIB values (e.g., by establishing thresholds beyond which alerts are created).

MIC (Management Integration Consortium)

MIC (media interface connector)
A fiber distributed data interface (FDDI) connector.

MIC (memory in cassette)
A media feature with which Sony has differentiated its Advanced Intelligent Tape (AIT) drive. It is a 16-Kbit E2PROM chip that indexes file locations, thus enabling faster access to data, and stores metadata about the media, allowing enterprises to track media life cycles in the physical cartridge.

MIC (microwave integrated circuit)

MICR (magnetic-ink character recognition)
Machine recognition and digitization of magnetically charged characters printed on paper (typically bank drafts and deposit slips).

Micro Channel Architecture (See MCA)

microcode
The microinstructions, especially of a microprocessor, that govern the details of operation. For example, the hardware of the 3081 fetches and executes 108-bit microinstructions wholly different

from the instruction set of System/370. Yet IBM supplies a microprogram that causes the 3081 to act like a System/370. The instructions in such a program are referred to as microcode. The execution of each System/370 instruction puts the hardware into a subroutine of microinstructions that execute the function defined for that instruction. Microcoded functions can improve performance but add a layer of complexity. For example, microcode errors appear to software as being hardware failures.

microfilm
A high-resolution film used to record images reduced in size from the original.

micro-marketplace (See MM)

microprocessor
A central processing unit (CPU) on a single chip. Desktop and portable computers one microprocessor, while more powerful computers often make use of multiple microprocessors.

Microsoft Certified Professional (See MCP)

Microsoft Certified Systems Engineer (MCSE) (See MCP)

Microsoft Cluster Server (See MSCS)

Microsoft Commercial Internet System (See MCIS)

Microsoft Disk Operating System (See MS-DOS)

Microsoft Management Console (See MMC)

Microsoft Message Queue Server (See MSMQ)

Microsoft Transaction Server (See MTS)

microwave
1. The portion of the electromagnetic spectrum above about 760 megahertz (MHz).

2. A term describing high-frequency transmission signals and equipment that employ microwave frequencies, including line-of-sight open-air microwave transmission and, increasingly, satellite communications.

middleware
Originally, middleware was defined broadly as the runtime system software layered between an application program and the operating system. In that sense, database management systems (DBMSs) and transaction processing (TP) monitors represent middleware, but development tools or system management utilities do not, because they do not directly support the application at runtime. Now, middleware is more commonly and narrowly defined as the network-aware system

MIC

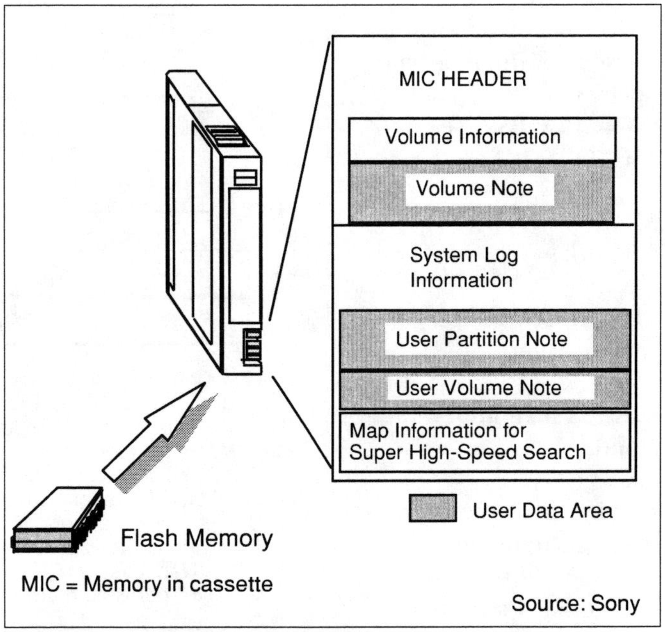

Memory-in-Cassette Features

software, layered between an application, the operating system and the network transport layers, whose purpose is to facilitate some aspect of cooperative processing. Examples of cooperative middleware include directory services, message-passing mechanisms, distributed TP monitors, object request brokers (ORBs), remote procedure call (RPC) services and database gateways.

midrange computer
A computer with an architecture similar to that of the minicomputer, which is used for multiple users.

Midrange System End-User Query
An end-user query facility on the midrange system that allows direct access to System/370 Virtual Storage Access Method (VSAM) or Database-2 (DB2) data using remote-access facilities.

MIF (management information file)

million instructions per second (See MIPS)

millions of floating-point operations per second (MegaFLOPS) (See MFLOPS)

MILNET (military network)

MIL-SPEC (military specification)

MIL-STD (military standard)

MIMD (multiple instruction, multiple data)
A design for parallel computers characterized by the simultaneous execution of many different instruction streams (programs) where the instructions in each stream handle different data.

MIME (Multipurpose Internet Mail or Messaging Extensions)
MIME functions enable the transport of attachments and non-ASCII text via the Simple Message Transport Protocol (SMTP). They cover most (but not all) of the features of X.400, and interface with X.400 via the MIME-X.400 Enhanced Relay (MIXER) specification.

MIME Object Security Services (See MOSS)

MIMIC (millimeter-wave monolithic IC)

Middleware

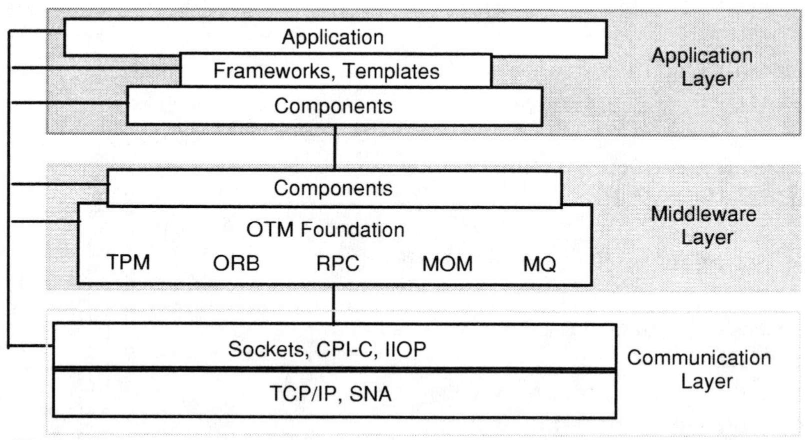

CPI-C = Common Programming Interface for Communications
IIOP = Internet Inter-ORB Protocol
MOM = Message-oriented middleware
MQ = Message queuing
ORB = Object request broker
OTM = Object transaction monitor
RPC = Remote procedure call
SNA = Systems Network Architecture
TCP/IP = Transmission Control Protocol/Internet Protocol
TPM = Third-party maintenance

Source: GartnerGroup

Middleware's Role in the Topology of Component Applications

minicomputer
A computing device that is typically more powerful than a PC, but less powerful than a mainframe, and is therefore often referred to as "midrange." The minicomputer can support a single user or multiple users.

MiniMAP
A simplified subset of the Manufacturing Automation Protocol (MAP) covering Open Systems Interconnection (OSI) Layers 1, 2, and 7 only.

minimum cell rate (See MCR)

Minimum Interoperability Specification for PKI Components (See MISPC)

Minitel
Minitel, which appeared in France in the 1970s, was the world's first electronic information system for public use — a forerunner of today's Internet.

MIPS (million instructions per second)
An approximate measure of a computer's raw processing power. MIPS figures can be misleading because measurement techniques often differ, and different computers may require different sets of instructions to perform the same activity.

MIPS RISC
A reduced instruction set computer (RISC) processor architecture designed and licensed by MIPS Computer Systems (now part of Silicon Graphics). Used by a number of midrange suppliers, it was the basis for the Advanced RISC Computing (ARC) definitions endorsed by the now-defunct Advanced Computing Environment (ACE) consortium

MIS (management information systems)
This was once the predominantly used name for the central data processing organization in a commercial enterprise. Today, information systems (IS) is the more commonly used term.

MIS (market or marketing information system)

MISPC (Minimum Interoperability Specification for PKI Components)
An initiative, led by the National Institute of Standards and Technology (NIST), to address interoperability and cross-certification among certificate authorities. It seeks to encourage the development of commercial, off-the-shelf software for public-key infrastructures (PKIs). The intent is to leverage standards and the activities of the public-key community of interests. The effort also recommends support for multiple digital signature and nonrepudiation methods as a way to ensure interoperability among products. Interoperable testing is to be done by members of the CommerceNet consortium. NIST also addresses the issues of certificate authority policies, practice statements and accreditation of certificate authorities as they relate to interoperability.

MISSI (Multilevel Information System Security Initiative)

MIME

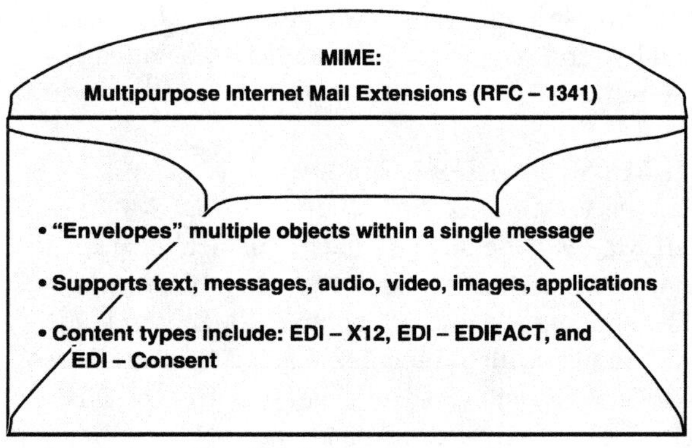

EDI = Electronic data interchange
EDIFACT = Electronic Data Interchange for Administration, Commerce and Transportation
RFC = Request for comment

Source: GartnerGroup

Multipurpose Internet Mail Extension Functions

mission-critical
Applications that are critical to the survival of an organization. Mission-critical services require a combination of several factors, such as availability, reliability, serviceability and performance. Each of these must be weighted in importance to fit the particular mission to be supported.

MITI (Ministry of International Trade and Industry — Japan)

Mixed Object: Document Content Architecture (See MO:DCA)

M-JPEG (Motion JPEG)
A version of Joint Photographic Experts Group (JPEG) for compression of motion video, as opposed to still images. Frame-to-frame redundancy is ignored, resulting in less compression than Motion Picture Experts Group (MPEG). The advantages are simplicity and fast access to individual images.

MLA (Master License Agreement — Novell)
Novell's most popular licensing option under its "Customer Connections" program.

MLC (monthly license charge)
A pricing structure for software licensing. Users can usually terminate their software licenses with a 30-day notice.

MLM (Medical Logic Module)
The Arden Syntax for Medical Logic Modules (MLMs) is a de facto standard in healthcare for coding clinical information (e.g., to generate clinical alerts, suggest interpretations or diagnoses, guide compliance with protocols). Each MLM encodes only one decision and evaluates as true or false. Although an MLM can call another MLM, in practice, this rarely occurs.

MLR (Multichannel Linear Recording 1 — Tandberg)
A technology developed jointly by Tandberg, IBM and Imation based on quarter-inch tape cartridge recording.

MM (materials management)

MM (micro-marketplace)
A type of electronic marketplace that helps buyers within a particular industry, geographic region, or affinity group make informed purchasing decisions by aggregating content, providing value-added services and offering multiple vendor alternatives.

MM (multimedia)
Applications and technologies that manipulate text, data, images, and voice and full-motion-video objects. Multimedia is typically associated with personal computers (PCs) but increasingly associated with network-based applications such as those residing on the Internet. Given the usage of multiple formats, multimedia is capable of delivering a stronger and more engaging message than standard text. Multimedia files are typically larger than text-based information and are therefore usually stored on compact disc read-only memory (CD-ROMs). Games and educational software commonly use multimedia.

MMC (Microsoft Management Console)
A Windows-based multiple document interface application that uses Internet technologies. MMC does not provide any management functionality, but rather a common management environment. It relies on independent software vendors (ISVs) developing snap-ins to provide management functionality. Snap-ins are Microsoft- or ISV-developed software modules that integrate with MMC to enhance its functionality.

MMDS (multipoint multichannel distribution service)
A wireless technology used for broadcasting, personal communications and interactive-media services.

MMI (man-machine interface)
End-user interface.

MMIS (materials management information system)
A software suite packaged as an integrated solution for meeting-materials management, human resources and back-office needs. MMISs should at least be designed to interface readily with other mission-critical information systems in the organization.

MML (Mathematical Markup Language)

MMMC (minimum monthly maintenance charge)

MMS (Manufacturing Message Service)
Part of Layer 7 in the Open System Interconnection (OSI) seven-layer network protocol stack. MMS creates a common communications interface between application software and factory devices such as programmable logic controllers, numerical controllers and robots.

MMT (model-mapping tables — Toolbus)
MMTs are developed using a mapping language that is custom-coded by Toolbus for each tool pair. The tables direct the behavior of each program as they fill the Toolbus file with metadata from one tool while performing adaptations to a neutral state, or while they pull metadata from the Toolbus file and format it into an acceptable form for the target tool. Some of the bridges can handle sophisticated situations with features that include filtering, defaulting and overriding to facilitate the selective bridging of metadata.

MMU (memory management unit)

MNC (mobile network computer)
A network computer distinguished, according to Mobile Network Computing Reference Specification (MNCRS) sponsors, "by characteristics that include disconnected operations when a network connection is not available (or desirable) and the ability to easily transition between different types of connections (or reconnections) and disconnected mode."

MNCRS (Mobile Network Computing Reference Specification)
A standard for network computers to dynamically adjust to a broad range of user devices under varying connectivity conditions (i.e., low bandwidth, offline and online), all without intervention on the part of the application programmer. Proposed in 1997, it defines a high-level set of requirements that sketch out some of the architectural underpinnings by which network computing will support offline and poorly connected and well connected users.

M/NET
An electronic-commerce (e-commerce) initiative acquired by PSI through the purchase of the ARM Group. It helps track purchases and inventory.

MNP (Microcom Networking Protocols)

MNS (managed network services)
The vendor delivery of primarily operational support for a new environment in which the hardware assets, financial obligations and personnel still remain on the books of the customer.

MO (magneto-optic)
Information stored by local magnetization of a magnetic medium, using a focused light beam to produce local heating and consequent reduction of coercivity so that a moderately strong, poorly localized magnetic field can flip the state of a small region of high coercivity material. Reaching is done either magnetically, with inductive heads in close proximity to the medium, or optically, through

rotation of the plan of polarization of probing light via the Faraday effect or Kerr effect.

Moab
Code name for the next generation of NetWare.

mobile earth station
A radio transmitter and/or receiver situated on a ship, or aircraft or other vehicle and used for satellite communications.

mobile IP
Defines a packet-forwarding mechanism for mobile and remote hosts so that remote users can connect into their networks over the Internet. It can work with Dynamic Host Configuration Protocol (DHCP). See also ATMP.

mobile network computer (See MNC)

MNCRS

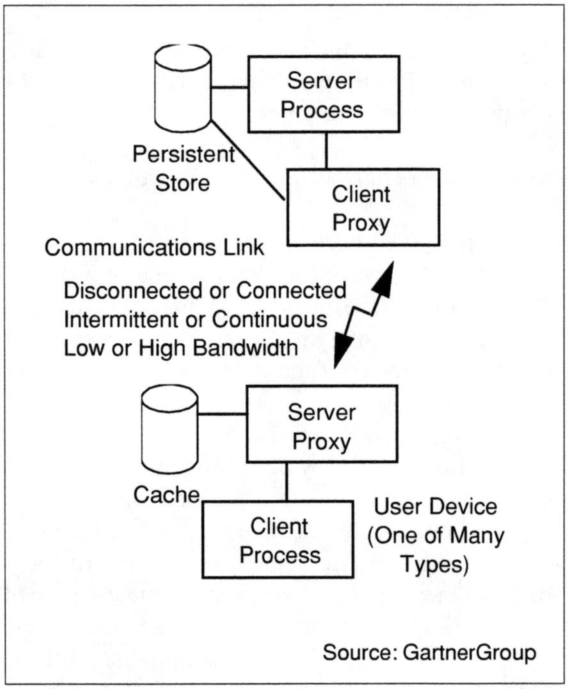

MNCRS Proxy Architecture

Mobile Network Computing Reference Specification (See MNCRS)

mobile satellite communications
Satellite-based services to ships, motor vehicles and aircraft.

mobile satellite service (See MSS)

mobile telephone service (See MTS)

mobile telephone switching office (See MTSO)

MOCVD (metal organic chemical vapor deposition)

modal bandwidth
Optical fiber capacity measure in megahertz per kilometer.

modal dispersion
Signal distortion in an optical fiber cable that causes the light to spread so much that the signal cannot be received.

MO:DCA (Mixed Object: Document Content Architecture)
The definition of the interchange data stream for documents containing a mixture of information types, such as text, image and graphics.

mode

1. The most common or frequent value in a group of values.
2. One of many energy propagation patterns through a waveguide.

model-mapping tables (See MMT)

modem (modulator-demodulator)
A conversion device installed in pairs that allows a computing device to transmit information over analog communication lines (for example, traditional

phone lines) through a modem at the opposite end by converting information that is digitally stored on the computer into transmission signals. The transmitting-end modem modulates digital signals received locally from a computer or terminal and sends analog signals over the line. The receiving-end modem demodulates the incoming signal, converting it back to its original (i.e., digital) format and passes it to the destination business machine.

Modem speeds are measured in bits per second (bps). The most common modems can transmit at speeds from 28.8 Kbps to 56 Kbps. "Digital modems," using Integrated Services Digital Network (ISDN), which are not true modems, provide access speeds of 56 Kbps to 125 Kbps. Cable modems that use cable television wires offer speeds 20 to 150 times greater, but their availability and use is still limited.

Modem-7
Similar to Xmodem; found mainly on Control Program for Microcomputers (CP/M) bulletin boards.

modem-sharing unit (See MSU)

Modified Accelerated Cost Recovery System (See MACRS)

modified final judgment (See MFJ)

modular

1. Made up of replaceable units that can be added together to make the system larger or modify its capabilities.
2. A type of cable connector used in telephone and data communication systems (see RJx).

modulation
The application of information onto a carrier signal by varying one or more of the signal's basic characteristics (frequency, amplitude or phase); the conversion of a signal from its original (e.g., digital) format to analog format. Specific types include:

- AM (amplitude modulation)
- differential pulse code modulation (see also ADPCM/adaptive differential pulse code modulation)
- FM (frequency modulation)
- PAM (pulse amplitude modulation)
- PCM (pulse code modulation)
- PWM (pulse width modulation; also called PDM/pulse duration modulation)

modulator
A device that converts a signal (voice or other) into a form that can be transmitted.

modulator-demodulator (See modem)

MOF (Meta Object Facility)

MOLP (Microsoft Open License Pak)

MOM (manufacturing operations management)

MOM (message-oriented middleware)
A model that programs the delivery of a message or a reply that must be deferred. MOM differs from other forms of program-to-program middleware, such as remote procedure cells (RPCs) and conversational services, because MOM communication is connectionless — i.e., the sending and receiving programs do not interact directly. A program sends the message to the MOM, which then takes responsibility for delivering it to the proper receivers.

MOMA (Message-Oriented Middleware Association)

monitor (display)
Computer hardware used for displaying digital output.

monomode
With fiber optic cable, this enables light to enter at a single angle only. This provides high bandwidth at the expense of needing a light source with a narrow spectral width. Also called single-mode fiber. See also multimode.

monthly license charge (See MLC)

Moore's Law
The idea that computing power doubles every 18 months, originally conceived by Intel co-founder Gordon Moore in 1965.

MOS (metal-oxide semiconductor)

Mosaic
A user-friendly Internet front end developed at the University of Illinois. The prototype for most Web browsers.

MOSFET (metal-oxide semiconductor field-effect transistor)

MOSP (Multiple Operating System PR/SM Charge Option — IBM)

MOSPF (Multicast OSPF)
Extensions to open shortest path first (OSPF) routing that allows Internet Protocol (IP) multicasts.

MOSS (MIME Object Security Services)
An Internet secure messaging method.

Motif
Graphical user interface (GUI) specified by the Open Software Foundation (OSF) and built on the Massachusetts Institute of Technology's (MIT's) X Windows.

Motion JPEG (See M-JPEG)

Motion Picture Experts Group standard (See MPEG)

MO/TO (mail order/telephone order)

moves, adds, changes and remove (See MAC/R)

MP (multiprocessor)
A computer that incorporates multiple processors with access to common storage.

MP3 (MPEG Layer III)
An open Motion Picture Experts Group (MPEG) standard for digital audio compression. Different from MPEG-3, MP3 is an audio-coding scheme that is part of MPEG and is defined within the audio segment of international standards MPEG-1 and MPEG-2.

MPC (massively parallel computer)

MPC (Multimedia PC)
Specifications for a multimedia personal computer (PC) from the Multimedia PC Marketing Council, first published in 1990. It requires adherence to minimum random-access memory (RAM), processor, compact disc read-only memory (CD-ROM) transfer rate, sound-sampling, video and port standards.

MPDSP (microprogrammable digital signal processing)

MPE (Multiprogramming Executive)
A multitasking operating system that is used on the Hewlett-Packard 3000 series.

MPEG (Motion Picture Experts Group)
The group responsible for setting the standards for the coding of moving pictures and audio. MPEG operates under the joint direction of the International Organization for Standardization (ISO) and the International Electro-Technical Commission (IEC).

MPEG (Motion Picture Experts Group standard)
A digital video standard for compression of full-motion images driven by the same committee as the Joint Photographic Experts Group (JPEG) standard. The compression ratios achieved with MPEG encoding make it an ideal standard for delivery of digital video data. It makes smaller files than motion JPEG because redundancies from frame to frame are also compressed, but this process makes it difficult to access individual frames for editing.

MPEG-1 deals with mono and two-channel stereo sound coding, at sampling frequencies commonly used for high-quality audio. MPEG-2 contains an extension to lower sampling frequencies, providing better sound quality at the low bit rates, and an extension for multichannel sound. MPEG-3 and MPEG-4, with further improvements, are under development.

Both MPEG-1 and MPEG-2 have a three-layer structure. Each layer represents a family of coding algorithms.

Layer 3 deals with sound encoding, and can't be used by itself to encode audio files. In this form, it is known as MP3.

MPEG Layer III (See MP3)

MPI (master person index)

MPLA (Multiport Link Aggregation — 3Com)

MPN (multiprotocol network)

MPOA (multiprotocol over ATM)
A routing option that combines the second phase of local-area network (LAN) emulations with a route server, a route set cache of protocols where routing intelligence resides on the set server, and route cache devices or edge devices that maintain route tables updated by the server and that can forward traffic without going to the route server to obtain path information.

MPOS (message-passing operating system)
An operating system that enables a process anywhere in a network to communicate via messages with any other process in the network.

MPP (massively parallel processing)
An architecture that uses hundreds or thousands of parallel processors.

MPP (Multichannel Point-to-Point Protocol)
A protocol developed by Ascend Communications that is similar to PPP (Point-to-Point Protocol) but operable over multiple network channels in an inverse multiplexed scenario.

MPPC (multipurpose parallel computing)

MPPL (Multipurpose Processing Language)

MPR (microperipheral)

MPS (master production scheduling)

MPTN (Multiprotocol Transport Networking)
Multiprotocol network support, including Transmission Control Protocol (TCP) over Systems Network Architecture (SNA), and SNA over Internet Protocol (IP), designed by IBM.

MPU (microprocessing unit or microprocessor)

MQI (Message Queue Interface — IBM)

MQM (message-queuing middleware)
A model to store and forward messages, thereby enabling asynchronous operations.

MQS (Message Queuing Series)

MRCF (multiple RAID coupling facility)

MRO (maintenance, repair and operations)
The activities and material purchased to support those activities associated with the operation and repair of any facility, equipment or asset.

MRP (material requirements planning)
Original manufacturing business software that focused only on planning the manufacturing materials and inventories and did not integrate planning for other resources, such as people and machine capacity.

MRP II (manufacturing resource planning)
A method for effective planning of all the resources of a manufacturing company. Ideally, it addresses operational planning in units and financial planning in dollars, and has a simulation capability to answer "what if" questions. It is made up of a variety of functions, each linked together: business planning, production planning, master production scheduling (MPS), material requirements planning (MRP), capacity requirements planning (CRP) and the execution systems for capacity and priority. Outputs from these systems will be integrated with financial reports, e.g., the business plan, purchase commitment report, shipping budget, and inventory projections in dollars. MRP II is a direct outgrowth and extension of MRP. MRP II is now migrating toward enterprise resource planning (ERP).

MRT (Multiple Rectangle Technique)
MRT intercepts the graphic primitives that cause screen output and identifies screen changes in predefined rectangular grids during each poll (frequencies start at one millisecond), which results in a fluid presentation of the captured information.

ms (millisecond)

MSB (most significant bit)

MSCS (Microsoft Cluster Server)
Previously known as Wolfpack Phase 1, this provides two-node server failover for enterprises seeking high-availability NT Server (NTS) solutions. Specific certified hardware configurations are required to support MSCS.

MS-DOS (Microsoft Disk Operating System)
An operating system written by Microsoft for personal computers that was the basis for IBM's PC-DOS. MS-DOS was used by all IBM PC-compatible machines. It was originally designed to organize how a computer reads, writes and interacts with its disks — floppy or hard — and how it talks to its various input/output (I/O) devices, such as keyboards, screens, printers and modems. Until the introduction of Windows-based operating systems, the most popular operating system for PCs was MS-DOS. Unlike its successors, MS-DOS was character-based and did not use a graphical user interface (GUI).

MSE (midsize enterprise)

MSF (Multiple Server Feature — Amdahl)
An Amdahl S/390 complementary metal-oxide semiconductor (CMOS) optional feature that allows a single system to be divided into smaller systems, each with a unique serial number.

MS-HUG (ActiveX)

MSI (medium-scale integration)
Fewer than 100 circuits built onto a single chip. MSI is used frequently in third-generation systems.

MSM (Microsoft Systems Management)

MSMQ (Microsoft Message Queue Server)
Originally called Falcon, MSMQ is a message-queuing middleware (MQM) product, or, more accurately, an operating system service that provides store-and-forward connectivity between two application programs. MSMQ is unlike most other MQM products in that it runs only on Windows NT and Windows 95.

MSN (Microsoft Network)

MSN (multiservice network)

MSNF (Multisystem Networking Facility)
A facility of IBM's Network Control Program (NCP) that is used to control a multiple-domain network. It was an optional feature of telecommunications access method (TCAM) and Virtual Telecommunications Access Method (VTAM) version 1.

MSO (managed services organization or management services organization)

MSP (managed-service provider)

MSP (Message Security Protocol)
An X.400-like protocol that can be used over Transmission Control Protocol/Internet Protocol (TCP/IP) networks.

MSS (mobile satellite service)
Mobile earth stations (e.g., on ships, survival stations and positioning radio beacons) that provide location identification using satellite service.

MSU (message signal unit — ISDN)

MSU (million service units)

MSU (modem-sharing unit)
A device that permits two or more terminals to share a single modem.

MSW (most significant word)

MTA (message transfer agent)
The storing and forwarding part of an electronic-mail system.

MTBDU (mean time between data unavailability)

MTBE (mean time between errors)

MTBF (mean time between failures)
The cumulative average time that a manufacturer estimates between failures or occurrences in a component, complete telephone system or printed circuit board.

MTF (mean time to failure)

MTO (master terminal operator)

MTP (Message Transfer Part — ISDN)
Contains the mechanism that ensures reliable functional signal message transmission. It corresponds to the first three layers of the Open Systems Interconnection (OSI) reference model.

MTS (Microsoft Transaction Server)
Microsoft's NT-based transactional middleware.

MTS (mobile telephone service)
Telephone service provided between mobile stations and the public switched telephone network; radio transmission provides the equivalent of a local loop. See also cellular radio.

MTSO (mobile telephone switching office)
A U.S. term for the central switch that controls the entire operation of a cellular system. It is a sophisticated computer that monitors all cellular calls, keeps track of the locations of all cellular-equipped vehicles traveling in the system area, arranges handoffs and keeps track of billing information.

MTTI (mean time to install)

MTTI (mean time to isolate)

MTTR (mean time to repair)
An estimated average time, by either the vendor or the manufacturer, required to do repairs on equipment.

MTX (mobile telephone exchange)

MU (message unit)
The U.S. term for the unit of measure for charging local calls. It details the length of call, the distance called and the time of day.

MUD (multiuser domain)

MUI (multimedia user interface)

mu-law encoding
Encoding according to International Telecommunication Union (ITU) recommendation G.711, used with 24-channel (PCM) systems in the United States. It is similar to a-law encoding, but the two differ in the size of the quantizing intervals.

MULC (Measured Usage License Charge)
An S/390 software licensing arrangement offered by IBM. It yields charges based on the amount of processing capacity being used by selected software products.

multiaccess
The ability to have several users communicate with a computer at the same time.

Multibus
Intel's central path (channel) for transmitting electrical signals and data in 8- and 16-bit computer systems.

multicast
Multicast, as opposed to broadcast, is a signal transmitted to only a subset of potential destinations.

multicast OSPF (See MOSPF)

Multichannel Linear Recording 1 — Tandberg (See MLR)

Multichannel Point-to-Point Protocol (See MPP)

multichannel publishing
The publishing of similar content in both printing and Internet formats.

multidrop
A communications arrangement where multiple devices share a common transmission channel, though only one may transmit at a time. See also multipoint.

multifrequency (MF) (See DTMF)

Multifunction Interpreter (See MFI)

multileaving
The transmission of a variable number of data streams between user devices and a computer, usually via bisynchronous facilities and using bisynchronous protocols.

multimedia (See MM)

Multimedia and Hypermedia Information Coding Expert Group (See MHEG)

Multimedia Cable Network System (See MCNS)

Multimedia PC (See MPC)

multimedia workstation
A workstation that can process multimedia applications.

multimode
With fiber optic cable, the ability to transmit multiple frequencies of light. See also monomode.

multimode fiber
A fiber supporting propagation of multiple modes. The cable has a core diameter of 50-100 microns. It causes more distortion and gives less bandwidth than single-mode (monomode) fiber.

multiple
A system of wiring arranged so that a circuit, a line, or a group of lines is accessible at a number of points. Also called multipoint.

multiple console operation
A private branch exchange (PBX) supporting more than one attendant's position to handle heavy traffic. Call traffic is distributed evenly among the consoles in use.

multiple customer group operation
A public branch exchange (PBX) that can be shared by several different companies, each having separate consoles and trunks. Stations are assigned to one company or the other and are then capable of reaching only that company's trunks and attendants.

multiple instruction, multiple data (See MIMD)

Multiple Rectangle Technique (See MRT)

Multiple Server Feature (See MSF)

Multiple Virtual Storage (See MVS)

Multiple Virtual Storage/Enterprise Systems Architecture (See MVS/ESA)

multiplexer (See MUX)

multiplexing
Division of a transmission facility into two or more channels either by splitting the frequency band transmitted by the channel into narrower bands, each of which is used to constitute a distinct channel (frequency division multiplexing), or by allotting this common channel to several different information channels, one at a time (time division multiplexing).

multipoint
Pertaining or referring to a communications line to which three or more stations are connected. It implies that the line physically extends from one station to another until all are connected. See also point to point.

multipoint line
A single communications channel (typically a leased telephone circuit) to which more than one station or logical unit is attached, though only one can transmit at a time. Such arrangements usually require a polling mechanism under the control of a master station to ensure that only one device transmits data at a time. Also called a multidrop line.

multipoint multichannel distribution service (See MMDS)

multiprocessor (See MP)

multiprogramming
A computer system operation whereby a number of independent jobs are processed together. Rather than allow each job to run to completion in turn, the computer switches between them so as to improve the use of the system hardware components.

Multiprogramming Executive (See MPE)

multiprotocol over ATM (See MPOA)

Multiprotocol Transport Networking (See MPTN)

Multipurpose Internet Mail or Messaging Extensions (See MIME)

Multistation Access Unit (See MAU)

Multisystem Networking Facility (See MSNF)

multitasking
Two or more program segments running in a computer at the same time.

multithreading
Concurrent processing of more than one message (or similar service request) by an application program.

multiuser
A term that describes a computer that can support several workstations operating simultaneously.

multivendor network management
Support for integration of network management on a common workstation. The network management facility should enable user organizations or third-party vendors to integrate additional network management tools.

MUX (multiplexer)
A device that combines inputs from two or more terminals, computer ports or other multiplexers, and transmits the combined data stream over a single high-speed channel. At the receiving end, the high-speed channel is "demultiplexed," either by another multiplexer or by software.

MVC (multiport video controller)

MVIP (Multivendor Integration Protocol)

MVLP (Microsoft Variable License Pak)

MVS (Multiple Virtual Storage)
IBM's flagship operating system. Essentially all the device support, software functions, time-sharing aids and reliability improvements that IBM produces are positioned most firmly within MVS. Many Virtual Machine (VM) microcode "assists" were designed so that MVS guests can run more effectively in that environment. Of all of IBM's software products, MVS has by far received the greatest investment for development, documentation and support.

MVS/370
A version of MVS limited to 24-bit addressing and lacking the dynamic channel subsystem. Dropped from support in the early 1990s.

MVS/ESA (Multiple Virtual Storage/ Enterprise Systems Architecture)
A version of MVS introduced by IBM in 1988. Capable of addressing up to 16 terabytes (Tbytes) of data. Runs on the 3090 E and S models, as well as on the 4381 E. Consists of MVS/SP1.3 plus the latest Data Facility Product (DFP) data management system.

N

N+1 disk shadowing/mirroring
A system or storage subsystem-level facility to provide significantly improved apparent disk reliability without the cost of two-times disk shadowing (e.g., N+1 redundant array of independent disks — RAID).

NAB (Name and Address Book)

NAB (National Association of Broadcasters)

NACD (National Association of Computer Dealers)

NACHA (National Automated Clearing House Association)

Nagle's algorithm
Two control algorithms that may be used in Transmission Control Protocol (TCP)-based networks; one reduces the sending window, the other limits small datagrams.

nailed-up connection
A slang term for a permanent, dedicated path through a switch. This often refers to lengthy, regular data transmissions going through a private branch exchange (PBX).

NAK (negative acknowledgment)
A return signal that reports an error in the method of error control that relies on repeating any message received with detectable errors.

NAM (number assignment module)
The electronic memory in the cellular phone that stores the telephone number and electronic serial number. Phones with dual- or multi-NAM features offer the user the option of registering the phone so that it will have two or more phone numbers.

named pipes
One of several operating-system facilities for interprocess communications.

naming service
A program that provides a mapping between a logical name and a physical address. It can be extended by a directory service (DS).

NAP (network access point)
The points from which Internet service providers (ISPs) drop down their lines and establish peering arrangements to provide Internet connectivity to their customers.

NAPLPS (North American Presentation Level Protocol Syntax)
A standard approach using vector graphics for the display and communications of text and graphics in a videotext system.

narrowband channels
Subvoice grade pathways characterized by a speed range of 100 to 200 bits per second (bps).

Narrowband ISDN (See N-ISDN)

narrowband PCS (See N-PCS)

NAS (NetWare Access Server)

NAS (Network Applications Support — Digital Equipment)
A collection of Digital Equipment architectures and development programs intended to provide a high degree of affinity between Virtual Address Extension (VAX) systems (both VMS-and Ultrix-based)

and a variety of workstations, including Apple's Macintosh and IBM's PCs running MS-DOS and Operating System/2 (OS/2).

NAS (network-attached storage)

NAS (Networked Application Services — IBM division)

NAS (Numerical Aerodynamic Simulation — NASA program)
Located at NASA's Ames Research Center.

NASD (network-attached storage device)

NAT (Network Address Translation)
A functionality provided through the gateway Network Control Program (NCP) to protect the internal Internet Protocol (IP) addressing structure from the Internet IP addresses.

NATA (North American Telecommunications Association)

National Computer Security Center (See NCSC)

national healthcare identifier (See NHID)

National Industrial Information Infrastructure Protocols (See NIIIP)

National Institute of Standards and Technology (See NIST)

national language support (See NLS)

National Security Agency (See NSA)

native code compiler for Java (See NCCJ)

natural-language understanding (See NLU)

NAU (Network Addressable Unit)
Any presentation-level service in IBM's Systems Network Architecture (SNA).

NAV (Norton Antivirus)

NBS (narrowband sockets specification)

NC (network computer)

NC (Numerical Control)

NCA (Network Computing Architecture)
Oracle's implementation of an Object Transaction Manager (OTM).

NC-C (network computer-client)

NCCJ (native code compiler for Java)
Translates byte code into a file format and binary-code representation that can be linked (using a static linker) with pre-compiled libraries and resources to form the executable program. An NCCJ provides the opportunity to optimize the structure of the program code to eliminate redundant code as well as to fine tune code sequences (e.g., loops, jumps and substitutions).

NCCS (network computing client/server)
An emerging set of technologies and architectures that will enable dynamic (and, to some extent, adaptive) application deployment, execution and management. NCCS is largely based on existing elements including Internet-derived technologies — e.g., Hypertext Markup Language (HTML), Hypertext Transport Protocol (HTTP), Java, ActiveX and Internet Inter-ORB Protocol (IIOP); various forms of middleware — e.g., message-oriented middleware (MOM), Common Object Request Broker Architecture (CORBA) and Component Object Model+ (COM+); and architectures (e.g., multitier client/server). However, it will foster a whole set of new technologies and architectural patterns.

NCD (networked computing device)

NCDM (National Center for Database Marketing)

NCF (network-computing framework)

NCGA (National Computer Graphics Association)

N-channel metal-oxide semiconductor (See NMOS)

NCL (Network Control Language)

NCOP (Network Code of Practice)
A code of standard practices for network design, intended to maintain technical standards.

NCP (Network Control Program — a. k. a. ACF/NCP)
The IBM-licensed program that controls the operation of an IBM 37xx front-end processor (FEP). Communication with the host is through Advanced Communication Function/Virtual Telecommunications Access Method (ACF/VTAM) via a channel interface, and communications with terminals or another FEP is via telecommunications lines. NCP offloads certain line protocol and routing functions from the host central processing unit (CPU). Version 5 includes PU 2.1 support.

NCQA (National Committee for Quality Assurance)
An accreditation body for healthcare plans.

NCRP (Network Computer Reference Platform)
A specification defining the minimum standards for a network of computers.

NCS (National Communications System)

NCS (Network Computing System — from Hewlett-Packard)

NCSA (National Center for Supercomputer Applications)

NCSA (National Computer Security Association) (See ICSA)

NCSA (network computer system architecture)

NCSC (National Computer Security Center)
A branch of the U.S. National Security Agency

NCSD (IBM's Network Computing Software Division)

NCTP (Next Compatible Tape Product — Philips)

NCVHS (National Committee on Vital and Health Statistics)

NDF (Network Distributed Function)

NDF (network dynamic functionality)
A software development and execution technology that allows applications to be written to a model designed from the outset to achieve platform independence. It affords dynamic movement and invocation of code resources over a network at runtime.

NDIS (Network Device Interface Specification)
Specification for the Ethernet adapter/NETBIOS liaison.

NDL (Network Data Language)
The skeletal standard developed by the Conference on Data Systems Languages (CODASYL) for an application programming interface (API) to network model database management systems (DBMSs). It has since been abandoned.

NDMP (Network Data Management Protocol)

NDS (Novell Directory Service)
A globally oriented service that maintains information about network resources, (including users, groups, servers, volumes, printers and multiple servers) and provides a naming service. NDS replaces the binary file used in previous versions of Novell's NetWare network operating system. (Previously called NetWare Directory Service.)

near-end crosstalk (See NEXT)

near-letter quality (NLQ)

NEDA (National Electronic Distribution Association)

negative acknowledgment (See NAK)

Neper
The basic unit of a logarithmic scale used for the expression of ratios of voltages, currents and similar quantities.

NetBEUI (NetBIOS Extended User Interface)
A device driver and transport protocol, originally developed by Microsoft, that can bind with up to eight Media Access Control (MAC) drivers.

NetBIOS (Network Basic Input/Output System)
An extension of IBM's PC BIOS. It was developed as the interface for the PC Network program, but is supported on the Token Ring Network (TRN) and a number of non-IBM systems. It will likely be a long-term tactical solution for local networking; the long-term strategic solution will be Advanced Program-to-Program Communications/Logical Unit 6.2 (APPC/LU 6.2).

NetBIOS Extended User Interface (See NETBEUI)

NetIPC (Network Interprocess Communications)
Permits intercentral processing unit (CPU) program sharing and enables programs running on different systems to exchange data through a set of programmatic calls. This peer-to-peer service is important for developing distributed applications.

netiquette (network etiquette)
The term used to describe the proper way to behave on the Internet. Users must follow netiquette to avoid being flamed. See also flame.

netizen
A network citizen — someone who uses the Internet quite frequently and essentially "lives" part of his or her life on the World Wide Web. Netizens are different from Web surfers in that they use specific Internet services for longer periods rather than visit many sites in short increments.

NetMeeting — Microsoft
A data conferencing and groupware facility for Microsoft Windows.

net present value (See NPV)

NETs (Normes Européennes de Télécommunications)
Pan-European communications equipment type approval standards agreed to by the European Telecommunications Standards Institute (ETSI).

NetView (See NV)

NetView/PC Connect
A network management interface to IBM's NetView network management system through the IBM NetView/PC service point.

NetView Peer Interface
Network management as a peer Systems Network Architecture (SNA) node to the focal point of IBM's NetView.

NetWare
A network operating system (NOS) by Novell. The dominant local-area networking system for peripheral sharing and application communications.

NetWare Loadable Module (See NLM)

network
Any number of computers (e.g., PCs and servers) and devices (e.g., printers and modems) joined together by a physical communications link. In the corporate context, networks allow information to be passed between computers, irrespective of where those computers are located. Networks provide the roads for information traffic (e.g., sending files and e-mail) within a corporate environment, and allow users to access databases and share applications residing on servers. If a network does not go outside of a company building, or campus, then it is known as a local-area network (LAN). If it has a bridge to other outside networks, usually via lines owned by public telecommunications carriers like AT&T, then it is known as a wide-area network (WAN).

network access point (See NAP)

Network Address Translation (See NAT)

Network Addressable Unit (see NAU)

network and systems management (See NSM)

Network Applications Support — Digital Equipment (See NAS)

network-based storage backup facilities — midrange
A system facility for defining and executing predetermined backup processes of data from other midrange systems of the same supplier in the network.

Network Basic Input/Output System (See NetBIOS)

Network Caching Servers
In contrast to proxy servers, the biggest difference is the network caching server's ability to listen on the network and intercept protocol requests on its associated Transmission Control Protocol (TCP) ports. This alleviates the need to have the enterprise's browser configured to "know" where the server sits on the network.

N

Network Code of Practice (NCOP)

network computer
Often called a "thin client," a network computer is a limited-function desktop computer that is designed to easily connect to networks. NCs include a keyboard, mouse, monitor, memory and a network connection but only limited, if any, local disk storage. When end users want to access software or databases using an NC, they would use a graphical user interface (GUI), much as they do now with a PC. However, the software would be downloaded from a central server instead of being resident on the desktop PC; large databases would also be maintained on the central server. All software backups, upgrades and maintenance would therefore be performed centrally on the network server.

Network Computer Reference Platform (See NCRP)

network computing
A new client/server application architecture with dynamic application deployment, execution and management. NC is characterized by four properties: dynamic cached propagation; write once, run anywhere; automatic platform adjustment; and network context storage. While these properties do not constitute a formal definition of NC and need not be present for an enterprise to have NC, the four properties constitute the backbone of the NC paradigm.

Network Computing Architecture (See NCA)

network computing client/server (See NCCS)

Network Control Program — a.k.a. ACF/NCP (See NCP)

network database
A database organized according to ownership of records, allowing records to have multiple owners and thus providing multiple access paths to the data. Database management systems (DBMSs) providing such capabilities are also known as CODASYL (Conference on Data Systems Languages) DBMSs.

Network Data Language (See NDL)

Network Device Interface Specification (See NDIS)

network dynamic functionality (See NDF)

network etiquette (See netiquette)

Network File System (See NFS)

Network Independent File Transfer Protocol (see NIFTP)

network information service — Sun Microsystems (See NIS)

networking (See also network)
The linking of a number of devices, such as computers, workstations and printers, into a network (system) for the purpose of sharing resources.

network interface card (See NIC)

Network Interprocess Communications (See NetIPC)

network layer
In the Open Systems Interconnection (OSI) model, the logical network entity that services the transport layer. It is responsible for ensuring that data passed to it from the transport layer is routed and delivered through the network.

network management
Administrative services performed in managing a network — e.g., network topology and software configuration, downloading of software, monitoring network performance, maintaining network operations, and diagnosing and troubleshooting problems.

Network Management Center (See NMC)

Network Computing

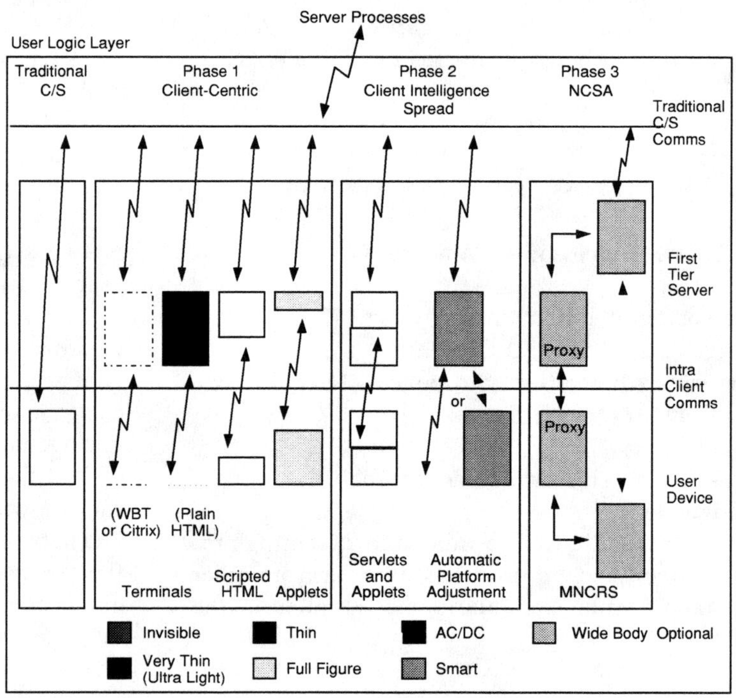

AC/DC = Alternating current/direct current
C/S = Client/server
HTML = Hypertext Markup Language
MNCRS = Mobile Network Computing Reference Specification
NCSA = Networking computing systems architecture
WBT = Windows-based terminal

Source: GartnerGroup

Network Computing Evolutionary Phases

Network Management Forum (See NMF)

Network Management System (See NMS)

network management vector tables (See NMVT)

Network News Transport Protocol (See NNTP)

Network OLE — Microsoft (See NOLE)

network operating system (See NOS)

network performance tuning/configuring facilities
The ability to configure combinations of local-area networks (LANs) and wide-area networks (WANs) centrally and dynamically based on anticipation and prioritization of data traffic volumes. Physical data paths could be configured based on data traffic content (i.e., transaction type). This is particularly important for online transaction processing (OLTP) applications.

network redundancy
A communications pathway that has additional links to connect all nodes in case one link goes down.

network security
Measures taken to protect a communications pathway from unauthorized access to, and accidental or willful interference of, regular operations.

Network Series (See NS)

Network Series 8 (See NS8)

network service access point (See NSAP)

network service provider (see NSP)

Network Terminating Unit (See NTU)

network-to-network interface (See NNI)

network topology
Describes the physical and logical relationship of nodes in a network, the schematic arrangement of the links and nodes, or some hybrid combination thereof.

network virtual terminal
A communications concept describing a variety of data terminal equipment (DTE), with different data rates, protocols, codes and formats, accommodated in the same network. This is done as a result of network processing where each device's data is converted into a network standard format, then converted into the format of the receiving device at the destination end.

neural net or neural network
An artificial-intelligence processing method within a computer that allows self-learning from experience. Neural nets can develop conclusions from a complex and seemingly unrelated set of information.

newbie
A person new to the Internet or some part of it.

NeWS
Sun Microsystems' initial graphical user interface (GUI) product.

newsgroup
On the Internet, one of over 16,000 discussion forums collectively known as Usenet.

NewWave
An environment that was developed by Hewlett-Packard in cooperation with Microsoft and built on Windows 2.0.

NewWave Office
Hewlett-Packard's third-generation office information system (OIS), which was built around the NewWave user environment on the workstation and HP-UX-, MPE/XL-and OS/2-based servers.

N

NEXT (near-end crosstalk)
Unwanted energy transferred from one circuit, usually to an adjoining circuit. It occurs at the end of the transmission link where the signal source is located, with the absorbed energy usually propagated in the opposite direction of the absorbing channel's normal current flow. It is usually caused by high-frequency or unbalanced signals and insufficient shielding.

Next-Generation Internet (See NGI)

Next-Hop Resolution Protocol (See NHRP)

NFS (Network File System)
A method of sharing files across a computer network. Pioneered by Sun Microsystems, it is now a de facto standard in the Unix environment. NFS is built on Transmission Control Protocol/Internet Protocol (TCP/IP) and Ethernet.

NFT (Network File Transfer)
Copies files between any two nodes on a network, either interactively or programmatically. It enables the user to copy remote files, translate file attributes and access remote accounts.

NGI (Next-Generation Internet)
The federal government project to fund research and to build a high-speed network designed to provide performance guarantees.

NHID (national healthcare identifier)
An identification code unique to each person, mandated by the Health Insurance Portability and Accountability Act of 1996 (HIPAA), that provides a way to seamlessly aggregate data on a given person regardless of the location of the data or the systems used to access it.

NHRP (Next-Hop Resolution Protocol)
Protocol defined for the Internet Engineering Task Force (IETF) to determine shortcuts through a routed infrastructure. The protocol has been incorporated in multiprotocol over ATM (MPOA) for asynchronous transfer mode (ATM) as well as for proprietary layer 3 implementations.

NIC (network interface card)
The bus-specific adapter that connects an end station or server to a local-area network (LAN). It plugs into an expansion slot on a workstation or server that is to be networked and has a connector for the network cabling.

nickel metal hydride (See NiMH)

NIFTP (Network Independent File Transfer Protocol)
Part of the Color Book protocol suite, which preceded Open Systems Interconnection (OSI) but is still widely used.

NIH (not invented here)

NIIIP (National Industrial Information Infrastructure Protocols)
The NIIIP-Smart activity, sponsored by the National Institute of Standards and Technology, is the technical standards aspect of the U.S. Department of Commerce's Consortium for Intelligent Integrated Manufacturing Planning and Execution project, part of the Advanced Technology Program. The thrust of this effort is an object-oriented framework with modular plug-and-play capability to facilitate the integration of open control systems (OCS), manufacturing execution systems (MES) and enterprise resource planning (ERP) applications. This effort will go beyond traditional standards activities in not only defining but demonstrating feasibility. Applicable to a broad range of discrete manufacturing from engineer-to-order to make-to-stock, this activity has broad appeal to all discrete manufacturers.

NiMH (nickel metal hydride)
A type of rechargeable battery used in portable computers and cell phones. NiMH batteries have greater charge density than nickel-cadmium batteries.

NIPRnet (Nonclassified Internet Protocol Router Network)
A subset of the Internet used by the U.S. military.

NIS (network information service — Sun Microsystems)
A Unix repository for user and resource configuration information.

N-ISDN (narrowband ISDN)
Integrated Services Digital Network (ISDN) speeds up to 1.544 megabits per second (Mbps). As speeds get faster, the definition of narrowband ISDN applies to faster speeds.

NIST (National Institute of Standards and Technology)
An agency of the U.S. Department of Commerce. Previously called the National Bureau of Standards.

NLM (NetWare Loadable Module)
Software that provides additional functions to a NetWare server — for example, an application (such as a DBMS) running directly under NetWare.

NLP (natural language processing)

NLQ (near-letter quality)
A designation for high-quality dot-matrix printers. Now largely obsolete.

NLS (national language support)
Mechanisms provided for the straightforward internationalization of both system and application user-visible interfaces.

NLS (network licensing server)

NLSP (Network Layer Security Protocol)

NLU (natural-language understanding)
The comprehension by computers of the structure and meaning of human language (e.g., English, Spanish, Japanese), allowing users to interact with the computer using natural sentences.

NMC (Network Management Center)
The center used for control of a network. It may provide traffic analysis, call detail recording, configuration control, fault detection and diagnosis and maintenance.

NMF or NM Forum (Network Management Forum)
A consortium of more than 100 equipment vendors and carriers that are developing implementation specifications for Open Systems Interconnection (OSI)-based network management. NMF was formerly known as OSI/Network Management Forum (OSI/NM Forum). It was joined in 1992 by the Association for the Integration of Network Management Systems (AIMS).

NMI (nonmaskable interrupt)

NMOS (N-channel metal-oxide semiconductor)
A microelectronic circuit used for logic and memory chips and in complementary metal-oxide semiconductor (CMOS) design. NMOS transistors are faster than the P-channel metal-oxide semiconductor (PMOS) counterpart, and more of them can be put on a single chip.

NMR (nuclear magnetic resonance)
A medical imaging technology that can "see" soft tissue.

NMS (Network Management System)
A central software-based set of programs for control of disparate hardware elements; also the software and hardware used in bridging, routing, etc., together with the Network Management Center.

NM/SIG
The Network Management Special Interest Group of the Open Systems Interconnection (OSI)

Implementer's Workshop (OIW), sponsored by the National Institute of Standards and Technology (NIST).

NMVT (network management vector tables)
A Systems Network Architecture (SNA) management protocol which provides alert problem determination statistics and network management data. See national number.

NNI (network-to-network interface)

NNM (network node manager)

NNTP (Network News Transport Protocol)
The discussion database standard that governs Usenet newsgroup distribution on the Internet.

NOC (network operations center)

node
A termination point for two or more communications links. The node can serve as the control location for forwarding data among the elements of a network or multiple networks, as well as performing other networking and, in some cases, local-processing functions. In Systems Network Architecture (SNA), it is an end point of a link or a junction common to two or more links in a network. Nodes can be host processors, communications controllers, cluster controllers, workgroup computers or terminals.

noise
Unwanted electrical signals, introduced by circuit components or natural disturbances, that tend to degrade the performance of a communications channel.

NOLE (Network OLE — Microsoft)
An early name for Distributed Component Object Model (D-COM).

nonblocking
Describes the state of a telephone switch where a through traffic path always exists for each attached station. Generically, it describes a switch or switching environment designed to never experience a busy condition due to call volume.

Nonclassified Internet Protocol Router Network (see NIPRnet)

noncompliant products
A hardware product that has not been submitted to rigorous authentication and testing with various configurations and parameters, including numerous clock settings and time/date stamps. Noncompliant products may run, but the level of risk associated with them is unknown because of a lack of test data.

non-real-time variable bit rate (See nrtVBR)

nonreturn to zero inverted (See NRZI)

nonstandard Java VM
A Java virtual machine (VM) not certified by Sun Microsystems as conforming to the VM specification. It may have extended functionality or the lack of support for some Java language and Java VM features. Nonstandard Java VM may extend the application programming interfaces (APIs) or replace Sun's APIs entirely.

NonStop SQL (NonStop Structured Query Language)
Leading-edge relational database management system (RDBMS) software from Tandem Computers. Working in concert with Tandem's message-passing Guardian operating system, NonStop SQL supports near-linear expandability and high uptimes for applications by tolerating single points of failure. NonStop SQL was the first DBMS to support engine-based (as opposed to front-end-tool-based), truly distributed databases.

NonStop Structured Query Language (See NonStop SQL)

Nonuniform Rational B-Spline (See NURBS)

nonvolatile (See NV)

nonwireline cellular carrier
A U.S. term referring to Block A carriers. Nonwireline or Block A systems operate on radio frequencies from 824 to 848 megahertz (MHz).

Normes Européennes de Télécommunications (See NETs)

North American Presentation Level Protocol Syntax (See NAPLPS)

NOS (network operating system)
A set of software utilities that, working in conjunction with an operating system (OS), provides the local-area network (LAN) user interface and controls network operation. A network operating system communicates with the LAN hardware and enables users to communicate with one another and to share files and peripherals. Typically, a NOS provides file-to-print services, directory services and security.

notary
An Internet standard defining message status capabilities and delivery notification.

Novell Directory Service (See NDS)

Novell NetWare Implementation
A facility that provides server functions and program-to-program application programming interfaces (APIs) on the midrange system.

NOW Index
A GartnerGroup metric that measures normalized cost and work produced in an IS facility.

NPA (Network Professional Association)

N-PCS (narrowband personal communications services)
N-PCS is similar to paging since it is used for short-message applications with a small "palm-of-the-hand" form factor. The addition of a response channel enables two-way paging capability and allows N-PCS to serve users that have more robust data and reliability requirements. N-PCS has been allocated a total of three megahertz (MHz) of spectrum in the 900-MHz block by the Federal Communications Commission (FCC).

NPSI (NCP Packet Switching Interface)

NPV (net present value)
Given an initial investment, a series of expected cash flow returns per period and an internal opportunity cost of capital (OCC), NPV analysis helps determine whether an investment should be made.

NRC (nonrecurring charge)

NRE (nonrecurring engineering)

nrtVBR (non-real-time variable bit rate)
An asynchronous transfer mode (ATM) service category, defined by the ATM Forum, that provides latency or bandwidth guarantees for traffic with no strict timing requirements. Good uses of this service are for legacy Systems Network Architecture (SNA) traffic or frame relay committed information rate (CIR) trunking.

NRZ (nonreturn-to-zero)

NRZI (nonreturn to zero inverted)
Encoding by inverting a signal on a high-voltage (on) pulse, leaving the signal unchanged for the low (off).

NS (Network Series)
A tape drive based on Travan technology. The features that differentiate it from Travan are read after write and hardware compression.

NS8 (Network Series 8)
A tape drive based on Travan technology. The feature that differentiates it from NS is native 8 gigabyte (GB) capacity. NS8 is manufactured by Seagate, Tecmar and AIWA.

NSA (National Security Agency)
A U.S. government agency responsible for electronic intelligence.

NSAP (network service access point)
In the semantics of the Open Systems Interconnection (OSI) addressing scheme, the point at which the OSI network service is made available to the transport entity.

NSAPI (Netscape Server API)

NSF (National Science Foundation)

NSF (Notes Files)

NSM (network and systems management)
The intersection of networking, network management and systems management. The vision of NSM is to enable the management of a distributed set of systems in a fashion similar to that in which many centralized data centers are managed. This vision remains far from fulfillment.

NSO (Network Server Option)

NSP (network service provider)
Any provider of network services, including regional Bell operating companies (RBOCs), interexchange carriers (IXCs), Internet service providers (ISPs), etc.

NSTL (National Software Testing Lab)

NT (See Windows NT)

NT1
An Integrated Services Digital Network (ISDN) Basic Rate Interface (BRI) line-terminating device at the subscriber's location that provides line maintenance access, timing and echo cancellation. NT1s may be built into other pieces of equipment or may stand alone.

NTFS (NT File System)

NTHSM (NT Hierarchical Storage Management)

NTL (narrow track longitudinal)

NTS (NT Server)
A multipurpose server operating system (OS) with the ability to function as a general-purpose application platform (e.g., as a Web server, a messaging server and a departmental SQL server). NTS also has the ability to serve as an enterprise's network operating system (NOS).

NTSC (National Television System Committee)

NTS/E (Microsoft Windows NT Server Enterprise Edition)
A bundling of Microsoft server technologies.

NT Server (See NTS)

NTU (Network Terminating Unit)
The part of the network equipment that connects directly to the data terminal equipment.

nuclear magnetic resonance (See NMR)

null modem
A configuration that enables two DTEs (data terminal equipment) to intercommunicate.

NUMA (nonuniform memory access)

number assignment module (See NAM)

Numerical Aerodynamic Simulation — NASA program (See NAS)

NURBS (Nonuniform Rational B-Spline)
An algorithm used in 3-D modeling software.

NV (NetView)
An IBM Systems Network Architecture (SNA) network management product that includes some of the functions of NCCF, NLDM, NPDA, NMPF and Virtual Telecommunications Access Method (VTAM) node control application. It was a key enabler to IBM's overall systems management strategy.

NV (nonvolatile)
A data store which retains data when power is off.

NVRAM (nonvolatile RAM)

NW/IP (NetWare Internet Protocol)

NWO (network outsourcing)

O

OAG (Open Applications Group)

Oakley Key Determination Protocol
A protocol that uses a hybrid Diffie-Hellman technique to establish session keys on Internet hosts and routers (encryption).

OASIS (Open Access Same-Time Information System)

OBI (Open Buying on the Internet)
An evolving consortium-developed standard for World Wide Web-based procurement of maintenance, repair and operations (MRO) goods.

object
In its simplest terms, it means nothing more than "thing" or "entity." In the world of object-oriented programming and databases, it signifies an instance of a class, such as "IBM" being an instance of the class "hardware vendor." An object is the unit of information interchange in third-generation (3GL) office systems. An object contains both content and semantics describing how the content is to be interpreted or operated on. A network object is any entity in a network (e.g., a node, printer or file server). Software objects may be files or pieces of data.

object-based middleware
Runtime software that enables objects (components) to work cooperatively with a container program or another object, even if the software is distributed across multiple computers.

object-based technologies
Technologies in which objects have encapsulation.

object class
A grouping of objects that can be described in terms of the attributes its members have in common. Generic electronic mail (e-mail) is a class. All e-mail systems have certain things in common. WordPerfect documents are a class.

object code (see object program)

Object Content Architecture (See OCA)

Object Database Management Group (See ODMG)

Object

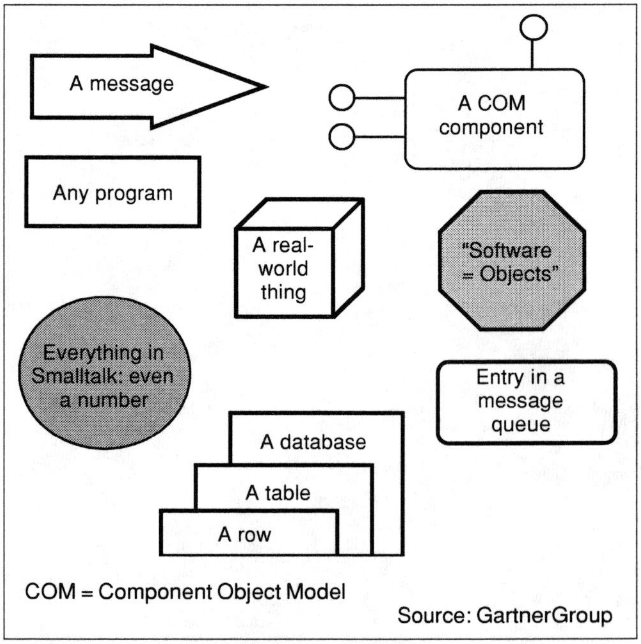

The Many Meanings of "Object"

object data model
A data model based on object-oriented programming, associating methods (procedures) with objects that can benefit from class hierarchies. Thus, "objects" are levels of abstraction that include attributes and behavior. An object-oriented data model is one that extends the individual program space into the world of persistent object management and shareability.

object encapsulation
Hiding complexity. Data and procedures may be encapsulated to produce a single object.

Object File System (See OFS)

object inheritance
Inheritance defines a relationship among classes in which a subclass shares, overrides or supplements operations or data values from one or more superclasses. A subclass is a specialization of one or more superclasses.

object instance
A specific occurrence of an object. For example, a specific mail message document is an instance.

object late binding
Runtime interpretation of messages. Using late binding, objects are integrated at runtime, as opposed to compiling an integrated object. This greatly enhances flexibility.

object management
Middleware that manages the naming, location and invocation of objects in a system.

Object Management Group (See OMG)

object message passing
In object-oriented systems, one object never operates on another. Instead, one object may pass a message to another object requesting invocation of a method — e.g., "print yourself," "display yourself" or "file yourself."

object method
Methods define what can be done with an object. Methods for an electronic-mail document may be display, send, file or print.

object orientation, object-oriented (See OO)

object-oriented database management system (See OODBMS)

object-oriented programming (See OOP)

object-oriented system
In an object-oriented system, all data is represented as discrete objects with which the user and other objects may interact. Each object contains data as well as information about the executable file needed to interpret that data. An object-oriented system allows the user to focus completely on tasks rather than tools. Examples of object-oriented programming languages include C++ and Smalltalk.

object-oriented technology (See OOT)

object program
A fully compiled or assembled program that is ready to be loaded into the computer. It is the result of processing a source program through an assembler or compiler. Also called object code.

object-relational mapping tools (See OR mapping tools)

object request broker (See ORB)

object role modeling (See ORM)

Object Structured Query Language — Hewlett-Packard (See OSQL)

object transaction monitor (See OTM)

OBS (organization breakdown structure)

OCA (Object Content Architecture)
The definition of the components, or objects, containing the data that comprises the document information carried by a Mixed Object: Document Content Architecture (MO:DCA) data stream.

OCC (opportunity cost of capital)

OCE (Open Collaboration Environment) (See AOCE)

OCF (Open Connection Feature)

OCI (Oracle Call-Level Interface)

OC-N (Optical Carrier at Rate N)
The range of incremental rates defined for Synchronous Optical Network (SONET)-based fiber-optic transmission. A SONET/SDH term identifying the place in the hierarchy or speed of such a channel (e.g., OC-3 is 155 Mbps).

OCR (optical character recognition)
The ability of a computer to recognize written characters through some optical-sensing device and pattern recognition software.

OCS (open control system)
Systems used to control the manufacturing processes in manufacturing industries and similar industries (such as utilities). Key elements are sensors for input, actuators for output, controllers to execute control algorithms, and interfaces with humans for operational control and engineering configuration. An OCS is distinctive in that it uses commercially available technology to interface with other IT systems in an organization and may contain both purpose built hardware and generic computing platforms driven by specialized software.

OCS

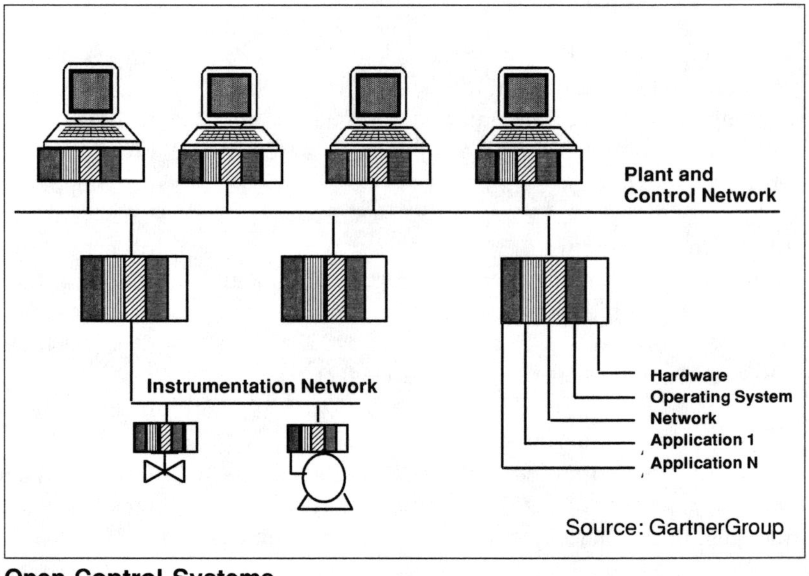

Open Control Systems

OCSP (Online Certificate Status Protocol)
A method of certificate revocation.

OCT (object code translation)

OCX (OLE Custom Controls)
Visual Basic add-on components based on the OLE set of interfaces.

ODA (Open Document Architecture)
An international standard that enables users to exchange texts and graphics generated on different types of office products.

ODBC (Open Database Connectivity)
A vendor-neutral interface based on the Structured Query Language (SQL) Access Group specifications. Announced by Microsoft in December 1991,

ODBC accesses data in a heterogeneous environment of relational and nonrelational databases.

ODBMS (object-oriented database management system)
See OODBMS. Alternative acronym.

ODD (optical disk drive)

ODETTE (Organization for Data Exchange Through Teletransmission in Europe)
An electronic data interchange (EDI) project for the European Automotive Industry.

ODIF (Open Document Interchange Format)
Defines the Open Document Architecture (ODA) format in terms of interchanged data elements.

ODM (Open Document Management)

ODMA (Open Document Management API)
Provides standard interface between document management systems and end-user applications. ODMA is becoming a desktop application integration de facto standard.

ODMG (Object Database Management Group)
A group of object-oriented database management system (OODBMS) vendors assisting the Object Management Group (OMG) in defining object standards.

ODS (Online Dynamic Server — Informix)

ODS (operational data store)
A new articulation of the perennial concept of shared production data. Different from a data warehouse, the ODS is an alternative to having operational decision support system (DSS) applications access data directly from the database that supports transaction processing (TP).

While both require a significant amount of planning, the ODS tends to focus on the operational requirements of a particular business process (for

ODBC

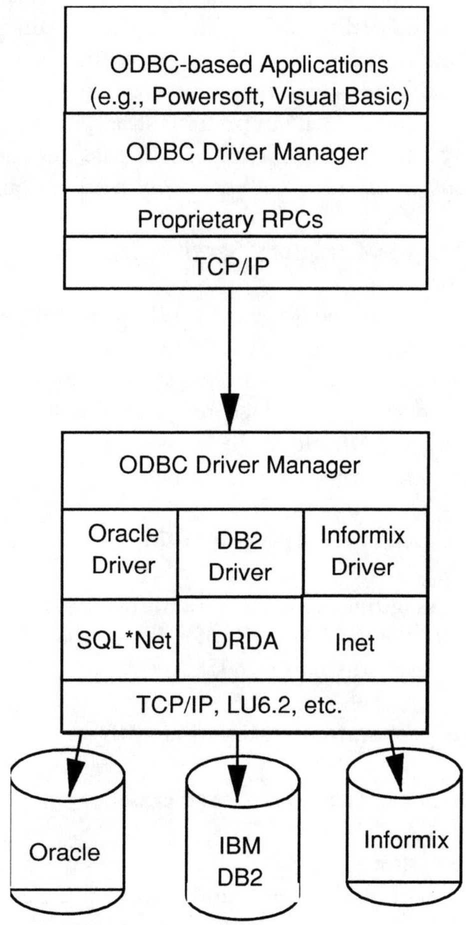

Within this three-tier architecture, an RPC may be used between the client and second tier (i.e., function-sharing), and a native DBMS call is used between the middle tier and the DBMS (i.e., data-sharing).

DB2 = Database 2
DBMS = Database Management System
DRDA = Distributed Relational Data
ODBC = Open Database Connectivity
RPC = Remote procedure call
SQL = Structured Query Language
TCP/IP = Transmission Control Protocol/Internet Protocol

Source: GartnerGroup

Server-Based ODBC Driver Architecture

O

example, customer service), and on the need to allow updates and propagate those updates back to the source operational system from which the data elements were obtained. The data warehouse, on the other hand, provides an architecture for decision makers to access data to perform strategic analysis, which often involves historical and cross-functional data and the need to support many applications.

ODSI (Open Directory Services Interface — Microsoft)
A standard in the Microsoft Windows operating system that provides a generic application interface to any of a number of database systems that have a service provider interface (SPI) available in the architecture. Additional SPIs may be provided by the database vendor or a third party.

OEC (open enterprise computing)

OEM (original equipment manufacturer)
Refers to the manufacturer of a device that another vendor resells as part of a system.

Office information system (See OIS)

Office Server Extension (See OSE)

OfficeVision
The name for IBM's Systems Application Architecture (SAA) office program, introduced in 1989.

offline
1. Equipment or devices not under the direct control of the central processing unit (CPU).
2. Terminal equipment not connected to a transmission line.

offshore programming
The contracting by a company for software services to be carried out in a country other than its own — e.g., a user located in North America may choose to have applications maintenance work carried out in India.

off-the-shelf
Equipment already manufactured and available for delivery from stock.

OFS (Object File System)
A file system conceived by Microsoft as a base for the directory in a future version of Windows NT, in which the name spaces of its file system and its Exchange electronic mail (e-mail) system would be unified.

OFX (Open Financial Exchange)
A specification that creates the presentment of a bill. It defines two fundamental capabilities for billing: communication of sign-up information from consolidator to biller, and communication of bill summary information from biller to consolidator. OFX does not define standards for the look of a bill. It merely provides a control channel for information about the bills.

OIG (Open Interoperability Group)

OIS (office information system)
The architectural reference frame for the construction of an office solution that meets the needs that originate at all levels (individual, departmental and corporate), integrating them in a functional sense.

OLAP (online analytical processing)
A definition of multidimensional business intelligence (BI) servers that originated with a Code and Date white paper that defined 12 "OLAP product-evaluation rules" as the basis for selecting multidimensional products. OLAP is, in truth, only a new name for a class of BI products, some of which have existed for decades. The 12 evaluation rules for providing OLAP to user-analysts are:

1. Multidimensional conceptual view
2. Transparency
3. Accessibility
4. Consistent reporting performance
5. Client/server architecture
6. Generic dimensionality

7. Dynamic sparse matrix handling
8. Multiuser support
9. Unrestricted cross-dimensional operations
10. Intuitive data manipulation
11. Flexible reporting
12. Unlimited dimensions and levels

OLCP (online complex processing)
An extension of online transaction processing (OLTP) to include concurrent ad hoc query and batch processing.

OLE
A Microsoft protocol that enables creation of compound documents with embedded links to applications, so that a user does not have to switch from one application to another to make revisions. With OLE:

- Users can create compound documents using multiple applications.
- Compound documents may contain text and spreadsheet objects, graphic and chart objects, sound objects, and video and animated objects.
- Objects that support OLE automation may be scripted by OLE controllers, such as Visual Basic, and used in end-user-developed applications.

OLE Custom Controls (See OCX)

OLE DB (OLE Database)

OLE DS (OLE Directory Services)

OLE for Process Control (See OPC)

OLL (online learning)

OLS (online service)

OLTP (online transaction processing)
A mode of processing that is characterized by short transactions recording business events and that normally requires high availability and consistent, short response times. This category of applications requires that a request for service be answered within a predictable period that approaches "real time." Unlike traditional mainframe data processing, in which data is processed only at specific times, transaction processing puts terminals online, where they can update the database instantly to reflect changes as they occur. In other words, the data processing models the actual business in real time, and a transaction transforms this model from one business state to another. Tasks such as making reservations, scheduling and inventory control are especially complex; all the information must be current.

OLTP monitor
Midrange system software designed to enhance the efficiency of online transaction-processing applications by providing screen mapping, transaction queuing, service prioritization, communications buffering and security.

OLTP screen-formatting front end
A cooperative processing facility that offloads screen formatting from a midrange system-resident online transaction processing (OLTP) system to a PC. The application programmer should be able to define a single set of screen-formatting maps without regard to whether the formatting is performed at the midrange system or at the PC.

OMAP (Operations and Maintenance Application Part — ISDN)
Provides network management functions.

OMF (object management facility)

OMF (open media framework)

OMG (Object Management Group)
A group, primarily of vendors, set up in 1990 to foster common definitions, understanding and standards for object-oriented computing. It has more than 100 members.

OMNIPoint (Open Management Interoperability Point)
A set of specifications, processes, and technology defined by the Network Management (NM) Forum within its Open Management Roadmap. OMNIPoints are planned at two-year intervals, allowing vendors time to develop products based on each set of guidelines.

OMR (optical mark recognition)

OMS (opportunity management system)
A system tied closely to the sales process; it is the framework for any sales force automation (SFA) design. All other applications are subordinate to the OMS. Transactions flow from the OMS to other applications on the users' portable computers. Applications can be integrated among vendors.

OMS (order management system)
Provides the order-taking capability within the supply chain environment. The OMS typically provides the orders to a warehouse management system for execution — i.e., picking, packing, and shipping.

OMT (Object Modeling Technique)

ONA (Open Network Architecture — from the FCC)

ONC (Open Network Computing — Sun Microsystems)

ONC (Open Network Connectivity)

ONE (Open Network Environment — Netscape)

One-Time Charge (See OTC)

online analytical processing (See OLAP)

Online Certificate Status Protocol (See OCSP)

online complex processing (See OLCP)

online documentation
A consistent, system-supplied mechanism for online documentation of system and application programs, including provision of such documentation of vendor-provided software.

online processor hardware replacement
Replacement of failed processor components without disrupting system operation.

online services
These provide access to exclusive data, information and communications resources. Customers of online

OMS

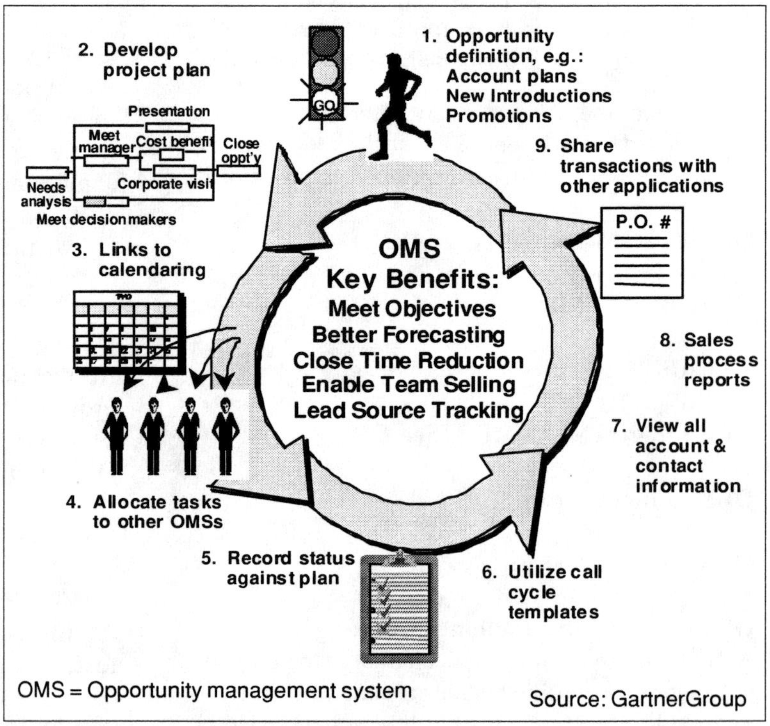

Opportunity Management Systems

services often must use proprietary software to access these resources. Online services often provide access to the Internet in addition to their exclusive resources. America Online, Microsoft Network, Prodigy and Lexis-Nexis are examples of online services.

online transaction processing (See OLTP)

online transaction-processing monitor (See OLTP monitor)

online transaction-processing screen-formatting front end (See OLTP screen-formatting front end)

OO (object-oriented or object orientation)
An umbrella concept used to describe a suite of technologies that enable software to be highly modular and reusable; applications, data, networks and computing systems are treated as objects that can be mixed and matched flexibly rather than as components of a system with built-in relationships. As a result, an application need not be tied to a specific system or data to a specific application. The four central object-oriented concepts are encapsulation, message passing, inheritance and late binding.

OO4GL (object-oriented fourth-generation language)

OOA (object-oriented analysis)

OOA&D (OO analysis and design)

OOD (object-oriented design)

OODBMS (object-oriented database management system)
A database management system (DBMS) that applies concepts of object-oriented programming, and applies them to the management of persistent objects on behalf of multiple users, with capabilities for security, integrity, recovery and contention management. An OODBMS is based on the principles of "objects," namely abstract data types, classes, inheritance mechanisms, polymorphism, dynamic binding and message passing.

OOP (object-oriented programming)
A style of programming characterized by the identification of classes of objects closely linked with the methods (functions) with which they are associated. It also includes ideas of inheritance of attributes and methods. It is a technique based on a mathematical discipline, called "abstract data types," for storing data with the procedures needed to process that data. OOP offers the potential to evolve programming to a higher level of abstraction.

OOT (object-oriented technology)
A software design model in which objects contain both data and the instructions that work on the data. It is increasingly deployed in distributed computing.

OPC (OLE for Process Control)
A specialized implementation of Microsoft OLE objects related to manufacturing, the specification of which is a function of the OPC Foundation.

open architecture
A technology infrastructure with specifications that are public as opposed to proprietary. This includes officially approved standards as well as privately designed architectures, the specifications of which are made public by their designers. The IBM PC, for example, was based on an open architecture, and spawned an entire industry of IBM clones.

Open Buying on the Internet (See OBI)

OpenCIM
Hewlett-Packard's open-system manufacturing initiative, which serves as an umbrella for products like OpenMFG, Hewlett-Packard's Unix-based MRP II software.

Open Client/Open Server
A product (and set of interfaces) marketed by Sybase that allows for gateways to foreign information environments. It is flexible, and licensable, but still proprietary, and thus not truly "open."

open control systems (See OCS)

Open Database Connectivity (See ODBC)

Open Directory Services Interface — Microsoft (See ODSI)

Open Document Architecture (See ODA)

Open Document Interchange Format (See ODIF)

Open Document Management API (See ODMA)

Open Financial Exchange (See OFX)

Open Look
An X Windows-based graphical user interface (GUI) developed primarily by Sun Microsystems.

Open Management Interoperability Point (See OMNIPoint)

OpenMFG
Hewlett-Packard's Unix-based manufacturing resource planning (MRP II) software.

Open Network Computing (See ONC)

Open Server Offering (See OSO)

Open Shortest Path First (See OSPF)

Open Software Description (See OSD)

Open Software Foundation (See OSF)

open source
Describes software that comes with permission to use, copy and distribute, either as is or with modifications, and that may be offered either free or with a charge. The source code must be made available.

open-source software (See OSS)

open system
A system whose interfaces — for example, application programming interfaces (APIs) or protocols — conform to formal, multilateral, generally available industry standards. "Formal" implies that the standard is selected and maintained using a structured, public process (i.e., de facto standards, such as those developed by the Open Software Foundation). "Multilateral" implies that, while nothing is ever completely vendor-neutral, the standard is not controlled by a single vendor. "Generally available" implies that the specifications are fully published (preferably with source code of a reference implementation), and that anyone can readily obtain license rights for free or at low cost.

Open Systems Interconnection (See OSI)

OpenView
A network management system from Hewlett-Packard.

Open Workgroup Repository (See OWR)

operating lease
A lease agreement that does not meet any of the criteria of a capital lease as defined by FASB 13 (Financial Accounting Standards Board Statement 13).

operating system (See OS)

Operating System/2 (See OS/2)

Operating System/400 (See OS/400)

operational data store (See ODS)

operational resource management (See ORM)

Operational Support Agreement (See OSA)

Operations and Maintenance Application Part — ISDN (See OMAP)

opportunity management system (See OMS)

OPS (optical proximity connection)

OPS (Oracle Parallel Server)

Optical Carrier at Rate N (See OC-N)

optical character recognition (See OCR)

optical disc
A disk read or written by light, generally laser light; such a disk may store video, audio or digital data.

optical magnetic reader (OMR)

OR (object-relational)

OR (object-relational) mapping tools
Tools that attempt to automate the mapping from object-oriented (OO) programming structures to relational storage structures. They are similar in intent to application integration middleware, which is designed to enable the interoperation of heterogeneous systems. However, they are different in the following important ways:

- The mapping layer is not runtime software that can be adjusted after deployment. OR mapping is done at development time, producing a compiled translation between objects and relational database management systems (RDBMSs).
- OR mapping tools map between data models, application integration middleware maps, message protocols and occasionally message contents. In this way, OR mapping tools seek to integrate at a deeper level than most other forms of middleware.

ORB (object request broker)
Middleware that allows objects to communicate with other software.

ORDBMS (object-relational DBMS)

order management system (See OMS)

Organization for Data Exchange Through Teletransmission in Europe (See ODETTE)

original equipment manufacturer (See OEM)

ORM (object role modeling)
A proprietary method that uses English to convey data design elements. The object is to enable developers to easily present the elements to end users who are unfamiliar with modeling notation.

ORM (operational resource management)
A method of managing of an organization's operating resources.

OS (operating system)
The operating system is the main control program that runs a computer and sets the standard for running application programs. It is the first program loaded when the computer is turned on, and it resides in memory at all times. An operating system is responsible for functions such as memory allocation, managing programs and errors, and directing input and output. It may be developed by the computer vendor or by a third-party independent software vendor.

OS/2 (Operating System/2)
An IBM operating system for personal computers that featured capabilities for large memory, multitasking and virtual machines.

OS/400 (Operating System/400)
An IBM operating system for midrange computers.

OSA (Open Software Associates)

OSA (Open System Adapter)

OSA (Operational Support Agreement)
IBM's Extended Service Agreement (ESA) offering in the United Kingdom.

OSA2 (Open System Adapter 2)

OSD (Open Software Description)
A specification that enables developers to specify attributes of their products, including how various pieces work together and when they were last updated, so that desktops are using current versions of software.

OSE (Office Server Extension)
OSEs enable users to create uniform resource locator (URL)-addressable threaded discussions that can resemble Network News Transfer Protocol (NNTP) threaded dialogues or be can embedded inside documents.

OSF (Open Software Foundation)
A consortium formed to develop formal, multivendor standards. Its founding members included IBM, Digital Equipment, Hewlett-Packard, Apollo Computer (since acquired by HP), Siemens Nixdorf and Groupe Bull. OSF was founded in reaction to the pact between AT&T and Sun Microsystems to develop a Unix standard that favored Sun's hardware. Its role has since evolved to address issues of common technology beyond Unix environments.

OSF/1
The first Open Software Foundation operating system, based on Carnegie-Mellon's Mach kernel and shipped in 1992.

OSF/Motif
The user interface developed by the Open Software Foundation (OSF). It is based on Digital Equipment's graphical user interface (GUI) toolkit, with a look and feel ported by Hewlett-Packard and Microsoft from Presentation Manager. It conforms to the X Windows standard, and is an implementation of the Motif GUI as defined by the Open Software Foundation Application Environment Specification User Environment Volume and Motif Style Guide.

OSI (Open Systems Interconnection)
A model developed by the International Organization for Standardization (ISO) for communications. It is similar in structure to Systems Network Architecture (SNA), but more open. A standard, modular approach to network design that divides the required set of complex functions into manageable, self-contained, functional layers. These layers, starting from the innermost, are:

1. Physical layer — concerned with the mechanical and electrical means by which devices are physically connected and data is transmitted.
2. Link layer — concerned with how to move data reliably across the physical data link.
3. Network layer — provides the means to establish, maintain and terminate connections between systems. Concerned with switching and routing information.
4. Transport layer — concerned with end-to-end data integrity and quality of service.
5. Session layer — standardizes the task of setting up a session and terminating it. Coordinates the interaction between end application processes.
6. Presentation layer — relates to the character set and data code that is used, and to the way data is displayed on a screen or printer.
7. Application layer — concerned with the higher-level functions that support application or system activities.

OSI environment
Those resources that enable information-processing systems to communicate openly, that is, to conform to the services and protocols of Open Systems Interconnection (OSI).

OSI FTAM
Support for Open Systems Interconnection File Transfer, Access and Management protocols verified under the Corporation for Open Systems Mark program.

OSI management
The facilities to control, coordinate and monitor the resources that enable communications in an Open Systems Interconnection (OSI) environment.

OSI/NM Forum (OSI/Network Management Forum)

OSIS (operating-system-independent server)

OSI TP (OSI Transaction Processing)

OSI X.400
Support for Open Systems Interconnection X.400 Message Handling System protocols verified under the Corporation for Open Systems Mark program.

OSM (operating-system service module)

OSO (Open Server Offering)
A process and marketing program from IBM, similar to its long-established Entry Server Offering (ESO), but with a focus on the network-computing and operating-systems environment.

OSPF (Open Shortest Path First)
An Interior Gateway Protocol (IGP) that transfers packets from one network to an adjacent one.

OSQL (Object Structured Query Language — Hewlett-Packard)
An extension to Structured Query Language (SQL) pioneered by Microelectronics & Computer Technology and delivered by Hewlett-Packard. It provides object management capabilities to the SQL relational language.

OSR (OEM Service Release)

OSS (open-source software)
"OSS" and "free software" are terms applied to software that can be run, distributed and modified without a fee. Restrictions are often applied — in the form of an "open-source license" — to profits or commercial fees for any product built on a base of free software (e.g., the GNU General Public License).

OST (offline store)

OT (object technology)

OTC (One-Time Charge)
An IBM single charge for purchasing or upgrading a product, as opposed to ongoing fees.

OTM (object transaction monitor)
An application program — similar to the mainframe Customer Information Control System (CICS) in function, but not in spirit — that represents a consistent model of an application for a modular and potentially highly distributed environment.

OTS (Object Transaction Service)

outsourcing
A contractual relationship with an outside vendor that is usually characterized by the transfer of assets, e.g., facilities, staff or hardware. It can include facilities management (data center and/or network), applications development/maintenance functions, and end-user computing services.

End-user-computing outsourcing includes all services to support end users from the workstation up to the front-end router. The scope ranges from the end user's workstation to the shared LAN and local network infrastructure of an enterprise's distributed computing architecture. It includes desktop services (implementation, operations and management of desktop hardware, software and peripherals), network systems management (implementation and management of LANs, network-enabling hardware and software) and help desks.

overflow

1. In telephony, excess traffic, on a particular route, that is offered to another (alternate) route.
2. In computing, a condition where data is presented to a buffer or port faster than it can be processed, resulting in lost data.
3. Also, in computing, a condition where a computational result is greater than the capacity of its location, resulting in an error condition.

overlapping VLAN
A virtual local-area network (VLAN) type where one user may belong to more than one VLAN at a time.

override
Seizure of a circuit that is already occupied.

overspeed
The condition in which the transmitting device runs faster than the data can be presented for transmission.

OWR (Open Workgroup Repository)
A local-area network (LAN)-based repository from Manager Software Products. OWR was originally called InfoSpan.

P

P7
X.400 protocol.

P42
The protocol created by the National Security Agency (NSA) by which the Defense Message System (DMS) Message Security Protocol (MSP) is described under the X.400 standards.

PA (Precision Architecture — Hewlett-Packard)

P/A (physical asymmetric)
A method of system partitioning that allows different-size increments of system resources to be divided physically into two or more partitions of different sizes. Some shared resources may be available.

PABX (private automatic branch exchange)
A telephone switch located at the site of the enterprise.

packet
An information block identified by a label at Layer 3 of the International Organization for Standardization (ISO) reference model for Open Systems Interconnection (OSI). It is a collection of bits that contains both control information and data, and is the basic unit of transmission in a packet-switched network. Control information is carried in the packet, along with the data, to provide for such functions as addressing sequence, flow control and error control at each of several protocol levels. A packet can be of fixed or variable length, but generally has a specified maximum length.

packet assembler/disassembler (See PAD)

packet format
The exact order and size of a packet's various control and information fields, including header, address and data fields.

Packet Level Protocol (See PLP)

packet overhead
A measure of the ratio of the total packet bits occupied by control information to the number of bits of data, usually expressed as a percentage.

packet switching
A technique in which a message is broken into smaller units called packets, which may be individually addressed and routed through the network, possibly using several different routes. The receiving-end node ascertains that all packets are received and in the proper sequence before forwarding the complete message to the addressee.

Packet Transfer Mode (See PTM)

PACS (Picture Archive and Communication System)
The hardware and software required for the storage and management of digital images, as well as the management of workflow within the radiology department. It has added functionality, compared to teleradiology, as it can provide historical context for current radiographs (old studies) and is an enabling technology that allows for the creation of the digital department.

PAD (packet assembler/disassembler)
An interface device that buffers data sent to and from character mode devices, and assembles and disassembles the packets needed for X.25 operation.

page (See Web page)

page description language (See PDL)

page, nonimpact, plain paper (See PNPP)

PAL (Phase Alternate Line)
A color television broadcasting system developed in West Germany and the United Kingdom that uses 650 picture lines and a 50-hertz (Hz) field frequency. See also NTSC (National Television System Committee) and SECAM (Séquential Couleur á Mémoire).

PAL (programmable array logic)

PAM (pulse amplitude modulation)
The encoding of information in a signal based on the fluctuation of carrier waves. The amplitude of the pulse carrier is varied in accordance with successive samples of the modulating signal.

PAMS (parallel application management system)

PAP (Password Authentication Protocol)
A security protocol without encryption that uses password authentication to allow access to a network or host. See also Challenge Handshake Authentication Protocol.

Parallel Enterprise Server (See PES)

parallel processing
The solution of a single problem across more than one processor. Little parallel processing is done today outside of research laboratories, because it is difficult to decompose tasks into independent parts, and the compiler technology does not yet exist that will extensively parallelize applications code.

Parallel Query Server (See PQS)

Parallel Reduced Instruction Set Multiprocessor (See PRISM)

Parallel Sysplex
The cornerstone of IBM's large-systems operating-system strategy. It is designed to allow multiple central electronics complexes (CECs) to share a common database so a transaction can execute on one of several processors that share a single view of the data. This implementation substantially improves parallelism, and therefore overall system throughput, at a multitasking level.

Parallel Sysplex License Charge (See PSLC)

parallel systems
Hardware configurations having nine or fewer central processing units (CPUs). Compare with highly parallel systems (HPS) and massively parallel systems.

Parallel Transaction Server (See PTS)

parallel transmission
Simultaneous transmission of the bits making up a character or byte, either over separate channels or on different carrier frequencies on one channel. See also serial transmission.

PARC (Palo Alto Research Center — Xerox)

parcel manifesting system (See PMS)

PA-RISC (Precision Architecture Reduced Instruction Set Computer)
Hewlett-Packard's RISC-based processor architecture, the basis for its desktop-to-mainframe processor products. It serves as a single design point to consolidate Hewlett-Packard's three computer families: Hewlett-Packard 9000/800 Unix multiuser system and servers; Hewlett-Packard 9000/700 Unix servers and workstations; and Hewlett-Packard 3000 commercial MPE/XL multiuser system and servers.

parity bit
A check bit appended to an array of binary digits to make the sum of all the binary digits, including the check bit, always odd or always even.

parity check
The addition of noninformation bits to data to make the number of ones in a grouping of bits either always even or always odd. This procedure enables detection of bit groupings that contain single errors. It can be applied to characters, blocks or any specific bit grouping.

partitioned data set (See PDS)

partitioning code
Applications can be broken into three logical parts — presentation, logic and data. These are areas in which the program can be separated to facilitate execution of each logical piece on a different machine. Each segment is known as a partition. For example, the thin-client Web model requires that interface presentation be handled by the browser, application logic by the World Wide Web server and other application servers, and data by a database server. Developers are responsible for determining where the separation occurs.

Passive Optical Network (See PON)

password
A code used to restrict access to database and other sources of computerized information. The use of passwords is a commonly used security measure, but it has limitations, because a computer can only verify the accuracy of the password, not the authenticity of the person using the password.

With the explosion of the Internet and extranets, passwords are becoming the security measure of choice to guard against unauthorized access to protected areas. Unfortunately, the same reasons that make passwords a popular security measure — easy distribution and administration — also make them undependable. Other procedures, such as certification processes used in combination with passwords, provide better security for critical interactions.

Password Authentication Protocol (See PAP)

patch
1. A temporary electrical connection.
2. To make an improvised modification; to change a software routine in a rough or expedient way.

Path Overhead — Sonet Term (See POH)

P

Parallel Sysplex

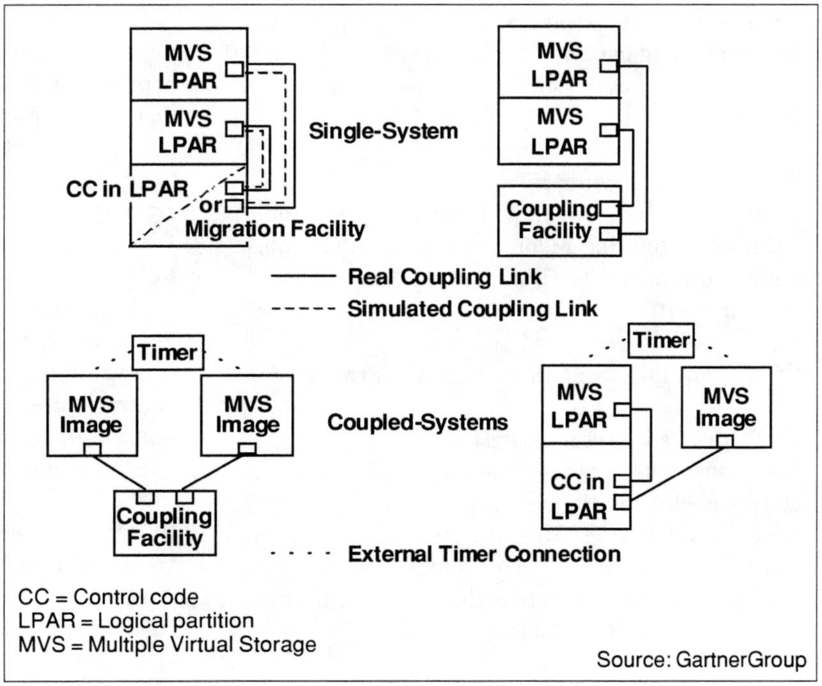

Parallel Sysplex Alternatives

PATX (private automatic telex exchange)

PAX (private automatic exchange)

payload pointer
Indicates the beginning of a synchronous payload envelope (a Sonet term).

PB (PowerBuilder)

PBA (production business application)

PBN (policy-based networking)
The application of business rules to govern network performance.

PBX (private branch exchange)
A telephone switch located on a customer's premises that primarily establishes voice-grade circuits (over tie lines to a telephone company central office) between individual users and the public switched telephone network. The PBX also provides switching within the customer premises local area, and usually offers numerous enhanced features, including least-cost routing and call detail recording.

PC (personal computer)
A microcomputer designed primarily for individual use. Sharing resources with another computer is optional. The first PCs were introduced in the late 1970s.

PCA (planning, control and administration)

PCB (printed circuit board)
A flat board made of fiberglass or plastic, on which chips and electronic components are interconnected via copper pathways. The primary PCB in a system is called a system board or motherboard, while smaller ones that plug into the slots in the main board are called riser boards or cards.

PC-Card (Personal Computer Memory Card) (See PCMCIA)

PC-DOS
The original operating system that IBM supplied with its personal computers, licensed from Microsoft.

PCI (Peripheral Component Interconnect)
The industry standard system bus architecture that is used in most desktop and server models. PCI provides faster communications between the processor and components (such as memory, disk and video) than the original IBM bus, now called Industry Standard Architecture (ISA).

PCL (Printer Control Language)
The set of commands used by Hewlett-Packard and compatible printers that governs how a document will be printed. Similar to, but less powerful and complex than PostScript.

PCM (plug-compatible manufacturer)
A hardware vendor whose products are direct replacements for the products of a computer system manufacturer. Initially PCMs provided peripherals that were "plug-for-plug" compatible with IBM peripherals, but the PCM industry has since grown to include IBM-compatible mainframes and peripherals for other vendors' systems.

PCM (pulse code modulation)
A digital technique that involves sampling an analog signal at regular intervals and coding the measured amplitude into a series of binary values, which are transmitted by modulation of a pulsed, or intermittent, carrier. It is the standard technique in telecommunications transmission.

PCMCIA (Personal Computer Memory Card International Association)
A nonprofit trade association founded in 1989 to standardize the PC card. The PCMCIA standard has since been renamed the PC Card standard. The standard cards are removable modules that can hold

memory, fax/modems, radio transceivers, network adapters, solid-state disks or hard disks in personal digital assistants (PDAs) and other lightweight or portable systems.

PCN (personal communications network)
A two-way digital cellular network. DCS1800, the PCN standard, is based on the Global System for Mobile Communications (GSM) standard. The user terminal is a light, handheld, portable device that remains with the individual as he or she moves among office, home and mobile environments.

P-code
An intermediate representation of a program that is file format independent and is executed by a virtual machine interpreter.

PCR (peak cell rate)
An asynchronous transfer mode (ATM) parameter used to determine the maximum number of cells permitted in a specified time period.

PCR (preventive cyclic retransmission)
The cyclic retransmission of all unacknowledged frames on an idle link. The term pertains to satellite and high-propagation delay links.

PCS (packet-controlled switching)

PCS (personal communications services)
A new, lower-powered, higher-frequency competitive technology to cellular service. Whereas cellular technology typically operates in the 800 to 900 megahertz (MHz) range, PCS operates in the 1.5 to 1.8 MHz range.

PCS (Personal Conferencing Specification)

PCTE (Portable Common Tool Environment)

PC-to-host communications products
Software or software/hardware products that enable a personal computer (PC) to communicate with a host or mainframe.

PCX (private communications exchange)
A high-capacity evolution of the digital private branch exchange (PBX), which incorporates a cell-based switching fabric or asynchronous (ATM) interfaces, an open client/server architecture and a high dependence on computer telephony integration (CTI) to deliver advanced functionality while retaining enterprise investment in PBX line cards and terminal equipment.

PDA (personal digital assistant)
A handheld, wireless computer that serves as an organizer, electronic book or note taker. It typically uses a stylus or pen-shaped device for data entry and navigation. Apple's Newton was an early example of a PDA.

PDC (Personal Data Cartridge)

PDC (Primary Domain Controller)

PDES (Product Data Exchange Specification)
A standard format for the exchange of data between advanced computer-aided design (CAD) and computer-aided manufacturing (CAM) programs. It describes a complete product, including the geometric aspects of the images, manufacturing features, tolerance specifications, material properties and finish specifications.

PDF (Portable Document Format)
The title format used by Adobe Systems to convert textually rich documents into files that can be easily transported and viewed with an Adobe Acrobat "reader."

PDH (Plesiochronous Digital Hierarchy)
The initial structure for organizing the hierarchy or possible bit rates in synchronous time-division multiplexing. It is now superseded by Synchronous Digital Hierarchy (SDH). PDH is defined by the International Telecommunication Union (ITU) in the G.703 standard.

PCX

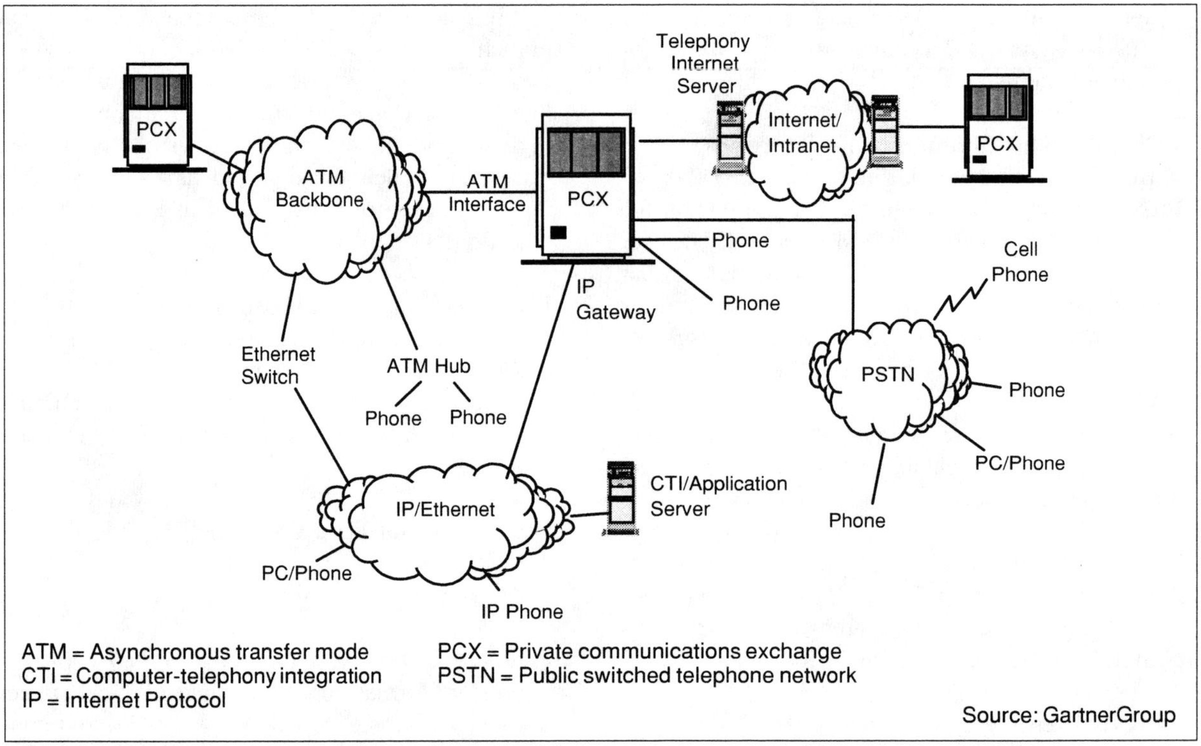

One Manufacturer's Interpretation of the PCX Concept

PDI (personal data interchange)

PDL (page description language)
The programming language used to specify the way a document will be printed or displayed.

PDM (exPress Data Mover — IBM)

PDM (product data management)
A set of technologies and capabilities for comprehensively managing design intent and product development processes across the enterprise. The three fundamental PDM technologies used are document vaulting, workflow and configuration management.

PDM (pulse duration modulation) (See PWM)

PDM II (product development management)
A new strategy for managing the interenterprise product development process from concept through production. The goal of a PDM II strategy is to provide the proper combination of people, processes and technologies to support the management of the entire interenterprise product development commercialization process to enhance competitiveness. The PDM II vision provides a framework for rationalizing the roles of virtual product development management (VPDM), product development management (PDM) and enterprise resource planning (ERP) technologies.

PDN (public data network)
A shared-use X.25 packet-switched network operated by a carrier. PDNs may offer value-added services at a reduced cost because of communica-

tions resource sharing and usually provide increased reliability due to built-in redundancy.

PDO (Portable Distributed Objects — Apple)

PDQ (Parallel Data Query)

PDS (partitioned data set)
A data set that is divided into physically distinct units, or members, which contain data or partial or complete programs.

PDU (Protocol Data Unit)
An Open Systems Interconnection (OSI) term for the data to be transmitted with the headers and trailers attached by each layer.

PDX (private digital exchange)

PDXI (Process Data Exchange Institute)
The organization standardizing the representation of process data for exchange among companies involved in the design and construction of process manufacturing facilities.

PE (phase encoding)

PE (project executive)

PEA (purchased enterprise applications)
Large, enterprisewide applications software purchased as a standardized packaged offering and typically customized by third-party or in-house developers. Examples include PeopleSoft and SAP R/3.

peak cell rate (See PCR)

peering agreement
A reciprocal arrangement between Internet providers that allows subscribers to access newsgroups and File Transfer Protocol (FTP) sites particular to a provider.

Peer Process — APPC
LU 6.2 support. Midrange system peer communications support using IBM's Advanced Program-to-Program Communications (APPC) protocols.

Peer Process — CPI-C API
Support is provided for applications that use IBM's Common Programming Interface for Communications (CPI-C) for peer-to-peer communications.

peer-to-peer
Access to application-to-application communication facilities between network-attached systems on the same level of a client/server hierarchy.

peer-to-peer remote copy (See PPRC)

PEM (privacy-enhanced mail)
A method of interenterprise e-mail messaging that works with existing e-mail systems to ensure the authenticity, integrity and optional confidentiality, through encryption, of messages.

performance monitoring and tuning tools
Facilities that enable users to monitor midrange-system performance, identify system and application performance bottlenecks, and set optimal performance-tuning parameters.

Performance Optimized With Enhanced RISC — IBM (See POWER)

PDM II

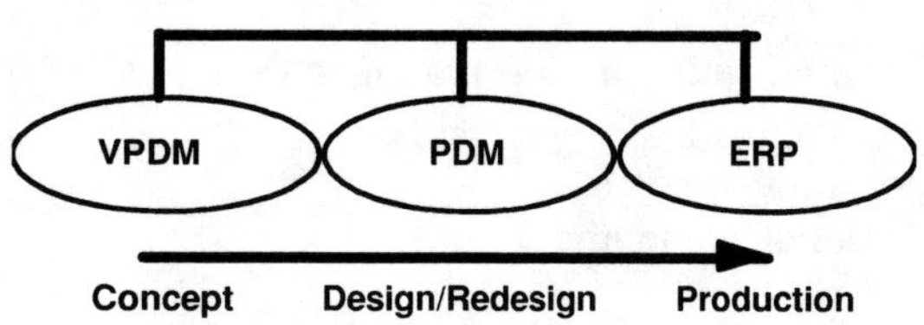

ERP = Enterprise resource planning
PDM = Product development management
VPDM = Virtual product development management

Source: GartnerGroup

Product Development Management II Model

Peripheral Component Interconnect (See PCI)

peripheral device
A piece of hardware that is connected to a computer. Examples are:

- Monitor
- Keyboard
- CD-ROM drive
- Modem
- Floppy disk drive

Peripheral Interchange Program (See PIP)

PERL (Practical Extraction Report Language)
A Unix scripting language for high-level system control, often used to manage Web servers.

permanent virtual circuit (See PVC)

personal communications network (See PCN)

personal communications services (See PCS)

personal computer (See PC)

Personal Computer Memory Card (PC-Card) (See PCMCIA)

Personal Computer Memory Card International Association (See PCMCIA)

personal digital assistant (See PDA)

personal information manager (See PIM)

personalware
Personal productivity tools.

PERT (Program Evaluation and Review Technique)
A management tool for graphically displaying projected tasks, milestones, schedules and discrepancies.

PES (Parallel Enterprise Server)
A label used by IBM for its CMOS-based mainframes.

PFM (personal financial manager)

PFS (process-flow scheduling)
Adds network process schedule planning and optimization functionality to a process-control system.

PGA (pin grid array)
An interconnection system for getting electrical signals into and out of a large integrated circuit (IC) such as a microprocessor.

PGML (Precision Graphics Markup Language)
An application proposed to the World Wide Web Coalition (W3C) to define 2-D graphics in Extensible Markup Language (XML).

PGP (Pretty Good Privacy)
Public-key encryption software sold by Network Associates (NA). PGP began as an open standard for message encryption. Add-ons are available for a

PERL

```
print "Content-type: text/plain", "\n\n";
$count_F = "/usr/local/bin/httpd/
sitecount.txt";
if (open (FILE, "<" . $count_F)) {
            $thehitcount = <FILE>;
            close (FILE);
            if (open (FILE, ">" . $count_F)) {
                  $thehitcount++;
                  print FILE $thehitcount;
                  close (FILE);
                  print $thehitcount;
            } else {
  print " [File Open failed! ]", "\n";
            }
} else {
  print "[ File Read Failed!]", "\n";
}
exit (0);
```

Source: GartnerGroup

A Sample Practical Extraction Report Language Counter Program

number of desktop products. The underlying protocol has been designated a military weapon by the United States and some other countries, in an effort to regulate its distribution, but similar software is widely available on the Internet.

PGS (proposal generation system)

Phase Alternate Line (See PAL)

phase jitter
In telephony, the measurement, in degrees out of phase, that an analog signal deviates from the referenced phase of the main data-carrying signal. It is often caused by alternating current components in a network.

phase modulation
One of three ways of modifying a sine wave signal to make it carry information. The sine wave or "carrier" has its phase changed in accordance with the information to be transmitted. Also known as Phase-Shift Keying (PSK) or Differential Phase-Shift Keying (DPSK).

phase shift
Errors that occur when the clock and data signals become unsynchronized.

Phase-Shift Keying (See PSK)

PHIGS (Programmers' Hierarchical Interactive Graphics Standard)
A graphics system and language used to create 2-D and 3-D images that interface between the application program and the device-independent graphics subsystem. Graphics objects are managed in a hierarchical manner so that a complete assembly can be specified with all of its subassemblies. High-performance workstations and host processing are required to handle the standard.

PHY (Physical Layer Protocol)
One of two sublayers of the Fiber Distributed Data Interface (FDDI) physical layer. See also PMD (Physical Medium Dependent).

physical asymmetric (See P/A)

physical layer
Within the Open Systems Interconnection (OSI) model, the lowest level of network processing concerned with the electrical, mechanical and handshaking procedures over the interface that connects a device to a transmission medium (e.g., RS-232-C).

Physical Layer Convergence Procedure (See PLCP)

Physical Layer Protocol (See PHY)

Physical Medium Dependent (See PMD)

Physical Unit (See PU)

PI (performance indicator)

PI (performance or process improvement)

PIC (programmable interrupt controller)

Picture Archive and Communication System (See PACS)

picture element (See pixel)

P&ID (piping and instrumentation drawing)
A style of drawing used in process manufacturing which depicts key process and control elements and is often used as a basis for construction, operation and maintenance of a facility.

PIDS (Patient Identification Services)

PIM (personal information manager)
Software that organizes and manages random information for fast retrieval on a daily basis. It provides a combination of features, including telephone list with automatic dialing, calendar and scheduler.

PIMS (process information management system)
A class of applications often referred to as manufacturing execution systems (MES) for process industries.

PIN (personal identification number)

PIN (Processor Independent NetWare)

Ping
A Transmission Control Protocol/Internet Protocol (TCP/IP) procedure that uses the Internet Control Message Protocol (ICMP) echo to check whether a network device is active.

PIP (Peripheral Interchange Program)
A Control Program for Microcomputers (CP/M) utility that allows files to be transferred between devices.

piping and instrumentation drawing (See P&ID)

PIR (protocol-independent routing)
A method in which routing decisions are made with no reference to the protocol in use. Protocol-independent routers have the functionality of protocol-specific routers, but can also route nonroutable protocols.

PIS (product information system)

PIT (programmable interval timer)

PITC (point-in-time copy)

PIX (private Internet exchange)

PIXBLT (pixel block transfer)

pixel (picture element)
The smallest resolvable dot in an image display.

Pixtext
Image-oriented document management product from Excalibur Technologies.

PKCS (Public-Key Cryptography Standard)

PKI (public-key infrastructure)
The software and/or hardware components necessary to manage and enable the effective use of public-key encryption technology, particularly on a large scale.

PKIX (Public-Key Infrastructure Exchange)
An initiative, led by the Internet Engineering Task Force (IETF) Public-Key Infrastructure Exchange (PKIX) subcommittee, addressing interoperability and cross-certification among certificate authorities.

PL/1 (programming language one)
An early scientific programming language now rarely used.

PLA (programmable logic array)

platform
An individual hardware or software architecture or an operating system.

platform-independent
Software that can run on a variety of hardware platforms or software architectures. Platform-independent software can be used in many different environments, requiring less planning and translation across an enterprise. For example, the Java programming language was designed to run on multiple types of hardware and multiple operating systems. If Java platform-independence becomes a reality, organizations with multiple types of computers will be able to write a specialized application

once and have it be used by virtually everyone, rather than having to write, distribute and maintain multiple versions of the same program.

PLC (programmable logic controller)
A specialized industrial computer used to programmatically control production and process operations by interfacing software control strategies to input/output (I/O) devices.

PLCP (Physical Layer Convergence Procedure)
The specification for mapping asynchronous transfer mode (ATM) cells onto the physical media.

PLD (programmable logic device)

Plesiochronous Digital Hierarchy (See PDH)

Plesiochronous network
A network that makes use of more than one clock source. It consists of different portions of the network where the signal may have the same nominal digit rate but does not stem from the same clock.

PLL (phase-locked loop)

PLP (Packet Level Protocol)
Network Layer protocol in the X.25 protocol stack.

PL/SQL (Programming Language/Structured Query Language)
One of the two deliverables of Oracle Systems' Transaction Processing Option (TPO). It is a 3GL-level extension of Structured Query Language (SQL) that groups SQL statements for transmission across the tools/database management system (DBMS) interface or across a network. PL/SQL must be used to take advantage of the Oracle version 6 performance enhancements.

plug-compatible manufacturer (See PCM)

PM (practice management)

PM (Presentation Manager)
The OS/2 graphical user interface, which includes windowing, graphics, standards for the keyboard interface, and editors for icons and fonts. It was the first manifestation of IBM's User Interface Architecture, consistent with the Common User Access (CUA) component of Systems Application Architecture (SAA).

PM (preventive maintenance)
A practice to reduce hardware or software downtime by replacement of components prior to failure via:

- A set of periodic inspections to highlight and repair functions prior to failure.
- Pre-emptive replacement based on mean time between failure (MTBF) statistics.

PMBX (private manual branch exchange)

PMCC (project management center of competency)

PMD (Physical Medium Dependent)
One of two sublayers of the Fiber Distributed Data Interface (FDDI) physical layer, PMD interfaces directly with the media. See also PHY.

PMD (programmable multilevel logic device)

PMH (product marshaling and handling)
An application suite that provides tight integration of warehouse and transportation operations and planning.

PMI (Project Management Institute)

PMLCD (passive-matrix liquid crystal display)

PMMU (paged memory management unit)

PMO (program management office)

P

PMOS (p-channel metal-oxide semiconductor)

PMP (Project Management Professional)
An information technology (IT) certification by the Project Management Institute (PMI) requiring two years of work experience and eight 50-minute sections testing on project scope, quality, time, cost, risk, human resources, procurement and communications management.

PMR (private mobile radio)

PMR (projection microradiography)

PMS (parcel manifesting system)
A system that provides the ability to weigh and rate small parcel shipments. The PMS contains the rate tables of the various parcel carriers such as UPS, RPS and Fed-Ex. The PMS also provides a detailed manifest of all parcel shipments.

PM/X (Presentation Manager/X)
A graphical user interface (GUI) product developed by Hewlett-Packard and Microsoft that provides an OS/2 Presentation Manager-compatible application programming interface (API) on Unix workstations.

PNNI (Private Network-to-Network Interface)
A standard that maps out the network from an asynchronous transfer mode (ATM) standpoint and, through multiple phases of the specification, will become the router-to-router protocol implementation in ATM switches.

PNPP (page, nonimpact, plain paper)
A laser- or LCD-type printer.

POC (Policy Oversight Committee)
Formerly the Internet International Ad Hoc Committee (IAHC), the POC is carrying out and expanding the policies outlined in the Genetic Top-Level Domain-Memorandum of Understanding (gTLD-MoU). The POC is composed of members from Council of Registrars (CORE), Internet Architecture Board (IAB), Internet Assigned Numbers Authority (IANA), Federal Networking Council (FNC), International Trademark Association (INTA), Internet Society (ISOC), International Telecommunication Union (ITU) and World Intellectual Property Organization (WIPO).

PMH

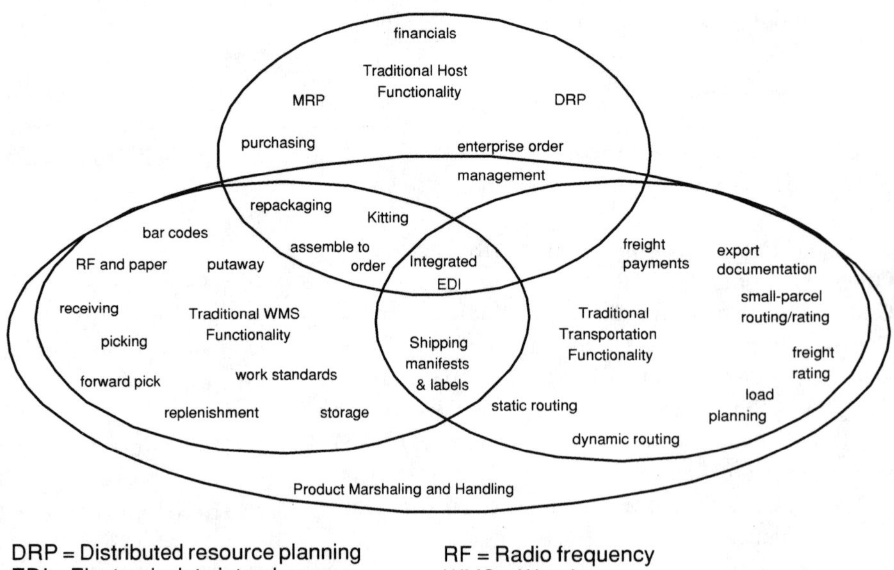

DRP = Distributed resource planning
EDI = Electronic data interchange
MRP = Material requirements planning
RF = Radio frequency
WMS = Warehouse management systems

Source: GartnerGroup

Warehousing Plus Transportation — Product Marshaling and Handling

POCSAG
A U.K. standard for radio paging formulated by the Post Office Coding Standards Advisory Group in 1982, now adopted by the Conference on European Posts and Telecommunications (CEPT) as a Pan-European standard.

POE (physician order entry system)

POE (point of entry)

POEMS (Platinum Open Enterprise Management System)

POH (path overhead — Sonet term)
Used for payload transport functions, the path overhead is assigned and transported with a payload until it is demultiplexed.

Point of Presence (See POP)

point of sale (See POS)

point to point
Describes a circuit that connects two points directly, where there are generally no intermediate processing nodes, although there could be switching facilities. See also multipoint.

Point-to-Point Protocol (See PPP)

Point-to-Point Tunneling Protocol (See PPTP)

polarization
A property of an electromagnetic wave characterized by the direction of the electric field.

polar keying
A technique of current loop signaling in which current flow direction establishes the two-level binary code.

policy-based networking (See PBN)

policy-based routing
The forwarding of packets to specified destinations based on user configurations.

Policy Oversight Committee (See POC)

polling
A means of controlling communications lines. When many stations are connected to the same circuit, polling from the center is used to ensure an orderly flow of data to the central location. Polling is an alternative to contention that makes sure no terminal is kept waiting for a long time.

POLS (private online service)

polymorphism
The capability of an operation to accept arguments of different or unknown types. Parametric polymorphism executes the same operation on different types. Overloading polymorphism selects appropriate operations according to the type.

POMS (Process Operations Management System)
An IBM-and customer-supported initiative to link manufacturing resource planning (MRP) applications running on AS/400 minicomputers and shop floor data collection systems running on PS/2 computers. It is not an IBM product, although IBM funded its development and has exclusive marketing rights.

PON (Passive Optical Network)
A fiber-based access system to customer premises for the delivery of video services such as video-on-demand that allows multiplexed traffic to be distributed to a number of users in such a fashion as to limit the number of optical terminations required.

POP (Point of Presence)
1. Since divestiture, the physical access location within a local access and transportation area

(LATA) of a long-distance and/or interLATA common carrier.

2. Thc point to which the local telephone company terminates subscribers' circuits for long-distance, dial-up, or leased-line communications.

3. An Internet provider's node that allows subscribers to dial in using modems and voice lines.

POP (Post Office Protocol)
An application protocol that provides a mailbox-retrieval service for Internet PC users. It is being replaced by Internet Message Access Protocol (IMAP).

POP3 (Post Office Protocol 3)
An access path for browser-enabled users to communicate with "mail to" requests from Hypertext Markup Language (HTML).

port
The entrance or physical access point to a computer, multiplexer, device or network, where signals may be supplied, extracted or observed.

portability
The ability to move software easily to computers from multiple vendors.

Portable Document Format (See PDF)

portal
A Web site that provides an entry point into the Internet as well as value-added services such as directories and search tools. Because of its high visibility, a portal is a prime position for advertising and preferred positioning of links and products. Fees for these services are used to support the portal. The portal concept is also relevant to enterprise intranets.

ported proprietary
Refers to a system that is a compliant implementation of an evolving set of proprietary or vendor-neutral specifications (or both) for interfaces, services, protocols and formats. These specifications let a user configure and operate a system, its applications and its components only with other equally compliant implementations available from the same vendor or with licensed implementations from different vendors.

Portfolio of Technology Solutions (See POTS)

porting
Modifying code that runs on one hardware platform or operating system so that it will properly execute on another hardware platform or operating system.

POS (point of sale)
POS systems use personal computers or specialized terminals in combination with cash registers, optical scanners or magnetic-stripe readers to capture and record data at the time of transaction. POS systems are usually online to a central computer for credit checking and inventory updating. Alternatively, they may be independent systems that store daily transactions until they can be transmitted to the central system for processing.

POSI (Promoting Conference for OSI)
A Japanese vendor organization for standards promotion.

Posix
A Unix-based standard developed by the Institute of Electrical and Electronics Engineers (IEEE) Posix committee. Posix has been adopted as a Federal Information Processing Standard (FIPS), and is included in the Open Software Foundation's (OSF's) and X/Open's basic specifications.

Posix 1003.1 compliance
Operating-system compliance with the Institute of Electrical and Electronics Engineers (IEEE) Posix 1003.1 system services standard.

POST (power-on self test)
Diagnostic tools that run automatically when a hardware device is turned on.

postal, telegraph, and telephone (See PTT)

Post Office Protocol (See POP)

Post Office Protocol 3 (See POP3)

PostScript printer support
Support for the printing of document information, including "rich text," on PostScript printers.

POTS (plain old telephone service)

POTS (portfolio of technology solutions)
A business model wherein vendors interface with major customers through solution-focused groups. These groups deliver repeatable solutions that address specific processes in specific industry sectors and are composed of consulting and implementation services based on leading-edge technologies and market-leading applications. The solution groups are supported by resources such as corporate services, technology centers of expertise, and industry and process centers of expertise. The vendor can treat these solution groups as profit-and-loss centers that are then easily valued for investment, incentive, and divestiture purposes.

POWER (Performance Optimized With Enhanced RISC — IBM)
IBM's proprietary reduced instruction set computer (RISC) processor technology used in the RS/6000 and selectively licensed to other suppliers, including Motorola.

powerfail restart
Automatic restart initiation upon restoration of power after a power failure.

power-on self test (See POST)

PPA (personal productivity application)

PPC (plain paper copier)

ppm (pages per minute)

PPMS (physician practice management system)

PPP (Point-to-Point Protocol)
A proposed Internet standard specified in Request for Comments (RFC) 1331.

PP-PI (production planning for process industries)
A module intended to provide vertical integration between the enterprise resource planning (ERP) elements of SAP R/3 and the production floor in batch/continuous manufacturing.

PPRC (peer-to-peer remote copy)
A synchronous controller-to-controller remote-copy capability. It uses standard Enterprise Systems Connection (ESCON) links to communicate between control units.

PPS (pulses per second)

PPTP (Point-to-Point Tunneling Protocol — Microsoft)
An extension to the standard Point-to-Point Protocol (PPP) that is used to create multiprotocol Virtual Private Networks (VPNs) via the Internet.

PQS (Parallel Query Server)
A product announced by IBM in April 1994 that uses complementary metal-oxide semiconductor (CMOS) technology to provide parallelism to Information Management System/Database Manager (IMS/DM) applications.

Practical Extraction Report Language (See PERL)

P

Precision Architecture Reduced Instruction Set Computer (See PA-RISC)

Precision Graphics Markup Language (See PGML)

predicate
A clause within a Structured Query Language statement (query) that specifies a constraint that the selected data (rows) must satisfy.

predicate transitive closure
The practice of adding semantically redundant predicates to a Structured Query Language (SQL) statement (query) to help the optimizer perform better. This can be done by application programmers or by the optimizer itself.

predictive behavior analysis
The use of techniques such as data mining, data visualization, algorithm clustering, and neural networking to find patterns or trends in data. These patterns or trends are used to forecast future behavior based on current or past behavior. Uses of predictive behavior analysis include identifying customers likely to drop out or default; identifying products customers are likely to buy next; developing customer segments or groups; and product development.

preparation, review, inventory, order, reference, installation, testing and year 2000 (See PRIORITY)

preprocessor
A program that converts data from the format of an emulated system to the format accepted by an emulator.

presentation layer
In the Open Systems Interconnection (OSI) model, the layer of processing that provides services to the application layer, enabling it to interpret the data exchanged, as well as to structure data messages to be transmitted in a specific display and control format.

Presentation Manager (See PM)

Presentation Manager/X (See PM/X)

Presentation Text Object Content Architecture (See PTOCA)

Pretty Good Privacy (See PGP)

Preventive Cyclic Retransmission (See PCR)

preventive maintenance (See PM)

PRI (Primary Rate Interface — PRA in Canada and Europe)
An Integrated Services Digital Network (ISDN) interface that connects private branch exchanges (PBXs) to the network at the North American 1.544 megabits per second (Mbps) T1 rate. It is electrically identical to the ISDN Basic Rate Interface (BRI). North American standards for this interface specify 23 64-kilobit-per-second (Kbps) B, or bearer, channels, plus one 64-Kbps D, or delta, channel. Thus, it is also referred to as 23B+D. European standards call for 30B+D.

Primary Rate Access (See PRA)

Primary Rate Interface (See PRI)

primary station
The data terminal in a network that selects and transmits information to a secondary terminal and has the responsibility to ensure information transfer.

primitive
A simple process, object or action. In Open Systems Interconnection (OSI) terms, an interaction between adjacent layers of the Reference Model, such as "request" or "response."

printed circuit board (See PCB)

Printer Control Language (See PCL)

print server
A network device allowing sharing of printers on a network without using the file server.

PRIORITY (preparation, review, inventory, order, reference, installation, testing and year 2000)
A GartnerGroup model to address the process of achieving year 2000 compliance in telecommunications and networking systems.

priority indicator
In data communications, a group of symbols that specifies the relative urgency of a message and its order of transmission.

PRISM (Parallel Reduced Instruction Set Multiprocessor)
A reduced instruction set computer (RISC) architecture developed by Apollo for its high-end workstation products.

privacy-enhanced mail (See PEM)

private automatic branch exchange (See PABX)

private branch exchange (See PBX)

private communications exchange (See PCX)

private exchange (See PX)

Private Network-to-Network Interface (See PNNI)

problem management
The core function of a customer service and support (CSS) application used by call centers. It coordinates a multitier, multiowner service and support environment, enables pattern analysis, provides management reports, and facilitates requesting additional service and support resources by providing hard numbers on the service workload and its changing nature. Because PM tools can also track service-level agreements (SLAs), they are valuable for monitoring compliance.

process
An interconnected network of activities that begins at the specification of a requirement for a product or service and terminates with the acceptance of consideration for providing the product or service.

process control
The regulation of variables that influence or control the conduct of a process so that a specified quality and quantity of product are obtained.

process coordination
The class of applications that exploits workflow technology.

Process Data Exchange Institute (See PDXI)

Process-Flow Scheduling (See PFS)

process information management system (See PIMS)

processing, batch
A method of computer operation in which a number of similar input items are accumulated and sorted for processing.

processing, line
The processing of transactions as they occur, with no preliminary editing or sorting before they enter the system.

process management
A management concept that describes the goal of increasing intraenterprise coordination of separate business functions. Business process re-engineering is a form of process management that focuses

on replacing traditional functions (e.g., sales, marketing and service) with functionally integrated processes (e.g., customer relationship management). The growth in the demand for enterprise software reflects the need for increased integration and sharing of business information throughout an enterprise.

Process Operations Management System (See POMS)

Processor Resources/ Systems Manager (See PR/SM)

procurement handbook
A handbook published by organizations such as Government OSI Procurement Specification (GOSIPs) to aid the buying process of Open Systems Interconnection (OSI) systems.

Product Data Exchange Specification (See PDES)

product data management (See PDM)

product development management (See PDM II)

production planning for process industries (See PP-PI)

product marshaling and handling (See PMH)

PR/OEE (Platinum Repository/Open Enterprise Edition)

Professional Office System (See PROFS)

PROFS (Professional Office System — IBM)
Office system facilities for the Virtual Machine (VM) environment. The e-mail function is particu-

Problem Management

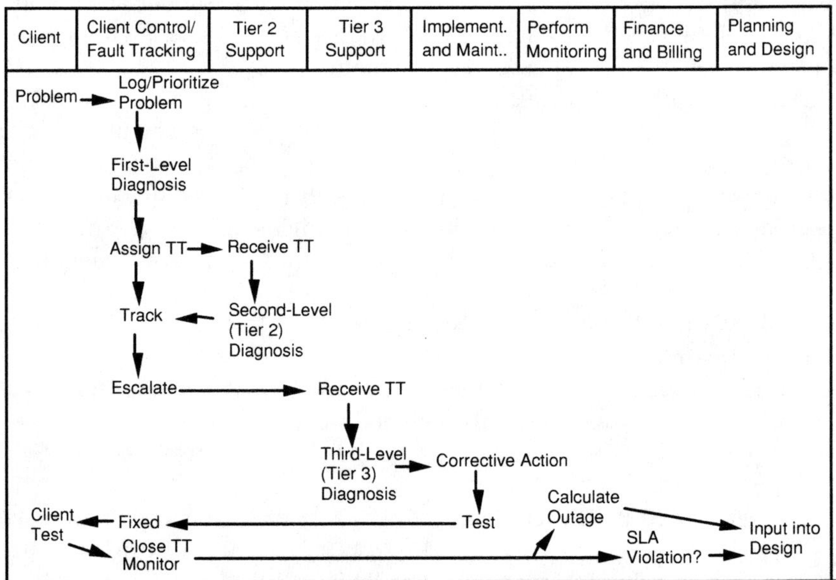

	Daytime Hours				Off Hours				Weekend			
	SL1	SL2	SL3	SL4	SL1	SL2	SL3	SL4	SL1	SL2	SL3	SL4
Help Desk Mgr.	1h	2h	8h	24h	1h	3h	10h	24h	1h	12h	24h	48h
Operations Mgr.	2h	4h	12h	36h	2h	6h	24h	36h	4h	18h	36h	72h
CIO	6h	12h	24h	48h	8h	12h	36h	48h	12h	24h	48h	96h
CEO	8h	24h	48h	96h	24h	48h	72h	96h	48h	72h	96h	120h

Severity Level (SL)

SL 1: **Severe problem has disrupted user service. Business risk is high.**
SL 2: **Problem affecting production. Customer or IT service has been impacted. User can continue to process but at an inconvenience. Business risk is moderate to low.**
SL 3: **Low to moderate impact. Service has not been impacted. Low business risk.**
SL 4: **Low to negligible impact. Problem deferred to when time allows.**

SLA = Service-level agreement
TT = Trouble ticket

Source: GartnerGroup

The Problem Management Process

larly strong, but the user interface is not oriented toward novice users.

PROFS Document Exchange
A facility to exchange documents to or from the midrange system with IBM's Professional Office System (PROFS). PROFS document content can be compatible with DISOSS (Document Content Architecture), although distribution and exchange of documents or notes requires a different approach.

program
An organized list of instructions that, when executed, causes a computer to behave in a predetermined way. Without programs, computers are useless. A program is like a recipe that contains a combination of two things:

1. A list of ingredients (called variables). Variables represent numeric data, text or graphical images.
2. A list of directions (called statements). Statements provide the instructions for what to do with the variables. There are many programming languages that are used to create this combination of variables and statements.

Program Evaluation and Review Technique (See PERT)

program library
A collection of computer instruction packages and routines.

programmable logic controller (See PLC)

Programmers' Hierarchical Interactive Graphics Standard (See PHIGS)

programming language
A defined group of commands and syntax that a program developer uses to write software. Languages range from primitive (similar to machine code) to high-level (closer to standard written language and somewhat automated) and have been classified into generations, the fifth being the most recent. C, C++, Pascal, BASIC, FORTRAN, COBOL, LISP and Java are examples of programming languages.

programming language one (See PL/1)

Programming Language/Structured Query Language (See PL/SQL)

program sharing
In a network, the ability for several users or computers to use a group of instructions stored at another connection point.

project management professional (See PMP)

PROM (programmable read-only memory)

Promoting Conference for OSI (See POSI)

prompts
Messages from a computer that give instructions to the user.

propagation delay
The period between when a signal is placed on a circuit and when it is recognized and acknowledged at the other end. Propagation delay is of great importance in satellite channels because of the great distances involved.

proprietary software
Software that is owned by an organization or an individual, as opposed to "public-domain software," which is freely distributed. The explosion in the use of the Internet has expanded the reach of public-domain software since it is now much easier to transmit these programs. While many commercial software developers have developed software that has become the de facto standard (e.g., Microsoft's Windows programs), proprietary software that is based on proprietary protocols, or standards, can

create obstacles for applications development and usage.

protected mode
A mode of the Intel 80286, 80386 and 80486 microprocessors with hardware memory protection, which has been important for multitasking and for escaping the 640K memory barrier.

protector
The interface between the inside and the outside plant, which protects against hazardous voltages or currents.

protocol
A set of procedures in telecommunications connections that the terminals or nodes use to send signals back and forth. Transmission Control Protocol/Internet Protocol (TCP/IP) is the standard protocol for the Internet and related networks such as intranets and extranets. Local-area networks (LANs) often rely on a different protocol. Networks and systems cannot communicate unless they use the same protocol or make use of a gateway.

protocol conversion
The process of translating the protocol native to an end-user device (e.g., a terminal) into a different protocol (e.g., ASCII to BSC), allowing that end-user device to communicate with another device (e.g., a computer) with which it would otherwise be incompatible. Protocol conversion can be performed by a dedicated device (a protocol converter); by a software package loaded onto an existing system, such as a general-purpose computer, front-end processor, or private branch exchange (PBX) system; or by a value-added network, such as Telenet.

Protocol Data Unit (See PDU)

protocol-independent routing (See PIR)

protocol stack
A defined protocol with options applicable for specific functions that can be implemented as a product. Also called a functional standard or functional profile.

protocol transparent
A device's capability to perform its function independent of the communications protocol.

proxy agent
A network management agent that comes between an unmanaged device and a management system, allowing management by proxy, i.e., on behalf of the device.

proxy servers
Devices that process and filter all Internet Protocol (IP) packets that are directed to them and decide which protocols and services can be served out of their caches. Proxy servers tend to offer the greatest range of protocol and caching support since they cache Hypertext Transport Protocol (HTTP), Secure Hypertext Transport Protocol (HTTPS), File Transfer Protocol (FTP) and, in some cases, streaming content such as RealAudio and PointCast. Each workstation addresses the proxy server directly by setting specific parameters in each browser on each workstation.

PR/SM (Processor Resources/Systems Manager)
IBM's logical-partitioning facility that allows the computer architecture to be separated from its physical implementation to provide a logical organization of resources that allows multiple operating systems (or copies of the same system) to run on one physical central processing unit (CPU) or complex.

PRX (program)

PS (Professional Services — IBM)

PSDI (Project Software and Development)

PSDN (public switched data network)

PSE (Packet-Switching Exchange)

PSF (print service facility)

PSFT (PeopleSoft)

PSK (Phase-Shift Keying)
Phase modulation that uses discrete, present changes of phase.

PSLC (Parallel Sysplex License Charge)
A software licensing arrangement available to vendors if the pieces making up their Parallel Sysplex (PS) complex have been qualified by IBM. Charges are based on the total machine capacity.

PSM (purchasing and supply management)

PSN (private switching network)

PSS (Product Support Services — IBM)

PSTN (public switched telephone network)
A worldwide voice telephone network.

PTA (post and telecommunications administration)

PTAT (private transatlantic fiber-optic cables)

PTB (post and telecommunications bureau)

PTF (program temporary fix)

PTM (Packet Transfer Mode)
A "variable-length cell" transfer mode employed in IBM broadband networks built using IBM's broadband and asynchronous transfer mode (ATM) switching technology.

PTO (public telecommunications operator)

PTOCA (Presentation Text Object Content Architecture)
Describes character data, position, controls and attributes that represent a formatted text presentation.

PTS (Parallel Transaction Server)
A product announced by IBM in April 1994 that introduces CMOS-based parallelism to Information Management System/Database Manager (IMS/DB) applications.

PTT (postal, telegraph and telephone)
A term used to refer to the agency responsible for postal, telegraph and telephone services at a governmental level.

PU (Physical Unit)
A physical device used in IBM Systems Network Architecture (SNA) communications, including the software in an SNA node controlling the node's communications hardware. PU is synonymous with "node type" within SNA. PU 2 devices are intelligent cluster controllers/terminals. A PU 2.1 node enables local user ports to communicate without going through a host node's services.

PU (processor unit)

public data network (See PDN)

public-key encryption
Cryptography that uses a protected private key and a mathematically connected, openly shared public key. The public key enables the encrypted document, file, e-mail or data stream to be deciphered using the related private key. Public-key encryption requires more computing power than symmetric-key encryption. To improve throughput, many systems use a public key to protect a symmetric key which, in turn, is used to protect the material.

public-key infrastructure (See PKI)

Public-Key Infrastructure Exchange (See PKIX)

public switched telephone network (See PSTN)

Public Utilities Commission (See PUC)

publish and subscribe
A messaging model that leverages the basic functionality of message passing. The difference is that a program using publish-and-subscribe middleware does not know the identity of a message's recipient(s). Also, publish and subscribe supports one-to-one as well as one-to-many, many-to-one, and many-to-many distribution of messages.

PUC (Public Utilities Commission)
A state regulatory body.

pulse
A brief change of current or voltage produced in a circuit to operate a switch or relay or which can be detected by a logic circuit.

pulse amplitude modulation (See PAM)

pulse carrier
A series of identical pulses intended for modulation.

pulse code modulation (See PCM)

pulse width modulation, or pulse duration modulation (See PWM)

purchased enterprise applications (PEA)

push technology
Software that automates the delivery of information to users. In contrast, the World Wide Web is a "pull" environment that requires a user to seek information.

In a "push" environment, information is sent to a person proactively, through a Web browser, e-mail, or even voice mail or a pager.

In business, push technology can be used for the conveyance of time-sensitive information, like changes in commodity pricing or the introduction of promotional programs to a sales force. Enterprises can employ push technology to communicate externally with their clients or internally with their employees over a network.

PV (present value)

PVC (permanent virtual circuit)
A virtual circuit established through manual or protocol interaction rather than via a call establishment sequence.

PVC (private virtual circuit)

PVCS
A software configuration management product from Intersolv. PVCS was originally called Polytron Version Control System.

PWB(A) (printed wiring board/assembly)

PWM (pulse width modulation)
A method of encoding information based on variations of the duration of carrier pulses. Also called pulse duration modulation (PDM).

PX (private exchange)
An internal telephone exchange serving a single organization and having no connection with a public exchange. Also private automatic exchange (PAX). Other types of private exchange include:

1. Private automatic branch exchange (PABX): A private automatic telephone exchange that provides for the transmission of calls internally and to and from the public telephone network. Also private branch exchange (PBX).
2. Private automatic telex exchange (PATX): Provides telex service within and without an enterprise (largely obsolete).

3. Private manual branch exchange (PMBX): Private, manually operated telephone exchange that provides private telephone service to an organization and allows calls to be transmitted to or from the public telephone network.
4. Private digital exchange (PDX): Private exchange employing digital transmission techniques.

Px64

Expected to be the videoconferencing standard eventually accepted worldwide (for two-way, full-motion video).

Q

Q (queue)

Q.2931
The broadband out-of-band signaling standard for call management. Also known as Q.93 broadband.

QA (quality assurance)
The historic focus of the National Committee on Quality Assurance (NCQA), fundamentally based on measures of compliance to standards or processes.

QAM (quadrature amplitude modulation)
A combination of amplitude and phase modulation (and shift-keying) techniques used to transmit 9600 bits per second (bps) over a 2400 baud line.

QA/QC (quality assurance/quality control)

QAS (quasi-associated signaling — ISDN term)
In QAS, signaling links are separated from the transmission route but are switched via the signal transfer point (STP).

QBE (query by example)

QCIF (Quarter Common Intermediate Format)
Part of the International Telecommunication Union Telecommunications Standards Sector's (ITU) H.261 video format standard, centered on Common Intermediate Format (CIF), which is a compromise between National Television Standards Committee (NTSC) and phase alteration line (PAL). In the H.261 standard, only QCIF is specified (176x144 pixel resolution).

QCTC (Quad Channel I/O Controller)

QEMM (Quarterdeck Expanded Memory Management)

QFA (quick file access)

QI (quality improvement)

QIC (quarter-inch cartridge)

QLLC (Qualified Logical Link Control)
Routines that provide Synchronous Data Link Control (SDLC).

QM (Quality Module — SAP)

QMF (Query Management Facility)
IBM's strategic query and report-writing product for relational database management systems (RDBMSs). Its main objective is to widen the RDBMS user base, i.e., to allow anyone to use relational data. QMF has basic analysis and graphics features.

QOS (quality of service)
A negotiated contract between user and network that renders some degree of reliable capacity in the shared network.

QphD (TPC-D "query per hour" metric)

QppD (TPC-D "power" metric)

QPSX (Queued Packet Synchronous Exchange)
A metropolitan-area network (MAN) based on the Institute of Electrical and Electronics Engineers (IEEE) 802.6 Distributed Queue Dual Bus (DQDB) standard for speeds up to 150 megabits per second (Mbps).

QR (queuing requirements)

QR (quick response)

QSAM (Queued Sequential Access Method)
An extended version of the Basic Sequential Access Method (BSAM), which queues up input data blocks pending processing and output data blocks pending transfer.

Q-SIG
A private automatic branch exchange (PABX) networking protocol produced by the European Computer Manufacturer's Association (ECMA) in line with the International Telecommunication Union (ITU) Integrated Services Digital Network (ISDN) recommendations.

QthD (TPC-D "throughput" metric)

quad
A cable of four separately insulated conductors, twisted together in such a way as to provide two pairs.

quadrature amplitude modulation (See QAM)

Qualified Logical Link Control (See QLLC)

Quality
Used by GartnerGroup to refer to elements of a system to support International Organization for Standardization (ISO) 9000 compliance.

quality assurance (See QA)

quality of service (See QOS)

quantization noise
Signal errors caused by the process of digitizing a continuously variable slope.

Quarter Common Intermediate Format (See QCIF)

quartet signaling
The part of the 100BASE-VG proposed standard that orders transmission of data over four wires simultaneously, enabling the increase in speed to 100 megabits per second (Mbps).

quasi-associated signaling — ISDN term (See QAS)

Quel (Query Language)
A relational data manipulation language that was a rival to Structured Query Language (SQL) but has now fallen into general disuse.

Query Language (See Quel)

Query Management Facility (See QMF)

query/report tools
Basic interactive and batch facilities that allow users to query files and databases and create terminal and printed-report output.

queue
1. Telephony. A series of telephone calls, arranged in sequence, the two ends being the head and tail. New calls are added to the tail. Calls can be removed either from the head or tail.
2. Any series of data streams such as a print queue, waiting to access a device.

Queued Packet Synchronous Exchange (See QPSX)

Queued Sequential Access Method (See QSAM)

Queued Telecommunications Access Method (See QTAM)

queuing
1. In telephony, a feature that allows calls to be "held" or delayed at the origination switch while waiting for a trunk to become available.
2. Sequencing of batch data sessions.

Q.x series
Any of several International Telecommunication Union (ITU) specifications for data communication standards that include:

1. Q.93B: Specification for establishing, maintaining, and clearing Broadband Integrated Digital Services Network (B-ISDN) network connections.
2. Q.920/Q.921: Specifications for the ISDN user-to-network interface (UNI) datalink layer.
3. Q.922A: Specification for Frame Relay encapsulation.
4. Q.931: Specification for establishing, maintaining, and clearing ISDN network connections.

R

R/2 (See SAP R/2)

R/3 (See SAP R/3)

RAAD (rapid architected applications development)
An approach to large-scale applications development (AD) that includes the following phases, which are executed by up to 10 teams of 10 people each during a period of no more than 18 months:

- Phase 1: Business and technical architecture reconciliation.
- Phase 2: Functional requirements gathering and specification.
- Phase 3: Initial architecture design, building and implementation.
- Phase 4: First building and testing of application, including user interface, data access and business logic.
- Phase 5: Initial installation of application.
- Phase 6: Concurrent engineering for subsequent builds.
- Phase 7: Rapid release plan.

RACE (R&D for Advanced Communications in Europe)

RACF (Resource Access Control Facility)
The IBM product offering back-end security in the System/370 Multiple Virtual Storage (MVS) and Virtual Machine (VM) environments. RACF had been difficult to use, but release 1.7 achieved a level of flexibility and usability close to what is offered by leading-edge, third-party software. Computer Associates' Top Secret and Access Control Facility-2 (ACF2) are the leading independent software vendor (ISV) offerings.

rack
A framework or structure on or in which an apparatus is mounted, usually by means of shelves or mounting plates. Also known as a bay or a chassis.

RAD (rapid application development)
An applications development (AD) approach that includes small teams (typically two to six people, but never more than 10) using joint application development (JAD) and iterative-prototyping techniques to construct interactive systems of low to medium complexity within a time frame of 60 to 120 days.

RADIO (Reliable Architecture for Distributed I/O)

radio channel
A frequency band allocated to a service provider or transmitter.

radio circuit
A physical circuit consisting of two unidirectional radio links and connections to terminal exchanges.

radio communications
Any telecommunications by means of radio waves.

radio determination
The use of radio waves to determine the position or velocity of a remote object. Also used to collect information.

Radio Determination Satellite Service (See RDSS)

radio frequency (See RF)

radio frequency identification (See RFID)

radio frequency interference (See RFI)

radio information system (See RIS)

RADIUS (Remote Authentication Dial-In User Service)
A security protocol used to transport passwords between the access device and the authentication server.

RAID (redundant array of independent disks)
A method of mirroring or striping data on clusters of low-end disk drives; data is copied onto multiple drives for faster throughput, error correction, fault tolerance and improved mean time between failures.

With the exception of RAID 0, all RAID levels provide automated recovery of data in the event of a disk failure. The RAID levels and their key features are:

- RAID-0 — provides disk striping without parity information; data is written by segment across multiple disks sequentially until the end of the array is reached, and then writing starts at the beginning again. Provides greater logical disk capacity with faster access time on reads (multiple segments read simultaneously). However, RAID-0 provides no data redundancy — if one drive fails, the entire disk array subsystem is unavailable.
- RAID-1 — provides fault tolerance by using disk mirroring (also called shadowing). Each byte of data on a disk is duplicated on another physical drive, providing 100 percent data redundancy. RAID-1 provides immediate access to data when either the primary or secondary drive fails, but it has the highest cost of all RAID types, since duplicate hardware is required.
- RAID-2 — eliminates the 100 percent redundancy overhead of RAID-1 by using a powerful error detection and correction code (Hamming),

RAD

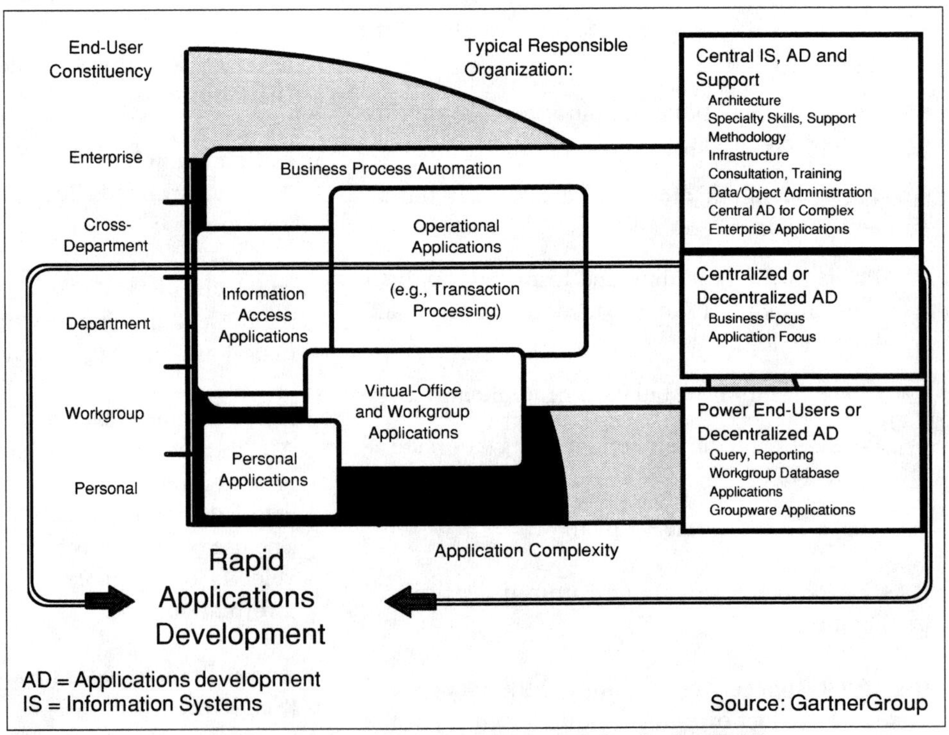

Application Complexity and User Constituency Criteria for RAD

with bits of the data pattern written across multiple disks.

- RAID-3 — similar to RAID-2, but uses a single check disk per group that contains the bit parity of the data disks; data is interleaved across all disks. Because disk reads are performed across the entire array and all data is transferred to the controller in parallel, RAID-3 is well suited for applications that require high data read/write transfer rates for large sequential files.
- RAID-4 — instead of interleaving blocks of data across all drives, writes the first block on drive 1, the second block on drive 2, and so on. This technique dramatically improves read time, since many reads are single block (single drive), freeing other drives for additional read requests.
- RAID-5 — eliminates the dedicated parity drive by writing parity with the data across all drives in the array. Consequently, the single-write restriction and some performance degradation of RAID-1 through RAID-4 are eliminated. If a drive fails, the controller can rebuild the data from the parity and data on the remaining drives.
- RAID-6 — provides two-disk parity and one spare, so that two simultaneous disk failures per array of disks can be tolerated. With the occurrence of a failure, a spare is brought online and transparent reconstruction begins automatically in the background with negligible impact on performance.
- RAID-10 — a combination of RAID-0 and RAID-1 that provides the benefits of striping and fault tolerance (disk mirroring).

Raike Public Key (See RPK)

RAM (random-access memory)
The primary memory in a computer. Memory that can be overwritten with new information. The "random access" part of the name comes from the fact that the next bit of information in RAM can be located — no matter where it is — in an equal amount of time.

RAMAC
IBM's remote copy technology product.

RAMP-C
An IBM proprietary benchmark constructed to measure performance on online transaction processing (OLTP) workloads. IBM has used RAMP-C both to measure the relative performance of its processors and architectures and to compare its processors to the competition. It has not released the code, so independent judgments on the relevance of the benchmark are impossible.

random access
A storage device that allows information or blocks of information to be read in any order, e.g., a disk or solid-state memory.

random-access memory (See RAM)

rapid application development (See RAD)

rapid architected application development (See RAAD)

RARP (Reverse Address Resolution Protocol)
A Transmission Control Protocol/Internet Protocol (TCP/IP) protocol for translating a Data Link Control address to an Internet Protocol (IP) address. RARP can be used to obtain a logical IP address. Responding to a RARP broadcast from a workstation, a RARP server can send back the IP address.

RAS (reliability, availability and serviceability)
A reference to a product's quality, availability of optional features, and ease of diagnosis and repair.

RAS (Remote Access Server — Microsoft)
A remote-node access feature of NT.

raster
Originally a German word naming the screen used in photoengraving; now, the array of scan lines used to cover a planar area to read or depict image information on that area. The electron beam of a TV picture tube writes a raster on the phosphor screen.

raster image processor (See RIP)

rate
The charge for a particular service or equipment usage.

rate averaging
A telephone company's method for establishing uniform toll rates based on distance rather than on the relative cost and/or volume of telephone traffic on a given route.

rate base
The total invested capital on which a regulated company is entitled to a reasonable rate of return.

rate center
A defined geographic point used by telephone companies in determining distance measurements for interLATA mileage rates.

RAW (read after write)

RBOC (regional Bell operating company)
Local or regional telco in one of seven regions of the United States formed by the divestiture of AT&T. Also known as Bell operating company (BOC) or, colloquially, as Baby Bells.

RBRS (resource-based relative value scale)

R/C (requisitions/confirmations)

RC2, RC4, RC5 (Rivest Code 2, 4 and 5)
Alternatives to Data Encryption Standard (DES). RC2 (Rivest Cipher 2) is an exportable Rivest, Shamir Adelman (RSA) proprietary variable — key-size cipher for bulk encryption.

RCC (radio common carrier)

RCM (reliability-centered maintenance)

RCP (Remote Copy Protocol)
Allows file copies to and from a remote host or server on a network; uses Transmission Control Protocol (TCP) to ensure the safe delivery of data.

RCS (Revision Control System)
A Unix utility that provides version control. The majority of Unix developers rely on basic utilities such as RCS for version control.

R&D (research and development)

RDA (Remote Data Access)
A standard (ISO/JCTI/SC21 WG3) to address the interconnection of applications and databases. The standard originally attempted to cover any kind of data access and concerned itself only with effective dialog management, but inherent complexity has encouraged it to focus more on Structured Query Language (SQL).

Rdb
Digital Equipment's strategic database management system (DBMS). Rdb is integrated with the other Virtual Address Extension (VAX) Information Architecture products, and is designed to provide true multiplatform, distributed-database capabilities.

RDBMS (relational database management system)
A database management system (DBMS) that incorporates the relational-data model, normally including a Structured Query Language (SQL) application programming interface. It is a DBMS in which the database is organized and accessed according to the relationships between data items. In

a relational database, relationships between data items are expressed by means of tables. Interdependencies among these tables are expressed by data values rather than by pointers. This allows a high degree of data independence.

RDD (rigid disk drive)

RDF (Resource Description Framework)
A proposed World Wide Web Consortium (W3C) standard for metadata descriptions.

RDLAP (Radio Data Link Access Protocol)

RDM (Relational Document Manager — Interleaf)

RDM (remote data management)
A form of cooperative-processing in which the database management system (DBMS) or file management system executes on a different node than the rest of the application logic.

RDP (Remote Desktop Protocol)
Microsoft's protocol for remote presentation.

RDRAM (rambus dynamic random-access memory)

RDS (report distribution system)

RDSS (Radio Determination Satellite Service)

RDT (recall dial tone)

read-only memory (See ROM)

real time
The description for an operating system that responds to an external event within a short and predictable time frame. Unlike a batch or time-sharing operating system, a real-time operating system provides services or control to independent ongoing physical processes. It typically has interrupt capabilities (so that a less important task can be put aside) and a priority-scheduling management scheme.

real-time clock (See RTC)

real-time collaboration (See RTC)

real-time document sharing (See RTDS)

real-time variable bit rate (See rtVBR)

reasonableness checks
Tests made on information reaching a real-time system or being transmitted from it to ensure that the data in question lie within a given range.

received line signal detector (See RLSD)
A signal indicating connection has been made. Also known as carrier detect (CD).

receive only (See RO)

record
Any information-bearing media generated or received by an organization — e.g., documents, spreadsheets, images, Web pages and e-mail.

record communication
Communication that produces a hard-copy record of the transmission, such as teletypewriter and facsimile.

recording density
The number of bits that can be written on a specific area of magnetic media; generally measured in bits per inch (bpi).

Record Management System — part of VMS (See RMS)

records management
The systematic organization and managed storage of diverse information sources through the end of

their life cycles. Records management can be viewed as a subset of integrated document management (IDM) and is one of the five most important IDM library service functions. The others are check-in/check-out, version control, document-level security and attribute, and full-text index search and retrieval.

records management application (See RMA)

recovery from fallback
When the system has switched to a fallback mode of operation and the cause of the fallback has been removed. This is the process that restores the system to its former condition.

recovery point objective (See RPO)

recovery time objective (See RTO)

Red Book
CCITT (now International Telecommunication Union/ITU) standards approved in 1984.

red, green, blue monitor (See RGB)

reduced instruction set computer (See RISC)

redundancy

1. Portion of the total information contained in a message that can be eliminated without loss of essential information.

2. Provision of duplicate, backup equipment or links that immediately take over the function of equipment or transmission lines that fail.

redundancy check
Automatic or programmed check based on the systematic insertion of components or characters used for checking purposes.

redundant array of independent disks (See RAID)

redundant processor
A computer that duplicates or partially duplicates the operation of another computer to substantially reduce the possibility of system failure.

redundant routing
By using an algorithm for redundant routing, a network management system automatically uses spare capacity to route by alternative paths in case of line failure.

reed switch
A special type of relay consisting of five moving, reed-like contacts controlled by an electromagnet where the reeds themselves are part of the magnetic as well as the electrical circuit being controlled.

referential integrity
The underlying rules defining the semantic interdependencies among items in a database. The goal is to define those items declaratively (i.e., as business-oriented assertions) rather than through procedural logic. A relational database management system (RDBMS) should enforce referential integrity as defined by Addendum 1 (X3.135.1-1989) to the American National Standards Institute (ANSI) Structured Query Language (SQL) standard.

Reflective Memory Technology (See RMT)

refresh rate
The speed at which an image is painted onto a monitor screen.

regenerative repeater

1. Repeater used in telegraph applications to retime and retransmit the received signal impulses and restore them to their original strength. These repeaters are speed- and code-sensitive and are used with standard telegraph speeds and codes.

2. Repeater used in pulse code modulation (PCM) or digital circuits which detects, retimes, and reconstructs the bits transmitted.

regenerator
Equipment that takes a digital signal that has been distorted by transmission and produces a new signal in which the shape, timing, and amplitude of the pulses are the same as those of the original before distortion.

regional Bell operating company (See RBOC)

regional center
Class of exchange.

regional (computer) network
A communications pathway with connections limited to a defined geographic area.

regional holding company (See RHC)

ReGIS (Remote Graphics Instruction Sets)
A graphics file transfer protocol.

register
First unit in the assembly of common control equipment in an automatic exchange. The register receives address information in the form of dial pulses or dual-tone multifrequency (DTMF) signals and stores it for possible conversion or translation.

registered jack (See RJ)

reinitiation time
The time required for a device or system to restart (usually after a power outage).

relational database management system (See RDBMS)

relationship manager (See RM)

relay
An electronically operated device that causes abrupt changes in an electrical circuit, such as breaking the circuit, changing the circuit connection, or varying the circuit characteristics.

reliability, availability and serviceability (See RAS)

remote access
The ability to log on to a network from a distant location. Generally, this requires a computer, a modem and remote-access software to allow the computer to dial into the network over a telephone line and connect.

Remote Access Server — Microsoft (See RAS)

R

Relationship Manager

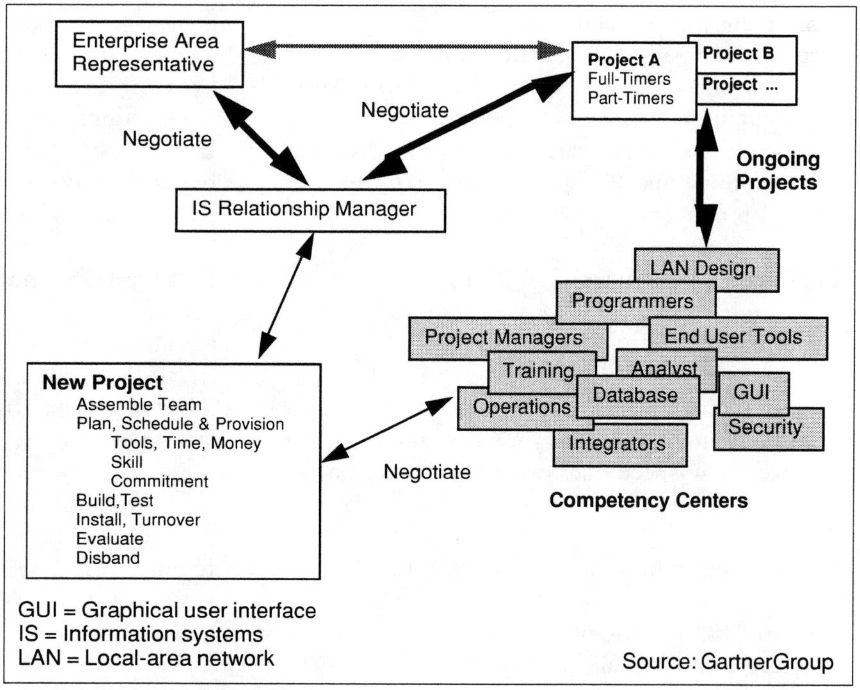

Relationship Manager Roles

remote-access software
Sometimes called remote-control software, this type of program is a superset of the asynchronous communications software market. Remote-access software allows a PC to have complete control over another PC at a different site.

Remote Authentication Dial-In User Service (See RADIUS)

remote batch
Transmission of bulk information stored by a distant terminal or computer.

remote computing
Using a distant processor to manipulate data.

remote console operation
A remote-operator console facility that enables the remote operator to perform normal operational tasks, including storage backup, on a running system.

remote control method
Application resides at the central location and the remote worker executes it via presentation software running on the remote device. The concept describes legacy applications as accessed over a 3270 terminal and PC applications using remote control products.

Remote Copy Protocol (See RCP)

Remote Data Access (See RDA)

remote data concentration
Communications processors used for multiplexing data from low-speed lines or terminals onto one or more high-speed lines. See also multiplexing.

remote data management (See RDM)

Remote DB2 Read-Only Access
Program-level calls allowing midrange-system applications remote but direct access to IBM Database-2 (DB2) databases on a System/370 mainframe. At least read-only access is supported.

Remote DB2 Update Access
Program-level calls allowing midrange-system applications remote but direct access to IBM Database-2 (DB2) databases on a System/370 mainframe. Both read-only and update are supported.

Remote Desktop Protocol (See RDP)

remote environmental monitoring
Hardware and software facilities to permit monitoring of computer room environment from a remote site, and to notify remote operators and sound alarms on conditions outside of selectable parameters.

Remote File Access (See RFA)

Remote File Sharing (See RFS)

Remote Graphics Instruction Sets (See ReGIS)

Remote IMS Read-Only Access
Program-level calls allowing midrange-system applications remote but direct access to IBM Information Management System (IMS) databases on a System/370 mainframe. At least read-only access is supported.

Remote IMS Update Access
Program-level calls allowing midrange-system applications remote but direct access to IBM Information Management System (IMS) databases on a System/370 mainframe. Both read-only and update are supported.

remote initial program load
A remote-operator console facility that enables the remote operator to initiate as well as continue systems operation after power-on or abnormal system failure.

remote job entry (See RJE)

Remote Job Entry — Binary Synchronous Communication (See RJE — BSC)

Remote Login (See Rlogin)

remote log-on
A facility that allows an interactive user on one midrange system to log on to any other midrange system of the same supplier in the network.

Remote Method Invocation (See RMI)

Remote Monitoring (See RMON)

Remote Monitoring Management Information Base (See RMON MIB)

remote-node method
Users connect remotely, but have the status of a full node on the local-area network (LAN). In theory, these remote users may run the same applications that are available to LAN-based users, albeit at a much lower speed.

remote operation
An action started by one application entity and performed by another.

remote peripheral access
The ability to attach peripherals logically on other midrange systems in the network to a user's local process or program.

remote power-off
A system command facility that when executed results in a full power-off of the midrange system. The command could be invoked by local or remote terminal access to the system or could be time-released as an unattended processing task.

remote presentation
A form of cooperative processing in which the presentation executes on a different node than the rest of the application logic and data management.

remote procedure call (See RPC)

remote software maintenance — applications
A form of cooperative processing that allows user support groups to control updates and distribution of application system libraries. A facility for predefining the selection and distribution criteria that should be included.

remote software maintenance system
A facility available to a user support group providing for distribution to selected remote midrange-system nodes of both new versions and "fixes" to midrange system software (e.g., operating system, database and communications).

remote SQL database calls
The availability of Structured Query Language (SQL) database calls on a PC that provide cross-network access to a relational database on a midrange system. The calls most likely would be syntactically and semantically equivalent to similar calls available on the midrange system.

remote storage device management
A function that reduces an enterprise's dependency on local operational support for storage by providing the ability to configure, monitor and administer remote storage devices over a network connection.

remote system monitoring
Software facilities to enable monitoring of systems operation from a remote site, and to notify remote operators on conditions outside of selectable parameters.

Remote VSAM Read-Only Access
Program-level calls allowing midrange-system applications remote but direct access to IBM Virtual Storage Access Method (VSAM) files on a System/370 mainframe. At least read-only access is supported.

Remote VSAM Update Access
Program-level calls allowing midrange system applications remote but direct access to IBM Virtual Storage Access Method (VSAM) files on a System/370 mainframe. Both read-only and update access are supported.

Removable Storage Management (See RSM)

REN (Ringer Equivalence Number)
A measurement of the load on a telephone circuit; if overloaded, not all handsets on the circuit will ring.

REOS (Real-Time Electronic Online System)

repeatable solutions
Replicable, pre-partnered, integrated solutions to a specific process improvement or application requirement. A repeatable solution typically exhibits the following characteristics:

- Fixed pricing, sometimes with a shared business-benefit upside.
- Fixed delivery schedule with rapid implementation.
- Specified performance.
- Initial pilot solution with rapid prototype, followed by roll-out and incremental additions.
- A prime contractor with one point of contact for the client.
- Long-standing and battle-proven partner relationships.
- Joint research and development (R&D) and joint marketing among the partners.
- Opportunity for residual values in the form of royalties, licensing, etc.

Repeatable solutions, as the basis for the portfolio of technology solutions (POTS), must be targeted at specific processes, technologies, subindustries or topical issues. They require high-end professional services such as business process reengineering, system and network integration and software customization.

repeater
1. In digital transmission, this equipment receives a pulse train, amplifies it, retimes it, and reconstructs the signal for retransmission.
2. In fiber optics, a device that decodes a low-power light signal, converts it to electrical energy, and retransmits it via a light-emitting diode (LED) or laser light source, often including some form of signal amplification.
3. A device on a local-area network (LAN) that extends the range by reamplifying and retiming the signal. See also regenerative repeater.

replicated-site applications
Identical versions of applications that are distributed to remote sites (e.g., sales offices, bank branches, field service offices, insurance agencies, supermarkets and pharmacies) to perform identical roles.

repository
A facility for storing descriptions and behaviors of objects in an enterprise, including requirements, policies, processes, data, software libraries, projects, platforms and personnel, with the potential of supporting both software development and operations management. As a single point of definition for all system resources, it should stimulate both program and installation management productivity. A system repository would include configuration definitions, tuning parameters and performance goals, while an application repository would include data definitions.

requester/server
A type of relationship between two independent programs in which:

- Two programs interoperate to carry out the processing for a single unit of application work.
- One directs the other; i.e., the requester program specifies a function to be performed and the server program fulfills that service.

request for comment (See RFC)

request for information (See RFI)

request for proposal (See RFP)

request for quotation (See RFQ)

resale carrier
A company that redistributes the services of another common carrier and retails the services to the public.

residual error rate, undetected error rate
The ratio of the number of bits, unit elements, characters, or blocks incorrectly received but undetected or uncorrected by the error-control equipment to the total number of bits, unit elements, characters or blocks sent.

resolution
The measure of the capability of a visual system, e.g., television, facsimile, etc., to reproduce detail. Usually given as resolution along the scanning lines and parallel to the scanning lines, as these two may differ.

resource
Any means available to system users, including computational power, programs, data files, and storage capacity.

Resource Access Control Facility (See RACF)

resource accounting and chargeback
Mechanisms for recording the use of resources such as processor time, physical memory, transactions, logical or physical input/output (I/O) operations, disk storage and licensed software, and reporting the utilization charged against users, projects, applications or cost centers.

Resource Description Framework (See RDF)

resource requirements planning
The process of converting the production plan or the master production schedule into the impact on key resources, e.g., man hours, machine hours, storage, standard cost dollars, shipping dollars and inventory levels.

Resource Reservation Protocol (See RSVP)

response time
The time period between a terminal operator's completion of an inquiry and the receipt of a response. Response time includes the time taken to transmit the inquiry, process it by the computer, and transmit the response back to the terminal. Response time is frequently used as a measure of the performance of an interactive system.

Restructured Extended Executor (See REXX)

return on equity (See ROE)

return on information technology (See ROIT)

return on investment (See ROI)

reuse
An applications development methodology that catalogs and makes available application components so that they may be incorporated into other applications.

Reverse Address Resolution Protocol (See RARP)

reverse-battery signaling
A type of loop signaling in which battery and ground are reversed on the tip and ring of the loop

to give an off-hook signal when the called party answers.

reverse channel
A simultaneous data path in the reverse direction over a half-duplex facility. Normally, it is used for positive/negative acknowledgments of previously received data blocks. See also half duplex.

Revisable Form Text: Document Content Architecture (See RFT: DCA)

Revised IP Security Option (See RIPSO)

Revision Control System (See RCS)

REXX (Restructured Extended Executor)
A "command language" (job control language). A structured, interpretive language used to create operator-level command streams to manage and link applications. Introduced in the Virtual Machine (VM) environment.

RF (radio frequency)

1. The electromagnetic frequencies used for radio communications: electromagnetic waves of frequencies between approximately 20 kilohertz (KHz) and 3 gigahertz (GHz).

2. RF is also used to refer to a class of peripheral devices communicating with a warehouse management system (WMS) on a local-area network (LAN) or a shipping system on a wide-area network (WAN) via RF communications means. It allows real-time interaction between the peripheral devices and the server without physical connection via wire.

RFA (Remote File Access)
Permits user applications in most languages, as well as most Hewlett-Packard-provided utility programs, to access remote files and remote peripherals transparently.

RFC (request for comment)
A document submitted for comment and put through a review process under the auspices of the Internet Engineering Task Force (IETF). When accepted, it has the weight of a standard in the Internet community. Each RFC is given a tracking number.

RFC 822 describes the address format and data definitions for addressing electronic messages over the Internet).

RFC 1490 is a standard specification for encapsulating multiple protocols over a wide-area frame relay network. This specification increases the capability for frame relay devices from different vendors to interoperate on a network shared disk system. See also clustered system.

RFI (radio frequency interference)
Signal interference generated at or near a received wavelength. The Federal Communications Commission (FCC) establishes RFI standards to reduce RFI.

RFI (request for information)
Notification of an intended acquisition sent to potential suppliers to determine interest and gather general descriptive product materials, though not prices.

RFID (radio frequency identification)
A hardware security technology.

RFP (request for proposal)
An invitation for vendors to bid on supplying goods and services.

RFQ (request for quotation)
Solicitation for pricing for a specific component software product, service or system.

RFS (Remote File Sharing)
Permits multivendor access to data on remote machines.

RFT (request for technology)

RFT: DCA (Revisable Form Text: Document Content Architecture)
The data stream for passing text documents in revisable form under IBM's second-generation Document Content Architecture.

RGB (red, green, blue monitor)
A color display screen for computers.

RHC (regional holding company)
RHCs are the companies that were created from the AT&T divestiture (originally, there were seven; now there are five). Each RHC acts as a holding company within a region of the United States for one or more of the divested Bell operating companies, as well as for their unregulated subsidiaries. The RHCs are: Ameritech, Bell Atlantic, BellSouth, SBC Communications and US West.

RHIN (regional healthcare information network)

Rich Text Format (See RTF)

RIF (Routing Information Field)
A token ring header field used by a source-routing bridge to determine through which segments it must send a packet.

ring

1. Ring-shaped contact of a plug usually positioned between, but insulated from, the tip and sleeve of a connector.
2. Audible alerting signal on a telephone line.
3. A network topology in which stations are connected to one another in a closed logical circle, with access to the medium passing sequentially from one station to the next by means of polling from a master station or by passing an access token from one station to another. Also called a loop.

Ringer Equivalence Number (See REN)

Ring In/Ring Out (See RI/RO)

ring network
A network topology in which each node is connected to two adjacent nodes to form a continuous ring configuration. Used particularly in the context of local-area networks.

RIP (raster image processor)
A device that converts computer graphics into a raster image — grids of small dots — from which the printing device will recreate them on paper.

RFP

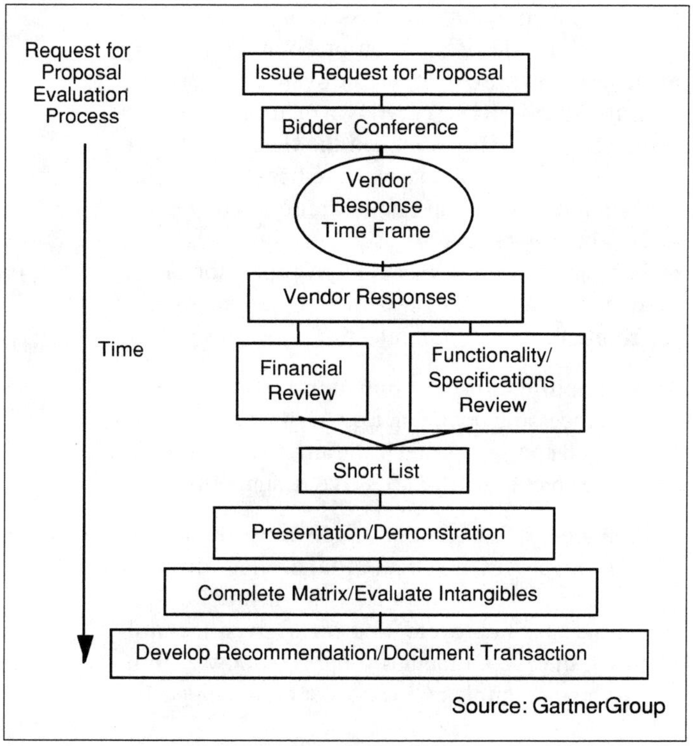

The Request-for-Proposal Process

RIP (Routing Information Protocol)
An internal router protocol used for informing network computers of changes in configuration.

RIPSO (Revised IP Security Option)
Internet Engineering Task Force Request for Comment (IETF RFC) 1108 specifies an optional Internet Protocol (IP) header field that contains a security classification and handling label.

RI/RO (Ring In/Ring Out)
A method of joining token rings.

RIS (radiology information system)
A system that supports the information-processing and business requirements of radiology departments and freestanding image centers.

RISC (reduced instruction set computer)
A processor architecture that shifts the analytical process of a computational task from the execution or runtime to the preparation or compile time. By using less hardware or logic, the system can operate at higher speeds. RISC cuts down on the number and complexity of instructions, on the theory that each one can be accessed and executed faster, and that less semiconductor real estate is required to process them. The result is that for any given semiconductor technology, a more powerful microprocessor can be produced with RISC than with complex instruction set computer (CISC) architectures.

This simplification of computer instruction sets gains processing efficiencies. That theme works because all computers and programs execute mostly simple instructions. RISC has five design principles:

- Single-cycle execution — In most traditional central processing unit (CPU) designs, the peak possible execution rate is one instruction per basic machine cycle, and for a given technology, the cycle time has some fixed lower limit. Even on complex CPUs, most compiler-generated instructions are simple. RISC designs emphasize single-cycle execution, even at the expense of synthesizing multi-instruction sequences for some less-frequent operations.
- Hard-wired control, little or no microcode — Microcode adds a layer of interpretive overhead, raising the number of cycles per instruction, so even the simplest instructions can require several cycles.
- Simple instructions, few addressing modes — Complex instructions and addressing modes, which entail microcode or multicycle instructions, are avoided.
- Load and store, register-register design — Only loads and stores access memory; all others perform register-register operations. This tends to follow from the previous three principles.
- Efficient, deep pipelining — To make convenient use of hardware parallelism without the complexities of horizontal microcode, fast CPUs use pipelining. An n-stage pipeline keeps up to "n" instructions active at once, ideally finishing one (and starting another) every cycle. The instruction set must be carefully tuned to support pipelining.

RISC System 6000 (See RS/6000)

Rivest Code 2, 4 and 5 (See RC2, RC4, RC5)

Rivest-Shamir-Adelman (See RSA)

RJ (registered jack)
A connector type used for telephone and network connections. See also Rjx series.

RJE (remote job entry)
Refers to a set of communications protocols for input and output of information to a mainframe in a batch mode (as opposed to interactive).

RJE — BSC (Remote Job Entry — Binary Synchronous Communication)
Emulation in the midrange system of IBM bisynchronous 2780 or 3780 protocols allowing terminal operators to exchange job control and job output with the mainframe processing queues.

RJx series
From "registered jack"; any of several physical specifications for telephone and other modular connectors. This includes:

1. RJ11: Wiring jack commonly used in U.S. telephone systems and modems worldwide.
2. RJ12: Wiring jack for six-wire modular connectors.
3. RJ14: Similar to RJ11; used for connection of two telephone lines.
4. RJ45: Wiring jack for eight-wire modular connectors; used in data-and telecommunications.
5. RJ48C: Wiring jack with eight-wire modular connections as used in the DSX-1 interface.

RLL (run length limited)

Rlogin (Remote Login)
An Internet service similar to Telnet, developed for use between Berkeley Unix-based systems attached to the same local-area network (LAN). It was developed when Telnet did not support all the services that users required. Berkeley's Unix development program intends to phase out this protocol.

RLSD (received line signal detector)
Signal indicating connection has been made. Also known as carrier detect (CD).

RM (relationship manager)
A staff member who acts as an organizational liaison, typically between an information services (IS) department and business-unit or function. The relationship manager may fulfill a combination of roles that correspond to the degree of trust and authority granted to the person in that role by his/her customer. The job content of the position (in order of increasing business trust and responsibility) is classified in four levels:

- Level 1: Inform and Communicate
- Level 2: Advise and Influence
- Level 3: Coordinate and Integrate
- Level 4: Manage and Oversee

Relationship management is essentially a matrixed position, with reporting requirements to at least two managers (typically a chief information officer — CIO — and business function or division manager). In practice, however, the position is usually linked more strongly to one side than another, and is most often aligned to the business management side.

RM (repository-mentor)

RMA (records management application)
An application that enables enterprises to manage electronic and paper-based records throughout the life cycles of those records.

RMF (Resource Measurement Facility)

RMI (Remote Method Invocation)
A specific type of application component that allows one application process to invoke services existing in another remote application environment that relies on specific Java code.

RMON (Remote Monitoring)
A network management protocol that remotely manages networks providing multivendor interoperability between monitoring devices and management stations.

RMON1
The RMON1 specification builds on the functionality of Simple Network Management Protocol (SNMP) by extending the definition of the SNMP Management Information Base (MIB). The extended

RMON1 MIB definitions enable network managers to monitor sub network devices (via the SNMP MIB). In addition, RMON1 enables the local collection of device data therefore helping network administrators address the bandwidth constraints imposed by SNMP's device polling design.

RMON2
Version two of a Remote Monitoring extension to the Simple Network Management Protocol (SNMP). It is used by management applications to collect statistics from network analysis probes. Statistics include traffic levels by application, across data circuits and between node pairs. RMON-1 products can assist in tasks involving load balancing, capacity planning, troubleshooting, security and accounting.

RMON MIB (Remote Monitoring Management Information Base)
An extension of the Simple Network Management Protocol (SNMP) Management Information Base II (MIB II) which provides a standard-based method for tracking, storing, and analyzing remote network management information. Developed by the Internet Engineering Task Force (IETF).

RMS (Record Management System — part of VMS)
The basic data management system under Digital Equipment's Virtual Memory System (VMS).

RMT (Reflective Memory Technology)
A high-speed memory-to-memory bus with very little overhead.

RNI (Raw Native Interface)

RO (receive only)
1. A printer terminal without a keyboard for data entry.
2. A satellite earth station capable of receiving but not transmitting a signal.

ROE (return on equity)
A measure of a company's financial performance (net income divided by the value of the stockholders' equity, and expressed in percent).

ROI (return on investment)
Financial gain expressed as a percentage of funds invested to generate that gain.

ROIT (return on information technology)
Financial gain expressed as a function of an enterprise's investment in information technology.

rollback
A programmed return to a prior checkpoint or rerun point.

rollback recovery
"Before" and "after" images of a transaction are maintained in a log file so that if the system fails, the unsuccessful updates can be backed out, or rolled back.

ROM (read-only memory)
Data stored in computer memory that can be accessed and read by the user but not modified. ROM is often permanent, and stores system-control software.

root bridge
Within a spanning tree domain, the bridge designated to provide topology information to other bridges.

ROS (Remote Operation Service)

round-robin lookups
A feature in the Domain Naming System (DNS) — post-BIND 4.8.3 — implemented by many enterprises in order for Web servers to share the client connection load. Essentially, the DNS tables contain multiple addresses (or "A" records) for a single name, such as www.athena.com, that correspond to

multiple Web servers with identical content. When a client makes a uniform resource locator (URL) request, the DNS response shuffles the list of addresses returned to the client, redirecting the connection to successively different machines each and every time.

router
A device that connects two networks, performing a function similar to a local or remote bridge. Routers receive packets of information from computers or other routers on the network; they then send these packets to their destinations based on "addresses" at the beginning of the packets and a road map of the other computers and peripherals on the network.

routing
Assignment of the communications path by which a transmission will reach its destination.

routing code
The address or group of characters in the heading of a message defining the final circuit or terminal to which the message has to be delivered. Also called routing indicator.

routing indicator (See routing code)

Routing Information Field (See RIF)

Routing Information Protocol (See RIP)

routing metric
How a routing algorithm determines the best route for a packet. The resulting information is stored in routing tables.

routing table
A table associated with a network node that states for each message (or packet) destination the preferred outgoing link that the message should use.

RPC (remote procedure call)
A mechanism that extends the notion of a local (i.e., contained in a single address space) procedure call to a distributed computing environment, enabling an application to be distributed among multiple systems in a way that is highly transparent to the application-level code. Examples of RPCs are Sun Microsystems' Open Network Computing, Sybase's Open Client/Open Server and the Open Software Foundation's (OSF's) Distributed Computing Environment (DCE) RPC.

RPG
A procedural programming language most commonly used on the AS/400 family of computers.

RPK (Raike Public Key)
An algorithm being forwarded by a New Zealand-based company operating in the United States as RPK, Inc. Based on the Diffie-Hellman public-key algorithm, it uses patented "Mixture Generator" technology, a combination of long linear feedback shift registers to do high-speed exponentiation using the keys to synchronize the RPK "Encryptonite" engine to a randomly generated state. It then uses the high-speed keystream output of the same engine to encrypt the data.

RPM (relative performance measurement)

RPO (recovery point objective)
The point in time until which data can be recovered using backups, journals or transaction logs. It defines what is an acceptable loss of data.

RPQ (request for price quote)

RRS (resource recovery services)

RS/6000 (RISC System/6000)
IBM's 32-bit technical workstation introduced in mid-1990. It is based on reduced instruction set computer (RISC) architecture and runs the Unix-

based Advanced Interactive Executive (AIX) operating system.

RSA (RAMAC Scalable Array — IBM)

RSA (Rivest-Shamir-Adelman)

1. An encryption software company owned by Security Dynamics.
2. The public-key algorithm invented by Rivest, Shamir, and Adelman. It gets its security from the difficulty of factoring large numbers. RSA is slower than Data Encryption Standard (DES) but widely deployed in commercial products, often in conjunction with DES.

RSA (Rural Service Area)
A U.S. term used by the Federal Communications Commission (FCC). For licensing purposes, the FCC divided the U.S. into Metropolitan Statistical Areas (MSAs) and Rural Service Area markets. There are 428 designated rural markets.

RSM (Removable Storage Management)
Provides access serialization for libraries and drives, library slot management and removable media catalog services. It also implements the tape and library device driver abstraction layer that simplifies vendor development and application certification.

RSP (remote store procedure)

RSVP (Resource Reservation Protocol)
A quality-enhancing protocol for improving the performance of a network.

RS-x series
Any of several interface specifications administered by the Electronic Industries Association (EIA). It includes:

1. RS-232-C: Physical interface, with associated electrical signaling, between Data Circuit-terminating Equipment (DCE) and Data Terminal Equipment (DTE); the most commonly employed interface between computers and modems. Now known as EIA/TIA-232.
2. RS-366: An EIA standard for providing dialing commands to network access equipment that uses RS-232 electrical specifications but different connector pinouts and signal functions.
3. RS-422-A: Specification for electrical characteristics of balanced-voltage digital interface circuits. Now known as EIA-530.
4. RS-423-A: Specification for electrical characteristics of unbalanced-voltage digital interface circuits. Now known as EIA-530.
5. RS-443: A standard describing electrical characteristics for unbalanced-voltage digital interface circuits.
6. RS-449: Specification for general-purpose, 37-position and 9-position interface for Data Terminal Equipment (DTE) and Data Circuit-terminating Equipment (DCE) employing serial binary data interchange. RS-449-1 includes Addendum 1. Now known as EIA/TIA-449.

RT (reorder tone)

RTC (real-time clock)
A hardware clock system powered by battery when the PC is switched off. This clock is paced by a quartz crystal and operates in a similar fashion to a digital watch, maintaining information for year, month, day, hour, minute and second.

RTC (real-time collaboration)
RTC consists of real-time document sharing (application sharing, shared whiteboard, chat), audio and videoconferencing.

RTCP (Real-Time Control Protocol)

RTDS (real-time document sharing)
Real-time document-sharing applications enable two or more individuals to share documents. RTDS functionality includes application sharing, file transfer, whiteboard and chat. Some of these applications also include audio- and videoconferencing, but real-time document sharing is the central functionality.

RTF (Rich Text Format)
A file format that encodes documents so their messages include boldface, italics and other limited text stylings across platforms and applications. Differences exist between implementations by Lotus and Microsoft.

RTMP (Routing Table Maintenance Protocol)

RTO (recovery time objective)
Often called the recovery window, RTO defines how quickly information systems, services and processes must be operational following some kind of incident such as fire, flood, or hardware failure.

RTOS (real-time operating system)

RTP (Real-Time Transport Protocol)

RTR (Reliable Transaction Router — Digital Equipment)

RTS (Reliable Transfer Service)

RTS (runtime system)

rtVBR (real-time variable bit rate)
An asynchronous transfer mode (ATM) service category, defined by the ATM Forum, that provides service guarantees for traffic with timing constraints (usually for compressed voice or video).

rule-based systems
Systems that apply a collection of rules to recorded facts to deduce or infer new facts, using an interface engine. Applications include diagnosis, underwriting, regulatory compliance and customer service.

run-length encoding
A lossless compression technique where sequences of repetitive characters are compressed. Suitable for still and motion video.

runtime component
A dynamically bindable package of one or more programs managed as a unit and accessed through documented interfaces that can be discovered at runtime.

RUOW (remote unit of work)

Rural Service Area (See RSA)

RV (residual value)

RVA (RAMAC Virtual Array — IBM)

RWR (read while write)

S

S3 (stand-alone shared storage)

S.100
Defines a client/server model and a set of services for voice/call processing. It is derived from Signal Computing System Architecture (SCSA), and controlled by the Enterprise Computer Telephony Forum (ECTF).

S/370 (See System/370)

S/390 (See System/390)

SA (System Architect)
An applications development (AD) tool suite from Popkin Software.

SAA (Systems Application Architecture)
IBM's name for the architecture once intended to unify its disparate computer architectures.

SAD (slow applications development)

SA/DA (Source Address/Destination Address)
The combination of source and destination Media Access Control (MAC) addresses which determine a flow over shared media such as Ethernet.

SAG (Software AG)

SAIC (Science Applications International)

sales force automation (See SFA)

SAM (software asset management)
A process for making software acquisition and disposal decisions. It includes strategies that identify and eliminate unused or infrequently used software, consolidating software licenses or moving toward new licensing models.

SAN (storage or server-area network)

SAP (SAP AG: Systeme, Anwendungen, Produkte in der Datenverarbveitung/Systems, Applications and Products in Data Processing)

SAP (Service Advertising Protocol)
In routing, broadcasts a message used to identify which servers and end stations are available to which end stations.

SAP (System Assist Processor)

SAPI (Server API)

SAPI (Speech Application Programming Interface — Microsoft)

SAP R/2
A mainframe enterprise-management suite from SAP AG. The architecture allows for the applications and the database to reside on one mainframe computer.

SAP R/3
SAP AG's integrated software solution for client/server and distributed open systems. Ported (with enhancements) from R/2.

SAPs
Standard SAP performance units of measure. One hundred SAPs equal 2,000 sales-and-distribution order line items fully processed in one hour at a specified central processing unit (CPU) utilization. (This requires 6,000 dialog steps and 2,000 actual postings, or 2,400 R/3 transactions.)

SAR (Segmentation and Reassembly)
A function of the lower half of Broadband ISDN (BISDN) Layer 3 by which the higher-layer data is broken up and put back together.

SAS (sales analysis system)

SAS (shared application services)

SAS (Statistical Analysis Software)

SASD (server-attached storage device)

SA/SD (structured analysis/structured design)

SASI (Shugart Associates Standard Interface)

SATAN (Security Administrator Tool for Analyzing Networks)

satellite communications
The use of geostationary orbiting satellites to relay transmissions from one earth station to another or to multiple earth stations.

satellite computer
A programmable machine that relieves a primary processor of such time-consuming operations as compiling, editing, and controlling input/output devices.

SBA (strategic business application)

SBM (skills-based management)
A program that objectively defines what skills an enterprise possesses, what skills it will need in the future, when it will need those skills, what strategic value it will place on those skills and how the information technology (IT) employees' competency levels match the value of the strategically significant skills. It is, in effect, a road map for developing competency improvement programs and other methods to fill any skill gaps.

SBS (satellite business systems)

SBU (strategic business unit)

SBus (Sun Bus)

SCADA (supervisory control and data acquisition)
A system to enable real-time monitoring of events occurring in remote locations, and transmittal of data to a database to provide alert and process management control information. SCADA data can be used to build a computerized model of the process, establish alarm criteria and prepare management reports on the performance of the system. Applications for SCADA include pipeline management, environmental management and industrial process management. Components of SCADA systems include a remote terminal unit, a central-site computer system (ranging in size from a PC to a mainframe, depending on processing requirements) and associated SCADA management software. Communications alternatives for SCADA systems run the gamut from none, (i.e., the service personnel collect data manually) to satellite communications. Microwave, very small aperture terminals (VSATs), telephone lines and mobile radio are also used.

scalability
The measure of a system's ability to increase or decrease in performance and cost in response to changes in application and system processing demands. Examples would include how well a hardware system performs when the number of users is increased, how well a database withstands growing numbers of queries, or how well an operating system performs on different classes of hardware. Enterprises that are growing rapidly should pay special attention to scalability when evaluating hardware and software.

Scalable Processor Architecture (See SPARC)

scanner
A device that resolves a two-dimensional object, such as a business document, into a stream of bits by raster scanning and quantization.

scattering
A cause of lightwave signal loss in optical fiber transmission. Diffusion of a lightbeam caused by microscopic variations in the material density of the transmission medium.

SCC (shipping container code)

SCC (specialized common carrier)

SCCS (Source Code Control System)
A Unix software configuration management utility used for source code version control.

SCE (supply chain execution)
A framework of execution-oriented applications that enables the efficient procurement and supply of goods, services and information across enterprise boundaries for the purpose of meeting customer-specific demands.

SCE (System Control Element)
The SCE's major function is to provide paths and controls for the communications between the major functional units and central storage within the IBM 308, 3090 and ES/9000 processor families.

schematic
A diagram that details the electrical elements of a circuit or system.

SCIV (supply chain inventory visibility)
Systems that enable companies to monitor and manage events across the supply chain to plan their activities more effectively and pre-empt problems. SCIV allows companies not only track and trace inventory globally on a line-item level, but also to submit plans and receive alerts when events deviate from expectations. SCIV systems accessed through enterprise transportation management system (TMSs) typically offer the same point of view and user interface as the TMS. They are appropriate for managing low volumes of events through a small, stable group of trading partners. By comparison, SCIV systems based on a concurrent logistics system architecture support multidimensional points of view that are configurable by end users. These systems are appropriate for managing high volumes of events in a large, dynamic trading partner community.

SCM (Select Component Manager — Select Software Tools)

SCM (software configuration management)
A methodology that includes problem/change request initiation and tracking; change impact analysis; version control; security administration of software assets; software promotion; quality reviews; and software distribution.

SCM (supply chain management)
Involves management and technical cooperation between buying and supplier organizations to optimize design, planning, production, delivery of materials, parts and other resources used in manufacturing and production. Supply chain applications can provide benefits such as reduced costs, improved quality and product design, and effective inventory management.

SCO (The Santa Cruz Operation)

SCOPE (Supply Chain Optimization, Planning and Execution)

SCOR (Supply Chain Operations Reference Model)

SCORE (supplier cost reduction effort)

SCP (service control point)
The database machine at the apex of the Signaling System 7 (SS7) network containing information on how to process, route and bill calls.

SCP (supply chain planning)

SCPC (Single Channel Per Carrier)
A transmission system in which a physical channel is allocated solely to one carrier for the duration of the transmission.

SCR (Sustainable Cell Rate)
In asynchronous transfer mode (ATM), the average cell rate a source is allowed to maintain.

scrambler
A coding device applied to a digital channel that produces an apparently random bit sequence. A corresponding device is used to decode the channel, i.e., the coding is reversible.

screening
Prevention of electric, magnetic, or electromagnetic fields from escaping or entering an enclosed area by means of a barrier. Also called shielding.

screen sharing
Similar to application sharing, but not all parties can update the document simultaneously.

scrolling
The vertical movement (up or down) of lines of data displayed on a cathode ray tube (CRT) screen.

SCS (sales configuration system)

SCSA (Signal Computing System Architecture)
A hardware and software architecture, defined by Dialogic, that specifies interfaces between components of a call-handling system, including media control. Media management is a missing component of Computer Supported Telephony Architecture (CSTA), Telephony Application Programming Interface (TAPI) and Telephony Services Application Programming Interface (TSAPI). Applications must make assumptions about the type of call (i.e., voice, data, fax or image) or interface with another piece of hardware to determine the type of call. SCSA can mesh with CSTA, TAPI and TSAPI. SCSA can provide computer-telephony integration (CTI) applications with the interfaces needed to identify and manage different call types.

SCSI (Small Computer Systems Interface)
A peripheral interface for up to seven devices. SCSI provides a high-speed, parallel data transfer of up to 40 megabits per second (Mbps) and has the advantage of connecting multiple peripherals while taking up only one slot in the computer.

SCSL (Sun Community Source License)
The Sun Microsystems license model for Java. The new agreement leverages a community-based development model similar to "free software" initiatives that have existed in several forms for many years.

SCT (Semantic Connection Technology — ViewSoft)
A technique to access class interfaces of an application to facilitate communication between two semantically linked elements without writing code. Semantically linked elements can be automatically updated based on each other's actions. For example, a scroll bar that is semantically linked to an integer value is updated visually if the value changes, and likewise updates the integer value if the scroll bar is repositioned.

SD (sales and distribution)

SD (software distribution)

SDA (Source Data Automation)
The capturing of information for machine entry.

SDDI (Shielded Distributed Data Interface)
A proposal by IBM, and backed by several other vendors, for transmitting Fiber Distributed Data Interface (FDDI) signals over copper media. SDDI competes with Copper Distributed Data Interface (CDDI), which runs on both shielded and unshielded twisted-pair media.

SDH (Synchronous Digital Hierarchy)
The European equivalent of the Synchronous Optical Network (SONET) standard, with transmission speeds and network management suited to the European standards.

SDK (software development kit)
A set of development utilities for writing software applications, usually associated with specific environments (e.g., the Windows SDK).

SDLC (Synchronous Data Link Control)
IBM's subset of High-Level Data Link Control (HDLC). The protocol is used for serial (by bit) information transfer over a data communications channel. Concerned with the lower two layers of the Open Systems Interconnection (OSI) model (physical and link control), SDLC was half of the Systems Network Architecture (SNA) attack on the diverse link controls, access methods and terminal types that existed in the pre-SNA era.

SDLC (systems development life cycle)

SDLT (SuperDLT-Quantum)
A product architecture that extends the capacity and transfer rate of digital linear tape (DLT) drives beyond the DLT 7000 tape drive.

SDM (System Data Mover)
The software component of extended remote copy (XRC) that runs under Multiple Virtual Storage (MVS).

SDMI (Secure Digital Music Initiative)
A framework to address new secure digital music technologies that will protect copyrighted material through all delivery channels. Announced on 15 December 1998 by the Recording Industry Association of America (RIAA) and endorsed by the major industry record labels and the technology community, the SDMI plans to create a digital music security specification. The SDMI's objectives are to answer consumer demand for online content access to quality recordings, while ensuring copyright protection for artists' work.

SDMS (Symmetrix Data Migration Service — EMC)
A controller-based feature that requires the target volume(s) to be contained within a Symmetrix or 7700 subsystem, respectively. Depending on customer configuration, the recabling required to support data migration may or may not be disruptive.

SDN (software-defined network)

SDRAM (synchronous dynamic random-access memory)

SDSAF (Switched Digital Services Applications Forum)
A consortium of equipment vendors, service vendors, and users with the goal of advancing the state of switched digital services.

SDSL (symmetric digital subscriber line)
A digital subscriber line (DSL) technology that operates over voice-grade lines at 1.5 megabits per second (Mbps) asymmetric or 768 kilobits per second (Kbps) both ways over 8,000 feet distance.

SDV (switched digital video)

SEAL (Software-Optimized Encryption Algorithm)
A cipher designed and patented by IBM scientists for 32-bit processors.

Sealink
A version of xmodem.

SEA-ME-WE 2
The Southeast Asia/Middle East/Western Europe 2 fiber-optic link. A fiber-optic submarine systems operating on two fiber pairs at 560 megabits per second (Mbps), providing 16,000 nominal voice grade telephone circuits between Singapore and France.

search
Software used for randomly accessing textual information.

search engine
A very large, searchable index of the World Wide Web that is automatically updated by spiders or webcrawlers and housed on a central server connected to the Internet. Search engines such as Yahoo, Lycos, and AltaVista offer the user a friendly front end to access their stored information.

SEAS (Signaling Engineering and Administration System)
Part of the Operations and Maintenance Application Part (OMAP) of Integrated Services Digital Network (ISDN).

SECAM (Séquential Couleur á Mémoire)
A color television broadcasting system using 625 picture lines and a 50-hertz (Hz) field frequency, in which the two color-difference signals are transmitted sequentially instead of simultaneously. Developed and used in France and also used in the former Soviet Union. See also NTSC and PAL.

SECC (Single Edge Contact Cartridge)

secondary channel
A low-speed channel established on a four-wire circuit over which diagnostic or control information is passed. User data is passed on the primary, high-speed channels of the circuit.

secondary station
On a communications pathway, a terminal device that has been selected to operate under the control of another terminal device.

second generation
The class of multiuser time-sharing integrated office systems including Digital Equipment's ALL-IN-1, IBM's PROFS and Data General's CEO. These products, introduced around 1983, were largely superseded by client/server third-generation products in 1989.

SECS (Semiconductor Equipment Communications Standards)
The oldest of the standards activities within the realm of the marketing encyclopedia system (MES): SECS I, SECS II, and the SECS Messaging Standard. This collection of standards dealing with the supervisory control and data acquisition interfaces are very specific to the semiconductor manufacturing industry.

Secure Digital Music Initiative (See SDMI)

Secure Electronic Network for Travelers' Rapid Inspection (See SENTRI)

Secure Electronic Transaction (See SET)

Secure Hash Algorithm (See SHA)

Secure MIME (See S/MIME)

Secure Network Communications (See SNC)

Secure Sockets Layer (See SSL)

Secure Store and Forward (See SSF)

SED (stream editor)
A Unix text parser.

S

segment
A physical section of a network bounded by internetworking devices.

Segmentation and Reassembly (See SAR)

SEI (Software Engineering Institute)
A recognized source of research, process models and appropriate practices surrounding applications development, the Software Engineering Institute (SEI) at Carnegie Mellon University uses its Capability Maturity Model (CMM) as a framework for examining the adequacy of an enterprise's processes and improving those processes. SEI also provides hands-on experience to practitioners through groups — e.g., software process improvement networks (SPINs).

selector
The last octet of an asynchronous transfer mode (ATM) address.

self-describing messages
A message that contains data as well as the metadata that describes the format and the meaning (i.e., the syntax and the semantics) of that data. For example, Extensible Markup Language (XML) is a self-describing message format that consists of tag/value pairs (e.g., cust_numberle).

self-relocating program
A group of instructions capable of assigning blocks of memory as they are needed.

self-test and fault isolation
Most systems include a processor-check capability that allows the controlling computer to test itself and the rest of the system. If a fault is found, an alarm light is lit and a message is given on the system printer teletype, if one is provided. This feature also expedites service since the computer can pinpoint faulty equipment, saving diagnostic time.

SEM (scanning electron microscope)

Semantic Connection Technology — Viewsoft (See SCT)

semantic data model
A method of organizing data that reflects the basic meaning of data items and the relationships among them. This organization makes it easier to develop application programs and to maintain the consistency of data when it is updated.

Semantic Nets
A type of knowledge representation that uses nodes (representing objects or events) and links (representing relationships between those objects or events).

Semiconductor Equipment Communications Standards (See SECS)

Senior Officials Group — Telecommunications (See SOGT)

SENTRI (Secure Electronic Network for Travelers' Rapid Inspection)
A face recognition system developed by Visionics under contract to the U.S. Department of Transportation (DOT) and the Immigration and Naturalization Service (INS) for U.S. ports of entry to Mexico and the Caribbean.

Sequenced Packet Exchange (See SPX)

Sequenced Packet Protocol (See SPP)

Sequenced Routing Update Protocol (See SRTP)

Séquential Couleur á Mémoire (See SECAM)

sequential function chart (See SFC)

serial
One bit following another over a single pathway.

serial, impact, dot matrix (See SIDM)

serial, impact, fully formed (See SIFF)

serial, nonimpact, direct thermal (See SNDT)

serial, nonimpact ink jet (See SNIJ)

serial interface
An interconnection that transmits information bit by bit rather than a whole character at a time. It is much slower and cheaper than a parallel interface.

Serial Storage Architecture (See SSA)

serial transmission
A method whereby the bits of a character are sent sequentially on a single transmission channel. See also parallel transmission.

server

1. A system or a program that receives requests from one or more client systems or programs to perform activities that allow the client to accomplish certain tasks. A processor that provides a specific service to systems on a network. Routing servers connect subnetworks of like architecture; gateway servers connect networks of different architectures by performing protocol conversions; and terminal, printer and file servers provide interfaces between peripheral devices and systems on the network.

2. Can refer to a physical computer ("the server is down..."), but more commonly to any machine that serves applications or information on the World Wide Web.

Service Advertising Protocol (See SAP)

service bureau
A company that processes various types of data for a client for a fee. Station message detail reporting (SMDR) and call-costing reports are typically provided.

service control point (See SCP)

service desk
A help desk that is equipped with the resources for resolving service requests and problem calls. It gives the customer service representative or end user the ability to efficiently diagnose, troubleshoot and correct technical-support problems, rather than being a "pass through."

service-level agreement (See SLA)

service-level reporter (See SLR)

service order
Request to a vendor for service or equipment.

service organization
Any company that contracts to provide for and operate computers not owned or leased by the company.

service-oriented architecture (See SOA)

Service Profile Identifier (See SPID)

service switching point (See SSP)

serving area

1. The region surrounding a broadcasting station where signal strength is at or above a stated minimum.

2. The geographic area handled by a telephone exchange, generally equivalent to a local access and transport area (LATA).

servlet
A form of server-based Java that operates in conjunction with a Web server and offers an alternative to using Common Gateway Interface (CGI) and server application programming interfaces (SAPIs) to communicate with Web server processes. In addition, servlets are independent of a given type of Web server, as the most prominent Web servers support servlets.

SES (severely errored seconds)
Any second with more than 1,544 bit errors.

SESAME (Secure European System for Applications in a Multivendor Environment)

session

1. A period of time in which an end user engages in dialog with an interactive computer system.
2. Layer 5 of the International Organization for Standardization's (ISO's) Open Systems Interconnection (OSI) reference model for network architectures.

SET (Secure Electronic Transaction)
A standard conceived in 1995 to ensure that all Internet-based payment transaction details are encrypted, the parties authenticated, acknowledgments fully recorded and the customer payment details made available only to the bank. SET uses encryption for securing the payment details and makes use of digital certificates for consumer, merchant and bank identification.

severely errored seconds (See SES)

SF (single frequency)

SF (status field — ISDN term)

SF-36 (Short Form 36)

SFA (sales force automation)
Using technology to automate the sales process. Some technologies that can be used for sales automation are:

- Laptop computers
- Personal digital assistants
- Contact databases
- Interactive selling systems

SFC (sequential function chart)
A programming language for industrial logic controllers.

SFC (shop floor control)
The set of functionality in manufacturing associated with defining the steps to be taken, machines to be used, labor action required, and components to be used in manufacturing a product and then collecting data on actual usage during the manufacturing process. Most applications promoted and sold as manufacturing execution system (MES) applications are really SFC applications.

SFDR (software failure detection and recovery)
Should support the concept of a transaction, including atomicity (either all changes take place or none

Servlet

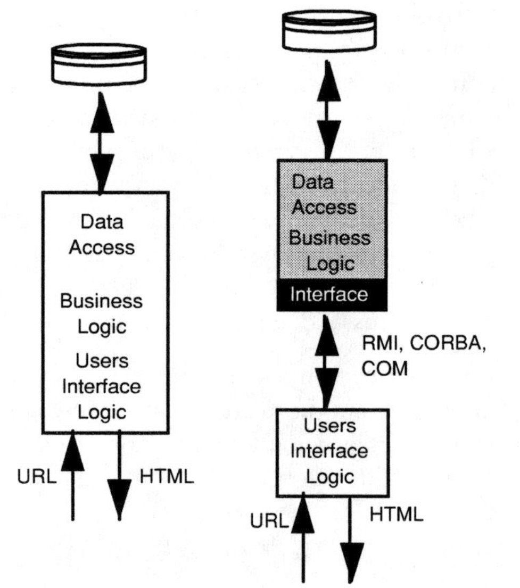

COM = Component Object Model
CORBA = Common Object Request Broker Architecture
HTML = Hypertext Markup Language
RMI = Remote Method Invocation
URL = Uniform resource locator

Source: GartnerGroup

Two Styles of Servlet Applications

take effect) to enable operating-system or application data recovery mechanisms to be implemented.

SFDSP (special-function DSP)

SFL (S/MIME Freeware Library)

SFS (Structured File Server — Transarc)

SG&A (selling, general and administrative)

SGML (Standard Generalized Markup Language)
An international standard of identifying the basic structural elements of a text document. SGML addresses the structure of a document, not its format or presentation.

SGRAM (synchronous graphics random-access memory)

SHA (Secure Hash Algorithm)
Designed by the National Institute of Standards and Technology (NIST) and National Security Agency for use with the digital signature standard. Similar to Message Digest hash function MD5.

shadow/mirror databases
A system-level facility to enable shadowing or mirroring (i.e., duplication) of selected databases to a separate disk or disk set. The purpose is to minimize the space required for backup data while providing for the continuation of critical processing in the event of the loss of a disk containing related databases.

shared-solution center (See SSC)

ShareNET
Formed by a number of clearinghouse participants in September 1997, ShareNET is a not-for-profit consortium promoting the creation of a virtual private network for healthcare electronic data interchange (EDI) administrative transactions. Initially, the strategy was to create direct links between participant networks. However, in February 1998, ShareNET augmented its initial connectivity strategy by selecting Electronic Data Systems (EDS) to develop a hub communications infrastructure.

shell
A cross-application operating environment accessed through a single user interface. A network connec-

SFA

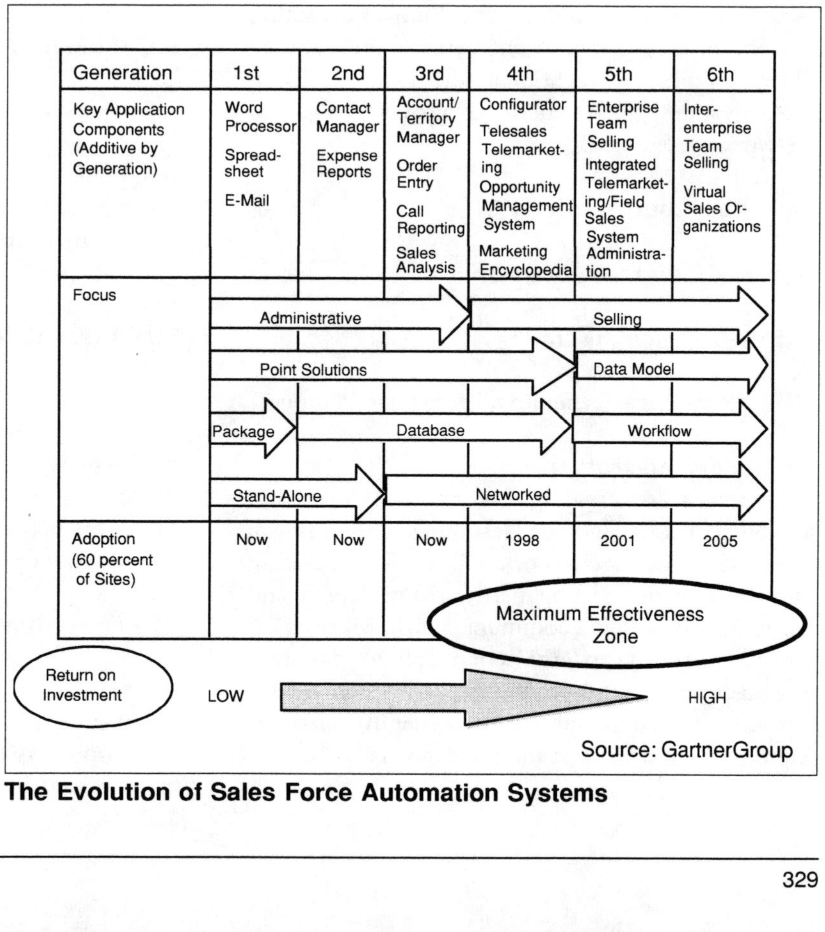

The Evolution of Sales Force Automation Systems

tivity shell is the environment used to access network resources — e.g., a suite with a single user interface for host, Transmission Control Protocol/Internet Protocol (TCP/IP) and Web access.

SHF (super-high frequency)
Denotes frequencies from 3 gigahertz (GHz) to 30 GHz.

Shielded Distributed Data Interface (See SDDI)

shielded pair
A pair of conductors in a cable that are wrapped with metallic foil designed to insulate the pair from interference.

shielded twisted pair (See STP)

shim
A software modification inserted into an operating system or application, to intercept the normal data flow and provide additional functionality. Often used by third party vendors to provide enhanced networking features.

shop floor control (See SFC)

Shortest Path First (See SPF)

SHT (short holding time)

SHTTP (Secure Hypertext Transport Protocol)

SI (system integration)
The process of creating a complex information system that may include designing or building a customized architecture or application, integrating it with new or existing hardware, packaged and custom software, and communications. Most enterprises rely on an external contractor for program management of most or all phases of system development. This external vendor generally also assumes a high degree of the project's risks.

SI (system integrator)
An organization or an individual that integrates two or more systems so that they work together. For example, an organization can integrate its payroll system with its check-processing system to process paychecks. System integration can be done internally or through an external contract. It requires specific technical knowledge of the programming languages. Major system integration projects often require the assistance of a specialty firm that has the resources and expertise to manage a project plan that could last for several months or even years.

SIA (Semiconductor Industry Association)

SIAC (Securities Industry Automation Corporation)

SIB (Securities and Investment Board)

SIC (Standard Industrial Code)

SID (Security ID)

sideband
A frequency band on either the upper or lower side of the carrier frequency within which fall the frequencies produced by the process of modulation.

SIDM (serial, impact, dot matrix)
A type of printer, suitable for making carbon copies, but now largely obsolete.

SIFF (serial, impact, fully formed)
A type of printer using a character wheel similar to a typewriter. Suitable for making carbon copies, but now largely obsolete.

SIG (special-interest group)

signal
A physical, time-dependent energy value used for the purpose of conveying information through a transmission line.

Signal Computing System Architecture (See SCSA)

signaling
The process by which a caller or equipment on the transmitting end of a line informs a particular party or equipment at the receiving end that a message is to be communicated.

Signaling, Engineering and Administration System (See SEAS)

Signaling, Protocols, and Switching (See SPS)

Signaling System 7 (See SS7)

signal-terminating equipment (See STE)

signal-to-noise ratio (See SNR)

significant digit
The integer of a number that represents the largest percentage.

sign off
Log off.

sign on
Log on.

silicon on sapphire (See SOS)

SIMAC
A Center for Facilitation of Procedures and Practices, Administration, Commerce and Transport (CEFACT) working group focused on simplifying electronic data interchange (EDI) to be of use by small to midsize businesses. SIMAC is derived from the Simpl-EDI, Forms and Web-Based Ad Hoc EDI group.

SIMD (single instruction, multiple data)
A design for parallel computers characterized by instructions that can directly trigger a large number (in parallel) of data operations on different data. Vector processors fall into this category.

SIMM (single in-line memory module)
A small printed circuit board that plugs into a socket on a personal computer and increases the available random-access memory (RAM).

Simple Internet Protocol Plus (See SIPP)

Simple Mail Transfer Protocol (See SMTP)

Simple Multicast Routing Protocol (See SMRP)

Simple Network Management Protocol (See SNMP)

Simple Workflow Access Protocol (See SWAP)

simplex
Pertaining to the capability to transmit in one direction only. See also half duplex and full duplex.

simplex circuit
A circuit permitting the transmission of signals in one specified direction only. Also known as single duplex.

simulation
The use of a mathematical or computer representation of a physical system for the purpose of studying constraint effects.

SIN (Status Indication Normal — ISDN term)
Link test feedback indicating normal operation.

Single Channel Per Carrier (See SCPC)

single-image mode
A mode of operation in which multiple physical central processing units (CPUs) within a complex logically appear as one system running under control of a single copy of the operating system.

single in-line memory module (See SIMM)

single instruction, multiple data (See SIMD)

single large expensive disk (See SLED)

single-mode fiber
A fiber with a small core diameter allowing the propagation of a single light path.

single-sideband (SSB) transmission
To make efficient use of the frequency band available, the carrier and the unwanted sideband of an amplitude-modulated wave can be filtered out so that only the sideband that contains all the information is transmitted.

single sign-on (See SSO)

single threading
A group of instructions that completes the processing of one message before starting another. See also multithreading.

SINIX (Siemens' version of Unix)

SINIX (Singapore user group)

sink
The terminal connection that collects overflow transmissions on a communications pathway.

S-Interface
In Integrated Services Digital Network (ISDN), the standard four-wire connection between the terminal adapter and the network.

SIO (serial input/output)

SIOS (Status Indication Out of Service — ISDN term)
Link test feedback indicating an error condition in the tested circuit.

SIP (SMDS Interface Protocol)
A frame-based protocol for access to a Switched Multimegabit Data Service (SMDS) by customer premises equipment based on Distributed Queue Dual Bus (DQDB) technology.

SIPP (Simple Internet Protocol Plus)
A proposed revision to the Internet Protocol (IP). IP must be modified to support an address threshold capable of supporting the exponential growth of the Internet. SIPP would increase the address space to eight bytes.

SIPRnet (Secret IP Router Network)

SITA (Societe Internationale de Telecommunications Aeronautiques)

SITE (strategy, iteration, testing, enablement — GartnerGroup)
Information systems (IS) departments have a history in applications development of following a design process of planning, prototyping, testing and development, resulting in justifiable design decisions. SITE seeks to build upon this long-established IS department practice in creating a structured framework within which both business unit (BU) managers and IS staff see clearly identified roles maximize their talents and skills. As a result, issues such as staffing, success factors, return on investment (ROI) guidelines, request for proposals (RFPs), interface design and graphic design are addressed in an environment where decisions are not arbitrary. Whether final execution is in-house or outsourced, adhering to SITE principles provides a project blueprint meaningful to multiple audiences

S/KEY
A one-time password authentication technology.

skills-based management (See SBM)

SKIP (Simple Key Management for Internet Protocols)

SKU (stock-keeping unit)
An inventory control code, generally used in the retail and wholesale industries. Generally embodied in a barcode.

SLA (service-level agreement)
An agreement that sets the expectations between the service provider and the customer and describes the products or services to be delivered, the single point of contact for end-user problems and the metrics by which the effectiveness of the process is monitored and approved.

slave
A terminal or computer controlled by another computer.

SLC (subscriber line charge)
An access charge paid by all telecommunications customers, developed by the Federal Communications Commission (FCC) to help local-exchange carriers (LECs) pay for their installed network infrastructure and for new network developments after the split-up of AT&T in 1984.

SLED (single large expensive disk)
Traditional disk drive. That is, a conventional large-system disk system that has, on average, almost twice the diameter of a lower-cost redundant array of independent disks (RAID) system and, as its name implies, is significantly more expensive to manufacture.

SLIC (Subscriber Line Interface Circuit)

slice architecture
A method of using several dedicated subprocessors to provide full processing capabilities.

SLIP (Serial Line Internet Protocol)

SLM (software license management)
A mechanism for systematically ensuring compliance with system vendor and independent software vendor (ISV) software licenses — for example, maximum users, maximum nodes and maximum MIPS. Examples include Digital Equipment's License Management Facility and Hewlett-Packard's Network License Server.

SLO (service-level objective)

SLOC (source lines of code)

SLR (service-level reporter)
An IBM product that provides direct-access storage device (DASD) administrators with predefined storage report formats. (Storage reports are used for identification of exception conditions, capacity planning, trend analysis, cost accounting and standards enforcement.)

SLR (Single-Channel Linear Recording 5 — Tandberg)

SLS (Signaling Link Selection — ISDN term)

SMA (Systems Management Architecture)

Small Computer Systems Interface (See SCSI)

small-systems consultant (See SSC)

Small Value Payments Co. (See SVPCo)

SMART (Self-Monitoring Analysis and Reporting Technology)

SMART (strategies for managing resources and technology)

smart card
A plastic card that contains a microprocessor and a memory chip or just a memory chip. The microprocessor card has the ability to add, delete and manipulate information on the card. A memory-chip card, such as a phone card, can only add information. By maintaining all necessary functions and

S

information on the card, smart cards do not require access to remote databases. Growing interest in smart cards crosses barriers of geography, industry and business functions. However, the variety of smart card applications belies the fact that smart cards are capable of only three functions:

1. Information Storage and Management: Storing data off-line is an important feature of the smart card. It can maintain, for example, all of an individual's health-related information. Data can be stored and updated continuously either in a write-once format (e.g., a patient's blood type or known allergies) or in a read/write memory (e.g., a patient's last visit to the doctor). Memory can store information that does not change, build a history of transactions, or maintain a current data value (as in a phone card). The ability to add and subtract data value from the card makes it particularly useful in financial transactions that use electronic cash or credit and debit. The basic technique is the same whether it is applied to monetary values or frequent-flyer miles. Because the records are always in the user's possession, privacy is enhanced since duplicate information may be stored at a secure, off-line site in case the card is lost or damaged.

2. Authentication: Smart cards can manipulate the data they contain to enable real-time transactions. Authentication is the process that determines whether the card will allow a transaction.

3. Encryption/Decryption: Encryption changes data into a form that can be read only by the intended receiver. To decipher the message, the receiver of the encrypted data must have the proper decryption key. By its very nature, data encryption and decryption must take place in a local, secure environment. The capability of smart cards to perform this function within the embedded chip means that secure data does not have to be transferred from the card to a reader or other device. This reduces the chance that information can be stolen from the card.

smart terminal
A display terminal that can operate in either conversational or block mode and can support a full range of local editing capabilities.

SMB (Server Message Block)

SMC (Select Component Manager — Select Software Tools)

SMDR (station message detail reporting)
A means of capturing telephone system information on calls made, including who made the call, where it went and what time of day it was made, for processing into meaningful management reports. With such information, it is easier to spot exceptions to regular calling patterns such as out-of-hours calling, international calls, significant variances from previous reporting periods and call destinations that do not reflect normal calling patterns for the enterprise.

SMDS (Switched Multimegabit Data Service)
A Bell Communications Research standard providing DS-1 and DS-3 access to a high-speed metropolitan-area network (MAN). It is based on the Institute of Electrical and Electronics Engineers (IEEE) 802.6 standard. SMDS is based on the data connectivity portion of the 802.6 MAN standard (but does not provide isochronous circuits). It is a high-volume, high-speed, switched digital service. Supported speeds range from 1.544 megabits per second (Mbps) to 45 Mbps (with 155 Mbps possible in the future).

Several local-exchange carriers (LECs) and interexchange carriers (IXCs) are now offering or testing SMDS services. Additionally, the service description for public networking includes an addressing capability, enabling users to interoperate with other SMDS users. Asynchronous transfer mode (ATM) is the underlying protocol of Broadband Integrated Services Digital Network (B-ISDN). It is dependent on the B-ISDN addressing scheme and must rationalize addressing schemes for non-B-ISDN implementations.

SMDS Interface Protocol (See SIP)

SME (small and midsize enterprises)

SMF (Standard Message Format)
A file format protocol for NetWare Message Handling Service (MHS).

SMF Min.
A message using the minimal submission format, or minimum set of header fields required by Standard Message Format (SMF).

SMG (Storage Management Group)

SMI (server management interface)

SMI (supplier-managed inventory — See VMI)

S/MIME or SMIME (Secure MIME)
The Secure Multipurpose Internet Mail Extensions standard for secure messaging. Promoted by RSA Data Security, the S/MIME method for protecting and digitally signing e-mail encapsulates a message within a MIME envelope and uses Rivest-Shamir-Adelman (RSA)'s PKCS #7 to encrypt it. S/MIME specifies that X.509 certificates validate the correspondent's public keys and electronic signatures. These certificates can come from the entity (i.e., self-certifying keys) or from a third-party certificate authority service such as VeriSign.

SMLI (stateful multilayer inspection)

SMP (symmetric multiprocessing)
A multiprocessor architecture in which all processors are identical, share memory and execute both user code and operating-system code.

SMR (specialized mobile radio)
A wireless communications technology in competition with analog cellular services. In an SMR system, the base station equipment supplier is the licensee of the transmitters. Users have access to the multiple channels of the network rather than the limited number of channels of a private mobile radio network. Many users share all of the available channels. Sharing is accomplished on a first-come, first-served basis. When users want to initiate a call, they activate the push-to-talk button on the handset. Assuming the portable unit (and dispatcher or other portable unit) is tuned to an available channel, a communication path is established. If channels that the sender and receiver can use are not available, the call cannot be completed, and the operator must wait for another opportunity to try again.

SMRP (Simple Multicast Routing Protocol)
Routes multicast data streams in conjunction with multicast extensions to AppleTalk.

SMS (Shared Medical Systems)

SMS (short-messaging service)

SMS (Storage Management Subsystem — IBM)
A component of IBM's Multiple Virtual Storage/Data Facility Product (MVS/DFP) that is used to automate and centralize the management of storage by providing the storage administrator with control over data class, storage class, management class, storage group and ACS routine definitions.

SMS (system-managed storage)
The term used for the conceptualization of an architecture for attachment, management and reconfiguration of secondary storage. Among the SMS basic design goals is the separation of logical-device management from physical-device management.

SMS (Systems Management Server — Microsoft)
SMS is systems management software that runs under Microsoft's Windows NT Server 3.5. It is used for the distribution of software, monitoring and analyzing network usage, and performing a variety of other network administration functions. Using SMS requires a Microsoft SQL Server database.

SMT (surface mount technology)
An integrated-circuit (IC) mounting system that uses flat pads instead of pins, eliminating the need to drill boards and making automated mounting easier.

SMTF (Symmetrix Multihost Transfer Facility)

SMTP (Simple Mail Transfer Protocol)
A messaging protocol governing electronic-mail transmission in Transmission Control Protocol/Internet Protocol (TCP/IP) networks. It is used to transfer e-mail between computers. It is a server-to-server protocol. SMTP supports only text and cannot handle attachments. It supports negative delivery notifications, not the positive notifications required by electronic data interchange (EDI).

SNA (Systems Network Architecture)
An IBM-developed layered network architecture. The layers isolate applications from system network services, enabling users to write applications independent of the lower networking software layer.

SNA APPN — Intermediate Node
Support for connecting and exchanging information with IBM systems using IBM's Advanced Peer-to-Peer Networking (APPN) protocols. Support should be extended to include an intermediate-node (data forwarding) role.

SNA Distribution Services (See SNADS)

SNADS (SNA Distribution Services)
An architecture for interchanging data through a Systems Network Architecture (SNA) network in a store-and-forward fashion. SNADS is an SNA extension that provides an asynchronous interface. It is mostly appropriate for applications without strong time requirements, such as document distribution, file transfer and e-mail. SNADS requires that Logical Unit (LU) 6.2, and the software that implements SNADS, reside in the same processor as the LU 6.2 support.

SNA LEN PU 2.1 End Node
Support for connecting and exchanging information with IBM systems using IBM's Low Entry Networking (LEN) PU 2.1 protocols. Support should be for at least an end-node LEN role.

SNAP (SubNetwork Attachment Point)
An extension of Logical Link Control (LLC) for network packets in Institute of Electrical and Electronics Engineers (IEEE) 802.3 format, a technique for multiplexing protocols on an 802.3 network using octets 14 and 15 with a Service Access Point (SAP) value of 0xAA.

SNC (Secure Network Communications)
A SAP AG initiative intended to identify products that will protect the communication links between the distributed components of SAP R/3 software. R/3 supports application-independent security products that adhere to the Generic Security Services Application Programming Interface (GSS-API) v.2 standard.

SNDT (serial, nonimpact, direct thermal)
A printer technology.

SNIA (Storage Networking Industry Association)

SNIJ (serial, nonimpact ink jet)
A printer technology.

SNMP (Simple Network Management Protocol)
A Transmission Control Protocol/Internet Protocol (TCP/IP)-derived protocol governing network management and the monitoring of network devices. Strictly speaking, SNMP is the Management Information Base (MIB) described in the SNMP standard; extensions to this MIB proposed by the Electronic Messaging Association permit the monitoring and reporting of all conforming messaging components through standard SNMP management tools for network components

SNOMED (Systematized Nomenclature of Human and Veterinary Medicine)

SNR (signal-to-noise ratio)
The power of a signal relative to channel noise.

SNTT (serial, nonimpact, thermal transfer)

SOA (service-oriented architecture)
A model for application construction that decouples server business functionality from client logic. The business functionality is organized as a collection of modules (services) that each have a clear business identity and strict formal interfaces. The identity allows a requester to map a function to a service, and the formal interface enables any qualified requester to invoke the service without any information regarding its internal design. Behind the interface, the implementation of the service may be a single program or a flow of multiple programs and may include calls to a message broker.

social-security systems
These systems help public-sector technology administrators to manage a host of tasks such as monitoring of fund dispersion, service status, and eligibility and benefits tracking, typically through the integration of what likely were, at one time, discrete social-security-related databases.

sockets
The Berkeley interprocess communications model. A socket specifies the end points of a two-way communications channel which connects two processes together so they can exchange information.

SOCKS
An NEC virtual private network (VPN) open protocol and Internet Engineering Task Force (IETF) standard.

SOD (statement of direction)
A vendor's announcement of future plans.

software
Programs that control computer hardware. The two primary categories are system software (which governs the workings of the computer itself, such as the operating system and utilities) and application software (which performs specific tasks for the user, such as word processing, spreadsheets and accounts payable).

software asset management (See SAM)

Software Asset Management Interest Group (See SWAMI)

software configuration management (See SCM)

software development
Project management, specifications, design, programming, testing, installation and training associated with a specific application development project of any size.

software development kit (See SDK)

Software Engineering Institute (See SEI)

software failure detection and recovery (See SFDR)

Software License Management (See SLM)

S

software maintenance
Updating software, adding new functions, fixing bugs and solving problems. Technology vendors often sell a maintenance contract with their software. This contract is usually calculated as an annual fee based on some percentage of the total software cost. It generally provides for overall support and maintenance of a software product, including applications. Support may include telephone assistance time as well.

Software-Optimized Encryption Algorithm (See SEAL)

software process improvement network (See SPIN)

SOGA (SNA Open Gateway Architecture)

SOGT (Senior Officials Group — Telecommunications)
An ad hoc committee composed of senior Member State and Commission Officials in the European Community to define, oversee, and agree on the technical work of the Groupe d'Analyse et Prevision (GAP) committees in telecommunications.

SOHO (small office/home office)

SOI (silicon on insulator)

SOI (statement of intent)

solid-state device
Electronic pathways made of solid materials, e.g., chips and bubble memories.

solid-state disk (See SSD)

SOM (System Object Model)
IBM's object model designed to provide users with scalability, portability and interoperability of distributed applications across Hewlett-Packard and IBM platforms.

SONET (Synchronous Optical Network)
A International Telecommunications Union Telecommunications standard for synchronous transmission up to multigigabit speeds. The standard includes multivendor interoperability, improved troubleshooting and network survivability. As a Layer 1 standard, it is a foundation for Broadband Integrated Services Digital Network (B-ISDN) services.

SOP 98-1
A standard used to account for the cost of developing and maintaining software in-house. For financial statements prepared for fiscal years beginning after 15 December 1998, the American Institute of Certified Public Accountants (AICPA) early in 1998 approved the Statement of Position (SOP) 98-1. Under the new guideline, maintaining legacy software is an internal maintenance expense — but if a company significantly enhances a system's functionality, then under SOP 98-1 that work may be capitalized. Thus, portions of euro or year 2000 compliance efforts may be capitalized, depending on how the upgrade is done.

SOP 98-1 establishes guidelines determining when applications development (AD) work should be expensed vs. when it may be capitalized. SOP 98-1 becomes part of the Generally Accepted Accounting Principles (GAAP) to which independent auditors adhere. Though the AICPA is an American professional body, SOP 98-1 will technically apply to all firms that adhere to GAAP, especially those that wish to trade on U.S. stock exchanges. It affects all nongovernmental entities, and applies to work in progress as of its adoption.

SOS (silicon on sapphire)
A semiconductor manufacturing term.

Source Address/Destination Address (See SA/DA)

Source Code Control System (See SCCS)

Source Data Automation (See SDA)

source encoding
A lossy or lossless compression technique that takes into account the nature of the information to be compressed. See entropy encoding.

source routing
A technique used in local-area networks (LANs) in which the source of the frame specifies the route that the frame has to follow; the source furnishes a routing information field that designates the entire route to the destination.

source-routing bridge
Used in IBM Token Ring networks. Source routing remote bridges use a combination of source routing and transparent bridging and can allow IBM and non-IBM types of nodes to share the same network.

source traffic descriptor
In asynchronous transfer mode (ATM), a set of parameters used during the setting up of a connection.

SOW (Statement of Work)
The Statement of Work includes an objectives section allowing the customer to emphasize the desired end state or performance metric to be achieved. It also mandates the assessment of past performance, technical approach and cost for each task order. The customer determines the relative importance of each criterion.

SP (service pack — Microsoft)
A minor revision to a software product that contains feature updates or bug fixes, but not enough new code to warrant a new version number.

SP (subportal)
A healthcare subportal (SP) provides highly targeted aggregate content and interactive capabilities and focuses on a specific vertical-market segment, as opposed to the broader market spectrum of portals (e.g., American Online, Excite or Microsoft Network). SPs are hybrid environments in that they can be deployed as intranet or Internet solutions, or a combination of both. SPs are linked to the healthcare organization (HCO) Web page and extend HCO branding — a desirable goal in that improved branding allows HCOs to recruit and retain the best providers, and establishes consumer loyalty that may give HCOs leverage in employer and payer negotiations.

SP (System Processor)

SP4 (Service Pack 4 — Microsoft)

space
The signal (communications channel state) corresponding to a binary zero.

space diversity reception
To reduce the effects of fading and attenuation, a radio signal is received at more than one site, the sites being separated by a few wavelengths. The signals are then combined, selected, or both.

space-division switching
A method for switching circuits in which each connection through the switch takes a physically separate path.

space segment
In a satellite circuit, the satellite itself, and necessary tracking, monitoring, and control functions. Excludes any ground equipment.

SPAG (Standards Promotion and Application Group)
Undertook much of the original information technology (IT) standardization work.

spam
Usenet messages flooded to many newsgroups indiscriminately. The term is also loosely applied to junk mail.

spamdexing
A severe form of Internet spamming wherein a spam "artist" hides as many as hundreds of words or phrases in a document to increase the hit count of a search engine.

Spanning Tree
The Institute of Electrical and Electronics Engineers IEEE 802.1D committee standard for bridging local-area networks (LANs) without loops. The algorithm ensures only one path connects any pair of stations, selecting one bridge as the root bridge from which all paths are considered to radiate.

SPARC (Scalable Processor Architecture)
A reduced instruction set computer (RISC) architecture developed by Sun Microsystems and used in the Sun workstation family. SPARC chips are available from several semiconductor manufacturers, as Sun positions SPARC as a de facto standard.

SPC (statistical process control)
The identification and control of process variations so that a change in some process parameter (and faulty outcome) can be avoided. In practice, significant inputs to a process are measured or sampled. Out-of-control conditions are recorded, either because the value of the measurement falls outside a control limit, or a pattern in the time series indicates an unusual and undesirable event, such as a trend or a process shift. When an out-of-control condition is identified, the production line can be stopped and an effort made to fix the process. SPC within manufacturing practices can reduce scrap/rework, reduce or eliminate inspection and increase production.

SPE (Sequenced Packet Exchange)

SPE (synchronous payload envelope) (See STS)

speakerphone
A telephone device that has a speaker-microphone unit, allowing hands-free conversation. Also called speakerset.

speaker verification
A superior biometrics-based alternative to typed passwords or personal identification numbers. A computer matches a person's spoken voice to an electronically-captured sample (analogous to a unique fingerprint) of their voice.

SPEC (System Performance Evaluation Cooperative)
A vendor consortium that selects and standardizes benchmark programs submitted by members or others, for the purpose of rating and comparing the performance of processors.

SPECfp (SPEC floating point)
A test of floating-point computations, established by the System Performance Evaluation Cooperative (SPEC).

specialized carrier
A company that provides value-added or limited communications facilities.

specialized mobile radio (See SMR)

specialty center
A specialty center, or center of excellence, is a group of people dedicated to identifying best practices in an area of expertise and to building an internal service organization around that expertise. A center of excellence is a central clearinghouse for knowledge capital that is used across all business transformation projects. Specialty centers are an excellent means to leverage specialized skill sets, and are typically staffed to address a known demand.

specification, tracking, evaluation, production (See STEP)

SPECint (SPEC integer)
A System Performance Evaluation Cooperative (SPEC) benchmark to measure the integer performance of a processor.

spectrum
A continuous range of frequencies, usually wide in extent, within which waves have some specific common characteristics.

speech circuit
A circuit designed for the transmission of speech, either analog or encoded, but which can also be used for data transmission or telegraphy.

speech recognition
A computer's ability to convert spoken input to text. Special software takes vocal sounds, digitizes them and then compares them to a library of sound patterns. When matches are found, the computer can use those words just as if they had been typed on a keyboard. Speech recognition can improve personal productivity in the workplace, increase the effectiveness of interactive voice response (IVR) systems, and bring computing to untraditional environments (e.g., a hospital emergency room). The term "voice recognition" is also commonly used to refer to the ability of a machine or program to recognize and carry out voice commands or take dictation.

Speech recognition software generally falls into three categories along a continuum:

- command systems were the earliest and simplest form; the computer learns a small number of voice commands like "open file" or "print document," freeing the user from having to use a keyboard or mouse to perform those tasks.
- discrete speech recognition, the second stage in this evolution, can be used for dictation and other natural speaking conditions, but pauses are required between words.
- continuous speech recognition software is emerging today. These systems understand natural speech without pauses, and their vocabularies and accuracy will continue to expand and improve.

speed dialing
A feature that enables a private branch exchange (PBX) or PBX station to store certain telephone numbers and dial them automatically when a short (one-, two- or three-digit) code is entered. Also called speed calling.

SPF (Shortest Path First)
A link-state protocol that uses a set of user-defined parameters to find the optimum route between two points. See also RIP.

SPI (service provider interface)

SPI (software process improvement)

SPID (Service Profile Identifier)
In Integrated Services Digital Network (ISDN), a number assigned to an ISDN line by the provider.

spider
A piece of software (also called a webcrawler) designed to follow hyperlinks to their completion and return Internet addresses passed.

SPIN (software process improvement network)
A best-practices group run by the Software Engineering Institute that provides hands-on experience to IT professionals.

splitter
A simple device that takes one input and sends it to several identical ports without amplification; commonly used residentially for sharing telephone lines between handsets and modems or for using two televisions on one antenna or cable point.

SPMD (single program, multiple data)

spoofing
1. A process whereby a router responds to keep alive messages from a host rather than passing them on the remote client, thus saving call

charges. Used mainly in Integrated Services Digital Network (ISDN).

2. Of a packet, falsely claiming to be from an address different from that from which it actually originated.

spool
Simultaneous online peripherals operations; software that manages access to peripherals, such as printers.

spooling
Temporary storage of batch input and output until the processor is ready.

spot beam
A satellite signal that is concentrated on a small geographic area.

SPP (Sequenced Packet Protocol)
Xerox's connection-based, flow-controlled packet transmission for client processes; part of the XNX suite.

SPS (Signaling, Protocols, and Switching)
One of the Conference on European Posts and Telecommunications' (CEPT's) working groups.

SPS (Standard Procurement System)
A procurement solution, based on a commercial package, to replace the Department of Defense's (DoD's) legacy systems with a single application capable of supporting the diverse computing needs of nearly 50,000 users across 900 contracting sites worldwide.

SPX (Sequenced Packet Exchange)
A Novell NetWare session-based communications protocol used to govern the transport of messages across a network. It is designed to provide reliable end-to-end data transport, including error detection between two end-user devices.

SQA (software quality assurance)

SQC (statistical quality control)

SQL (Structured Query Language)
A relational data language that provides a consistent, English keyword-oriented set of facilities for query, data definition, data manipulation and data control. It is a programmed interface to relational database management systems (RDBMSs). IBM introduced SQL as the main external interface to its experimental RDBMS, System R, which it developed in the 1970s. SQL statements include:

- Data manipulation language statements: SELECT, INSERT, UPDATE and DELETE
- Data definition language statements, including the CREATE and DROP statements for tables and indexes
- Statements that control data consistency, and grant and revoke authority

SQL statements are called "dynamic" when they are not completely specified until the program is executed. They are called "static" when they are completely specified when the program is compiled. SQL is precise, because it is based on predicate logic, but is difficult for average users to deal with, and its most fruitful position is as a protocol for software-to-software connectivity, rather than for human-to-software access.

SQL/400
The IBM relational database management system (RDBMS) for the AS/400.

SQL Access Group
A consortium of vendors set up in November 1989 to accelerate the development of Remote Data Access (RDA) standards, deliver protocols for interconnectivity among multiple SQL-based products, and define the application programming interfaces (APIs) necessary for the interoperability of heterogeneous SQL implementations in a network environment and the portability of applications developed for those same implementations.

SQL DB Access (SQL Database Access)
Availability of a relational interface to a midrange system database that is compliant with Level 1 of the American National Standards Institute (ANSI) X3.135-1986 or International Organization for Standardization (ISO) 9075 SQL standard. Both a command (interpretive) and programming (compiled) implementation of the interface should be available.

SQL/DS (SQL/Data System)

SQLJ
The larger database management system (DBMS) vendors (Oracle and IBM), which are also Vendors Against Microsoft (VAM) participants, have proposed SQLJ as the standard way of using embedded Structured Query Language (SQL) within Java applications.

SQLNet
Middleware automatically bundled into Oracle6 and Oracle7 to enable fat-client two-tier applications and masked from most users.

SQL Services
Digital Equipment's implementation of a Structured Query Language application programming interface (API) that was distributed from Virtual Memory System (VMS) servers to Disk Operating System (DOS), Macintosh, OS/2, VMS or Ultrix desktops.

SRAM (static RAM)

SRDF (Symmetrix Remote Data Facility)
Implements controller-to-controller remote copy. It can operate in synchronous, semi-synchronous or adaptive mode.

SRM (storage resource management)

SRM (System Resource Manager)

SRPI (server/requester programming interface)

SRT (Source Routing Transparent)

SRTP (Sequenced Routing Update Protocol)
Assists VINES servers in finding local addresses of peers and clients.

SS7 (Signaling System 7)
An out-of-band signaling scheme, typically with a 64-kilobit-per-second (Kbps) transmission rate, used in the United States. It is designed for digital networks, and is key to current Integrated Services Digital Network (ISDN) implementations. Also called Common Channel Signaling No. 7 (CCS7).

SSA (Serial Storage Architecture)
IBM's disk storage technology and product line of disk subsystems. For most purposes, it is a single-sourced proprietary interface, especially useful for users who have standardized on RS/6000 systems with applications that require very high data rates that are not particularly cache-friendly.

S

SRM

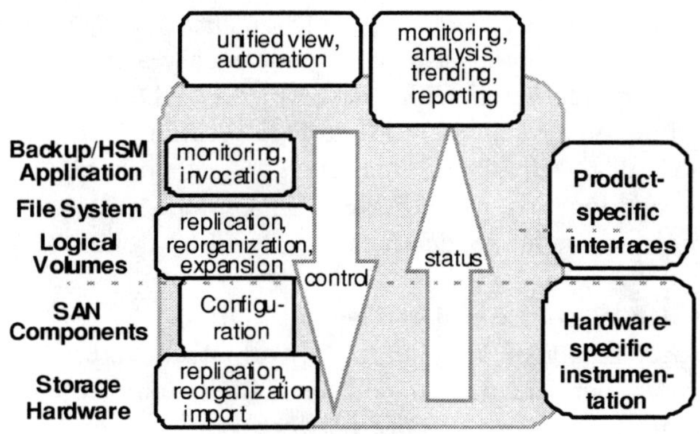

HSM = Hierarchical storage management
SAN = Storage area network

Source: GartnerGroup

Storage Resource Management Automation Functions and Current Interfaces

SSA (System Software Associates)

SSAP (Statements of Standard Accounting Practice — U.K.)

SSB (single sideband)
See single-sideband transmission.

SSC (shared-solution center)
In Stage 1, an SSC is primarily a "showcase" for software demos and training. In Stage 2, the SSC can be used for "jump starts," while the client builds its own infrastructure. In Stage 3, certain project phases such as report development are done at an SSC. In Stage 4, more project phases including testing are done at the SSC, and the SSC reaches "scale" — at any given time 20 or more clients are being serviced from an SSC. Finally, in Stage 5, there are phase-based "factories" where testing or data conversion specialists and tools can be leveraged across multiple projects, whether on SAP, Oracle or other software.

SSC (small-systems consultant)
The SSC facilitates the transfer of skills needed by business unit (BU) developers from part-time developers to end users. The role of an SSC is to provide and enthusiastically promote easy-access, user-friendly applications development (AD) consulting on a rapid, just-in-time basis. Although the SSC may be involved in the actual project work, his or her focus is to help the BU developers plan projects, model applications and "learn by doing."

SSCP (System Services Control Points)
Focal points of a Systems Network Architecture (SNA) network that contain the ability to manage configuration, coordinate network requests, and provide services.

SSD (solid-state disk)
A disk drive with no moving parts. It typically includes one or more circuit boards loaded with memory chips, and a controller that presents a standard disk drive interface to the computer system. Since it is on the peripheral side of the input/output (I/O) boundary, an SSD suffers the performance impacts of command overhead — typically less than 0.1 millisecond (ms) — and of I/O bus bandwidth. However, because it uses memory chips instead of mechanical access arms and rotating disk media, SSD eliminates the mechanical seek-and-rotation times that add 10 ms or more to the average access time of a hard-disk drive (HDD). Thus, while an HDD might deliver 100 I/Os per second, an SSD can do 4,000 I/Os per second. To emulate the permanence of magnetic disk storage, an SSD generally contains a battery backup power supply and an HDD that can save the contents of the memory in the event of a power failure.

SSC

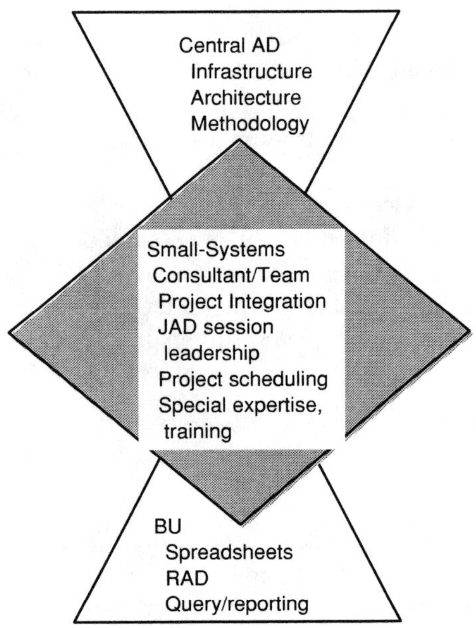

AD = Applications development
BU = Business unit
JAD = Joint applications development
RAD = Rapid applications development

Source: GartnerGroup

The Role of the Small-Systems Consultant

SSEM (system and server evaluation model)
A GartnerGroup model that focuses on the six major categories of differentiation that exist between server platforms: performance and scalability, high availability, software vendor enthusiasm, platform architectural longevity, systems and network management software, and maintenance.

SSF (Secure Store and Forward)
A SAP AG initiative to certify third-party products. Security functions supported by SSF include application-level end-to-end security, smart-card authentication and single sign-on. R/3 supports application-independent security products that adhere to the Generic Security Services Application Programming Interface (GSS-API) v.2 standard. SSF provides support for products that protect data and documents using such mechanisms as digital signatures and digital envelopes. The standard supported is PKCS 7.

SSI (single-system image)

SSI (subsystem interface)

SSL (Secure Sockets Layer)
An Internet security standard from Netscape Communications, used for its browser and server software.

SSN (Switched Service Network)
A telephone network consisting of terminals, transmission links, and at least one exchange, on which any user can communicate with any other user at any time.

SSO (single sign-on)
A term describing the function of consolidating the number of log-on processes for end users among deployed and planned, built and bought information technology (IT) resources.

SSP (service switching point)
The telecommunications switch in an intelligent network which handles a call with reference to supplementary routing and database information contained at a service control point (SCP).

SSSWG (Storage System Standards Working Group)

ST (synchronous transport)

stack
An area in memory for the temporary storage of information. Information stored here is not retrieved by address, but rather in chronological order, last in-first out (LIFO).

stackable
Network devices that may be stacked one on another but where the stack is managed as one, as opposed to daisychaining, where each device is viewed separately by the network management system. Types of devices available in this format are hubs, switches, and routers.

STAIRS (Storage and Information Retrieval System)
IBM's mainframe contextual search and library package (STAIRS/VS for MVS and STAIRS/CMS for VM).

standard
A document that recommends a protocol, interface, type of wiring, or some other aspect of a system. It may even recommend something as general as a conceptual framework or model (e.g., a communications architecture). De jure standards are developed by internationally or nationally recognized standards bodies or vendors. De facto standards are widely used vendor-developed protocols or architectures, such as IBM's Systems Network Architecture (SNA).

Standard for the Exchange of Product Model Data (See STEP)

Standard Generalized Markup Language (See SGML)

Standard Message Format (See SMF)

Standard Procurement System (See SPS)

standards
Specifications or styles that are widely accepted by users and adopted by several vendors. Standards are critical to the compatibility of hardware, software, and everything in between. Industry standards enable the essential elements of a computer and related infrastructure to work together. Standards provide specifications to hardware manufacturers and software developers that allow them to create products that will work together. Deviation from standards could result in the following problems:

- A plug on a keyboard does not fit into the related outlet on a computer.
- A piece of software does not work with a particular operating system.
- An Internet browser cannot read a certain page on the World Wide Web because the page is not formatted according the browser requirements.
- Proprietary software does not work on the Internet.

Standards Promotion and Application Group (See SPAG)

standby central control
A second control computer that can be provided to direct private branch exchange (PBX) operations if the primary one fails.

Starlan
A local network design and specification within IEEE 802.3 standards subcommittee, characterized by 1 megabit per second (Mbps) baseband data transmission over two-pair, twisted-pair wiring.

star network
A network topology in which each station is connected only to a central station by a point-to-point link and communicates with all other stations through the central station.

start-stop (signaling)
Signaling in which each group of code elements corresponding to an alphabetical signal is preceded by a start signal that serves to prepare the receiving mechanism for the reception and registration of character and is followed by a stop signal that serves to bring the receiving mechanism to rest in preparation for the reception of the next character.

statement of direction (See SOD)

Statement of Work (See SOW)

station
One of the input or output points of a communications system, e.g., a telephone set in the telephone system or the point where a business machine interfaces to a network also called a node.

station message detail reporting (See SMDR)

statistical multiplexing
A time-division multiplexing technique in which time slots are dynamically allocated on the basis of need (i.e., slots are allocated to equipment with data to be transmitted).

statistical process control (See SPC)

statistical quality control/statistical process control
A set of techniques based on statistical principles and methods used to regulate the quality of products and processes.

statistical time-division multiplexing (See STDM)

Status Indication Normal — ISDN term (See SIN)

Status Indication Out of Service — ISDN term (See SIOS)

STDM (statistical time-division multiplexing)
Time shared dynamically between active channels on a multiplexer.

STE (signal-terminating equipment)
A network node used in the interconnection of public data networks.

STEP (specification, tracking, evaluation, production)
The four stages on which essential activities in the successful deployment of advanced technology are based. They are:

- Specification — which aligns corporate strategy and technology focus
- Tracking — which assesses individual technologies for maturity and business impact
- Evaluation — which involves prototyping and other in-depth evaluation activities to further gauge the readiness and relevance of the technology
- Production — which sees the technology being piloted and, if successful, rolled out into full deployment.

STEP (Standard for the Exchange of Product Model Data)
An international standards effort for defining the exchange of complete, unambiguous product model data. The goal of STEP is not only neutral file exchange, but also to serve as the basis for implementing, sharing and archiving entire product databases.

S/T interface
The electrical interface between a network terminator (NT1) device and one or more Integrated Services Digital Network (ISDN) communications devices that do not contain their own NT1s. A U.S. term.

STM (synchronous transfer mode)
A technique for multiplexing several circuits over transmission links and switches whereby time is divided into slots or buckets, and circuits are given time units whether or not they have any data to transmit. See also asynchronous transfer mode.

STN (super-twisted nematic)
An LCD display-screen technology

stock-keeping unit (See SKU)

stop bit
The last bit of a character in asynchronous serial transmission, used to ensure recognition of the next start element.

S

STEP

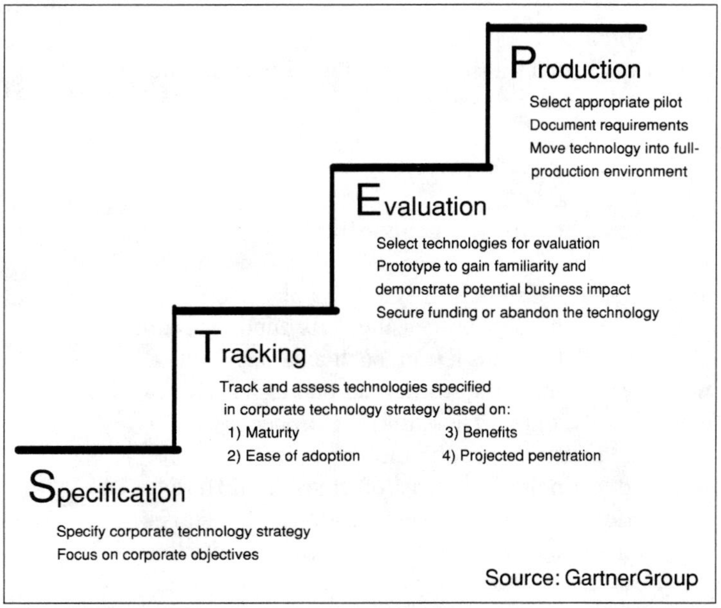

The STEP Process

stop element
In asynchronous transmission, the quiescent state following the transmission of a character. It is usually required to be at least 1; 1.42; 1.5; or 2 bit times long.

Storage and Information Retrieval System (See STAIRS)

Storage Management Subsystem — IBM (See SMS)

store and forward
A type of packet switching where the whole frame is processed before further transmission.

stored procedures
A limited form of remote procedure call (RPC) that enables procedural code (e.g., referential integrity constraints) to be stored and, thus, shared in the kernel of the database management system (DBMS). The DBMS provides a facility for storing procedural code associated with the database, and enforces its use during any database operation.

STP (shielded twisted pair)
A pair of twisted transmission wires with a metallic shield to minimize interference.

STP (signal transfer point)

STP (straight-through processing)
A popular strategy for financial institutions that is also pursued by some utility companies under the name "flow-through processing." Its fundamental premise is that a transaction, such as a payment, a trade, or a change to a residential phone service, is entered only once. Thereafter, it proceeds in an automated fashion through the rest of its life cycle, which may include dozens of steps in different application systems in various locations. The goal is to avoid re-keying information, thereby reducing input errors and shortening the time to completion.

straight-through cable
A cable with wires that have terminating ends with the same wire assignments. See also crossover cable.

straight-through processing (See STP)

strategy, iteration, testing, enablement — GartnerGroup (See SITE)

stream editor (See SED)

STREAMS
The Unix System V release 3 implementation of interprocess communications, which provides a flexible, layered mechanism for two or more processes to communicate with each other. STREAMS can support either Transmission Control Protocol/Internet Protocol (TCP/IP) or Open Systems Interconnection (OSI) implementations.

Structured Query Language (See SQL)

STS (synchronous transport signal)
The following terms are associated with STS signaling:

1. STS-1: The basic Sonet logical building block signal, with a transmission rate of 51.84 megabits per second (Mbps).
2. STS-3c: Synchronous Transport Signal level 3, concatenated. Sonet format specifying the frame structure for the lines used to carry asynchronous transfer mode (ATM) cells.
3. STS-n: Signal created with byte interleaving of "N" STS-1 signals together (Sonet term). The transmission rate is "N" times the STS-1 rate of 51.84 Mbps. See STS-1.
4. STS-Nc: Concatenated synchronous transport signal level N. An STS-N line layer signal combining the STS envelope capabilities from the "N" STS-1s forming an STS-Nc synchro-

nous payload envelope, which is transported as a single entity.

5. STS envelope capacity: The total bandwidth within the STS frame carrying the STS synchronous payload envelope (SPE). Total bandwidth is the combination of "N" STS-1s required to carry an STS-Nc SPE.
6. STS payload capacity: The maximum bandwidth of an STS SPE.
7. STS POH: STS Path Overhead. Starting with the first byte of an STS SPE, nine evenly distributed bytes per 125 microseconds. The STS POH provides the communication from the creation of an STS SPE to its disassembly.
8. STS PTE: STS Path Terminating Equipment. Network devices that multiplex and demultiplex the STS payload. These devices can originate, terminate, and modify the STS POH as required to transport the STS payload.
9. STS SPE: STS synchronous payload envelope. A generic term referring to both STS-1 SPEs, and STS-Nc SPEs which represent a 125-microsecond frame structure composed of STS POH and STS payload capacity.

STTL (Schottky transistor-transistor logic)

STX (start of text)

subnet
A portion of network that may be physically independent of another network portion, but both portions of the network share the same network address, and the portion is distinguished by a subnet number.

subnet mask
The bits of an Internet Protocol (IP) address used for a subnetwork.

subnet number
The portion of the Internet address that designates a subnet. It is used for intranet routing but is ignored for Internet-routing purposes.

SubNetwork Attachment Point (See SNAP)

subscriber line charge (See SLC)

subscriber loop
See subscriber line.

subvoice grade channel
A channel with a bandwidth narrower than that of voice-grade channels. Such channels are usually subchannels of a voice-grade line.

suite
A group of programs designed to work together, and often use the same underlying architecture.

Summit
Also referred to as FS/Summit. Summit is the name used to denote the IBM high-end processor series that follows the 3090. The FS/Summit processors are the ES/9000 Models 820 and 900.

Sun Community Source License (See SCSL)

Sun Microsystems Operating System (See SunOS)

SunOS (Sun Microsystems Operating System)
Based on Berkeley 4.2; merged with AT&T's SVR4 Unix operating system.

SuperDLT-Quantum (See SDLT)

Superframe
In T1 lines, a set of 12 frames for synchronous transmission.

supergroup
An assembly of five 12-channel groups occupying adjacent bands in the spectrum for the purpose of simultaneous modulation or demodulation, i.e., 60 voice channels.

super-high frequency (See SHF)

super-rate signal
A signal carried only by an STS-Nc (Sonet term). See STS-Nc.

superserver
Multiprocessor machines designed as network servers, combining input/output (I/O) capabilities of minicomputers with the capability to run industry-standard network operating systems.

Super Video Graphics Array (See SVGA)

supervisor
The part of an operating system that coordinates the use of resources and maintains the flow of central processing unit (CPU) operations.

supervisory control
Characters or signals that automatically actuate equipment or indicators at a remote terminal.

supervisory control and data acquisition (See SCADA)

supervisory programs
Computer programs designed to coordinate, service, and augment the machine components of the system and coordinate and service application programs. They handle work scheduling, input/output operations, error actions, and other functions. Also known as operating systems.

supplier-managed inventory (See VMI)

supply chain execution (See SCE)

supply chain inventory visibility (See SCIV)

Supply Chain Management (See SCM)

Supra
Cincom Systems' overall environment that includes productivity tools and database managers.

surface mount technology (See SMT)

Sustainable Cell Rate (See SCR)

SVC (switched virtual circuit)
A virtual connection with a call establishment and tear-down procedure to allow its temporary use.

SVDR (simultaneous voice and data recording)

SVGA (Super Video Graphics Array)
A Video Electronics Standards Association (VESA) display standard that provides higher resolution than the 640 x 480 Video Graphics Array (VGA) standard. It can support as many as 16 million colors, depending on the computer system and amount of available memory.

SVID (System V Interface Definition)
The specifications for Unix System V, set by AT&T. The fear that SVID might become a de facto standard, though not vendor-independent, was one reason for the creation of the Open Software Foundation (OSF).

SVPCo (Small Value Payments Co.)
A banking consortium, formed in July 1998, that is governed by 12 large U.S. banks and that plans to extend its board to 20 members. SVPCo is concentrating on Electronic Check Presentment (ECP), which requires cooperation from many banks in order to succeed.

SVR4 (System V Release 4)

SVVS (System V verification suite)

SW (software)

SWAMI (Software Asset Management Interest Group)
A worldwide network of influential users who are helping to shape more equitable software business practices and value-based pricing and licensing models. Working together, SWAMI members strive to understand and affect software licensing terms that provide long-term price protection and facilitate best-in-class deals. SWAMI holds general sessions annually in the United States and Europe.

SWAP (Simple Workflow Access Protocol)
An Internet-based protocol designed to provide a Hypertext Transport Protocol (HTTP)-based way to access a generic workflow service or a workflow enabled process or to interoperate with it. SWAP, which has been endorsed by the Workflow Management Coalition (WfMC), will offer a set of standard definitions for the type and structure of messages passed between cooperating workflow systems. SWAP will allow a workflow system to start, monitor, exchange data with and control workflow instances on a different workflow system. It will also provide a way to integrate workflow systems with other World Wide Web-based services.

SWIFT
A self-describing messaging format that is used within the banking/finance industry to support electronic funds transfer.

switch
A device that makes, breaks, or changes the connections in an electrical circuit; to shift to another electrical circuit by means of a switch. In the telecommunications industry, the term is often used as a synonym for private branch exchange (PBX) or central office (CO) switch.

Switched 56
A U.S. circuit-switched service offering 56 kilobits per second (Kbps).

Switched Digital Services Applications Forum (See SDSAF)

switched line
One of a series of lines that can be interconnected through a switching center; a line on the public telephone network.

Switched Multimegabit Data Service (See SMDS)

switched network
A multipoint communications pathway with circuit-switching capabilities, e.g., the telephone network.

Switched Service Network (See SSN)

Switched Virtual Call (See SVC)

switched virtual circuit (See SVC)

switching
The establishment of a transmission path from a particular inlet to a particular outlet of a group of such inlets and outlets.

switching center
A location that terminates multiple circuits and is capable of interconnecting circuits or transferring traffic between circuits.

switching matrix (See matrix)

switchover
When a failure occurs in the equipment, a switch to an alternative component can occur. Also called failover.

SWV (sampled write verify)

symmetric digital subscriber line (See SDSL)

S

symmetric-key encryption
Cryptography that involves sharing the secret that enables the encryption and decryption of plain text. Symmetric keys are problematic because of difficulty of ensuring the safety of the shared secret.

symmetric multiprocessing (See SMP)

Symmetrix Data Migration Service — EMC (See SDMS)

Symmetrix Remote Data Facility (See SRDF)

synchronization
Establishment of common timing between sending and receiving equipment.

synchronous
Having a constant time interval between successive bits, characters or events. Synchronous transmission uses no redundant information to identify the beginning and end of characters, and is faster and more efficient than asynchronous transmission, which uses start and stop bits. The timing is achieved by transmitting sync characters prior to data; usually synchronization can be achieved in two-or three-character times.

synchronous communications
High-speed transmission of contiguous groups of characters. The stream of monitored and read bits uses a clock rate.

Synchronous Data Link Control (See SDLC)

Synchronous Digital Hierarchy (See SDH)

synchronous network
A network in which all the communications links are synchronized to a common clock.

Synchronous Optical Network (See SONET)

synchronous transfer mode (See STM)

synchronous transmission
Timing is achieved by transmitting sync characters prior to data. It does not use such redundant information as the start and stop bits in asynchronous transmission to identify the beginning and end of characters and is thus faster and more efficient.

synchronous transport signal (See STS)

Synchronous Transport Signal level 3, concatenated (See STS-3c)

syntax
Message format or grammar (e.g., field lengths and delineators, headers, footers and optional fields).

Sysplex
A system complex of closely coupled Multiple Virtual Storage (MVS) processors sharing status information over a channel-to-channel link using the MVS Cross-System Coupling Facility (XCF) component. Sysplex became available with the first release of MVS/ESA SP 4.

System/370
A generic term for IBM's older mainframe architecture. Families with 370 architecture include 370/xxx, 9370, 43xx, 303x and 3090. The term System/370, if not qualified, generally refers to all large IBM computers except for the S/390 family.

System/390
The generic term for IBM's processor family announced in September 1990, which replaced the S/370 family. S/390 consists of the ES/9000 mainframes.

system and server evaluation model (See SSEM)

System Application Architecture (See SAA)

System Architect (See SA)

System Control Element (See SCE)

System Data Mover (See SDM)

system integration
The process of creating a complex information system that may include designing or building a customized architecture or application, integrating it with new or existing hardware, packaged and custom software, and communications. Most enterprises rely on an external contractor for program management of most or all phases of system development. This external vendor generally also assumes a high degree of the project's risks.

system integrator
An organization or an individual that integrates two or more systems so they work together. For example, an organization can integrate its payroll system with its check processing system to process paychecks. System integration can be done internally or through an external contract. It requires specific technical knowledge of the programming languages. Major system-integration projects often require the assistance of a specialty firm that has the resources and expertise to manage a project plan that could last over several months or even years.

system-managed storage (See SMS)

system management
Any of a number of "housekeeping" activities intended to preserve, maintain or correct the operation of a computer system. Included are such routine but critical processes as hardware diagnostics, software distribution, backup and recovery, file and disk integrity checking and virus scanning.

System Object Model (See SOM)

System Performance Evaluation Cooperative (See SPEC)

System R
Prototype version of the relational model developed by IBM, of which the important result was the precursor of Structured Query Language (SQL).

System Services Control Points (See SSCP)

systems integration or integrator (See SI)

Systems Management Server — Microsoft (See SMS)

Systems Network Architecture (See SNA)

System V
AT&T's Unix operating system, introduced in 1983.

SystemView
IBM's initiative for system management.

System V Interface Definition (See SVID)

T

T1/T1C/T2/T3/T4
A digital carrier system introduced in the United States by the Bell System in the 1960s. It was the first to successfully support DS-1 formatted digitized voice transmission that connected directly to a network. T1 and T3 lines are often used in Internet service provider (ISP) connections to the Internet

T-series speeds include:
1. T1: 1.544 megabits per second (Mbps)
2. T1C: 3.152 Mbps
3. T2: 6.312 Mbps
4. T3: 44.746 Mbps
5. T4: 274.176 Mbps

T.120
A key standard for real-time document sharing ratified by the International Telecommunication Union (ITU).

TA (telecommunications administration)
Also called a PTT (postal, telephone and telegraph), a TA is an agency in a European or Asian country that is usually a government-run monopoly. It is responsible for all postal, telegraph and telephone services. It also has certain regulatory functions for telecommunications, such as providing specifications for modems and certifying that equipment may connect to the telephone network. In some countries, the TA also provides its own line of equipment, e.g., modems. TAs are undergoing varying amounts of structural change.

TA (terminal adapter)
An interfacing device for an Integrated Services Digital Network (ISDN) environment. It enables non-ISDN terminals to connect at the physical layer.

TAB (tape-automated bonding)

table driven
1. A logical computer process, widespread in the operation of communications devices and networks, where a user-entered variable is matched against an array of predefined values.
2. A frequently used logical process in network routing, access security and modem operation.

TACACS (Terminal Access Controller Access Control System)
An authentication protocol from Digital Data Network (DDN) providing remote access security and related services.

tacit knowledge
In a knowledge management context, the personal knowledge resident within the mind, behavior and perceptions of individuals. Tacit knowledge includes skills, experiences, insight, intuition and judgment. Tacit knowledge is typically shared through discussion, stories, analogies and person-to-person interaction; therefore, it is difficult to capture or represent in explicit form. Because individuals continually add personal knowledge, which changes behavior and perceptions, tacit knowledge is, by definition, uncaptured. See also knowledge management (KM).

TACS (Total Access Communications System
A derivative of the AT&T-developed analog cellular radio standard AMPS (Advanced Mobile Phone Service) adopted by U.K. Cellnet and Racal-Vodaphone, operating at 900 megahertz (MHz).

Tag Control Information (See TCI)

Tag Image File Format (See TIFF)

Tag Protocol Identifier (See TPID)

tail
In satellite networks, any terrestrial extension used to connect end users to an earth station.

tandem
The connection of networks or circuits in series, i.e., the connection of the output of one circuit to the input of another.

tandem data circuit
A data circuit that contains two or more sets of data circuit-terminating equipment (DCE) in series.

Tandem Tie Trunk Network (See TTTN)

Tap1
Ethernet connection for coaxial wiring.

Tap2
Connection that can be in series or parallel to the main transmission media.

Tape Cartridge License
A format-specific Linear Tape Open (LTO) license package for media manufacturers.

Tape Mechanism License
A format-specific Linear Tape Open (LTO) license package for manufacturers that want to produce the drive.

TAPI (Telephony Application Programming Interface)
An interface standard from Microsoft and Intel that brings a well-defined computer/telephone application programming interface (API) to the desktop. The desktop linkage for TAPI can be accomplished via serial RS-232 interfaces. Additionally, it also allows for a board associated with the telephone to plug into the desktop computer's bus. The telephone station does not disappear from the desktop for several reasons (e.g., computer and application uptime, and handset requirement). The stable APIs that exist between Windows and the Nx64 Kbps circuit-switching systems are not limited to voice; they can accommodate data, images and video.

tariff
The formal process whereby services and rates are established by and for communications common carriers. Carriers submit tariffs to the appropriate regulatory agencies, which then review, amend and approve or disallow them.

TAT (transatlantic telephone cable)

TAXI (transparent asynchronous transmitter/receiver interface)
A 100-megabit-per-second (Mbps) multimode fiber interface.

TB/admin (terabytes-per-administrator ratio)
A metric that has become the standard measurement of data center storage management efficiency. The ratio is not a measurement of efficiency. It is merely a way of relating labor costs to the size of an organization's direct-access storage device (DASD) installed base.

Tbyte (terabyte)
One trillion bytes.

TC (Transaction Capabilities — ISDN term)

T&C (terms and conditions)

TCA (Telecommunications Association)

TCAM (Telecommunications Access Method)
An IBM macro language for creating communication application programs and message control.

TCAP (Transaction Capabilities Application Part — ISDN term)
Designed for transaction-type information transfer.

T carrier
Time-division multiplexed digital transmission facility, operating at an aggregate data rate of 1.544 megabits per second (Mbps) and above.

T-carrier services
High-speed, private-line digital transmission services that provide large-volume transmission between two stations. T1, the most common T-carrier service, operates at an aggregate data rate of 1.544 megabits per second (Mbps) and consists of 24 separate channels. (T2 and T3 are rated at 6.312 Mbps and 44 Mbps, respectively.) T1 channels are 6 to 30 times more cost-effective on a per-bit basis than voice-grade lines, but users must be able to fill the 1.544 Mbps channel to take full advantage of savings. Fractional T services, however, enable businesses to lease a fraction of a T line. Only T1 and T3 are widely supported. In Europe, e-carrier services are provided, although the corresponding data rates are not identical.

TCB (transaction control block)

TCF (transparent computing facility)

TCI (Tag Control Information)
Part of the virtual local-area network (VLAN) Tag Header in the Institute of Electrical and Electronics Engineers (IEEE) 802.1q draft standard.

TCI (Tele-Communications Inc.)

TCM (Thermal Conduction Module or Thermo-Conductive Module)
The basic building block technology of the IBM 308X, 3090 and ES/9000. The TCM is a sealed container enclosing a multiple-chip carrying substrate amid a chip interconnection structure.

TCMP (tightly coupled multiprocessing)
A configuration in which all processors share a single pool of memory.

TCO (total cost of ownership)
A comprehensive assessment of information technology (IT) or other costs across enterprise boundaries over time. For IT, TCO includes hardware and software acquisition, management and support, communications, end-user expenses and the opportunity cost of downtime, training and other productivity losses.

TCP (Transmission Control Protocol)
A communications protocol based on the U.S. Department of Defense's (DoD's) standards for reliable internetwork delivery of data.

TCP/IP (Transmission Control Protocol/ Internet Protocol)
A set of protocols covering (approximately) the network and transport layers of the seven-layer Open Systems Interconnection (OSI) network model. TCP/IP was developed during a 15-year period under the auspices of the Department of Defense. It has achieved de facto standard status, particularly as higher-level layers over Ethernet. TCP/IP implementations are available on products from more than 80 vendors, including IBM, Digital Equipment, AT&T, Data General and Sun Microsystems. The biggest issue for TCP/IP is potential migration to the International Organization for Standardization (ISO) protocols for Layers 3 and 4.

TCP/UDP (Transmission Control Protocol/ User Datagram Protocol)

TDI (technical data interchange)

TDM (time division multiplexing)
A data, voice and video communications technique that interleaves several low-speed signals into one high-speed transmission channel.

TDMA (time division multiple access)

TDMF (Transparent Data Migration Facility)
An Amdahl-developed Multiple Virtual Storage (MVS) application that nondisruptively migrates data between the geometry-like devices — 3380s to 3380s or 3390s to 3390s — from any vendor.

TDR (time domain reflectometry)
A technique used to track faults in networks, such as cable breaks or loose connections. A pulse of a known shape is transmitted over the network and an echo is created when the pulse hits an obstacle or cable end. The time lapsed between the sending of the pulse and receiving the echo can be used to locate the origin of the echo and therefore the break. Sophisticated testing equipment is available to perform this test and to analyze the results.

TDS (telecommunications data systems)
A frequency allocation technique based on allotting discrete time slots to users, permitting many simultaneous transmissions.

TE (Terminal Equipment)
One of the Conference on European Posts and Telecommunications' (CEPT's) working groups.

TEB (technology-enabled buying)
An integrated set of applications that improves both Web-buyer effectiveness and sales management efficiency. TEB solutions employ a mix of software applications, databases, middleware, operating systems, and hardware environments. TEB can help enterprises to integrate their Web-buying sites with other distribution channels; to use the Web as a medium to build longer-term customer relationships; and to use Web-based buying to influence customers, sellers and suppliers.

TEC (technology-enabled content)
The integration of content with information technology (IT) to create value-added information that directly supports a business process.

technical license management (See TLM)

technology-enabled buying (See TEB)

technology-enabled content (See TEC)

technology-enabled marketing (See TEM)

technology-enabled relationship management (See TERM)

TEB

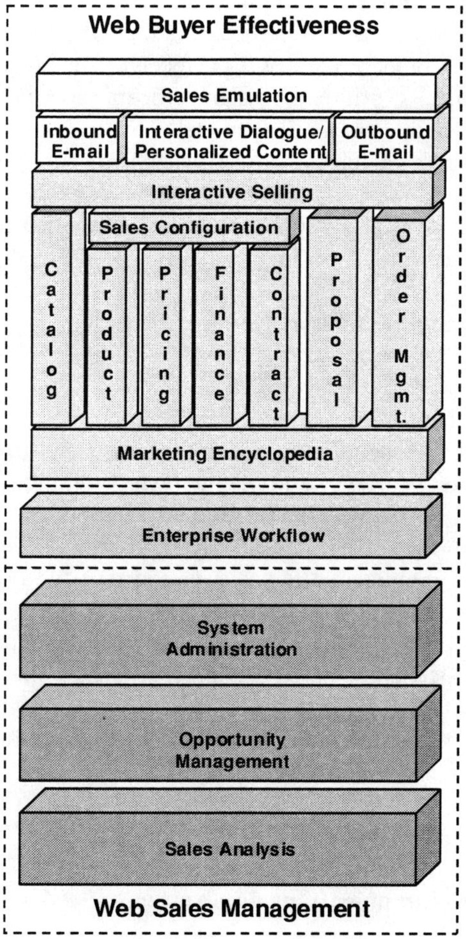

Source: GartnerGroup

Technology-Enabled Buying

technology-enabled selling (See TES)

telco
A contraction of the term "telephone company." It generally refers to the local-exchange carrier (LEC).

telecom (telephone company)
Slang, mainly used in Europe.

Telecom Act (See Telecommunications Act of 1996)

telecommunications
Any process that permits the passage of information from a sender to one or more receivers in any usable form (e.g., printed copy, fixed or moving pictures, and visible or audible signals) by means of any electromagnetic system (electrical transmission by wire, radio, optical transmission, waveguides, etc.). It includes telegraphy, telephony, video-telephony and data transmission.

Telecommunications Access Method (See TCAM)

Telecommunications Act of 1996
Besides opening up the local and long-distance markets to competition, the Telecommunications Act of 1996 was intended to fix many of the flaws in universal service and access charges. The new telecommunications law required that the Federal Communications Commission (FCC) separate access charges from universal service and that part of access charges be based on actual costs. The Telecommunications Act also made provisions to include Internet access for U.S. schools, libraries and hospitals as part of universal service.

telecommunications administration (See TA)

telecommunications data systems (See TDS)

Telecommunications Industry Association (See TIA)

telecommunications lines
Telephone and other communication pathways that are used to transmit information from one location to another.

Telecommunications Management Network (See TMN)

telecommuter
A work-at-home computer user who connects to the corporate local-area network (LAN) backbone using remote access technologies.

telecommuting
Any significant portion of working hours spent at a remote site (e.g., home) using communications lines to send and receive information, interact with customers and peers, and deliver work projects.

teleconference
Bidirectional audio on either a one-to-many or a many-to-many basis.

telecottage
A well-equipped, well-connected small office that may be used by people working remotely for the same or different companies.

telephone channel
A transmission path designed for the transmission of signals representing human speech or other telephone communication (e.g., facsimile) requiring the same bandwidth. The bandwidth allotted is usually 64 kilobits per second (Kbps), but can be reduced to 32 Kbps or even 16 Kbps with multiplexing techniques.

telephone circuit
An electrical connection permitting the establishment of telephone communication in both directions between two points. Also called telephone line.

telephone company (See telco, telecom)

telephone exchange
A switching center for the interconnection of lines that terminate therein. Also called central office (CO).

telephone frequency
Any frequency within the part of the audio-frequency range that is essential for the transmission of speech of commercial quality, i.e., 300 hertz (Hz) to 3,000 Hz. Also called voice frequency (VF).

telephony
A generic term for voice telecommunications.

Telephony Application Objects
The software model for Signal Computing System Architecture (SCSA), introduced by Dialogics. It includes the Enterprise Computer Telephony Forum (ECTF).

Telephony Application Programming Interface (See TAPI)

Telephony Services Application Programming Interface (See TSAPI)

Telephony User Part — ISDN term (See TUP)

telepoint
A means of accessing the public switched telephone network (PSTN) via low-cost, low-power radio base stations and compact, portable telephones. Access is obtained at up to 200 meters from base stations located in public places such as railway stations, airports and shopping centers.

teleprocessing
The processing of information that is received from or sent to remote locations by way of telecommunications lines. Such systems are necessary to hook up remote terminals or connect geographically separated computers. See also telecommunications.

teletext
Generically, one-way data transmission designed for widespread broadcasting of graphics and textual information for display on subscriber televisions or low-cost terminals.

telink
An enhanced version of xmodem, mainly used on Fido bulletin boards.

Telnet
The Internet standard protocol for remote terminal connection. It allows a user at one site to interact with a remote device or system that expects terminal-mode traffic.

TEM (technology-enabled marketing)
Automating aspects of the marketing process. It allows enterprises to improve the measurement and evaluation of their activities. The ultimate goal of technology-enabled marketing is to allocate marketing resources to the activities, channels and media with the best potential return and impact on profitable customer relationships.

Tempest
The U.S. military standard for electronic products that can withstand electromagnetic pulses.

TEN (total effect of networking)

terabyte (See Tbyte)

terabyte-per-administrator ratio (See TB/admin)

teraFLOPS (See TFLOPS)

TERENA (Trans-European Research and Education Networking Association)
A European Community (EC) organization promoting information and telecommunications developments in the EC.

TERM (technology-enabled relationship management)
The concept of forming one enterprisewide view of the customer across all customer contact channels (i.e., sales, marketing, and customer service and support). It is a complex area, requiring complex solutions to problems of integration, data flow, data access and marketing strategy. A critical component is the database that serves as the customer information repository.

terminal
A device, combining keyboard and display screen, that communicates with a computer. Terminals are divided into different classes depending on whether they are able to process data on their own.

- Dumb terminals — display monitor or simple input/output (I/O) devices that send and accept data from a network server or mainframe. They have no built-in processing capabilities. Workers enter data and commands, which are sent to a computer located elsewhere.
- Smart terminals — monitors that process limited amounts of information.
- Intelligent terminals — devices that contain main memory and a central processing unit (CPU) to perform special display functions. Examples include an information kiosk and AT&T Display Phones.
- 3270 terminals—IBM display stations used to communicate with mainframes made by IBM and other manufacturers. They are in widespread use, and are widely copied.

Terminal Access Controller Access Control System (See TACACS)

terminal adapter (See TA)

terminal emulation
Imitation of a specific terminal (VT100, for example) by a device, such as a PC, through software. PCs often use terminal emulation methods to connect to specific hosts, such as Digital Virtual Address Extensions (VAXs) or IBM mainframes, with which they would otherwise be incapable of communicating.

Terminal Equipment (See TE)

terminal job
In systems with time sharing, the processing done on behalf of one terminal user from log-on to log-off. See also time sharing.

terminal server
A local-area network (LAN) device that allows asynchronous dumb terminals to communicate with a host computer also attached to the LAN. It is useful in minimizing the amount of cabling

TERM

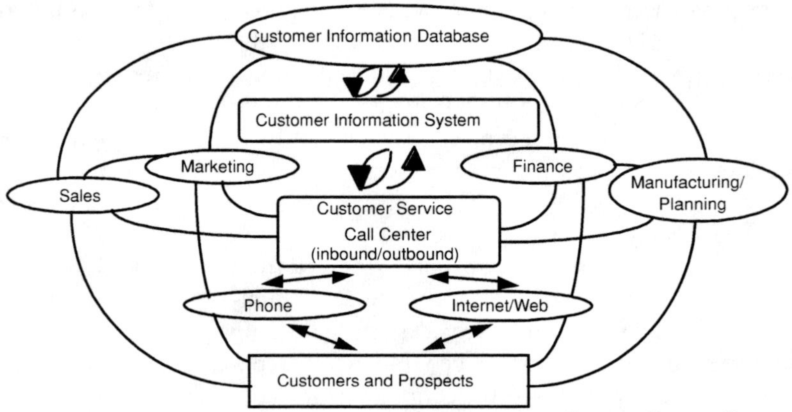

Source: GartnerGroup

Technology-Enabled Relationship Management

where several terminals need to be attached to a mainframe.

terminal user
In systems with time sharing, anyone who is eligible to log on. See also time sharing.

TES (technology-enabled selling)
TES systems employ a mix of software applications, databases, middleware, operating systems, hardware and applications development (AD) environments. Technology decisions in each of these areas determine application extendibility and integration capabilities over the long term.

Many enterprises employ TES, with field sales automation as a key component, to improve the effectiveness of their selling operations. Whereas first-generation TES applications focused on automating administrative tasks (e.g., expense reporting), newer applications (e.g., opportunity management systems) focus on shortening sales cycles and increasing sales revenue. These applications rely heavily on corporate and third-party data, which sales representatives use in the field. Although some applications require read-only access to the data, more-advanced TES applications are likely to support read-and-write access as field sales representatives perform tasks such as updating customer account information or taking orders.

test data generator
Communications instructions for forming files containing sets of information developed specifically to ensure the adequacy of a computer run or system.

test generators
A software aid used to help ensure the adequacy of new programs.

tethered remote access
A terrestrial or nonmobile connection of individual users or small workgroups to a data source or network interface beyond the boundary defined by a building or campus. The connection is generally via a wide-area network (WAN), which, in most cases, is outside the sphere of ownership and management of the enterprise making the remote connection.

text
The information portion of a transmitted message, as contrasted with the header, check characters, and end-of-text characters. Sometimes called the body of the message.

text editing
Manipulation of the information portion of a transmitted message by changing or rearranging symbols, words, sentences and paragraphs.

text information management system (See TIMS)

TES

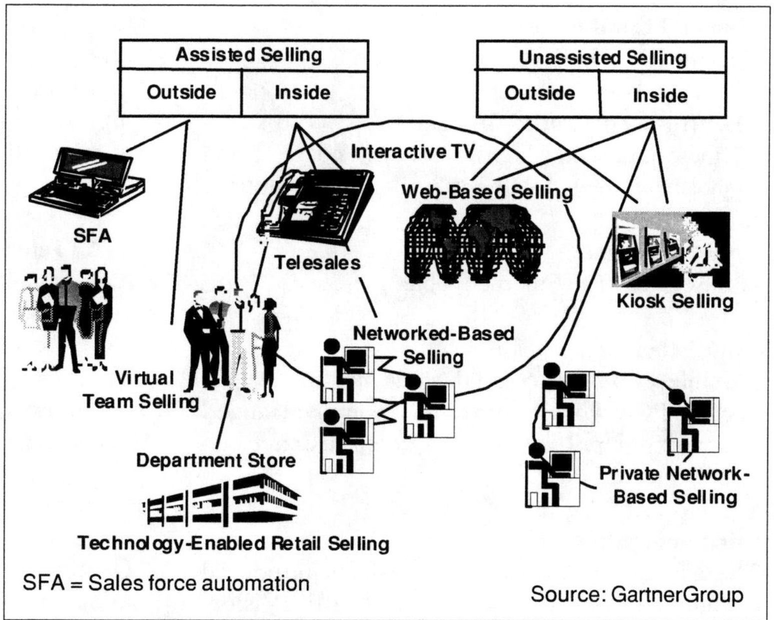

Technology-Enabled Selling

text retrieval
Software used for finding units of textual information such as documents by matching a user's search terms to those in a full-text index derived from the collection of textual units.

TFLOPS (teraFLOPS)
Trillion floating-point operations per second.

TFT (thin film transistor)

TFTP (Trivial File Transfer Protocol)
A protocol used for basic file transfers, as well as booting systems that communicate with the Transmission Control Protocol/Internet Protocol (TCP/IP) suite using the TFTP boot protocol. TFTP boot is similar to bootp, but contains an additional file transfer capability. This protocol is commonly used to provide configurations to remote routers, allowing network managers to centrally generate the remote router configuration file and then download that configuration once the router is powered up and connected to the wide area network.

Thermal Conduction Module or Thermo-Conductive Module (See TCM)

THF (time horizon to failure)
Defines the date on which an asset will not work and cannot be corrected without business interruption.

Thick Ethernet
10Base-5 coaxial Ethernet cable.

Thin Ethernet
Flexible 10Base-2 coaxial cable useful in connecting PCs, workstations and systems arranged in a workgroup. It supports segment distances up to 185 meters.

third generation
The class of client/server office systems introduced beginning in 1989, including IBM's OfficeVision, Digital Equipment's ALL-IN-1 Phase II and Hewlett-Packard's NewWave Office.

third-party maintenance
Maintenance performed by a service organization contracted by the owner of the system.

three-schema architecture
A framework for managing access to data that involves three layers or schemas: the external or programming view, the conceptual or data administration view, and the internal or database administration view. Such ideas were developed by an American National Standards Institute/Scalable Processor Architecture subcommittee in 1971 but received little practical implementation by database management system (DBMS) vendors. The principle is that the conceptual schema consists of business rules derived from a semantic data model, which provides independence between programs and data structures. The emphasis has since shifted to computer-aided software engineering (CASE) tools and "repository" standards.

throughput
A computer term for the volume of work or information flowing through a system. Particularly meaningful in information storage and retrieval systems, in which throughput is measured in units such as accesses per hour.

TIA (Telecommunications Industry Association)
An association that develops telecommunications standards.

TickIT
An initiative sponsored by the U.K. government. It is a scheme that adapts International Organization for Standardization (ISO) 9000 to the special needs of software development. TickIT is designed to make it easier for systems developers to apply Quality standards. TickIT is not a standard in itself; rather, it is a way of understanding and applying ISO 9000. Enterprises and information systems (IS)

departments that undertake software development in the United Kingdom can apply for certification under TickIT. This certifies that their software development procedures conform to Quality standards. It does not imply any approval of other processes in the department or the enterprise.

tie line (See TL)
U.S. term for allowing the system to handle tie lines that can be accessed either by dialing a trunk group access code or through the attendant. Tie lines link a private branch exchange (PBX) or a distant key system.

TIFF (Tag Image File Format)
A de facto standard format for bit-mapped image files.

tightly coupled multiprocessing (See TCMP)

Time-Assignment Speech Interpolation (See TASI)

time division multiplexing (See TDM)

time-division signaling
Signaling over a time-division multiplex system in which all voice channels share a common signaling channel, with time division providing the separation between signaling channels.

time-division switching
The switching method for a time-division multiplexing (TDM) channel requiring the shifting of data from one slot to another in the TDM frame. The slot in question can carry a bit, a byte, or, in principle, any other unit of data.

time domain reflectometry (See TDR)

time horizon to failure (See THF)

time out
The set time period before a terminal system performs some action. Typical uses include a poll release (when a terminal is disconnected if the time-out period elapses before keying resumes) or an access time out (when a terminal on a local area network using a Carrier Sense Multiple Access with Collision Detection — CSMA/CD) access method is prevented from transmitting for a specified time period after a collision occurs).

time sharing
Use of a computer facility by many users for different purposes at (apparently) the same time. Although the computer services the users sequentially, it allocates segments of time so that each user appears to have the dedicated resources of the machine. In the 1970s and 1980s, time sharing was common. With the introduction of more powerful, less expensive computers, it has become less common.

Time-Sharing Option (See TSO)

time slice
An interval on the central processing unit allocated to performing a specific task. Once the interval is expired, central-processing unit (CPU) time is allocated to another task. See also time sharing.

TIMS (text information management systems)
The genre of products that combines content-based retrieval and document database functions.

T-Interface
In Integrated Services Digital Network (ISDN), four-wire Basic Rate Interface (BRI) circuit connection.

TI RPC (Transport Independent Remote Procedure Call)

TL (tie line)
A private-line communications channel of the type provided by communications common carriers for

T

linking two or more points together, typically private branch exchanges (PBXs). Also called tie trunk.

TLF (trunk link frame)
See also crossbar switch.

TLM (technical license management)
The management and control of software via a platform-independent automated facility that:

1. Ensures that access and use are in alignment with associated licensing agreements.
2. Provides the basis for determining enterprise use requirements.
3. Integrates with systems and network management tools.

TLMS (tape library management system)

TLP (transmission-level point)
Any point in a transmission system at which the power level of the signal is measured.

TLS (transport layer security)
Internet-based transaction security provided by the Secure Sockets Layer (SSL) protocol.

T&M (time and materials)

Tmap
Developed by Nortel Networks with support from Intel, Microsoft and Novell, Tmap maps Telephony Application Programming Interface (TAPI) programming calls to Telephony Services Application Programming Interface (TSAPI), enabling TAPI applications to run on networks that support TSAPI.

TMN (Telecommunications Management Network)
Model defined in the International Telecommunication Union (ITU) Recommendation M30. TMN will form the standard basis for network management in such advanced networks as synchronous digital hierarchy (SDH) and Groupe Speciale Mobile (GSM). It defines management functions with standard interfaces using a management network which is separate from the transmission network and uses standard protocols such as Common Management Information Protocol (CMIP).

TMON (The Monitor)

TMS (transportation management systems)

TOA (technical office automation)

TOD (time of day)

token bus
A local network access mechanism and topology in which all stations actively attached to the bus listen for a broadcast token or supervisory frame. Stations wishing to transmit must receive the token before doing so; however, the next physical station to transmit is not necessarily the next physical station on the bus. Bus access is controlled by preassigned priority algorithms.

token passing
A LAN access technique in which participating stations circulate a special bit pattern that grants access to the communications pathway to any station that holds the sequence. It is often used in networks with a ring topology.

token ring
A local network access mechanism and topology in which a supervisory frame or token is passed from station to station in sequential order. Stations wishing to gain access to the network must wait for the token to arrive before transmitting data. In a token-ring, the next logical station receiving the token is also the next physical station on the ring. The ring may be a logical, rather than physical, ring in the case of switched token ring.

token-ring network (See TRN)

TOP (Technical Office Protocol)

TopN
In Remote Monitoring (RMON), conversation information that is imported from an external data collector.

topology
The logical or physical arrangement of stations on a network in relation to one another. See also bus, ring, star network and tree.

TORP (task order requirements package)

Total Access Communications System (See TACS)

total cost of ownership (See TCO)

total quality control (See TQC)

Total Solutions Lease (See TSL)

touch sensitive
Refers to the technology that enables a system to identify a point of contact on the screen by coordinates and transmit that information to a program.

Touch-tone
The registered AT&T trademark for push-button dialing. See also dual-tone multifrequency signaling (DTMF).

TP (teleprocessing)

TP (transaction processing)
A mode of processing characterized by short transactions recording business events that normally requires high availability and consistent, short response times. A category of application that requires a request for service to be answered within a predictable period that approaches real time, and a transaction that transforms this model from one business state to another. Tasks such as making reservations, scheduling and inventory control are especially complex; all the information must be current.

TPA (third-party administrator)

TPC (Transaction Processing Performance Council)
An organization that has developed several standardized transaction processing (TP) benchmarks, among which are TPC-A, TPC-B, and TPC-C. TPC prohibits testing systems that are specially optimized for benchmarking or lack real-world applicability.

TPC-A (Transaction Processing Performance Council Benchmark A)
A revised and superior version of the debit/credit online transaction processing (OLTP) benchmark. Ratified in late 1989, it came into widespread use in 1990. The major improvements in TPC-A were the requirements for full disclosure and the inclusion of the front-end network and terminals. TPC-A is intended to replace debit/credit as the only industrywide measure for OLTP performance and price/performance. It is a good test since it measures end-to-end performance, but it still is only one test reflecting a single type of transaction.

TPC-C (Transaction Processing Performance Council Benchmark C)
The Transaction Processing Performance Council (TPC) benchmark model for complex transaction-processing workloads. It is a well-defined set of programs and testing protocols that are used to derived consistent, repeatable benchmark results for online transaction processing. The TPC-C benchmark is most often used to define the maximum scalability supported by a database management system (DBMS) or an application server platform.

T

TPC-D (Transaction Processing Performance Council Benchmark D)
The Transaction Processing Performance Council (TPC) benchmark model for decision support workloads.

TPF (Transaction Processing Facility)
A high-availability, high-performance IBM system designed to support real-time, transaction-driven applications with maximum efficiency.

TPF2 (Transaction Processing Facility 2)
TPF2 is a low-function, high-cost set of control blocks and macro instructions that is positioned as IBM's highest-performance transaction-processing (TP) environment.

TPID (Tag Protocol Identifier)
Part of the virtual local-area network (VLAN) Tag Header in the Institute of Electrical and Electronics Engineers (IEEE) 802.1q draft standard.

tpm (transactions per minute)

TPM (third-party maintenance)

TPM (transaction-processing monitor)
A process whereby the computer handles each instruction or query individually as it is entered.

tpmC (transactions per minute of TPC-C)

TPP (third-party participant)

TP-PMD (Twisted Pair-Physical Media Dependent)
The American National Standards Institute (ANSI) standard for FDDI (Fiber Distributed Data Interface) over copper, replacing Shielded Distributed Data Interface (SDDI), which runs on shielded cable and Copper Distributed Data Interface (CDDI), which runs on unshielded cable.

tps (transactions per second)

TQC (total quality control)
A theory of quality whereby the maker of the part has responsibility for the quality of that part.

TQM (total quality management)

TR4 (Travan linear tape drives)

trace packet
In packet switching, a special kind of packet that functions as a normal packet but causes a report of each stage of its progress to be sent to the network control center.

track
A storage channel on a disk or tape that is made up of a series of sectors.

tracking, telemetry, control, and monitoring (See TTC&M)

Tradacoms
The United Kingdom's de facto Electronic Data Interchange (EDI) standard for the exchange of trading data between businesses. It is published and maintained by the Article Numbering Association (ANA).

traditional processing
The availability of traditional and basic data processing facilities at the midrange system. Examples include sequential and keyed files, compilers such as COBOL, FORTRAN, PL/I, BASIC and C, interactive access, batch processing, multiprocessing and multitasking.

traffic
1. Messages sent and received over a communications channel.
2. Quantitative measurement of the total messages and their length, expressed in hundred call seconds (CCS) or other units..

traffic flow
The measure of the density of traffic on a telephone network expressed in Erlangs.

traffic matrix
Matrix of which the X, Y element contains the amount of traffic originated at node X and destined for node Y. The unit of measurement may be telephone calls or data packets per second, depending on the kind of network.

train time
The initialization time for full-duplex operation on a modem.

transaction
A logical update that takes a database from one consistent state to another.

Transaction Capabilities Application Part — ISDN term (See TCAP)

transaction feed
The capability of passing, to the mainframe, midrange system transactions predetermined for Multiple Virtual Storage/Customer Information Control System (MVS/CICS) or Virtual Machine/Customer Information Control System (VM/CICS) processing with replies returned to the midrange system user. The IBM "intersystem communication" facility of CICS could be the technique used for implementation.

transaction logging
A concept in which a detailed record is kept of all operations in a transaction; in case of a failure, the transaction could be backed out and the former state reconstructed.

transaction monitor
A subsystem that ensures that all transactions against a database leave it in a consistent state or, in case of a transaction failure, returns the database to its pre-transaction state.

transaction processing (See TP)

Transaction Processing Facility (See TPF)

Transaction Processing Facility 2 (See TPF2)

transaction-processing monitor (See TPM)

Transaction Processing Performance Council (See TPC)

Transaction Processing Performance Council Benchmark A (See TPC-A)

Transaction Processing Performance Council Benchmark C (See TPC-C)

Transaction Processing Performance Council Benchmark D (See TPC-D)

transceiver
A device that can transmit and receive traffic. It is used to connect nodes to Ethernet (LAN).

transducer
A device for converting signals from one form to another, such as a microphone or a receiver.

Trans-European Research and Education Networking Association (See TERENA)

transfer rate
The speed at which information can be sent across a bus or communications link.

transit VLAN starvation
The condition a switch suffers in a non-ATM (asynchronous transfer mode) network when it becomes congested and cells or cell streams representing Layer 3 virtual local-area network (VLAN) packets are missed or dropped, leading to the VLAN becoming unstable. Also known as beatdown.

translator
A device that converts information from one system of representation into equivalent information in another system of representation.

transmission
Sending information in the form of electrical signals over electric wires, waveguides, or radio.

Transmission Control Protocol (See TCP)

Transmission Control Protocol/Internet Protocol (See TCP/IP)

Transmission Convergence Sublayer
In asynchronous transfer mode (ATM), protocol defined in the Physical Media Dependent for preparing cells for transmission.

transmission-level point (See TLP)

transmission speed
The rate at which information is passed through communications lines, generally measured in bits per second (bps).

transmit
To send information from one location to another.

transparency
If a signal passes through a network or facility unchanged, that network or facility is said to be transparent to it.

transparent asynchronous transmitter/receiver interface (See TAXI)

Transparent Data Migration Facility (See TDMF)

transponder
The receiver-transmitter combination that retransmits the received signal greatly amplified and at a different frequency. Communications satellites usually contain several transponders.

transport layer
In the Open Systems Interconnection (OSI) model, the network processing entity responsible — in conjunction with the underlying network, data link and physical layers — for the end-to-end control of transmitted data and the optimized use of network resources.

transport layer security (See TLS)

transport overhead
Overhead to the synchronous transport signal synchronous payload envelope (STS SPE) for transmission purposes (Sonet term). See STS.

traveling wave tube amplifier (See TWTA)

tree
A type of bus network topology in which the medium branches at certain points along its length connect stations or clusters of stations. Also called a branching bus.

Trellis Coding
A method of modulation that combines both amplitude and phase.

Triple DES (Triple Data Encryption Standard)
A variant of DES. It uses three different DES keys, in sequence, to encrypt a file.

Triple X
A colloquial name given to the three International Telecommunication Union (ITU) protocols (X.3, X.28 and X.29) connecting character mode terminals to packet switched networks using the X.25 packet definition.

Trivial File Transfer Protocol (See TFTP)

TRN (token-ring network)
Local-area network (LAN) topology and protocol in which all stations actively attached to the ring listen for a broadcast token or supervisory frame. Stations wishing to transmit must receive the token before doing so, and when done, must pass the token to the next station on the ring.

Trojan horse
A Trojan horse is a form of malicious code that may be deliberately planted to perform a destructive act on a computer. It is effective because it is not what it appears to be. That is, the execution of a Trojan horse may have an undesirable and unexpected effect on the user's work environment, but it is the user who initiates the execution of the code (e.g., by clicking on a button in a graphical user interface that appears harmless). Unlike a computer virus, a Trojan horse is unable to replicate and is not parasitic.

TRUSTe
A Web privacy group.

TS (transaction server)

TSAF (Transparent Services Access Facility)

TSAPI (Telephony Services Application Programming Interface)
A computer-telephony integration (CTI) application programming interface (API) developed by Novell and AT&T that provides a client/server implementation and supports first-and third-party call control. The major benefit of third-party call control is that, via the command link to the switch, it is possible to control calls between third parties (much like an operator does today). This permits CTI applications to provide multiparty services, call routing based on automatic number identification and other advanced features. However, TSAPI requires a Novell NetWare networking environment. TSAPI does not require additional hardware in each PC, but does require a server CTI connection to the private branch exchange (PBX) equipment.

TSE (Terminal Server Edition — Microsoft)

TSL (Total Solutions Lease)
An IBM ESO/ICC (Entry Service Offering/IBM Credit Corp.) marketing program that rolled the price of hardware, software, maintenance and certain services into a multiyear contract with a fixed monthly payment.

TSO (Time-Sharing Option)
The name originally given to IBM's compatible extension of Multiple Virtual Storage (MVS) background facilities into foreground execution. The name has stuck, although TSO is no longer an option in MVS.

TSO/E (Time-Sharing Option/Extended)

TSR (terminate and stay resident)

TSTN (triple-supertwist nematic)

TT (trouble ticket)

TTC&M (tracking, telemetry, control and monitoring)
Specialized ground stations used to track and control satellites and to monitor their performance.

TTL (time to live)

TTL (transistor-transistor logic)

TTP (trusted third party)

TTTN (Tandem Tie Trunk Network)
A private network making use of tandem switching.

TUA (Telecommunications Users Association)

tuning
The process of adjusting computer system control variables to make a system divide its resources most efficiently for a workload.

tunneling
Provides services on a point-to-point basis without the necessity to change the data to accommodate differing network types or protocols.

TUP (Telephony User Part — ISDN term)
Provides non-Integrated Services Digital Network (ISDN) call setup and control.

turnaround time
The time required to reverse the direction of transmission, e.g., to change from receive mode to transmit mode in order to acknowledge on a half-duplex line when individual blocks are acknowledged, as is required in certain protocols (e.g., IBM BSC). The turnaround time has a major effect on throughput, particularly if the propagation delay is lengthy, such as on a satellite channel.

turnkey system
A complete communications system, including hardware and software, assembled and installed by a vendor and sold as a total package.

TVML (TV markup language)
An open standard promoted by WebTV and Microsoft as an extension to open Hypertext Markup Language (HTML) standards.

TWAIN
A common interface standard for optical scanners that enables consistent scanner control.

twinax
Coaxial cable with two center conductors at each connection point.

twisted pair
Two insulated wires twisted together, which can be shielded (STP) or unshielded (UTP).

Twisted Pair-Physical Media Dependent (See TP-PMD)

two-phase commit
A method for coordinating a single transaction across two or more database management systems (DBMSs) or other resource managers. Two-phase commit guarantees the logical integrity of data by ensuring that transaction updates are finalized in all of the separate databases or are fully backed out of all participating databases, i.e., all or nothing based on transaction boundaries. Two-phase commit is a necessary component of distributed database and is implemented in transaction management software, which may be part of a DBMS, online transaction processing (OLTP) monitor, or front-end application tool.

Two-Phase Commit Protocol
Handshaking semantics across more than one participating node or database on a network involved in a transaction update such that, if a failure occurs at any point in the middle, all record updates are automatically rolled back.

two-wire circuit
A circuit formed by two conductors insulated from each other, providing "send" and "return" channels in the same frequency.

TWTA (traveling wave tube amplifier)
A satellite component used to amplify an incoming signal before transmitting to receiving earth station.

Type A, B and C Enterprises
A GartnerGroup framework that classifies enterprises or their subdivisions according to a technology adoption profile. Classification is based not only on an enterprise's current technology adoption strategy, but also on whether the strategy is supported by top management and is adequately funded.

- Type A organizations are typically technically aggressive, well-funded and use information technology (IT) for competitive advantage.

- Type B enterprises, which are in the majority, are mainstream IT users with adequate funding that use IT for productivity.
- Type C enterprises are conservative, risk-averse, and seek to control IT costs.

Recognizing an enterprise's type offers company strategists a meaningful way to compare an enterprise's use of technology against that of competitors, and to make decisions about when, how and where to adopt new technologies.

U

UART (universal asynchronous receiver/transmitter)
An integrated circuit attached to the parallel bus in a computer that conducts serial communications efficiently.

UAWG (Universal ADSL Working Group)
A vendor consortium promoting adoption of asymmetric digital subscriber line (ADSL) as a remote access method, with an emphasis on the adoption of International Telecommunication Union (ITU) standards.

UBR (unspecified bit rate)
An asynchronous transfer mode (ATM) service category, defined by the ATM Forum, that provides no service guarantees and therefore is a "best effort" service equivalent to a shared-media local-area network (LAN).

UCR (usual and customary rates)

UDB (Universal Database)

UDF (user-defined functions)

UDP (User Datagram Protocol)
A Transmission Control Protocol/Internet Protocol (TCP/IP) technology that enables an application to send a message to one of several applications running in a destination machine. Some problems arise because Internet applications are not exclusively TCP-based. UDP is stateless — it differentiates sources and destinations within hosts and provides no other services. Often services do not use predefined port numbers, so filtering on the basis of "well known ports" will not work.

UFDL (Universal Form Definition Language)
UWI.Com's technology for e-form management. The UFDL is an "open" protocol that defines a high-level language that can be used to construct, display and use e-forms. UWI.Com defines UFDL as open because the actual language syntax and description is published at the UWI.Com Web site. In 1998, UWI.Com released the UFDL version rewritten in Extensible Markup Language (XML) syntax.

UHF (ultra-high frequency)

UI (user interface)
The connection between the user and a computer's hardware or software that permits the user to work productively with a system or a program. User interface design requires significant skill and attention and has become a recognized specialty.

U Interface
In Integrated Services Digital Network (ISDN), a two-wire loop of twisted-pair cables.

UltraSCSI
A high-speed version of the Small Computer Systems Interface (SCSI) bus. It supports 40-Mbyte-per-second transfers.

ultraviolet (See UV)

Ultrix
Digital Equipment's version of Unix, built on a University of California at Berkeley 4.2 Berkeley Software Distribution (BSD) base.

UMB (upper memory block)

UML (Unified Modeling Language)
The industry standard language for specifying, visualizing, constructing and documenting the artifacts of software systems.

UMTS (Universal Mobile Telecommunications System)

unattended operation
Operation of a communications or data-processing system transmission that is controlled automatically and does not require a human operator. Also called "lights-out operation."

unbalanced-to-ground
In a two-wire circuit, the condition in which the impedance-to-ground on one wire is measurably different from that on the other. See also balanced-to-ground.

undetected error rate
Residual error rate.

UNI (user network interface)
In asynchronous transfer mode (ATM) environments, the point at which the user joins the network.

Unified Modeling Language (See UML)

Unified Network Management Architecture (See UNMA)

uniform resource locator (See URL)

uniform-spectrum random noise
Noise distributed over the spectrum in such a way that the power-per-unit bandwidth is constant. Also called white noise.

uninterruptible power supply (See UPS)

Universal ADSL Working Group (See UAWG)

universal asynchronous receiver/transmitter (See UART)

Universal Form Definition Language (See UFDL)

Universal Networked Object (See UNO)

universal queue
A process (and technology) whereby all contact channels and media — e.g., phone, interactive voice response (IVR), fax, Web and e-mail — are integrated into the same queue to standardize processing and handling.

Universal Serial Bus (See USB)

Universal Time-Sharing System (See UTS)

Unix
An operating system originally designed by Bell Laboratories, Unix has proven to be adaptable to a variety of platforms. Developed in 1969, Unix has gone through a multitude of upgrades and enhancements. It is the dominant operating system for critical applications, servers and high-end workstations, because of its scalability and support of complex processing. However, Microsoft's Windows NT has been gaining ground in this market segment since it was released in 1993.

Unix-to-Unix Copy Program (See UUCP)

Unix-to-Unix encoding (See uuencode)

UN/JEDI (UN Joint Electronic Data Interchange)
A working group set up by the United Nations (UN) Economic Commission for Europe (ECE), which established the Electronic Data Interchange for Administration, Commerce and Transportation (EDIFACT).

UNMA (Unified Network Management Architecture)
AT&T's scheme for integrated network management.

UNO (Universal Networked Object)
The Object Management Group's (OMG's) approval of the Universal Networked Object (UNO) proposal on 6 December 1994, mandates that CORBA2-compliant object request brokers (ORBs) must be able to interoperate with other, heteroge-

neous ORBs using a particular lightweight, Transmission Control Protocol/Internet Protocol (TCP/IP)-based protocol ("GIOP").

unshielded twisted pair (See UTP)

UNSM
An Electronic Data Interchange for Administration, Commerce and Transportation (EDIFACT) generic standard message.

unspecified bit rate (See UBR)

uplink
The portion of a satellite circuit extending from an earth station to the satellite. See also downlink.

upper-CASE tool
A tool for modeling applications requirements, systems analysis and data structure. Examples are Index Technologies' Excelerator and KnowledgeWare's Information Engineering Workbench.

UPS (uninterruptible power supply)
A device that provides temporary power upon failure of the main power source.

UR (utilization review)

UREP (Universal Repository — UNISYS)

URI (uniform resource identifier)

URL (uniform resource locator)
The character string that identifies an Internet document's exact name and location.

USART (universal synchronous/asynchronous receiver/transmitter)

USB (Universal Serial Bus)
A commercial desktop standard input/output (I/O) bus that provides a single peripheral connection and vastly increases bus speed. It simplifies peripheral connections via a "daisy chaining" scheme whereby the desktop system has only one I/O port to which all peripherals are connected in a series. Up to 120 peripherals can be connected to a single system.

Usenet
The part of the Internet that is made up of discussion forums or "newsgroups." The hierarchy is divided into mainstream — e.g., computing (comp) or country-specific; recreational (rec); and alternative (alt) groups before splitting into subgroups.

user
An individual who interacts with a computing device through applications. Technical personnel are not considered to be users when they are programming or operating the computer.

User Datagram Protocol (See UDP)

user-friendly
Any system, software or device that is easy to learn and use. Graphical user interfaces (GUIs) are designed to be user-friendly.

USB

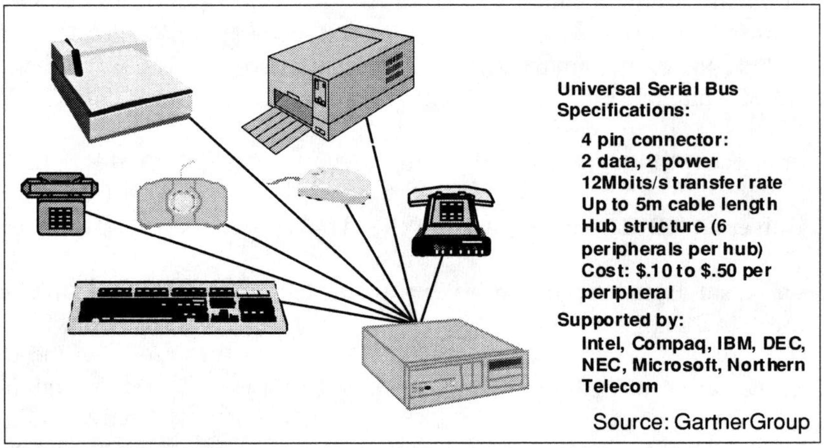

Universal Serial Bus

user interface (See UI)

username
The unique identifier for each user on a network.

user network interface (See UNI)

user workbench
A vision to guide the implementation of end-user computing, providing a multimedia integrated work environment, an omnipotent tool for gaining, using and communicating information, and a high level of job support to the office worker.

USITA (United States Independent Telephone Association)

USLI (ultra-large-scale integration)
More than 1 million transistors in a chip.

USO (UNIX Software Organization)

USOC (Uniform Service Order Code)

USS (Unix System Services)

USTA (United States Telephone Association)

UTP (unshielded twisted pair)
Two insulated wires twisted together, that is, wiring with one or more pairs of twisted insulated conductors housed in a single plastic sheath. The wires are twisted around each other to minimize interference from other twisted pairs in a cable bundle. UTP has no coaxial shielding.

UTS (Universal Time-Sharing System)
In January 1986, Amdahl introduced a version of its UTS that can run stand-alone (not just as a guest under VM) on Amdahl 580 Series processors. UTS has been verified by AT&T as a Unix System V implementation.

UUCP (Unix-to-Unix Copy Program)
A protocol used for communication between geographically dispersed Unix systems.

uuencode (Unix-to-Unix encoding)
Converts files from binary to American Standard Code for Information Interchange (ASCII) format for transmission onto the Internet as e-mail messages. Uuencode has been largely superceded by Multipurpose Internet Messaging Extensions (MIME), but still exists among older products.

UV (ultraviolet)
Part of the electromagnetic spectrum with higher frequencies than visible light.

V

VA (volt ampere)

V AC or VAC (volts alternating current)

VACC (virtual access call center)
Whereas call centers are predominantly focused on voice-based contact with customers, the VACC will manage voice, e-mail, voice mail, fax, Web sites and scanned paper mail images for customer interactions.

VAD (value-added distributor or dealer)

VAG (VisualAge Generator)

VAI (value-added internetwork)
Networks that offer distributed client/server computing services built on top of Internet protocols to enable electronic trading communities to flourish.

The differences between traditional value-added networks (VANs) and VAIs are less clear today, because VANs have started to accept transactions from the Internet. However, VAIs should not be confused with VAN offerings that treat Internet protocols as just another transport resource and fail to offer services that enable trading. VANs will continue to offer typical electronic data interchange (EDI) mailbox services for both Internet and VAN-originated interchanges. VAIs will focus on building an Internet-based technology infrastructure to enable distributed client/server computing within and outside the enterprise.

VAIS (value-added Internet service)

VAJ (VisualAge for Java)

value-added carriers
Vendors that enhance the phone network and resell the service.

value-added common carrier
A company that sells the services of a value-added network. It can be a postal, telegraph and telephone services (PTT) agent or subsidiary or an independent company.

value-added internetwork (See VAI)

value-added network (See VAN)

VACC

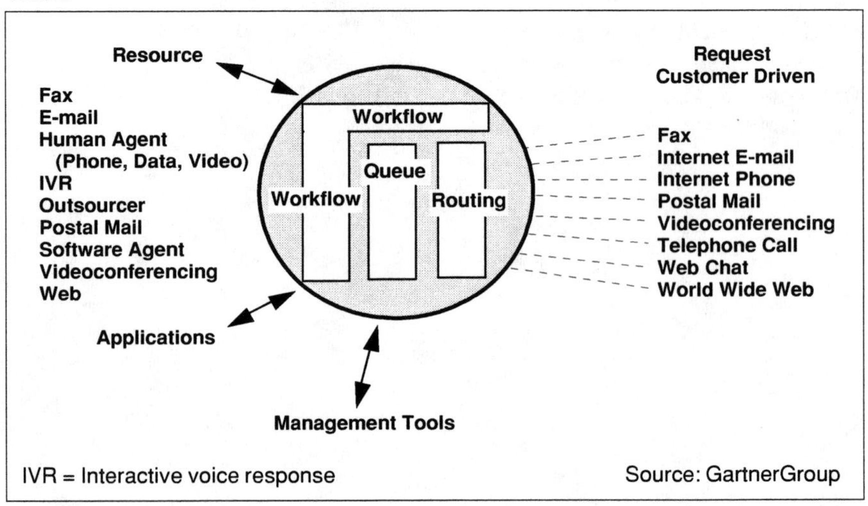

Virtual Access Call Center

value-added reseller (See VAR)

value-added service (See VAS)

Value Chain Initiative (See VCI)

VAM (Vendors Against Microsoft)
A de facto coalition that has formed around Netscape Communications, Sun Microsystems and Oracle, with dozens of informal members, loosely united against Microsoft. VAM has: engaged the imagination of entrepreneurs, inventors and some early adopters; fostered tremendous creativity, reinvention and relearning; and provided a new source of leadership attempting to counterbalance Microsoft. Intel is equally a target, since Microsoft and Intel control critical industry software and hardware standards.

vampire tap
Connection into an Ethernet cable by piercing.

VAN (value-added network)
A private network through which value-added carriers provide special data transmission services.

VANS (value-added network services)

VAR (value-added reseller)
An organization that buys equipment from a vendor at a discount, adds value (such as application software that is packaged and sold with underlying system software, often including a database management system) and remarkets it.

variable bit rate (See VBR)

VAS (value-added service)
A communications facility using communications common carrier networks for transmission and providing enhanced extra data features with separate equipment. Such extra features, including store-and-forward message switching, terminal interfacing and host interfacing, are common.

VAX (Virtual Address Extension)
The Digital Equipment architecture that was the company's principal product line prior to the Alpha. VAX was enormously successful in Digital's traditional engineering and scientific customer base and, more significantly, enabled Digital to penetrate the commercial data-processing and office-automation markets.

VAX IBM Data Access (See VIDA)

VAX unit of performance (See VUP)

VB (Visual Basic)
A high-level programming language used in developing applications for Microsoft Windows 95.

VBA (Visual Basic for Applications)
A Visual Basic system included with Windows 95 applications and used for creating basic and customized programs.

VBR (variable bit rate)
An asynchronous transfer mode (ATM) quality of service category, defined by the ATM Forum. Both real-time variable bit rate (rtVBR) and non real-time variable bit rate (nrtVBR) are defined. Apart from the traffic parameters for peak cell rate (PCR) and sustainable cell rate (which defines the average bit rate required by the application), additional quality-of-service parameters such as maximum cell transfer delay, cell delay variation and maximum burst size must be agreed upon. The typical application for which it is used is compressed voice and videoconferencing for rtVBR, and response-time-sensitive data such as Systems Network Architecture (SNA) for nrtVBR.

VBScript
A primary form of Microsoft's Visual Basic (VB). It has been introduced as Internet-oriented scripting language intended for providing client-side and server-capable processing within Web pages.

VBVA (visual builder of virtual applications)

VBX (Visual Basic Extension)
A Visual Basic add-on that Microsoft is converting to an Object Linking and Embedding (OLE) Custom Controls (OCX) infrastructure. The OCX/OLE standard interface is replacing the VBX interface.

VC (virtual channel)
In asynchronous transfer mode (ATM), a communications track between two nodes giving the bandwidth needed for a virtual connection across the network.

VC (virtual circuit)
In packet switching, network facilities that appear to users to be an end-to-end circuit, but are in fact a dynamically variable network connection in which sequential user data packets may be routed differently during the course of a "virtual connection." Transmission facilities may be shared by many virtual circuits simultaneously.

VC (Visual C++ — Microsoft)

VCC (Voyager Coupling Code)

VCI (Value Chain Initiative)
An effort by Microsoft and participating partners to define broadly accepted program interfaces to support the integration of applications across enterprises in specific vertical industries, such as banking, insurance and healthcare.

VCP (voice and call processing)

VCR (videocassette recorder)

VC starvation
The condition a switch in an asynchronous transfer mode (ATM) network suffers when it becomes congested and cells or cell streams representing Layer 3 virtual local-area network (VLAN) packets are missed or dropped, leading to the VLAN becoming unstable Also known as beatdown.

VCTO (vendor configure-to-order)

V DC or Vdc (volts direct current)

VDSL (very high-speed digital subscriber line)
Very-high-speed digital subscriber line (DSL) connections over short distances.

VDT (video display terminal)

VDU (visual display unit)

vector facility (See VF)

vector quantization
A source-encoding compression technique based on the division of the data stream into blocks called vectors, which are compared to vectors in a code book, the references of which are transmitted.

VEM (vendor evaluation model)

Vendor Independent Messaging (See VIM)

Vector Markup Language (See VML)

vendor-neutral
A state in which no one vendor can control the definition, revision or distribution of a specification. Vendor-neutral specifications encourage the development of competing yet compatible implementations, freeing the purchaser to choose from a multitude of vendors without suffering a loss of functionality. Vendor-neutral specifications must be comprehensive, consistent, and either publicly available or licensed at a nominal fee. Additionally, they must be defined by a multilateral association that is representative of a broad cross-section of the computer industry, open to new members, publishes the rules of membership and operates according to

democratic principles. Preferably, a vendor-neutral specification is supplemented with at least one reference implementation. This reference would be available in a format that allows re-creation — that format would be source code for software implementations — and a set of conformance tests that sufficiently ensure the implementation's integrity under all reasonable conditions of projected use.

Vendors Against Microsoft (See VAM)

vendor-unique MEI (See VUMEI)

Veronica
A search mechanism on the Internet using descriptive text, a precursor to the search engines of today.

very high frequency (See VHF)

very high-speed digital subscriber line (See VDSL)

very large database (See VLDB)

very large-scale integration (See VLSI)

very long instruction word (See VLIW)

very low frequency (See VLF)

very small aperture terminal (See VSAT)

VESA (Video Electronics Standards Association)

VESA local bus (See VL bus)

VF (vector facility)
An attachment to a processor that enables the processor to run programs that issue vector instructions, which are particularly useful in scientific calculations, but are not particularly useful for database operations.

VF (Visual FoxPro — Microsoft)

VF (voice frequency)

VFast
The precursor to V.34 from Rockwell International, originally endorsed by many modem manufacturers.

VGA (Video Graphics Array)
A hardware display and software resolution standard for personal computers.

VHDFDD (very high-density flexible disk drive)

VHDL (VLSI Hardware Description Language)
An industry standard format for describing integrated circuit logic and behavior.

VHDL Initiative for the Standardization of ASIC Libraries (See VITAL)

VHF (very high frequency)

VHS (video home system — videocassette format)

VHSIC (very high speed integrated circuit)

VI (Visual InterDev — Microsoft)

VICS (Voluntary Interindustry Communications Standards)

VIDA (VAX IBM Data Access)
Digital Equipment's Relational Database (Rdb) to DB2 interoperation software.

videoconferencing
Communication by individuals or groups using systems that support image, voice and data transfer over digital networks or telephone circuits. Videoconferencing systems can take the form of large, dedicated units for group meetings or can be integrated with desktop personal computers.

Video Electronic Standards Association (See VESA)

Video Graphics Array (See VGA)

Video On Demand (See VOD)

video random-access memory (See VRAM)

video server
A server that delivers streams of digital video and audio.

video signal
A signal comprising frequencies normally required to transmit pictorial information (1 to 6 MHz).

videotex
An interactive data communications application broadcast over the public switched telephone network and received on adapted television receivers. It is designed to enable unsophisticated users to converse with remote databases, enter data for transactions and retrieve textual and graphics information. Also called viewdata.

view
An alternative representation of data from one or more tables. A view can include all or some of the columns in these tables.

VIM (Vendor Independent Messaging)
An application programming interface (API) that allows the exchange of electronic mail among programs from different vendors. Members of the Vendor Independent Messaging (VIM) Consortium are in the process of internally standardizing on VIM across all their networking products as they roll out their new product releases. VIM is designed to work across desktop platforms on Windows, Macintosh, DOS and OS/2.

VIM (virtually interoperable manufacturing)
A way for manufacturers to gain competitive advantage by integrating business processes across core disciplines and the supply chain, while customizing and integrating the underlying business application products.

Vines
Banyan Systems' network operating system (NOS).

virtual access call center (See VACC)

Virtual Address Extension (See VAX)

virtual channel (See VC)

virtual circuit (See VC)

virtual LAN (See VLAN)

virtually interoperable manufacturing (See VIM)

Virtual Machine (See VM)

Virtual Memory System (See VMS)

virtual path (See VP)

virtual private data network (See VPDN)

virtual private network (See VPN)

virtual product development management (See VPDM)

virtual reality (See VR)

Virtual Reality Modeling Language (See VRML)

virtual storage
A computer that appears to have a much larger memory than its real memory. This is accomplished by software that moves pages rapidly in and out of

a high-speed, random-access storage device, usually a disk.

Virtual Storage Access Method (See VSAM)

Virtual Storage Extended (See VSE)

Virtual Source/Virtual Destinations (See VS/VD)

virtual tape subsystem (See VTS)

Virtual Telecommunications Access Method (See VTAM)

Virtual Terminal (See VT)

Virtual Terminal Protocol (See VTP)

Virtual Tributary (See VT)

virus
Software used to infect a computer. After the virus code is written, it is buried within an existing program. Once that program is executed, the virus code is activated and attaches copies of itself to other programs in the system. Infected programs copy the virus to other programs.

VIS (voice information services)

Visual Basic (See VB)

Visual Basic Extension (See VBX)

Visual Basic for Applications (See VBA)

visualization
To illustrate information objects and their relationships on a display. Strategic visualization graphically illustrates the strength of relationships by the proximity of objects on the display. Advanced technology can make a significant difference in users' ability to interface to large knowledge repositories. These advances use the distance between objects on the display to reflect the similarity of meaning, similarity of content or other relationships (e.g., association with a group).

Visual J++ — Microsoft (See VJ)

Visual Studio (See VS)

VITAL (VHDL Initiative for the Standardization of ASIC Libraries)
A standard for defining the format of integrated-circuit simulation libraries.

VJ (Visual J++ — Microsoft)
A variant of the Java language.

VLA (Volume License Agreement — Novell)
A software licensing option offered under the Novell "Customer Connections" program, with an entry point that opens discounts to smaller organizations.

VLAN (virtual LAN)
A virtual LAN (local-area network) is a set of systems, regardless of higher layer addressing or location, that is designated as a logical LAN and treated as a set of contiguous systems on a single LAN segment. Virtual LANs can be proprietary or standardized using the Institute of Electrical and Electronics Engineers (IEEE) 802.1Q. Typical grouping parameters for VLANs include the port number of the hub, switch, or router, the higher layer protocol such as Internet Protocol (IP) or Internetwork Packet Exchange (IPX), the Media Access Control (MAC) address, and the traditional subnet. The goal of VLANs is to provide simpler administration, simple moves/adds/changes to network devices, and partitioning at the MAC layer.

VL bus (VESA local bus)
A local bus architecture introduced by the Video Electronic Standards Association (VESA) to work with the Intel 486.

VLDB (very large database)
A database greater than 100 gigabytes.

VLF (very low frequency)

VLIW (very long instruction word)
A processor architecture in which each data word contains multiple instructions. Used in Intel's next-generation IA-64 ("Merced") products.

VLM (very large memory)

VLM (Virtual Loadable Module — Novell)

VLSI (very large-scale integration)
A technology that makes it possible to place the equivalent of between 100,000 and 1 million transistors on a chip.

VLSIC (very large-scale integrated circuit)

VLSI Hardware Description Language (See VHDL)

VM (Virtual Machine)
The IBM Virtual Machine (VM) set of operating system products (VM/SP, VM/HPO, VM/XA, VM Migration and VM/ESA) manages a system so that all its resources — processors, storage and input/output (I/O) devices — are available to many users at the same time. Each user has at his disposal the functional equivalent of a real dedicated system. Because this functional equivalent is simulated by VM and does not really exist, it is called a "virtual" machine.

VMA (Voice Mail Association)

VM/CP (voice messaging/call processing)

VMEbus
A high-speed parallel backplane system bus originally developed by Motorola, and now widely used on technical workstations and small multiuser systems.

VML (Vector Markup Language)
An application proposed to the World Wide Web Coalition (W3C) for defining 2-D graphics in Extensible Markup Language (XML).

VML (Veritas Media Librarian)

VMS (Virtual Memory System)
Digital Equipment's traditional mainstay operating system. Virtual Address Extension (VAX) computers that play a role for Digital similar to the one that Multiple Virtual Storage (MVS) plays for IBM.

VOD (Video On Demand)
A multimedia application with which a user can access motion or still video, which may be available as public or private services.

VOD (Voice Over Data)
Transmission of voice over digital lines.

voice band
A voice-grade channel.

voice digitization
Conversion of an analog voice signal into digital form for storage or transmission.

voice encryption
A function that enables a device to transport digitized voice signals.

voice grade
A telecommunications link with a bandwidth (about 3 kHz) appropriate for an audio telephone line.

voice-grade channel
A channel with bandwidth equivalent to a telephone line obtained through the public telephone network. The maximum potential bandwidth of a voice-grade channel is approximately 20 kilohertz (KHz); how-

ever, most voice grade channels in a transmission facility are usually spaced 4,000 hertz (Hz) apart, and not all of that bandwidth is generally available to a user due to the presence of noise-limiting loading coils. The telephone network itself is usually defined in terms of channels, with frequencies from 300 to 3,400 Hz.

voice mail
A service providing digitized voice message handling.

Voice Markup Language (See VoxML)

voice-messaging system
Also called voice mail and, incorrectly, voice-processing systems. Voice-messaging systems are hardware and software products that operate with most private branch exchange (PBX), hybrid, or key telephone systems, enabling users to send, receive, and redirect voice messages through office telephone systems and computers. Voice-messaging hardware includes a central processor, analog-to-digital converters, disk storage and input/output ports.

voice-operated device
A piece of equipment that can be controlled by spoken commands.

Voice Over Data (See VOD)

voice processing systems
Hardware and software products that encompass voice messaging, voice recognition, voice response and any other applications that deal with the processing of voice communications.

voice recognition
A hardware and software system that translates human speech into binary text. Also called speech recognition.

voice response system (See VRS)

voice response unit (See VRU)

Voice Store-and-Forward (See VSF)

VOIP (voice over IP)

Volume License Agreement — Novell (See VLA)

volume purchase agreement (See VPA)

volume source cardinality (See VSC)

volume table of contents (See VTOC)

VoxML (Voice Markup Language)
A markup language that encodes Web-site information so that it can be read over the telephone. VoxML was introduced in September 1998 by Motorola's Internet and connectivity services division. VoxML allows for an assortment of speech technologies to be incorporated so Web information on the Web can be relayed through any phone. Sites can convert the text of Web pages to computerized speech, play pre-recorded audio content or construct sentences out of pre-recorded words and phrases.

VP (virtual path)
In asynchronous transfer mode (ATM), the bandwidth between two points on a network used by one or more virtual channels (VCs).

VPA (volume purchase agreement)
An agreement between a computer vendor and a customer under which the vendor grants discounted prices in return for the customer's commitment to purchase a minimum quantity of products.

VPDM (virtual product development management)
A term describing the set of capabilities used for achieving product innovation competitiveness.

VPDM is the system used to transfer ideas into designs.

VPDN (virtual private data network)
A data networking service offered by the provider in a virtually private mode, using virtual private network (VPN) technologies.

VPN (virtual private network)
A system that delivers corporation-focused communications services on a shared public network infrastructure, and provides customized operating characteristics uniformly and universally across an enterprise. VPN is generically used to refer to voice virtual private networks. To avoid confusion, Internet Protocol (IP)-based data services are referred to as data VPNs. VPN service providers define a virtual private network as a wide-area network (WAN) of permanent virtual circuits, generally using asynchronous transfer mode (ATM) or frame relay to transport IP. VPN technology providers define a virtual private network as the use of encryption software or hardware to bring privacy to communications over a public or untrusted data network. VPN is also a trademarked voice service offered by Spring and GlobalOne.

VPO (Volume Purchase Option — Lotus)

VR (virtual reality)
A computerized process, usually including special equipment, that projects the user into a simulated three-dimensional space. It gives the user the sensation of being in the simulated environment and the ability to respond to the simulation.

VRAM (video random-access memory)
A type of dynamic random access memory (DRAM) used in high-speed processing of visual data.

VRML (Virtual Reality Modeling Language)
A means of rendering 3-D worlds from mathematical equations or descriptions. A VRML browser can create shapes and text within a navigable 3-D context. The v.2.0 specifications further enhance the immersive experience, allowing for such real-world events as interaction between "visitors" and collision-detection when a user bumps into an object or other users.

VRS (voice response system)
Specialized technologies designed for providing callers with verbal and faxed answers to inquiries without assistance from a person. They provide account information, fulfill requests for mailable items, pre-screen callers for script customization, interact with host systems (read and write) and produce reports.

VRU (voice response unit)
An automated telephone answering system consisting of hardware and software that allows the caller to navigate through a series of prerecorded messages and use a menu of options through the buttons on a touch-tone telephone or through voice recognition.

VS (Visual FoxPro — Microsoft)

VS (Visual Studio)
A Microsoft package of five applications development (AD) tools with complementary, albeit overlapping, focuses: Visual Basic (VB), Visual C++ (VC), Visual J++ (VJ), Visual InterDev (VI) and Visual FoxPro (VF).

VSAM (Virtual Storage Access Method)
IBM's chosen access method for direct-access files. It is optimized for a virtual storage environment. Multiple Virtual Storage (MVS), Data Facility Product (DFP), Information Management System (IMS), Customer Information Control System (CICS), and DB2 all use VSAM.

VSAT (very small aperture terminal)
Small earth station for data transmission to and from orbiting satellites.

VSC (volume source cardinality)
A model for the deployment of document scanners based on the volume of documents, the number of distinct document types (cardinality), and the source of the document (internal or external).

VSE (Virtual Storage Extended)
Formerly DOS/VSE. A multitasking, 370-architected operating system akin to Multiple Virtual Storage (MVS). VSE work runs in partitions rather than address spaces, and uses Performance Optimized With Enhanced RISC (POWER) for input/output (I/O) rather than Job Entry Subsystem (JES), but is largely similar to MVS. Subsequent VSE/ESA releases gave VSE the XA-370 channel architecture, 31-bit virtual and real storage support, and data spaces. VSE is the IBM operating system on one-third of installed 4381s and a significant proportion of 9370s as well. It offers transaction and batch processing capabilities well beyond Virtual Machine's (VM's) current capabilities, and has a close affinity with MVS.

VSF (Voice Store-and-Forward)
A processor-controlled system that enables voice messages to be created, edited, sent, stored and forwarded. Users access and operate the system by means of any 12-button dial pad in response to voice prompts from the system.

VSM (Virtual Storage Manager)

VSS (Versatile Storage Server — IBM)

VS/VD (Virtual Source/Virtual Destinations)
One of three types of feedback an asynchronous transfer mode (ATM) switch can provide.

VT (Virtual Terminal)
An application allowing interoperability between heterogeneous terminals (OSI term).

VT (Virtual Tributary)
A structure that transports and switches sub-synchronous transport signal-1 (STS-1) payloads (a SONET term). A VT can be described by size, such as VTx, with x representing 1.5, 2, 3 or 6.

VTAM (Virtual Telecommunications Access Method)
The main Systems Network Architecture (SNA) subsystem resident in an IBM mainframe that manages session establishment and data flow between terminals and application programs, or between application programs.

VT envelope capacity
Bandwidth that is part of the Virtual Tributary (VT) superframe and available for the VT synchronous payload envelope (a SONET term). See also Virtual Tributary.

VT group
A 108-byte structure that carries one or more Virtual Tributaries (VTs) of the same size.

VTOA (Voice and Telephony over ATM)

VTOC (volume table of contents)
The data structure on a direct-access volume that describes each data set on that volume.

VTP (Virtual Terminal Protocol)
The protocol driving the Virtual Terminal (VT) application.

VT path-terminating equipment (See VT PTE)

VT payload capacity
The maximum bandwidth within the Virtual Tributary synchronous payload envelope (VT SPE) that is available to transport a payload (a SONET term).

VT POH (Virtual Tributary path overhead)

VT PTE (VT path-terminating equipment — SONET term)
Network devices that multiplex and demultiplex the Virtual Tributary (VT) payload. VT PTEs can create, terminate, and modify the VT path overhead (POH) as required to transport the VT payload.

VTR (videotape recorder)

VTS (Virtual Tape Server — IBM)

VTS (virtual tape subsystem)
Tape library hardware and software extensions that utilize direct-access storage device (DASD) buffers to multiply the tape device count, throughput and storage density of tape library systems.

VT SPE (VT synchronous payload envelope — SONET term)
A 500-microsecond frame structure carried by the Virtual Tributary (VT). It provides Virtual Tributary path overhead (VT POH) and bandwidth for transporting payloads.

VT superframe
An organized 500-microsecond superframe structure overlaid on a 125-microsecond synchronous transport signal-1 synchronous payload envelope (STS-1 SPE — a SONET term). Within this structure are the Virtual Tributary (VT) payload pointer and the Virtual Tributary synchronous payload envelope (VT SPE).

VT synchronous payload envelope — SONET term (See VT SPE)

VUMEI (vendor-unique MEI)
A master enterprise identifier (MEI) that is generated in such a way that it is guaranteed to be unique across all of a vendor's enterprise master person index (EMPI) systems.

VUP (VAX unit of performance)
The average compute-bound performance of a Virtual Address Extension (VAX) processor relative to a VAX-11/780. One VUP is equivalent to between 0.7 and 1.0 IBM System/370 MIPS, depending on the compute-bound benchmarks chosen. Multiuser benchmark results vary much more widely, due to different input/output (I/O) architectures and software path lengths on Digital Equipment and IBM systems.

V.x series
A series of communications specifications administered by the International Telecommunication Union (ITU). It includes:

1. V.10: ITU recommendation for unbalanced high-speed communications.
2. V.11: ITU recommendation for balanced high-speed communications.
3. V.17: ITU fax ITU recommendation using TCM modulation.
4. V.21: ITU recommendation for full-duplex asynchronous modems up to 300 bits per second (bps) on dialup lines.
5. V.22: ITU recommendation for full-duplex asynchronous modems of 600 or 1,200 bps on dialup lines.
6. V.22bis: ITU recommendation for full-duplex modems of 2,400 bps on dialup or two-wire leased lines.
7. V.23: ITU recommendation for half-duplex asynchronous modems of 0-600 or 0-1,200 bps on dialup lines.
8. V.24: ITU definitions of interchange circuits between terminal and communications equipment (e.g., between a PC and a modem).
9. V.25bis: ITU definition of call procedures for call setup and teardown over a data terminal

equipment/date circuit-terminating equipment (DTE/DCE) interface.

10. V.26: ITU recommendation for full-duplex synchronous modems of 2,400 bps on four-wire leased lines.

11. V.26bis: ITU recommendation for full-duplex synchronous modems of 1,200 or 2,400 bps on dialup lines.

12. V.26ter: ITU recommendation for full-duplex modems of 2,400 bps on dialup and two-wire leased lines.

13. V.27: ITU recommendation for full-duplex synchronous modems of 4,800 bps on dialup lines.

14. V.27bis: ITU recommendation for full-duplex synchronous modems of 2,400 or 4,800 bps on four-wire leased lines.

15. V.27ter: ITU recommendation for half-duplex synchronous modems of 2,400 or 4,800 bps on dialup lines.

16. V.28: ITU recommendation defining the functions of the RS232 interface.

17. V.29: ITU recommendation for synchronous modems of 4,800, 7,200, or 9,600 bps on four-wire leased lines.

18. V.32: ITU serial line protocol for 4.8 kilobits per second (Kbps) or 9.6 Kpbs bidirectional transmission.

19. V.32bis: ITU recommendation that extends V.32 to speeds of 14.4 Kbps.

20. V.33: ITU recommendation for full-duplex synchronous modems of 12,000 or 14,400 bps on four-wire leased lines.

21. V.34: ITU recommendation for communications between a network access device and a packet network; a synchronous protocol driving speeds up to 48 Kbps. See also VFast.

22. V.34+: ITU recommendation that improves V.34 to achieve speeds up to 33.6 Kbps over dialup lines.

23. V.35: ITU recommendation for the transmission of data over the public switched telephone network.

24. V.36: ITU recommendation for four-wire communications at speeds greater than 48 Kbps.

25. V.42: ITU recommendation for error correction using Link Access Procedure for Modems (LAPM).

26. V.42bis: ITU recommendation for modem data compression using a ratio of 4:1.

27. V.52: ITU recommendation for Bit Error Rate Test (BERT) procedures on modem links.

28. V.54: ITU recommendation for loopback tests on modems.

29. V.110: ITU recommendation for supporting DTE equipment on Integrated Services Digital Network (ISDN).

30. V.120: ITU recommendation for asynchronous rate adaptation up to 64 Kbps over ISDN bearer channels.

W

W2P (Windows 2000 Professional — Microsoft)

W2S (Windows 2000 Server — Microsoft)

W3C (World Wide Web Consortium)

W-4GL (workgroup fourth-generation language)

WABI (Windows application binary interface)

WAC (Web authorization and control)
An access-control technology that works at the Web server, enabling an administrator to define generic user roles and authorize the user access to Web-based data and resources across multiple Web servers, generally at the sub-uniform-resource-locator (URL) level. Solutions are likely to include a central server where a user presents authentication credentials and then receives an encrypted "cookie" or embedded information in the URL. The URL or the cookie is then acknowledged by each of the Web servers in the systems running the WAC agent.

WAD (Web application development)

WAD (wide-area data)

WADN (wide-area data network)

WAIS (Wide-Area Information Service)
A full-text database system designed by Thinking Machines Corp. for information retrieval. WAIS is used widely on the Internet.

WAN (wide-area network)
A communications network that connects computing devices over geographically dispersed locations. While a local-area network (LAN) typically services a single building or location, a WAN covers a much larger area such as a city, state or country. WANs can use either phone lines or dedicated communication lines.

WAN performance monitor
A tool or toolset (hardware and software) to allow monitoring of wide-area network (WAN) traffic and problems.

WAPI (Workflow API)
The Workflow Management Coalition's (WfMC's) application program interface (API), designed to enable workflow application interoperability in a heterogeneous workflow environment in five key areas between: business process re-engineering (BPR)/modeling tools and workflow systems; workflow systems and workflow-client applications; workflow systems and desktop applications; workflow engines; and common workflow administration and monitoring services.

WARC (World Administrative Radio Conference)

warehouse management system (See WMS)

WAS (Web Application Server (See NCA)

WAS (Windows 2000 Advanced Server — Microsoft)

WATS (wide-area telephone service)
A telephone company service providing reduced costs for certain telephone call arrangements. It may be IN-WATS or 800-number service, for which calls can be placed to a location from anywhere at no cost to the calling party, or OUT-WATS, for which calls are placed from a central location. The cost is based on hourly usage per WATS circuit and

on distance-based zones, or bands, to which (or from which) calls are placed.

WATTC (World Administrative Telegraph and Telephone Conference)
An International Telecommunication Union (ITU) conference during which provisions are created for the interconnecting and interworking of the world's telecommunications networks.

wave division multiplexing (See WDM)

waveguide
A transmission path in which a system of boundaries guides electromagnetic energy. The most common of these are hollow metallic conducting tubes (microwave communications) or rods of dielectric material. See also fiber-optic waveguides.

wavelength
The distance between the crests of a wave in a radio signal, measured as the speed of light divided by the frequency in hertz (Hz).

WBEM (Web-Based Enterprise Management)
An initiative launched in July 1996 by a consortium of five vendors: BMC Software, Cisco Systems, Compaq Computer, Intel and Microsoft. Its intention was to create a new set of network and systems management (NSM) middleware services based on Internet technologies. As a part of the proposal, three components of an NSM architecture were introduced: Hypermedia Management Schema (HMMS), Hypermedia Management Protocol (HMMP) and Hypermedia Object Manager (HOMOM).

WCL (Windows Communication Library)

WCM (Web content or component management)
The process of creating, maintaining and managing content and components on a Web site.

WDCS (Windows 2000 Data Center Server — Microsoft)

WDM (wave division multiplexing)
Also called DWDM (dense wave division multiplexing). In fiber-optic networks such as Synchronous Optical Network (SONET), WDM permits several wavelengths (i.e., colors of light) to be placed on the same fiber. For each new wavelength, the capacity of the fiber increases 100 percent over the original capacity. The current generation of WDM will achieve 96 colors.

WDM (Windows Device Driver Model)

wearable computer
Typically consists of a belt-mounted PC and a head-mounted, voice-activated screen over one eye. Originating in the military, wearable sys-

WBEM

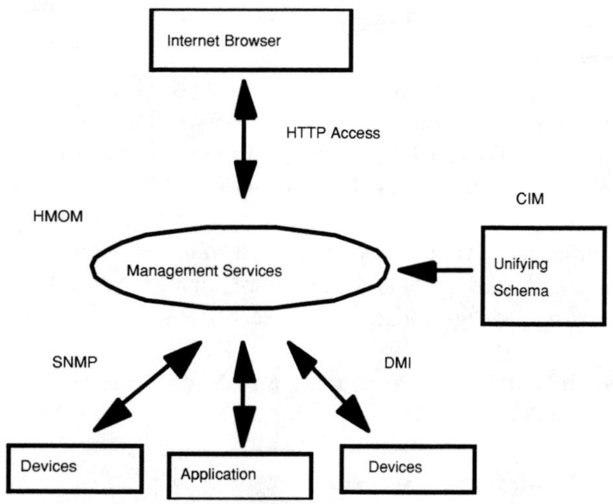

CIM = Common Information Model
DMI = Desktop Management Interface
HMDM = Hypermedia Object Manager
HTTP = Hypertext Transport Protocol
SNMP = Simple Network Management Protocol

Source: GartnerGroup

Components of the WBEM Initiative

tems are commercially available in the $5,000 to $10,000 price range.

Web (See WWW)

Web authorization and control (See WAC)

Web-Based Enterprise Management (See WBEM)

Web browser
A "client" (system or program) for use in accessing the World Wide Web on the Internet.

Web content or component management (See WCM)

webcrawler
A piece of software (also called a spider) designed to follow hyperlinks to their completion and to return to previously visited Internet addresses.

WebDAV (Web Distributed Authoring and Versioning)
An integrated document management (IDM) protocol proposed as an extension of Hypertext Transport Protocol (HTTP) 1.1 to provide library services for Web server resources. In a WebDAV IDM implementation, library services are executed on a resource basis rather than through a traditional relational database. This architecture enables shared locking, partial updates and reservations.

Web Distributed Authoring and Versioning (See WebDAV)

Web integration servers
Web servers that directly support Hypertext Transport Protocol (HTTP); execute a proprietary, high-level 4GL or scripting language; and include one or more adapters for databases, legacy systems and packaged applications. Extensible Markup Language (XML)-based Web integration servers are similar; however, they also use XML data internally within the server and externally with clients and other applications.

Webmaster
The person who maintains a Web site.

Web page
A World Wide Web document — usually based on Hypertext Markup Language (HTML) — that may contain text, graphics, online audio, video, Java or ActiveX objects. The most basic elements of Web marketing, these pages are linked to other pages using hypertext to form a Web site. Web pages can be designed for virtually any purpose, and many third-party organizations have evolved services that assist marketers in page content development and layout.

Web Request Broker (See WRB)

Web server
The central location that hosts Web pages or a Web site and enables a remote "client" (system or program) to access the material held.

Web site
A collection of files that covers a particular theme or subject and is managed by a particular person or organization. Its opening page is called a home page. A Web site is accessed through a Web address known as a uniform resource locator (URL).

A large Web site may reside on a number of servers located in different places. The server is connected to the World Wide Web and is able to format and send information requested by worldwide users 24 hours a day, seven days a week. Web sites typically use the Hypertext Markup Language (HTML) format to format and present information and to provide navigational facilities that make it easy for the user to move within the site and around the Web.

Web TV
Web TV services enable a user to access the Web on a television set using a special remote control and a

decoder that sits on top of the TV. Services are offered by various types of provider — e.g., TV broadcasters, satellite operators, and telecom operators. The connection can be provided over various media — analog or digital telephone lines, cable network or satellite links — depending on local infrastructure.

WEDI (Workgroup for Electronic Data Interchange)

wet line
A T1 line with span power.

WF (workflow framework)
A set of proposals that allow applications to deliver "workflow information" to a user or workflow engine.

WFC (Windows Foundation Classes)
Microsoft's object-oriented Java application framework and component model based on J/Direct Java Virtual Machine (JVM). The Java applications leveraging WFC and J/Direct can bypass much of the overhead of the Java runtime environment by directly accessing the Win32 application programming interface (API).

WfM (Wired for Management Initiative)
A blueprint, developed by Intel in partnership with and supported by leading information technology (IT) vendors, for making PC-based systems — including desktops, mobile systems and servers — universally manageable. The initiative encompasses advances in hardware and software that enable system management software applications that provide management to the desktop, mobile system or server, and the integration with systems management tools and frameworks. The innovations in hardware and software collectively enterprises should understand, evaluate and incorporate into all PC acquisitions.

WFM (work force management)
A system intended to maximize the use of agent labor by projecting incoming call volumes and scheduling staff to meet needs exactly, by time of the day, day of the week, week of the month, etc. WFM systems use historical calling records, which are collected from the automatic call distribution system, to project future calling patterns and volumes for specified time frames. Features include:

- Call volume forecasting.
- Calculation of the required number of agents, based on the desired average speed of answer.
- Agent scheduling.
- Meeting and vacation planning.
- Reporting.
- "What if" analysis.

WfMC (Workflow Management Coalition)
The Workflow Management Coalition, founded in 1993, is a nonprofit international organization of workflow vendors, users, analysts and university research groups. WfMC's mission is to promote and develop the use of workflow technology through the establishment of standards for software terminology, interoperability and connectivity between workflow products.

WfMC API (See WAPI)

WfMC Interface 1 (Workflow Management Coalition Interface 1)
The WfMC's interface between modeling and definition tools and runtime workflow management software. It consists of an interchange format and applications programming interface (API) calls, which can support the exchange of process definition information over a variety of physical or electronic interchange media. The interface may support the exchange of a complete process definition or a subset — e.g., a set of process definition changes or the attributes of a particular activity within the process definition. This interface is intended to be an integral part (as a specialization) of Interface 2 version 2.x.

WfMC Interface 2 (Workflow Management Coalition Interface 2)
The WfMC's interface designed to provide access from a workflow application to the workflow engine and work list, irrespective of the nature of actual product implementation.

WfMC Interface 3 (Workflow Management Coalition Interface 3)
The WfMC's interface intended for application agents and (longer-term) applications that have been designed to be "workflow enabled" (i.e., to interact directly with a workflow engine). This interface has been amalgamated into Interface 2.

WfMC Interface 4 (Workflow Management Coalition Interface 4)
The WfMC's interface designed to enable two or more workflow engines to communicate and work together to coordinate work. Interface 4 (i.e., WAPI4-WFMC-TC-1012) establishes the definition of all the requests and responses that two workflow engines must exchange to support processes that interoperate across a network. The exact coding used to transport those requests and responses is released in a separated binding specification. This separation allows the specification of different bindings using different network and encoding protocols. The first and only defined binding was released in March 1997, and is called WAPI4/MIME (WFMC-TC-1018). WAPI4/MIME uses Internet mail as the transport mean and Multipurpose Internet Mail Extensions (MIME) and Common Gateway Interface (CGI) for content encoding. See also JFlow.

WfMC Interface 5 (Workflow Management Coalition Interface 5)
The WfMC's interface designed to let an independent management application interact with different workflow domains, although alternative implementation scenarios are also feasible. For example, the management application may be an integral part of one enactment service, although capable of managing various functions across additional (heterogeneous) workflow domains.

WFQ (Weighted Fair Queuing)

WGS (workgroup systems)
A future-oriented, vendor-independent model for office information systems (OIS). Key WGS proposals include a complete, cohesive architecture, distributed-logic client/server technology and interenterprise-capable, enterprise-class platforms for communications, collaboration, word and knowledge reuse.

WGS

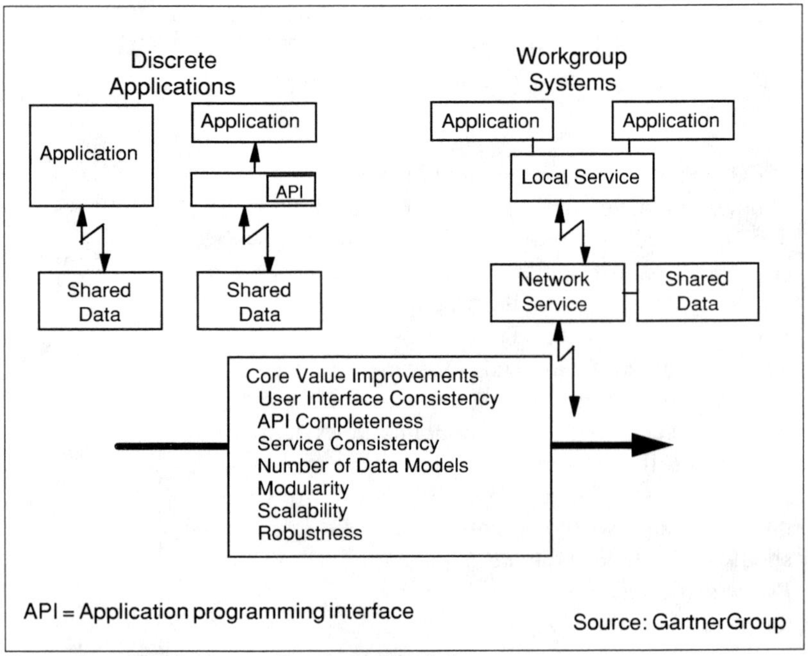

Emerging Workgroup Systems Model

what you see is what you get (See WYSIWYG)

White Pages
A lookup service that translates names of objects into their network addresses.

Whois
An Internet program that enables Internet users to access a database of users and information about Internet areas such as domains, networks and hosts. This database is housed in the network information center (NIC).

Wide-Area Information Service (See WAIS)

wide-area network (See WAN)

wide-area telephone service (See WATS)

wideband
See broadband.

wideband channel
A channel wider in bandwidth than a voice-grade channel.

wide frequency tolerant power plant
A plant providing private branch exchange (PBX) power facilities that operate from alternating current (AC) energy sources that are not as closely regulated as commercial AC power.

WIDL (Web Interface Definition Language)

WIMPS (windows, icons, menus, pointers, scroll bars)
A style of graphical user interface (GUI) originally developed by Xerox, popularized by the Apple Macintosh, and adopted by Microsoft for Windows.

windowing
A display technique that uses multiple screen segments to display different items of information. The display can take two forms: tiling (breaking up the screen into discrete segments) and overlapping (producing a three-dimensional effect by having a screen segment partially or fully obscure another segment).

Windows
The operating system developed by Microsoft for PCs. The first version of Windows was introduced in 1985, and although it presented a graphical user interface (GUI) rather than its text-based predecessor, MS-DOS, it was clumsy compared to Apple's Macintosh operating system. However, an overwhelming base of MS-DOS users combined with superior marketing tactics have since made Microsoft's Windows the dominant operating system for PCs, and the company claimed more than 90 percent of the market in 1997.

Windows 95
A 32-bit operating system introduced by Microsoft in 1995, it offered significant enhancements over prior releases of Windows, with features like memory protection, multithreading, integrated networking and pre-emptive multitasking.

Windows 2000
In 1998, Microsoft renamed its upcoming Windows NT Workstation version 5 to Windows 2000 Professional, and NT Server v.5 to Windows 2000 Server. Windows NT is Microsoft's high-end operating system that competes with Unix and Novell NetWare.

Windows CE (See CE)

Windows DNA
A Microsoft marketing umbrella term and road map for developers using Component Object Model (COM) and Windows.

Windows Foundation Classes (See WFC)

windows, icons, menus, pointers, scroll bars (See WIMPS)

Windows Internet Naming System (See WINS)

Windows NT
Microsoft's high-end 32-bit operating system for client/server computing. Offered in two versions: Windows NT Workstation for the client, and Windows NT Server for the server.

Windows Open Services Architecture (See WOSA)

WINS (Windows Internet Naming System)
A Windows NT Network utility that resolves named nodes to their IP addresses.

Wintel
Refers to the personal computer (PC) environments composed of a Microsoft Windows operating system running on an Intel microprocessor. This environment dominates the personal-computing market, and therefore Microsoft and Intel together control many aspects of the PC industry. The widely accepted standards of this environment have encouraged significant software development for this de facto standard platform, allowing software, files and data to be more easily shared among users and enhancing productivity. However, some have claimed that the dominance of Microsoft and Intel in the PC marketplace has reduced innovation and allowed Microsoft and Intel to set guidelines that enhance their corporate profits rather than benefit users.

WIP (Windows Interface Protocol)

WIP (work in progress)

WIPO (World Intellectual Property Organization)

Wired for Management Initiative (See WfM)

wireless data communication
A form of communication that uses the radio spectrum rather than a physical medium. It may carry analog or digital signals, and may be used in local-area networks (LANs) or wide-area networks and in one- or two-way networks.

wireless LAN (See WLAN)

wireline cellular company
A U.S. term referring to the Block B carrier. Under the Federal Communications Commission's (FCC's) initial licensing procedures, the Block B carrier is the local telephone company. Wireline or Block B systems operate on the frequencies ranging from 869 megahertz (MHz) to 894 MHz.

wiring closet
A dedicated room or enclosure serving as a central point for a data communications or a telecommunications network's equipment.

WK1
The specification for the structure of data stored on disk by Lotus 1-2-3 releases 1 and 2.

WK3
The specification for the structure of data stored on disk by Lotus 1-2-3 release 3.

WLAN (wireless LAN)
A local-area network (LAN) communications technology in which radio, microwave or infrared links take the place of physical cables. WLANs represent a full system extension to the enterprise network. Three physical media types of WLAN systems are available. The first two — direct-sequence spread spectrum (DSSS) and frequency-hopping spread spectrum (FHSS) — are based on radio technologies that are not interoperable. The third is based on infrared, a nonradio technology based on lightwaves. Infrared can coexist with DSSS and FHSS radio-based systems in one enterprise network. However, internetworking issues between access points (APs) prevent an enterprise from mixing and matching WLAN devices from multiple vendors. Other criteria are necessary for interoperability to occur. Also known as cableless LANs (CLANs).

WLL (wireless local loop)

WM (Warehouse Management — SAP)

WMF (Workflow Management Facility (See JFlow)

WMI (Windows Management Interface)

WMS (warehouse management system)
A real-time execution management system designed to receive, store and ship products in the most efficient, yet compliant, way possible. It enables the enterprise to ensure, with its own resources, that the customer receives what it wants when it wants, and in the form and by the methods specified. Also called a DMS (distribution management system).

WORA (write once, run anywhere)

workflow
The automation of work among users where the system is intelligent enough to act based on the definition of work types, users and tasks, and the recognition of dynamic processing conditions.

Workflow API (See WAPI)

workflow framework (See WF)

Workflow Management Coalition (See WfMC)

Workflow Management Coalition Interfaces 1, 2, 3, 4 and 5 (See WfMC Interface 1; WfMC Interface 2; WfMC Interface 3; WfMC Interface 4; and WfMC Interface 5)

work force management (see WFM)

workgroup systems (See WGS)

work in progress (See WIP)

work management
A set of software products and services that apply workflow structure to the movement of information as well as to the interaction of business processes and human worker processes that generate the information. Work management streamlines and transforms crucial business processes and thus can improve results and performance.

workstation

1. In general terms, a workstation is a human-to-machine interaction device, usually a PC, that is composed of coordinated input/output (I/O) devices (including video displays, keyboards and functional menus) and that may include offline storage capabilities. It may be used for graphics, text, data and retrieval functions.

2. More specifically, a workstation is the term often applied to a high-performance computer designed for use with personal applications that require significant processing power, such as graphics or computer-automated design. Many software programs originally designed for use on a workstation are designed to run using a Unix operating system.

World Administrative Telegraph and Telephone Conference (See WATTC)

World Wide Web (See WWW)

worm
A malicious software program able to distribute multiple copies of itself within monolithic or distributed systems. Unlike a computer virus, it does not have a separate executable payload. Therefore, the primary impact of this type of threat is to system availability.

WORM (write once, read many)
A digital, optical storage medium on which information can be recorded once and read many times. Provides for extremely compact storage of data at

W

relatively low prices compared to traditional magnetic storage.

WOSA (Windows Open Services Architecture)
An architecture and set of application programming interfaces (APIs) that position Windows as a universal client. It standardizes the interfaces that developers can use in accessing underlying network services.

WP (word processing)

WPBX (wireless private branch exchange)

wpm (words per minute)

WRAM (Windows Random-Access Memory)

wrap
Automatic action taken by a Fiber Distributed Data Interface (FDDI) network in case of failure. Stations on each side of a break create a single logical ring out of the primary and secondary rings so that the network can still run.

wrapper
A layer of software that provides a new interface to the program around which it is wrapped. The purpose of a wrapper is to make the underlying program accessible to an otherwise incompatible external requesting program. A wrapper is a custom proxy program that performs either or both of the following two functions:

- Protocol bridging, such as from an object request broker (ORB) to another ORB, a transaction processing (TP) monitor, a file or a messaging system.
- Message content transformation, e.g., American Standard Code for Information Interchange (ASCII) to Extended Binary-Coded Decimal Interchange Code (EBCDIC), data type translation or truncating, padding or dropping fields.

Sometimes the wrapper must reconcile dissimilar communication patterns. This might involve talking to a wrapped legacy application via conversational terminal emulation while displaying a message-queuing or ORB-style interface to external requesters.

WRB (Web Request Broker) (See NCA)

write once, read many (See WORM)

WS (Workgroup Solutions — IBM)

WSI (wafer scale integration)

WSTS (World Semiconductor Trade Statistics)

WWW (World Wide Web)
A hypertext-based global information system developed at the European Laboratory for Particle Physics (CERN) in Geneva. It is a subset of the Internet, technically defined as the community on the Internet where all documents and resources are formatted using Hypertext Markup Language (HTML). HTML, and the related Hypertext Transport Protocol (HTTP), makes it easy to find and view data and documents stored on computers connected to the Internet. HTML creates the links ("hyperlinks") that enable the user to move among many Web documents with the click of a mouse.

WYSIWYG (what you see is what you get)
A user interface that presents a screen image that closely matches the appearance of the printed document.

X

X12
A data interchange standard.

X.25 WAN
Support of the X.25 wide-area network (WAN) protocol for system and network interconnection.

X.400
An International Organization for Standardization (ISO) and International Telecommunication Union (ITU) messaging protocol that allows e-mail to move between different mail systems.

X.400 Application Programming Interface (See XAPI)

X.500
The International Telecommunication Union (ITU) standard for directory services.

X.509
The certificate authority standard administered by the International Telecommunication Union (ITU).

X.509 Certificate
An International Telecommunication Union (ITU) standards-based file format binding a user or device to a public key.

XA
A component of X/Open Distributed Transaction Processing standards, as defines the interface between the Resource Manager and the Transaction Manager.

XA (Extended Architecture)
System/370 XA is the second major extension of IBM's System/360 architecture. It was delivered in 1983 on the 308x processors, and is now available on the 3090 and 4381. The major new features in XA were 31-bit addressing and a more sophisticated input/output (I/O) subsystem. It is supported by the MVS/XA and VM/XA operating systems.

XAPI (X.400 Application Programming Interface)
APIs developed by the X.400 API Association (XAPIA) to sit on top of the X.400 protocols, simplifying the task of submitting and fetching X.400-compliant messages. The message submitted is transported by an X.400-compliant message transfer agent.

X.500

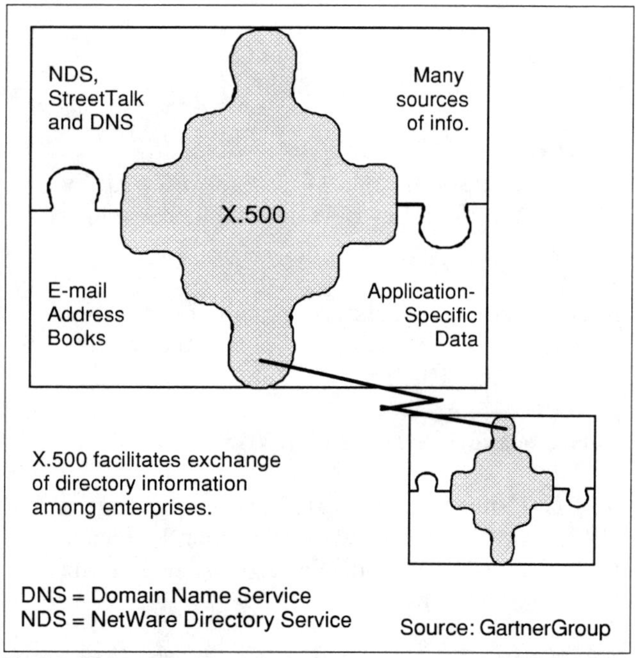

X.500 Directory Technology

XAPIA (X.400 API Association)

XAPI file-based API
An unofficial file-based application programming interface (API) used to submit and deliver messages with X.400 features to an X.400 message transfer agent.

Xbar
Crossbar.

XBDI (XML business data interchange)
The use of Extensible Markup Language (XML)-based standards and technologies not related to the X12 electronic data interchange (EDI) standards (see XML/EDI).

Xcert Universal Database (See XUDA)

XDS
An interface that connects to X.500 directory services, designed by the X.400 API Association XAPIA.

xDSL
Any of several variants of Digital Subscriber Line (DSL). See also ADSL and SDSL.

XENIX
A multiuser operating system developed by Microsoft. A subset of Unix, it is no longer sold.

Xeon
Intel's high-performance workstation processor, which is based on the same "P6" core as the Pentium II and Pentium III chips.

Xerox Network Systems (See XNS)

XFDL (Extensible Form Definition Language)
UWI.Com's Universal Form Definition Language (UFDL) version rewritten in Extensible Markup Language (XML) syntax.

XFN (X/Open Federated Naming)
Sun Microsystems' federated-naming service specification, similar to Messaging Application Programming Interface (MAPI) and Apple Open Collaborative Environment (AOCE), for the Unix environment. XFN first shipped with Sun's Solaris operating system in 1994. XFN was accepted as a prototype of an X/Open federated-naming service standard in 1995.

XICS (Xerox Integrated Composition System)

XIE (X-Windows Image Extensions)
Extensions that support client compression/decompression.

XIP (execute in place)

Xjack
A miniature RJ11 modem jack for the Personal Computer Memory Card Industry Association's PCMCIA/PC card modems.

XLink (XML Linking Language) (See XML standards)

XMI (Metadata Interchange Format)
A metadata interchange standard that allows the sharing of Unified Modeling Language (UML) and Meta Object Facility (MOF) objects between various development tools and repositories.

Xmit (transmit)

XML (Extensible Markup Language)
A metalanguage approved as a World Wide Web Coalition (W3C) Recommendation in February 1998. It is a simplified version of Standard Generalized Markup Language (SGML-ISO:8879) that captures the key (Standard Generalized Markup Language (SGML) advantages (e.g., extensibility) without its more obscure features. Because it is a metalanguage (a language to define languages), it

intrinsically offers Hypertext Markup Language (HTML) capabilities. HTML is just one instance of an SGML document while Extensible Markup Language (XML), like its "parent" SGML, is a language that can be used to create HTML. Today's mature SGML-aware tools (e.g., content-creation applications, composition engines, document component managers) are converted for XML compliance.

XML business data interchange (See XBDI)

XML data (See XML standards)

XML/EDI (Extensible Markup Language/ electronic data interchange)
Specifically refers to the effort being made by the Data Interchange Standards Association (DISA), CommerceNet, and the XML/EDI group, not only to use the XML standards and technologies for business data interchanges, but also to leverage the use of the existing X12 data dictionaries, code lists, semantics, and general business domain knowledge encapsulated in the 4010 version of the X12 EDI standards. Other efforts to use XML-based standards and technologies not related to the X12 EDI standards are referred to as XML business data interchange (XBDI).

The XML/EDI effort is being driven by the X12C Ad Hoc Task Group on the use of XML with X12 EDI. The group consists primarily of members from CommerceNet, DISA, and the XML/EDI group.

XML Linking Language (See XML standards)

XML Namespace (See XML standards)

XML Pointer Language (See XML standards)

XML standards
- The XML Linking Language (XLink) specifies constructs that may be inserted into Extensible Markup Language (XML) resources to describe links between objects. It uses XML syntax to create structures that can describe the simple unidirectional hyperlinks of today's Hypertext Markup Language (HTML) as well as more sophisticated multiended and typed links. The nearest analogy in HTML is the uniform resource identifier (URI).
- The XML Pointer Language (XPointer) specifies constructs that support addressing in the internal structures of XML documents. In particular, it provides for specific reference to elements, character strings, and other parts of XML documents, whether or not they bear an explicit ID attribute.
- The Extensible Style Language (XSL) specifies how XML documents will be rendered by associating presentation characteristics with specific XML tags in the XML document.
- XML Namespace qualifies tag names used in XML documents by associating them with their source.
- XML data standardizes schemas to define the characteristics of classes of objects. XML data schemas provide a common vocabulary for ideas that overlap between syntactic, database and conceptual schemas.
- The Document Object Model (DOM) specifies how programs and scripts can dynamically access and update the content, structure, and style of XML documents.

Xmodem
An 8-bit, public domain error-checking protocol developed in the late 1970s. The file transfer protocol uses a 128-byte data block and cyclic redundancy check (CRC) or checksum error-checking method.

XMP (X/Open Management Protocol)

XNS (Xerox Network Systems)
An Ethernet-based data communications protocol developed by Xerox.

X-on/X-off
A method of controlling data communications. It essentially enables a terminal to activate a line when it is ready to receive information and to suspend line activity when the terminal is overloaded. See also asynchronous.

X/Open
An international consortium of computer vendors working toward advancement in the employment of Unix. It aims to create and promote a vendor-independent interface standard called the Common Applications Environment (CAE). CAE addresses the operating system interface, data management and languages, and includes networking and graphical user interfaces (GUIs). X/Open was founded in Europe by European vendors, but has expanded to include a number of U.S. companies (AT&T, Digital Equipment, Hewlett-Packard, NCR, Unisys and Sun Microsystems) and an office in the United States.

X/Open branding
Verified midrange-system software compliance, in accordance with the X/Open branding program, with the X/Open consortium's Common Applications Environment (CAE) X/Open Portability Guide release 3 (XPG3) base profile.

X/Open Distributed Transaction Processing
An online transaction processing (OLTP) monitor compliant with the X/Open Extended Architecture (XA) distributed transaction-processing advance specification.

X/Open Federated Naming (See XFN)

X/Open ISAM
Support, compliant with X/Open Portability Guide (XPG) volume 5, for Indexed Sequential Access Method (ISAM) files.

X/Open NLS
National language support (NLS) compliant with the X/Open XPG3 NLS specification.

X/Open Portability Guide (See XPG)

X/Open Transport Interface (See XTI)

XPAF (Xerox Printer Access Facility)

XPE (Cross Platform Extension)

XPG (X/Open Portability Guide)

XPG3 (X/Open Portability Guide release 3)

XPG4 (X/Open Portability Guide release 4)

X/Open

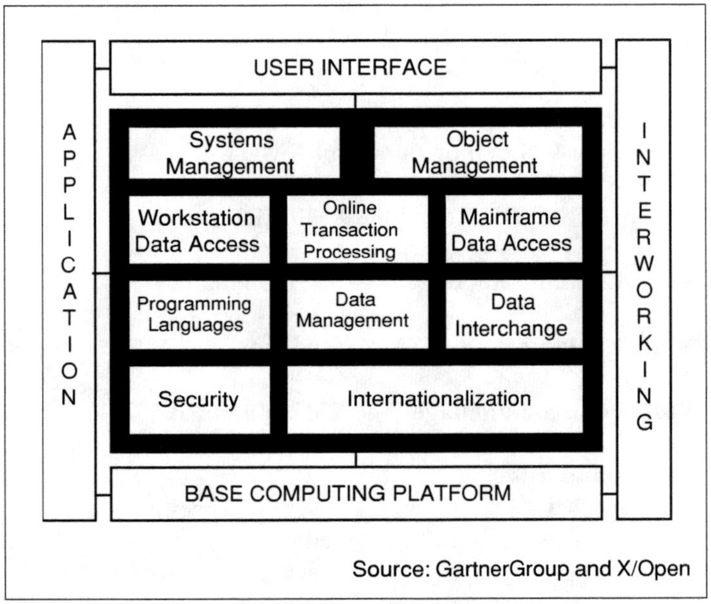

X/Open's Common Applications Environment

XPointer (XML Pointer Language) (See XML standards)

XPS (Cross Platform Server)

XRC (extended remote copy)
An asynchronous remote-copy capability that works with Multiple Virtual Storage (MVS).

XRF (Extended Recovery Facility)
A reliability enhancement for an Information Management System/Virtual Storage (IMS/VS) database/data communications environment. It provides the capability of creating a "mirror" IMS system and synchronizing it to the primary subsystem. The mirror IMS/VS system takes over the workload from the primary subsystem in the case of some, but not all, disruptive events, thereby improving availability. XRF will also facilitate testing and installation of new software releases. It has also been extended to Customer Information Control System (CICS).

XSL (Extensible Style Language) (See XML standards)

X Terminal
A workstation operating under X Windows.

XTI (X/Open Transport Interface)
Support provided for applications that use the X/Open XTI programming interface for peer-to-peer communications.

XUDA (Xcert Universal Database)
A programmer's interface technology product from Xcert. It is a Secured Socket Layer (SSL)-secured Lightweight Directory Access Protocol (LDAP) complain toolkit for developers, used for accessing disturbed, multiplatform encryption modules.

XUI
An X Windows-based graphical user interface (GUI) developed by Digital Equipment as part of its DECwindows program.

X Windows
The software system written for managing windows under Unix. A graphics architecture, application programming interface (API) and prototype implementation developed by the Massachusetts Institute of Technology, X Windows defines a client/server relation between the applications program and the workstation. It is not, however, a complete graphical user interface (GUI), but rather the basis upon which one can be built.

X-Windows Image Extensions (See XIE)

X.x series
Any of a number of technical specifications codified or administered by the International Telecommunication Union (ITU). It includes:

1. X.3: Packet assembler/disassembler (PAD) facility in a public data network (PDN).
2. X.21: A technical specification recommended by the ITU that describes the interface used in the ITU X.25 packet-switching protocol and in some types of circuit switched data transmissions.
3. X.21bis: Defines the physical layer protocol for data terminal equipment/circuit-terminating equipment (DTE/DCE) communication in an X.25 network.
4. X.25: ITU recommendation that specifies the interface between user DTE and packet-switching DCE.
5. X.26: ITU recommendation for unbalanced high speed data communications.
6. X.28: DTE/DCE interface of a start/stop mode DTE accessing the PAD on a PDN situated in the same country.

7. X.29: Procedures for exchange of control information and user data between a packet mode DTE and a PAD facility.
8. X.32: ITU recommendation that defines how X.25 connects to a packet network via a switched telephone system.
9. X.75: A standard for connecting X.25 networks, developed by the CCITT (now ITU).
10. X.121: International public data network numbering scheme.
11. X.400: ITU recommendation covering the handling of messages, such as the storage and forwarding of electronic mail (e-mail), over digital circuits.
12. X.435: ITU recommendation covering the transmission of electronic data exchange (EDI)-type messages by X.400 e-mail systems.
13. X.500: ITU recommendation covering the implementation of addressing databases for devices attached to a network.

Y

Y2K (year 2000)

yard management system (See YMS)

year 2000 compliance
Confirmation that applications are free from the year 2000 problem, i.e., that they do not abnormally end or produce erroneous results as the result of incorrectly interpreting the year 2000 as "00" due to the use of only two digits to represent the year.

year 2000 problem
The year 2000 problem is the result of an industry practice that for more than 35 years has represented years in dates as only two digits, assuming in application logic that the first two digits of the year are "19". A variety of errors are introduced once such applications must deal with dates beyond 31 December 1999.

yellow alarm
An alarm condition that occurs on a T1 line under the following conditions:

- D4 format: Starting with bit 2, every eighth bit of 256 or more consecutive channels is a zero.
- Extended superframe format (ESF): a pattern in which eight ones are followed by eight zeros.

Ymodem
A packet-based error-checking protocol using 128-kilobyte (Kbyte) or 1024-Kbyte blocks.

YMS (yard management system)
A logistic management system that provides the ability to monitor and track the movement and activities of vehicles entering and departing trailer yards. This capability allows enterprises to know the contents and location of all trailers within their facilities. A YMS also controls and directs the movement of trailers within a yard and between yard locations and dock doors.

YTD (year-to-date)

Z

ZAI (Zero Administration Initiative)
Microsoft's initiative to lower the total cost of ownership (TCO) necessary to manage its technology. ZAI consists of many components, including Zero Administration Kit, Systems Management Server (SMS), IntelliMirror and Common Information Model (CIM). Most of ZAI's functionality is included with Windows 2000.

ZAK (Zero Administration Kit)
A Microsoft product designed to reduce the management complexity associated with the Windows platform. Initially announced as an offering for Windows NT 4.0, ZAK is an early component of Microsoft's Zero Administration Windows (ZAW) initiative.

ZAK-A (Zero Administration Kit, Applications Support, AppStation Mode)

ZAK-E (Zero Administration Kit, Explorer Interface, TaskStation Mode)

ZAS (Zero Administration Server)

ZAW (Zero Administration Windows)
A Microsoft initiative to lower the total cost of ownership (TCO) associated with the Windows platform by reducing costs associated with administration. More extensive and comprehensive than the Zero Administration Kit, ZAW will be deployed across a variety of Windows platforms over a period of years.

Zero Administration Initiative (See ZAI)

Zero Administration Kit (see ZAK)

Zero Administration Kit, Applications Support, AppStation Mode (See ZAK-A)

Zero Administration Kit, Explorer Interface, TaskStation Mode (See ZAK-E)

Zero Administration Windows (see ZAW)

zero insertion force (See ZIF)

zero-latency enterprise (See ZLE)

zero suppression
The elimination of nonsignificant zeroes in a numeral.

ZIF (zero insertion force)
A type of chip socket that allows the chip to be removed and reinserted without damage.

Zip
The principle form of file-by-file data compression in the Windows environment.

ZIP (Zone Information Protocol)
A protocol that maps network numbers to zone names in an AppleTalk network.

ZLE (zero-latency enterprise)
Any strategy that exploits the immediate exchange of information across technical and organizational boundaries to achieve business benefit. For example, technical boundaries exist between different operating systems, database management systems (DBMSs) and programming languages. "Immediate" implies being fast enough to bring all of the business benefits that simultaneous knowledge can potentially achieve. Latency cannot literally be

zero in any real system because computers need time to "think."

Zmodem
A fast and reliable error-checking protocol that enables files to be transferred in one batch. If transmission is interrupted, file transfer is resumed from the point of interruption.

Zone Information Protocol (See ZIP)